CHINESE SHAKESPEARES

GLOBAL CHINESE CULTURE

CHINESE SHAKESPEARES

Two Centuries of Cultural Exchange

Alexander C. Y. Huang

Columbia University Press   New York

Columbia University Press wishes to express its appreciation for assistance given by
Penn State University and the Chiang Ching-kuo Foundation for International Scholarly
Exchange and Council for Cultural Affairs in the publication of this series.

Columbia University Press
Publishers Since 1893
New York   Chichester, West Sussex

Library of Congress Cataloging-in-Publication Data
Huang, Alexander C. Y. (Alexander Cheng-Yuan)
    Chinese Shakespeares : two centuries of cultural exchange / Alexander C. Y. Huang.
      p. cm. — (Global Chinese culture)
    Includes bibliographical references and index.
    ISBN 978-0-231-14848-1 (cloth : alk. paper) ISBN 978-0-231-14849-8 (pbk. : alk. paper)
ISBN 978-0-231-51992-2 (e-book)
    1. Shakespeare, William, 1564–1616—Appreciation—China. 2. Shakespeare,
William, 1564–1616—Adaptations—History and criticism. 3. Shakespeare, William,
1564–1616—Influence. 4. Chinese drama—English influences. 5. China—Civilization—
English influences. 6. Theater—China—History. 7. Performing arts—China—History.
I. Title. II. Series.
PR2971.C6H83 2009
822.3'3—dc22

                    2009000329

♾

References to Internet Web sites (URLs) were accurate at the time of writing. Neither the
author nor Columbia University Press is responsible for URLs that may have expired or
changed since the manuscript was prepared.

Title page: Lady Macbeth, a solo Sichuan-opera performance (Berlin, 2006) by Tian Mansha.
(Image courtesy of Tian Mansha)

Contents

Illustrations

Acknowledgments

Acknowledgments can be a self-referential genre, but a book on collaborations and exchanges will not be complete without retracing its author's intellectual debts beyond the impersonal format of endnotes and bibliography, even though it is impossible to summarize them all, much less repay, in these pages. I am pleased to acknowledge research sponsorship by Penn State University—Institute for the Arts and Humanities faculty research grant, College of Liberal Arts RGSO research funds and Minority Faculty Development Program—and the following institutions: Folger Institute, International Shakespeare Association, Chiang Ching-Kuo Foundation, Association of Asian Performance, and several divisions of Stanford University, including the Division of Literatures, Cultures and Languages, Department of English, Center for East Asian Studies, and Stanford Shakespeare in Asia initiative.

I am most grateful to Timothy Billings, Haun Saussy, and Patricia Parker, for their insightful feedback and support at crucial stages of the project. Haiyan Lee, Charles Ross, Xiaomei Chen, Peter Donaldson, Mark Thornton Burnett, and the anonymous reviewers have read with great care the manuscript in various stages and generously provided meticulous comments; Wilt Idema, David Palumbo-Liu, Eric Hayot, David Bevington, Thomas Cartelli, and Elizabeth Wichmann-Walczak generously offered time to read versions of different chapters with an attentive eye to detail. I have been fortunate enough to have Jennifer Crewe as my acquisitions editor at Columbia University Press, who—along with Irene Pavitt—graciously shepherded the book to completion. The final stage of writing has benefited from lively conversations in a semester-long research seminar codirected by Tom Cartelli and Katherine Rowe and funded by the Folger Institute, and from the good humor and sympathetic skepticism of Patrick Cheney, Barbara Hodgdon, Ton Hoenselaar, Colin Mackerras, Martin Orkin, Tom Bishop, Sun Huizhu, Kathy Foley, Michel Hockx, and Kuang-ming Wu. The project also benefited from the probing questions from audiences at a number of venues. I am indebted to Brett de Bary, Linda Hutcheon, Dennis Kennedy, Yong Li Lan, Stephen Greenblatt, Jean Howard, James Siemon, Susan Bennett, Irena Makaryk, Ryuta Minami, Yukari Yoshihara, Perng Ching-hsi, Leo Ou-fan Lee, Sukanta Chaudhuri, Chee Seng Lim, Barbara Mittler, Rudolf Wagner, and Chung Ming-der, for inviting me to give lectures or participate in colloquia or conferences they organized at Cornell and Harvard and in London, Heidelberg, Singapore, Taipei, Tokyo, Valencia, Brisbane, Chicago, Beijing, Bermuda, and elsewhere. All these colleagues and mentors are truly inspiring examples in the scholarly profession.

Portions of this book have appeared in print in different forms, although they have since changed substantially: "Lin Shu, Invisible Translation, and Politics," *Perspectives: Studies in Translatology* 14, no. 1 (2006): 55–65; "The Politics of an 'Apolitical' Shakespeare: A Soviet-Chinese Joint Venture, 1950–1979," *Borrowers and Lenders: The Journal of Shakespeare and Appropriation* 1, no. 2 (2005); "Site-Specific *Hamlets* and Reconfigured Localities: Jiang'an, Singapore, Elsinor," *Shakespearean International Yearbook* 7 (2007): 22–48; and "Shakespeare, Performance, and Autobiographical Interventions," *Shakespeare Bulletin* 24, no. 2 (2006): 31–47. My thanks to Routledge, Ashgate, University System of Georgia, and Johns Hopkins University Press for permission to use these materials.

For contributions of primary materials for analysis, I thank Michael Hill, Zhen Zhang, Li Ruru, Claire Conceison, Shen Lin, Sun Huizhu, Yang Shaolin, Yu Rongjun, Rossella Ferrari, and several distinguished playwrights, performers, and directors I am privileged to know, including Ong Keng Sen, Stan Lai, Li Jiayao, Wu Hsing-kuo, Tian Mansha, Wang Rongyu, Chung Chuan-hsing, Wei Haimin, David Tse, and the late Ma Yong'an. Archival research for this project would not have been as enjoyable and productive without the assistance of knowledgeable and patient librarians such as Anne Labitzky-Wagner (Ruprecht-Karls-Universität Heidelberg) and Don Marion (University of Minnesota), and staff members who graciously accommodated my requests for eccentric materials at the Shakespeare Institute Library in Stratford-upon-Avon, Folger Shakespeare Library, Library of the Central Academy of Drama in Beijing, Shanghai Theatre Academy Library, Penn State University Libraries Interlibrary Loan Department, Harvard-Yenching Library, Harvard Widener Library, Library of the Chinese National Academy of Arts in Beijing, TheatreWorks Archive in Singapore, National Library of Taiwan, National Library of China, Shanghai Dramatic Arts Centre Archive, Shanghai Library, Performance Workshop Archive, Contemporary Legend Theatre Archive, Archive of Wei Haimin Cultural Foundation, Tainaner Ensemble Archive, Shanghai Yueju Yuan Archive, Shanghai Jingju Yuan Archive, Shanghai Kunju Yuan Archive, and Stanford University Libraries.

Finally, I would have devoted this book to Liana, but she deserves so much more.

A Note on Texts and Translation

Scene and line references of Shakespearean plays are keyed to *The Riverside Shakespeare*, 2nd ed., edited by G. Blakemore Evans (Boston: Houghton Mifflin, 1997), with modernized spelling and punctuation. All translations are mine unless otherwise noted. I have adopted the *pinyin* romanization system for Chinese throughout, except for names or phrases that are commonly known in a different form. Historical or official names are also preserved (for example, Canton and Peking University).

Further transcriptions, translations, and critical notes for selected works (accompanied by streaming videos and photographs) will be available online through "Shakespeare Performance in Asia," a multilingual, freely accessible digital database at http://web.mit.edu/shakespeare/asia/.

Readers not familiar with the history of Shakespeare performance, Chinese cultural history under discussion, or the critical discourses in either field are invited to consult the select chronology and chapter notes.

CHINESE SHAKESPEARES

Prologue

Readers travel. Texts are passed to new territories. But myths tend to stay, which is why the space between China and Shakespeare as cultural tokens is exhilarating and frustrating in equal measure. These days, English-speaking metropolitan audiences and jaded cultural tourists have grown used to a Shakespeare who figured prominently in other national cultures, particularly that of Germany, where the notion of *unser* Shakespeare (our Shakespeare) needs no more illustration than the wedding march that Felix Mendelssohn composed for Ludwig Tieck's celebrated production of *A Midsummer Night's Dream* (1843). The story of Shakespeare's worldwide appeal may go like this: In Shakespeare's times, shortly after appearing on London stages, his plays migrated to foreign shores. The English Comedians toured Europe in the late sixteenth century, staging semi-improvised performances frequently attended by both the locals and British travelers who became outsiders to the once familiar plays.[1] In 1607, Shakespeare's plays were sailing east. *Hamlet* and *Richard II* were performed on a makeshift stage on board an English East India Company ship, the *Red Dragon*, anchored near Sierra Leone; *Hamlet* was performed again in 1608 on the island of Socotra, at the entry to the Gulf of Aden (now part of the Republic of Yemen).[2] The *Red Dragon* arrived in colonial Indonesia in 1609. Shakespeare's name and works spread rapidly to other parts of Asia. Prompted by the worldwide cultural phenomena that have materialized around Shakespeare's name and dramas, many directors and scholars have recognized the malleability and collaborative nature of Shakespeare's play texts.[3] Named the Writer of the Millennium, Shakespeare has come full circle and become a cliché, embraced by marketers and contested by intellectuals.[4] Similar narratives about China's rise in global stature have been told with equal gusto, championed and denounced in turn by optimists and critics.[5]

This seems to be old news. On the positive side, Shakespeare seems to belong to the whole world, representing the metropole and the Global South. But that sense of belonging is immediately problematic. Shakespeare's global career was not tied entirely to the spread and retreat of the British Empire or the rise of intercultural performance. Even in contemporary Anglophone culture, the persistence of Shakespeare's plays as popular material for the entertainment industry is an odd phenomenon.[6] While in our times the presence of Shakespeare in world cultures appears to be ordinary and commonplace, the global history of Shakespeare's afterlife reveals the limit of the universal as an artistic concept. If Shakespeare now has worldwide currency, how is the sense of belonging and betrayal configured chronologically and spatially? The old news—our journalistic familiarity with Shakespeare's provenance in global contexts—calls for careful reconstruction of a historical foundation for theorization.

Many people have seen one or more Asian performances, but few are aware that for almost two centuries, East Asian writers, filmmakers, and theater directors have also engaged Shakespeare in their works in a wide range of contexts. The ideas of Shakespeare and China have been put to work in unexpected places. Every year, hundreds of works emerge in Mandarin and a wide range of Chinese dialects, performing styles, and genres, including fiction, theater, cinema, and popular culture. The exchange goes both ways. Outside China, Asian theatrical idioms such as Beijing opera (*jingju*) are becoming more common in English- and European-language Shakespeare productions.[7] International productions have appeared in the Chinese-speaking world with increasing frequency, ranging from British burlesques in nineteenth-century Hong Kong and Soviet–Chinese productions in mid-twentieth-century China to a truly global array of approaches in contemporary Taiwan and rich intraregional citations in East and Southeast Asia. As more and more Chinese productions tour in Great Britain, the United States, and Europe, Shakespeare has evolved from Britain's export commodity to an import industry in the Anglo-European culture, giving birth to Asian-inflected performances outside Asia.

If meaning is shifting and debatable, what does "Shakespeare" *do* in Chinese literary and performance culture? Conversely, how do imaginations about China function in Shakespearean performances, and what ideological work do they undertake—in mainland China, Taiwan, and other locations?

It is best to begin with stories. In 1942, when China was at war with Japan, a Chinese-language production of *Hamlet*, set in Denmark, was staged in a Confucian temple in Jiang'an in southwestern China. The director, Jiao Juyin (1905–1975), wed the foreign setting to the allegorical space of the temple and the historical exigencies of the time. The balcony in front of the shrine of Confucius was used as a makeshift stage, and the audiences were seated in the courtyard—with a clear view of the shrine and the action on stage. The temple thus becomes both a fictive space of performance and a context for the reading of China and Hamlet's Denmark. This extraordinary moment has several implications. The meanings of this wartime *Hamlet* were complicated by the intruding presence of the Confucian shrine on the makeshift stage and the setting of the temple. Jiao insisted on the primacy of his locality, and the performance created a communal experience during the war intended to stir patriotic spirit in Confucian, moral terms. The production subscribed to a national agenda during a time that witnessed a deteriorating economy, intensified conflicts between the Chinese Communist (CCP) and Nationalist (KMT) parties, and major setbacks in the Chinese resistance to Japanese invasion. While Laurence Olivier's similarly jingoistic *Henry V* (1944) has been considered as an example of what Walter Benjamin called "the aestheticization of politics," Jiao's *Hamlet* is an exercise in the politicization of art. Shakespeare has been absorbed into the political life during times of war.[8]

While the temple *Hamlet* readily connected Shakespeare with the connotations of the local venue, other directors used allegory to reconfigure Shakespeare and Asian identity multinationally. In Ong Keng Sen's multilingual *LEAR* (1997), staged with English subtitles, actors from several Asian countries and their characters were poised for a search of cultural identities as the pan-Asian production played to full houses in Singapore, Tokyo, other parts of Asia, and Europe. The power-thirsty eldest daughter (performed cross-dressed), who spoke only Mandarin and employed *jingju* chanting and movements, confronted the Old Man (Lear), who

FIGURE 1   Umewaka Naohiko as the Japanese-speaking Old Man (Lear) and Jiang Qihu cross-dressed as the Mandarin-speaking Older Daughter (conflated from Regan and Goneril) in the multilingual *LEAR*, directed by Ong Keng Sen, TheatreWorks and Japan Foundation Asia Center, 1997. (Courtesy of TheatreWorks, Singapore)

spoke only Japanese and walked the stage in the solemn style of *nō* performance (figure 1). The subtitles defamiliarized (in Victor Shklovsky's sense) the Shakespearean lines and decorporealized Asian performance practices at once.[9] The sensual overload of the performance overwhelmed its international audiences, who, despite their best effort, would always miss something. While this uniquely multilingual performance recast the questions of race and nation in a new light, its bold experiments of hybrid Asian styles were controversial. The performance physicalized, in linguistic and dramaturgical terms, the promise and perils of globalization and the uneasy coalition among participants of this transnational project.[10] Seen afar from the European perspective, the contrasts between the Asian languages and styles were flattened by their similarities. However, seen from an Asian perspective, the difference between Asian cultures was accentuated by the performance. The production highlighted the discrepancy between Asian languages and styles, and between Chinese and Japanese perspectives on World War II.

Both Jiao's and Ong's intercultural productions stage contradictions and raise complex issues related to cultural politics and international touring. They register similar concerns about shifting localities. Jiao relates Shakespeare unabashedly to the Confucian tradition evoked by the temple. Ong notes that his project, a "multicultural playground," is a platform for him to "work through his ambivalence about tradition."[11] Are such theatrical encounters with a foreign-language Shakespeare and with a Shakespeare-inspired Asian director symptomatic of cultural tourism rather than the logics of internationalism? Does watching Shakespeare with subtitles overcome or simply redraw cultural boundaries? Shakespeare has been used to construct political relevance for Ong's project, local urgency for Jiao's, and many other meanings in Asia since the nineteenth century.

These intriguing cases constitute only the tip of an iceberg of larger questions and pervasive cultural practices that have yet to be admitted to the scholarly discourse on Shakespeare and Chinese modernity. Standing behind these practices is a long history of constantly reconfigured relationships that have connected and disconnected Shakespeare and China. The currency of Shakespeare in the modern world is partly determined by political and historical forces that are often located outside the plays but that have been claimed to be located within or derived directly from the text itself.

Special to Chinese Shakespeares and unexpected for English-language readers are not only the edgy or dissident voices but also Chinese artists and audience's unique (ab)use of cultural authorities and insistence on "authentic" Shakespeares in various forms. To say so is not to suggest that the Anglocentric view of Shakespeare ought to be replaced by a Sinocentric one, as in some nationalist imaginary or de rigueur celebration of ethnic authenticity. Much of this work will undermine the fantasies of cultural exclusivity of both "Shakespeare" and "China," attending to the fact that even though every reading is a rewriting, more rewritings of a canonical text do not always translate into more radical rethinking of normative assumptions. It is with this conviction that I examine the transnational imaginary of China in Shakespearean performance *and* Shakespeare's place in Chinese cultural history from the first Opium War in 1839 to our times.

Sites of Fixation

A long view of history will reveal the multidirectional processes that contribute to the mutually constructive grammar of the global and the local. Over a century of cross-fertilization has firmly rooted Shake-speare in Chinese cultural production and Chinese performance idioms in twentieth-century Shakespeare traditions.

The transmission of Renaissance culture in China began with the ar-rival of the first Jesuit missionaries in 1582, followed by the Dominicans and Franciscans in the 1630s.[12] Illustrated British travel narratives record British emissaries' experience attending theatrical productions in Tianjin and Beijing during the reign of the Qianlong Emperor (1736–1795), in-cluding the mission of Lord George Macartney.[13] Even though there are records of Europeans attending theatrical and ritual performances in the Chinese court, drama and literature was not a major concern for them. This is the case for a number of reasons.[14] The missions of Matteo Ricci (1562–1610), Nicolas Trigault (1577–1628), and Niccolò Longobardo (1565–1655) focused on understanding and converting religious differences into cross-cultural connections. The missionaries and their Chinese collabora-tors such as Xu Guangqi (1562–1633) were preoccupied with devotional writings, cartography, Renaissance objects (prisms, clocks, astronomical instruments), mathematics, the calendar reform, and the failed project to introduce Aristotelian philosophy into the Chinese education system. The focus on material culture and the prospect of trade persisted into the seventeenth and eighteenth centuries.[15] One diary entry briefly comments on the similarity between an unnamed Chinese play and Shakespeare's *Richard III*.[16] More references in Chinese to Shakespeare as the English national poet emerged during the first Opium War (1839–1842), a transi-tional period greatly different from the earlier eras.

With the decline of the Qing dynasty in the nineteenth century, Chinese interests in Western modes of thinking and political systems intensified. In the previous centuries, the Chinese had conducted exchanges with Eu-ropean merchants and missionaries almost solely in Chinese—with the exception of a few Chinese educated for the priesthood. The burden of learning a foreign language rested on the Europeans. But the dynamics changed in the mid-nineteenth century when the Western hegemony took the form of military power. Literary production was marked by the com-plicity and complexity of Chinese engagements with the imperial West in a time of transition when intellectuals questioned both the traditional and modern formations of Chinese culture. This was also a time when the West was both reviled and admired.[17] Early Chinese reactions to Shake-speare were informed by the double bind of the recourse to the West—a mode of thinking that was at once obligatory and detested.

Both Shakespeare and China were "translated"—to use the word to mean "transformed" or "metamorphosed," as Peter Quince does in *A Midsummer Night's Dream*—in the late nineteenth century according to powerful and at times mutually exclusive ideologies.[18] At this point in history, translation was freely practiced in China with little cultural differentiation between an "original" and a rewrite. Within China proper, intellectuals and reformers alternately saw the demands of cross-cultural understanding and the reassessment of Chinese values as a blessing and a curse. Along with John Milton and other "national" poets, Shakespeare's name entered the discourse of nationalism. Shakespeare was first mentioned in passing in 1839 in a compendium of world cultures translated by Lin Zexu, a key figure in the first Opium War. By the time Chinese translations became available and substantive critical engagements with Shakespeare were initiated, there was already over half a century of reception history in which Shakespeare was frequently evoked to support or suppress specific agendas—in the writings of both missionaries and Chinese reformers—all in the name of modernity and cultural renewal.

Two major literary events of the early twentieth century are the publication of a Chinese rendition of Charles and Mary Lamb's *Tales from Shakespeare* (1807) and the serialization of Shakespeare's history plays in a popular literary magazine. The Lambs' text was translated orally by Wei Yi and rendered freely into classical Chinese by Lin Shu as *An English Poet Reciting from Afar* (*Yingguo shiren yinbian yanyu*, 1904). Also influential in the early reception of Shakespeare in Korea and Japan, the *Tales* were reframed in China as a text intended for the male elite class that operated according to moralizing principles. Although Shakespeare's history and Roman plays were excluded from Lin's 1904 text, they were serialized as prose novels, also "translated" by Lin, in *Short Story Magazine* (*Xiaoshuo yuebao*) in 1916. While no full line-by-line translation of any play was available yet, these rewrites popularized "representative" plays in each of the Shakespearean genres by creatively transforming them into prose narratives.

In terms of performance style, Shakespeare has figured prominently in the shaping of modern and contemporary Chinese theater, where the genres of *xiqu* (stylized theater with more than 360 regional variations in dialect, aria type, and technique; commonly known as Chinese opera outside China) and *huaju* (post-1907 Western-influenced spoken drama theater, including obsolete subgenres) coexist.[19] Competing narratives about Shakespeare and China in *xiqu* and *huaju* theaters reflect a series of crises of representational practice that are complicated by ethics, aesthetics, politics, and the contingencies of live theater. Shakespeare has given occasion for innovations in both these performance genres, as well as other forms of representation.

While the initial spread of Shakespeare's reputation was connected to the Chinese elite who studied or traveled in Japan, Europe, or the United States, and to the presence of Anglo-European cultures in most coastal cities of the Chinese mainland, two cities stood out. Nineteenth-century Hong Kong saw more regular Shakespearean performances in English, while Shanghai remained the hub of much of the early Chinese-language publications and performance activities that initiated subsequent debates about old and new forms of drama.

The Merchant of Venice was a site of fixation of the Chinese imagination, as it provided inspiration for both the earliest documented cinematic and *huaju* Shakespeares, including *Shylock; or, the Merchant of Venice Preserved*, a travesty by Francis Talfourd (1828–1862) staged in 1867 and revived in 1871 by the Hong Kong Amateur Dramatic Club. The cover of the play contains a brief statement that it is "an entirely new reading of Shakespeare . . . printed from an edition hitherto undiscovered by modern authorities."[20] The choice of a mercantile-themed play in a trade colony may be coincidental, but the nostalgia and not-so-subtle reference to the modern "West" were articulated through the production and a number of other performances.

Gender roles in *The Merchant of Venice* and other plays were also reimagined. A silent film, *The Woman Lawyer* (also known as *A Bond of Flesh* [*Rou quan*]), premiered in Shanghai on May 29, 1927. Another notable cinematic Shakespeare from the same era was *A Spray of Plum Blossom* (*Yi jian mei*, 1931), a 110-minute silent film based on *The Two Gentlemen of Verona* in a hybrid genre of chivalric adventure and classic love story. While these films rescripted both the Shakespearean plays and modern Chinese ideals of womanhood to project cosmopolitan desires and to endorse the new woman's movement (in the context of education reform that allowed women to attend college and to enter the legal profession), other interpretations of *The Merchant of Venice* suppressed the racial and religious conflicts in the play that might have been relevant to early-twentieth-century Chinese audiences and instead highlighted China's revitalized yet, because of continuing wars, constantly threatened global trade. Rather than the questions of Jewishness or religious values, the play mirrored the emergence of women lawyers in Shanghai and new demands of the global trade.[21]

Hamlet, though, captured the Chinese imagination of a modern nation-state. A number of literary works addressed the supposed deficiencies of national character, such as procrastination and inaction, and problematized the place of the ghost in the new corpus of a national literature. Some of these concerns found expression through rewrites of Shakespeare's works. Lao She's short story "New Hamlet" (Xin Hanmuliede, 1936) follows a college student through a series of reverse cultural shocks after he returns home to face the decline of the family business. It reinvents the theme of procrastination, not revenge, to suit its purpose as a commentary on the Chinese imagination of Hamlet's intellectualism. Couched in coded ethical terms and bearing the imprint of the intellectual mandate of the time, such rewrites and early performances trouble the boundary between moral criticism and sociopolitical dimensions of artistic works. The ethical terms dictated not only the reception of many literary works— both Chinese and foreign—but also its attendant evaluative moves.

After the founding of the People's Republic of China in 1949, Shakespeare and Chinese writers alike were reinterpreted through the Soviet-Marxist critical lens. Marxist-Maoism dictated the construction of a Chinese self-image, which was accompanied by alternating periods of active cultural activities, setbacks, and revitalization. The Soviet influence throughout China's social infrastructures and Stanislavskian realism contributed to the politics of Soviet–Chinese Shakespeare in the first three decades after the founding of the People's Republic. Even though no foreign dramas and very few Chinese dramas were performed during the Cultural Revolution (1966–1976), Shakespeare and other authors were read privately in labor camps. The private life of once public plays politicizes and aestheticizes personal experiences. After the Cultural Revolution, Shakespeare again returned to the core of actor-training institutions as part of a boom in *huaju* and *xiqu* performances of Western dramas.

The situations in the other parts of the Chinese-speaking world were and still are different from those in mainland China. Kawakami Otojirō's (1864–1911) *Othello* in 1903 recast Taiwan as the outpost of the colonial Japanese Empire, moving Venice to Japan and Cyprus to the Penghu Archipelago, west of Taiwan.[22] When Muro Washiro (the Othello figure), a dark-faced Japanese colonial general in Taiwan, commits suicide at the end of the play, he compares himself to an "uncivilized" Taiwanese ab-original inhabitant (*seiban* [raw savage]).[23] An island off the southeast coast of mainland China, Taiwan has had complex relationships with the dominant "fatherland" (*zuguo*) across the strait and with Japan to the north.[24] While not directly responsible for the scarcity of Western dramas from the early to the mid-twentieth century, the island's intense focus on the essentialized aspects of Japan and China prevented the growth of translated dramas from European languages.[25] In the first half of the twentieth century, tours of Japan's all-female Takarazuka performances to Taiwan occasionally included Shakespeare. The earliest-documented Chinese-language performance of Shakespeare in Taiwan was *Clouds of Doubt* (*Yi yun*), staged by the Experimental Theater of Taipei (Shiyan xiao juchang) in February 1949 and based on *Othello*. A few other perfor-mances followed, but until martial law was lifted in 1987, Taiwan's theater remained shaped by political censorship in significant ways, first by the Japanese colonial cultural policy and then by the anti-Communist cultural policy of the KMT regime.

The presence of Shakespeare at theater festivals in Taiwan in the 1980s and 1990s took a different form from mainland China's postrevo-lutionary Shakespeare boom, which was initiated by state-endorsed and government-sponsored Shakespeare festivals in 1986 and 1994. The month-long "Shakespeare in Taipei" festival (May 2003), for instance, focused more on providing a platform for artistically innovative and com-mercially viable experimental works. As a multilingual society (Mandarin, Taiwanese, Hakka, and aboriginal languages), Taiwan has produced a sig-nificant number of mainstream performances either entirely in a dialect or with a mixture of Mandarin and a local dialect or English. Some of these works reflect Taiwan's multiply determined history, while others question that history and the much-contested "Chineseness" of the island's iden-tity. These tendencies provide interesting contrasts to the ways in which mainland Chinese artists imagine China. By the same token, while main-land China is certainly multilingual, it is Taiwan and Hong Kong that have established strong traditions of Shakespeare performances in one or more dialects. The few mainland Chinese performances of Shakespeare in local dialects were commissioned and sponsored by the government for festivals or produced by ethnic minority students in actor-training pro-grams. The linguistic diversity of Taiwan and Hong Kong theaters fosters distinctive views of "Shakespeare" and what counts as "Chinese."

With strong dual traditions of English and Cantonese Shakespearean performances in *huaju* and *yueju* (Cantonese opera), Hong Kong theater reflects the tension between southern Chinese culture and the British legacy. After Hong Kong was ceded to Britain for 150 years in the Treaty of Tianjin (1842), Englishness became an important element throughout the social structure. Under the British government, theater was supported and encouraged as "a wholesome diversion from the tedium of military life."[26] English literature was established as a subject of study in Hong Kong's school system, and in 1882 students began to study Shakespeare for exams, initiating a form of "domination by consent."[27] Shakespearean drama became part of the repertoire of the Hong Kong Amateur Dramatic Club, which was active in the 1860s and 1870s. The so-called amateur theater was in fact noncommercial theater rather than nonprofessional. Such performances entertained British expatriates and brought "a touch of the British culture" to Hong Kong residents.[28] As in Japan, nineteenth-century China and Hong Kong saw sporadic performances of "authentic" Shakespeare in English that exposed local residents to the contemporary English culture. What was meant by authentic Shakespeare was a performance style that purported to present Shakespeare as he was conceived to have been played in his lifetime. Shakespeare festivals (April 23, 1954; April 1964; January 24–29, 1984) and experimental Shakespearean performances emerged in the mid-twentieth century. Since the 1980s, a considerable amount of energy has been directed not toward the post-colonial question but toward Hong Kong's global status and its Chinese heritage, as evidenced by the productions of Hong Kong Repertory Theatre (founded in 1977), the largest professional theater in Hong Kong, and performances by students of Hong Kong Academy for Performing Arts and other universities.

Despite the association of Shakespeare and Englishness, Shakespeare was not resisted as an image of colonization. Political changes have hardly affected him. Some contemporary Hong Kong scholars are surprised to find that "local experimentations with Shakespeare in post-modernist and Chinese styles have continued to flourish [in Hong Kong]." This continued prominence, they argue, shows that "Shakespeare has transcended his British heritage and become part of the Hong Kong Chinese tradition."[29] While partly true, this view blurs the historical conditions surrounding early performances. One crucial reason why Shakespeare seems to transcend his British heritage is that Britain never colonized Hong Kong the way it did India. This special historical condition—an indirect colonial structure that Mao Zedong later called semicolonialism—informed Hong Kong's performance culture in the late nineteenth and early twentieth centuries.[30] If the practitioners of the new theater were resisting anything, it was the Chinese past. The same is true of other treaty ports, such as Shanghai, that were home to a host of European concessions but had no overarching colonial institution.

The first decade of the new millennium was for Asian cinematic Shakespeares as the 1990s had been for Anglophone Shakespeare on film. Shakespeare has been a part of the Chinese-speaking popular culture since the late twentieth century, with *Romeo and Juliet* and *Hamlet* at the center of cinematic imaginations. Anthony Chan's *One Husband Too Many* (*Yiqi liangfu*, Hong Kong, 1988) weaves *Romeo and Juliet* into a contemporary urban comedy, while Cheah Chee Kong's *Chicken Rice War* (*Jiyuan qiaohe*, Singapore, 2000), another comic film, engages such films as Baz Luhrmann's *William Shakespeare's Romeo + Juliet* (1996) and John Madden's *Shakespeare in Love* (1998) from an ironic distance.[31] Huo Jianqi also shifts *Romeo and Juliet* into comedy in *A Time to Love* (*Qingren jie*, China, 2005). Starring television idol-stars Zhao Wei and Lu Yi, the film bears a Chinese title with witty puns that can read as either *Valentine's Day* or *Valentine's Knot*.[32] More recently, two feature films with all-star casts experiment with the genre of period film. *The Banquet* (*Yeyan*, China, 2006), a martial-arts film in Mandarin Chinese, gives Gertrude and Ophelia, traditionally silenced women characters in *Hamlet*, a strong presence. *The Prince of the Himalayas* (*Ximalaya wangzi*, China, 2006), in Tibetan, reframes *Hamlet* in ancient Tibet.[33] More films are being planned. It remains to be seen if any of these films can achieve the circulation and status of Kurosawa Akira's (1910–1998) well-known *Ran* (1985) and *Throne of Blood* (*Kumonosu jō*, 1957), based on *King Lear* and *Macbeth*, respectively. The rash of new Shakespeare films from Asia may be the result of increasingly aggressive transnationalizing strategies in East Asian cinema since the 1990s.

Other Sights

The complexities of the cultural institution of Chinese opera and artists' and critics' philosophical investments in the visual sign in stylized performances warrant separate investigation. While there are stage productions that focus, however creatively and distantly, on Shakespeare and are done in the way Western audiences tend to think of a stage play, there are also performances in traditional Chinese theater that borrow a bit of Shakespeare to reinvent and expand the Chinese performance idiom. Chinese-opera performances of Shakespeare have provided "other" sights for both Chinese and non-Chinese audiences. The varied styles found under this umbrella term are further reconfigured by the "premodern," physicalized, nonillusionist, and actor-centered languages of the Chinese operatic stage. The Solo Experimental Chinese Opera Festival in Hong Kong (2002) and its sequel in Taipei (2003), where a number of influential solo performances were staged, offer an example of this relational approach to theater. As such, Chinese-opera Shakespeare performances often initiate heated debates over Shakespeare and Chinese theater.

The earliest-documented *xiqu* Shakespeare, *Killing the Elder Brother and Snatching the Sister-in-Law,* was based on *Hamlet* and performed in *chuanju* (Sichuan-opera) style.[34] Other artists followed suit. The Custom Renewal Society staged *A Pound of Flesh* (*Yi bang rou*) in the *qinqiang*-opera style in 1925 in Shaanxi Province in northern China.[35] Although stylized performances of Shakespeare in different genres of Chinese opera have existed since the early twentieth century, the 1980s were a turning point, when Shakespeare became more regularly performed in different forms of stylization in China, Taiwan, Hong Kong, and elsewhere, and entered the collective cultural memory of Chinese-opera performers and audiences. The revived interest in Chinese-opera Shakespeare was encouraged by increased exchanges among performers based in mainland China and in the Chinese diaspora. These exchanges were fueled by Deng Xiaoping's Open Door Policy (announced in 1978) and by the increasing economic ties among China, Hong Kong, Taiwan, and the rest of the world. After a few successful international tours in the 1980s of productions such as Huang Zuolin's *The Story of Bloody Hands* (*Xie-shou ji,* Shanghai Kun Opera Company) and Wu Hsing-kuo's *Kingdom of Desire* (*Yuwang chengguo,* Taiwan's Contemporary Legend Theatre), both inspired by *Macbeth,* the complexity of Chinese-opera styles was increasingly regarded by the performers and their sponsors not as an obstacle but as an asset in creating an international demand for visual creativity.

Chinese-opera performers were not the only ones experimenting with Shakespeare and expanding the repertoire of Chinese theater. Both at home and abroad, directors and performers of *huaju* and other theatrical genres have deployed *xiqu* elements in their works, although they tend to

privilege *jingju*—among the many Chinese-opera forms—as the representative genre. Ariane Mnouchkine's *Richard II* (Paris, 1981) and Ong's *LEAR*
appropriated traditional Chinese and Japanese theaters. William Huizhu
Sun and Fan Yisong codirected an English-language *jingju Othello* at the
"Shakespeare Through Beijing Opera Workshop" at Tufts University in
1994.[36] Tracy Chung directed an English-language *jingju The Taming of
the Shrew* at Denison University in 2003 as a Fulbright Visiting Scholar-
in-Residence.[37] While English-language Chinese opera as a hybrid form is
not new, these productions introduced an alien theater form to American
audiences through both a local language (English) and a "local" playwright
(Shakespeare).[38] The additional purchase gained through the rhetorically
created unfamiliarity of Chinese opera helped to offset the potentially dis-
orienting experience. Chinese opera has also been used in other types of
productions. In Taipei, a rock musical version of *The Taming of the Shrew*
titled *Kiss Me Nana* (*Wenwo ba Nana*, 1995) was staged in 1997 (contrary
to what the title suggests, it had no relation to Cole Porter's *Kiss Me Kate*).
The production incorporated Chinese-opera techniques, cross-dressing,
modern dance, and rock music. Ta-lung's (Petruchio) servants become
three androgynous acrobats tumbling *jingju* style on stage.[39]

Beyond Chinese opera, performances of Shakespeare that involve
China at their center of imagination frequently highlight linguistic differences. Languages served as markers of ethnic differences in a bilingual
Taiwanese–Mandarin *Romeo and Juliet* at the Shakespeare in Taipei festival
in 2003.[40] The Montagues and the Capulets are each assigned a different
language, complicating the experience of artists in the Chinese diaspora
and the play's capacity as a national allegory. Key scenes from *Romeo and
Juliet* were staged in two plays-within-a-play in Ning Caishen's *Romeo and
Zhu Yingtai*, directed by He Nian and produced by the Shanghai Dramatic
Arts Center (May 2008), in which French, Japanese, English, and Mandarin Chinese were spoken. In what Ning called "a tragedy told in comic
manners," the star-crossed lovers traversed 1937 Shanghai and present-
day New York in search of new personal and cultural identities. Other
bilingual or multilingual performances have taken place in the Chinese
and Asian diaspora. The Pan Asian Repertory Theatre staged a bilingual
Mandarin–English *A Midsummer Night's Dream* (New York, 1983) directed
by Tisa Chang, in which Mandarin was reserved for kings, queens, and
Puck, while other characters spoke mainly English except in moments of
stress.[41] British-Chinese director David Tse's futuristic Mandarin–English
King Lear reframed the epistemological gap between Lear and Cordelia

FIGURE 2   Matt McCooey (Edmund) and Daniel York (Edgar) duel in the Mandarin–English *King Lear,* directed by David Tse, Stratford, 2006. (Courtesy of Yin Xuefeng and Shanghai Dramatic Arts Center)

in linguistic difference. Part of the Royal Shakespeare Company's (RSC) Complete Works Festival (2006–2007), the production traveled to Shanghai, Chongqing, Stratford-upon-Avon, and other cities in Great Britain.[42] With British-Asian performers from Tse's London-based theater company, Yellow Earth (founded in 1995), and performers from the Shanghai Dramatic Arts Center, the production embodied the anxieties of diasporic artists. Regan and Goneril spoke fluent and elegant Chinese, but Cordelia—a member of the Chinese diaspora—spoke no Chinese and could say only *meiyou* (nothing). The idea of China was also symbolized in Tse's use of Chinese opera. The highly stylized duel between Edgar and Edmund was staged to *jingju* percussion beats (figure 2). Here Chinese opera functioned in a way similar to the video-game rhythm and music of RSC's *Romeo and Juliet,* directed by Nancy Meckler during the same season, providing a symbolic space for violence in productions that reframed Shakespeare's plays in contemporary settings.

Between 1839, when Shakespeare was part of a war of ideology, and the present time, when Chinese Shakespeares have become a vital force in many cultural locations, the distance between world cultures has shrunk (because of colonialism and globalization) and grown (because of war and misunderstanding). These intercultural readings continue to fascinate.

When performed in non-Anglophone countries in the twenty-first century, Shakespeare no longer seems to be "talking to himself" but has become "the substance of a global conversation."[43] Chinese Shakespeares contain some of the most interesting parts of these conversations.

Coda

There are three coexisting modes to engage ideas of China and Shakespeare. First, a trend to universalize rather than localize Shakespeare has produced plays performed "straight," with visual and textual citations of what was perceived to be authoritative classical performances (such as Laurence Olivier's versions). Early performances in Shanghai tended to follow this pattern. If the play seems foreign, according to advocates of this approach, that only guarantees its aesthetics have been preserved in a way that benefits the audience.

A second trend, to localize the plot, setting, and meanings of a play, assimilates Shakespeare into the fabric of local worldviews and representational practices. An example is Bu Wancang's *A Spray of Plum Blossom*. At the heart of this approach is a moral evaluation of the utility of the ideas contained in literature and arts—local or foreign. In nineteenth-century China, the motives for using Shakespeare's name to construct the Chinese dream of modernity was detached from Shakespeare's texts and attached to the perceived ethical insights of the modern represented by Shakespeare. Sufficiently familiar and valuable to local communities, Shakespeare's texts have been cited in varied ways by politicians and other cultural celebrities in mainland China and Taiwan, where there is no English heritage. Some Shakespeare allusions emphasized the moral lessons allegedly contained in the plays; others invoked a sense of cultural belonging and a shared recognition of values that were in an unspecified sense "universal" in the public life. On December 2, 1992, Jiang Zemin, then chairman of the Central Military Commission of the People's Republic of China, quoted from *Timon of Athens*, a play known to CCP cadres through Karl Marx's writing, during his address to the People's Liberation Army officers at the National Defense University:

> TIMON: Gold? Yellow, glittering, precious gold? . . .
> Thus much of this will make black white, foul fair,
> Wrong right, base noble, old young, coward valiant. (4.3.26–29)

Jiang urged the cadres to heed the lesson about the corrupting power of money in order to remain loyal and useful members of the party.[44] In March 1999, Chinese premier Zhu Rongji used *The Merchant of Venice* to endorse the legitimacy of market law for post–Deng Xiaoping China, glossing over the ontological, religious, racial, and ethical implications of the contract of a pound of flesh.[45] In November 2006, Taiwan's premier, Su Tseng-chang, quoted *Julius Caesar* at length to demonstrate his loyal support for President Chen Shui-bian, who was at the center of a political storm.[46] When other politicians responded enthusiastically by quoting other parts of the play to argue for or against Su's proposal, a highly allegorical discussion of *Julius Caesar* and Taiwan ensued.

The third tendency has prompted artists to truncate and rewrite Shakespeare's plays so as to relate them to images of China. An example is Lao She's "New Hamlet." Such a re-creation is deconstructive in the sense that it focuses on multiply determined localities in a polycentric world. Similar works from other parts of Asia have been hailed as "welcome developments" and as a liberating "free" form (pastiche or multilingual theater).[47] In the Chinese context, although such rewriting may be a means to counter stereotypical construction of local and foreign cultures, they do not always translate into effective resistance of the authority of Shakespeare and Chinese cultural forms. As retro as "straight" performances (the first trend) may seem, they do not always succumb to the perceived textual authorities as the artists embracing the third approach tend to argue. Although English-speaking audiences recognize the otherness or alternativeness of Chinese Shakespearean performances, many of these performances are far from alternative. They are commercially successful and regarded as mainstream productions in their local communities. Fredric Jameson's critique of the monopoly of late capitalism leads some scholars to hold a more pessimistic view of the interpretive capacity of commercially successful intercultural performances because, as they argue, these works often institutionalize cultural differences.[48] It may not always be the case. Each of the three approaches has produced interpretations that effectively complicate the conventions of authenticity and authority claims.

Underlying my study are three related lines of inquiry united by what might be called locality criticism—that is, analyses that focus on shifting localities that cluster around the artists, their works, and their audiences. The case studies in this volume examine the interplay between the locality where authenticity and intentionality is derived and the locality where

differences emerge, as evidenced by the works of intellectuals, theater artists, filmmakers, and writers, such as Lin Shu (Lin Qinnan, 1852–1924),
Lu Xun (Zhou Shuren, 1881–1936), Liang Qichao (1873–1929), Lao She
(Shu Qingchun, 1899–1966), Huang Zuolin (1906–1994), Li Jianwu
(1906–1986), Ruan Lingyu (1910–1935), Jiao Juyin (1905–1975), Yevgeniya
Konstantinovna Lipkovskaya (1902–1990), Stan Lai (Lai Sheng-chuan,
b. 1954), and Wu Hsing-kuo (b. 1953). Given the complexity of this cultural
history, it is important not to lose sight of the temporally and geographi-
cally expansive patterns of cross-cultural engagement. Therefore, the
opening chapter, "Owning Chinese Shakespeares," pursues the critical
concept of localization and critiques the fidelity-derived discourse about
cultural ownership. How were Chinese Shakespeares used as a kind of
staged utopia of modernity?

Part of the answer to this question is found in chapter 2, in which I
investigate the varied and often paradoxical cultural logics of constructing a hypercanonical presence of Englishness in China in the absence
of Shakespeare's texts from the first Opium War in 1839 to the turn of
the century. Leading Chinese thinkers valorized Shakespeare *before* any of
his plays were translated or performed in Chinese. Liang Qichao wrote a
play, *New Rome (Xin Luoma)*, that featured Shakespeare as a character; Lu
Xun, Xu Zhimo, and other writers searched in vain for a "Chinese Shakespeare," a national cultural figure; and reformers turned "Shakespeare"
into a fiction of moral space in which they found a ready home. In the
twofold defamiliarization of Shakespeare and China, utopian visions of
universal figures of modernity (Shakespearean or Chinese) were used to
construct cultural and political worthiness. While largely written out of
the master narrative of cultural history, the patterns of these early encounters are part of the multiply influenced local Shakespeare tradition that
emerged after 1900. Chapter 3 takes stock of the rapidly stretching ripples
of these encounters in the early twentieth century, when translation was
turned into ethical acts of interpretation. Shakespeare and his plays were
useful imported cultural packages that facilitated visions of a new China
in relation to the ongoing cultural reform. This moralistic and allegorical mode of reading has influenced the next generation of readers in the
mid-twentieth century, but Lin Shu's and Lao She's works have been sidestepped by the paradigm of evolutionary model in the field.[49]

The rhetorical strategies to articulate a cultural modernity also defined the transformation of the "new woman." Chapter 4 analyzes the
roles of women and urban elites in the construction of the usefulness of

Shakespeare in naturalist theater and silent films of the 1930s and 1940s. These works bear the traces of the shifting gender hierarchy and the anxieties of Western influence and, in the process, overlook the racial issues that have come to define Anglo-European productions and criticism of such plays as *The Merchant of Venice*. The new woman's movement is central to the self-identity of China's cosmopolitan urbanites and their imagination of Shakespeare's women characters[50] The hopeful yet unattainable gaze directed at Shakespeare's ambiguous Western values was replaced by an intensified interest in the cosmopolitan identity of China's urban centers, which leads us to the question of historicity. Chapter 5 addresses the intricate interplay between presentism and historicism through a comparative analysis of Jiao Juyin's *Hamlet*, staged in a Confucian temple in 1942; Wu Ningkun's reading of *Hamlet* in a labor camp during the Cultural Revolution; and a purportedly apolitical Soviet–Chinese production of *Much Ado About Nothing* (premiered in 1957 and revived in 1961 and 1979).[51] In all these cases, locality and the site of reading played major roles in the interpretation of Chinese history and Shakespeare. In the case of the Soviet–Chinese venture, although the influence of the well-known Russian tradition of filming such Shakespearean plays as *King Lear* and *Hamlet* is not immediately evident, the Stanislavskian method and Soviet ideologies helped Chinese theater artists to find a safe text.

That text acquired more diverse meanings in the next decade. Chapter 6 examines the ways in which the visual currency of Chinese opera and Shakespeare's textual authority were imagined, visualized, and consumed since the 1980s, a decade that saw a boom of *xiqu* Shakespeare performances and a revived interest in, if not obsession with, the ocular dimension of interculturalism. *Xiqu* has frequently been seen as an antithesis to *huaju*. I argue to the contrary; modern *xiqu* theater has always been a hybrid form of representation, incorporating idioms and styles from other traditions, including *huaju*. This chapter also touches on colorblind casting in China, an issue rarely discussed by theater historians. Chapter 7 delineates the theoretical and political consequences of disowning "Shakespeare" and "China" in the present time. Part of the question of consequence necessarily remains open-ended, as international circumstances continue to change. However, a number of new trends in performance since 1990 have gained momentum. Stan Lai's *Lear and the Thirty-seven-fold Practice of a Bodhisattva* (*Pusa zhi sanshiqi zhong xiuxing zhi Li'er wang*) and Wu Hsing-kuo's *Lear Is Here* (*Li'er zaici*) exemplify performances that are framed by the artists' autobiography and religious discourse. They signal the arrival of a new Asian identity in the global marketplace of cultures. The grand narrative of East meets West now co-exists with an account of the living, contemporary directors' personal engagement with Shakespeare, and with new but equally elusive categories such as "I" and "Shakespeare." The epilogue tackles the ramifications of these new modes of inscribing temporally and visually ambiguous articulations of Shakespeare and China into a global vernacular in theater (Lin Zhaohua's *Richard III*) and cinema (Feng Xiaogang's *The Banquet*). A paradox of infatuation with Asian visuality and rejection of ethnic authenticity emerged in the asymmetrical cultural flows.

It is my hope that *Chinese Shakespeares'* localization of the meanings of Shakespeare and China will break down the critical impasse surrounding cross-cultural entanglements, a crucial step toward reinventing the interpretive energy that has been dulled by ideological investments in various conventions of authenticity informed by notions of the original and the derivative. The scholarship that seeks to cross borders loses its intellectual punch when it is able to consider only one perspective, or when it merely seeks to add to, say, the already long list of Shakespeare's global reincarnations. It is important that Chinese Shakespeares as a new interpretive subject be analyzed so as to dislodge what China means and how Shakespeare is customarily interpreted, because multilocation perspectives bring to light the unpredictable and exciting fabric of cultural life that rarely conforms to institutional divisions of knowledge production. This displacement is necessary to keep roads passable and bridges open between different forms of cultural production and knowledge.

PART I

Theorizing Global Localities

1   Owning Chinese Shakespeares

... for the eye sees not itself
But by reflection, by some other things.
                        —*Julius Caesar*

One of the possibilities enhanced by the encounter between China and Shakespeare might be found in *The Tempest:*

ARIEL: Nothing of him that doth fade,
   But doth suffer a sea-change
   Into something rich and strange. (1.2.400–402)

Although one cannot say that nothing of Shakespeare or China fades in these historical processes, there has been a sea change in how the world sees them. The cultural space between "Shakespeare" and "China" is a space of (re)writing that is found outside of what is written. It subjects the artists and their local and foreign audiences to see, and be seen, from afar.

As the ideas of Shakespeare and China enter the global cultural marketplace, they initiate collaborative processes by which readers and audiences in different cultures grasp or exclude certain literary meanings and values. *Chinese Shakespeares* investigates what I suggest is a central moment in Shakespeare's afterlife and in the cultural alterity of China.[1] Attending to both the local and the transnational mechanisms through which the expressive and political values of literature emerge, I consider what the Shakespeare–China interrelations are, why they have been used to rhetorically construct narratives about difference and universality, and how such narratives have unleashed new interpretive energy.

The answers proposed in *Chinese Shakespeares* suggest that the rewrites of Shakespeare and China turn them into syntactical categories that are used to generate meanings. Like words and grammatical patterns, Shakespeare and China are used to generate specific meanings in different contexts. Focusing on how artistic interventions modify the transnational knowledge bank about ideas of Shakespeare and China, my case studies of several major cultural events and texts reveal that Shakespeare and China are narrative systems read and written within the framework of performance and cultural translation. The symbiotic "narrative system" consists of writers', directors', and audiences' (whatever their locations and cultural identities) uses of Shakespeare to accentuate the perceived uniqueness of Chinese culture and vice versa.

That is what the Shakespeare–China interrelations are and how they operate. The provenance of Shakespeare or China in different times has allowed the cross-cultural (for example, intercultural performance) and intracultural operations (for example, Chinese social reform) to be carried out. That is why these networks of meanings are dictated by artistic and ideological forces. However, textual fluidity is not a carte blanche for every reader to concoct his or her own meaning. Certain historical moments demand reading to be carried out in the reader's cultural context, while other historical junctures provoke interpretations that claim to depend on the "text" itself. These patterns of interpretation are informed by recursions to various sites of origin and the reinvention or repression of specific meanings within these sites.

It is commonly recognized that the history of Shakespearean performance is the history of "what we mean by Shakespeare."[2] The Shakespeare–China relations not only reveal what Asian and Anglo-European readers mean by "Shakespeare" and/or "China," but also constitute histories that, constructed over time, reveal shifting perspectives on the question of the migration of texts and representations. Shakespeare's plays have acquired a number of different political and aesthetic functions, allowing Chinese artists and audiences to see China through the eyes of the Other (Shakespeare). This, in turn, makes Chinese interpretations of Shakespeare a visual projection of the gaze of Shakespeare's Other (Chinese perspectives). This rich network of interpretations and positions enables multifaceted modes of reading both Shakespeare and China.

With the acceleration of economic and cultural globalization, the present time is particularly propitious to investigate the topic of Shakespeare and China. And yet the significance of multiple Chinese Shakespeares extends beyond the clichéd but frequently cited reasons, such as Shakespeare's connection to the formation of world cultures or China—making headlines with increasing frequency—as an important nation to know about in our century. For people who know, or think they know, what China and Shakespeare stand for, the questions are: Whose Shakespeare is it? Whose and which China?

Locality Criticism

The unnatural longevity of Shakespeare's viability begs the question of the value of local reading positions. The question of where Chinese Shakespeares are situated is ultimately connected to the question of where critics and audiences discover themselves. This question—along with the relationship between the local and the global—calls for a reexamination of Shakespeare and China as two amorphous discursive entities.

An awareness of the fetishization of the universal values of Shakespeare has prompted scholars to forsake the character criticism established by A. C. Bradley and G. Wilson Knight and turn to various forms of historical knowledge. Interpretive possibilities have multiplied when Shakespeare's text is lodged in its social networks, then and now. Elizabethan knowledge has been brought to bear on the operation of Shakespeare's theater.[3] Cultural materialism and new historicism have also transformed other fields through their attention to the interplay between decidedly local forces and artistic production.

However, the local knowledge that informed our contemporary performance has remained marginal in the scholarly inquiries into the meanings of "Shakespeare."[4] Many contemporary rewrites, especially non-Anglophone ones, are seen as obscure bits of Shakespeariana and too far removed from the core of Shakespearean knowledge to matter. Despite their recognized status as an integral part of postcolonial and performance criticism, literary and dramatic adaptations have long been regarded as secondary and derivative, and the field has accordingly been relegated to the status of an "[un]acknowledged genre in criticism."[5] To counter this bias, we need to consider the itinerant projections of Shakespeare and various localities where Shakespeare has been put to work.

As Konstantin Stanislavsky suggested, "spectators come to the theatre to hear [and *see*] the subtext, [because] they can read the text at home."[6] Elements of cultural politics, nationalism, revolution, and postmodernism form a prominent set of subtexts in which Shakespeare and China are read. Since literary interpretation is always done from specific cultural locations, at the center of my study lies the notion of locality. Artists and critics work through various cultural locations, some of which lie at the crossroads of fiction and reality, such as "Hamlet's castle," Kronborg Castle in Denmark.[7] I distinguish not only between historical hindsight and blind spots, but also between individuals reading in the same historical period but in different contexts. Any manifestation of Chinese Shakespeares must be understood in relation to the subtexts of the multiple deferrals to local and foreign authorities, authenticity claims, and unexamined silences.[8] Such an approach opens up the notions of Shakespeare and China to new temporalities and locations. As representations of Shakespeare multiply, so do the localities where these representations themselves are appropriated. These localities constitute a set of historically significant practices—the practices of locating global Shakespeares and transmitting such location-specific epistemologies as the idea of Chinese opera.

While Shakespeare in other locations often speaks simultaneously in the coercive voice of Prospero and the agonized accents of Caliban, the case of Shakespeare and China does not fit easily into the postcolonial theoretical models commonly used to interpret Asian rewrites of Anglo-European literature.[9] Michael Neill rightly observes that Shakespeare's plays were "entangled from the beginning with the projects of nation-building, empire and colonization" in many cases.[10] However, regions with more ambiguous relationships with the West can be doubly marginalized when dominant critical paradigms, such as postcolonial criticism, are deployed. There are two historical forces behind Chinese Shakespeares' unique mythology in the historical record of globalization. Except for Macao, Hong Kong, and a handful of treaty ports, China was never quite colonized by the Western powers in the twentieth century. In most parts of the Chinese-speaking world, Shakespeare has rarely been resisted as a dominant figure of colonialism. Further, throughout its modern and contemporary history, China often played multiple and sometimes contradictory roles simultaneously, including the oppressor and the oppressed. In relation to the paradox of China's status, one may legitimately ask:

"Is China a postcolonial nation?" or "Are contemporary Chinese cultural discourses too 'nationalistic' and potentially hegemonic to be included in that cultural frontier?"[11] Cultural production in the territories that were not directly influenced by European colonial forces has begun to attract the attention of scholars such as Gayatri Spivak and Prasenjit Duara.[12] While such locations as India, Africa, and Latin America continue to be the core of postcolonial criticism, my study suggests that it is precisely by virtue of being in an estranged, ambiguous relationship to the post-colonial question that Chinese Shakespeares can provide rich opportunities for reexamining the logic of the field.

Such rethinking may find its inspiration from the cultural-historical contexts of traveling texts and their readers. Locality is a useful concept to understand the audience–performer or reader–text interactions. The concept of locality is a lynchpin of sociological theory that is only beginning to be applied to literary and cultural criticism.[13] The term takes into account the cultural coordinates of a work, including the setting of a play, its performance venue, and the specificities of the cultural location of a performance such as Jiao Juyin's wartime *Hamlet* in 1942, in which parallel and antagonistic readings of local and world histories are evoked. The performance in a Confucian temple in rural China offered particular articulations of various localities recognized both in medias res and in retrospect: Hamlet's Denmark, Fortinbras's Norway, a China under Japanese invasion, and symbolically defined Chinese virtues. The crux of these readings of Confucianism and *Hamlet* emerges from the temple, a venue that becomes a fictive and historical space for reflection. These localities shape and define Shakespeare's extensive post-humous encounters with the world. While it has now been recognized that Shakespeare has occupied an international space for centuries, the theoretical implications of this international space remain unclear. The Shakespeare–China interrelations are determined by interactions between local histories embedded in and superimposed on the works of art, shaping an interchange repeatedly staged since the nineteenth century. The notion of locality recognizes that representations signify relationally. Cultural difference, as Homi Bhabha observes, often introduces into "the process of cultural judgment and interpretation the sudden shock of the successive, non-synchronic time of signification" rather than a simple contention between different systems of cultural value.[14]

The local is not always the antithesis to the global or an antidote to the hegemonic domination that has been stereotypically associated with the West in the shifting reconfigurations of Shakespeare and China in this history. We live in an age when global or universal claims are suspect and the local is often celebrated as a Quixotian hero resisting hegemony or guarded as an "endangered space" in need of being "produced, maintained, and nurtured deliberately."[15] In China, the global finds subtle articulation in the institution of cultural translation and in politically divisive discourses of modernity. There are indeed times when artists who appeal to Shakespearean universalism are deluded and complicit, although a performer can also let his or her politically driven agenda set up the work as alternative to dominant academic or artistic practices. Odd as it may seem, in other times, such as the Cultural Revolution, the local *is* the coercive and oppressive agent. Likewise, rampant Sinophobia in Taiwan's cultural institution subjugates *jingju* performers in the name of preservation of "local" performing arts. In those moments, the global represents a potential space for liberation. While the local is sometimes deployed to confront transnational values represented by Shakespeare's increasing, or decreasing, global clout, in other instances the additional purchase of the global is summoned to reduce the authority of the local. The dispersed nature of these transmissions necessarily detaches both the Shakespearean texts and Chinese cultural texts from their perceived points of origin. Contrary to what one might expect, such detachment does not always liberate these texts for reinterpretation. Far from threatening the canonical status of Shakespeare, some rewrites reinscribe the authorial authority and cultural essentialism into the discourse of cultural exchanges. As much as Shakespeare and China are powerful cultural institutions, they are also repositories of emotions and personal histories. Traditionally, the temporal dimension of Shakespeare's afterlife has received more attention. Locality criticism emphasizes the physical and geocultural dimensions of the processes of rewriting.

If we accept that cultural translation not only occurs in the space between these entities but also defines the interstices of global cultures, we must treat Asian- and European-informed conceptions of Shakespeare and of China as intertwining sets of formulations, as epistemic foundations for a critical understanding of Chinese Shakespeares. Only an adequate theory of what it means to localize Shakespeare can let us decide what does or does not succumb to the ideological forces driving these new works.

Other Shakespeares as a Theoretical Problem

It has become impossible to speak of Shakespeare without be-coming aware of other Shakespeares, the othering of Shakespeare, and the linguistic and political diaspora of Shakespeare. Since all interpreta-tions—including criticism and my own positions—bear the imprimatur of specific locations and historical moments, it takes both metacritical and historical modes of inquiry to effectively understand the institutional forces (academic, political, artistic) and cultural forms (fiction, theater, cinema) that produced Chinese Shakespeares. My aim of metacriticism is to examine the unique logic and structure of a work or an artistic claim, and its critical reception.[16]

There is little doubt that the field of cultural globalization has yet to properly define its object and grasp competing claims made in the name of local/global culture and the tradition of text-and-representation criti-cism. Since the 1990s, Shakespearean film and theater scholars have re-peatedly called for the necessary refinement and application of theories for cross-cultural appropriation, but not all scholars—even those critics on the lookout for new performance trends—agree on the implication of theorization.[17] Patrice Pavis, for example, cautions that it may be "too soon to propose a global theory of intercultural theatre" when we are "un-certain as to whether [intercultural performance], the tip of an iceberg, . . . signals a depth of startling proportions hidden from view, or whether it is already in the process of melting away."[18] Pavis's question of timing is an interesting one, but the obstacle to theorization is not the critic's temporal proximity to the events that may impede a full appreciation of the discur-sive fields. Even when critics find themselves within the structure being read, meaningful intellectual work can still be carried out. Rather, the lack of in-depth critical histories of these events impedes the development of any theory, which is why I have opted for a wider range of coverage of historical and critical issues to contextualize the case studies.

The differences and similarities between ideas of Shakespeare and of Asia, rather than the dynamics of the interstitial space, have historically received more critical attention. This in part has hindered the develop-ment of a theoretical model for global Shakespeare. The distance between Chinese and Shakespearean aesthetic principles bears dwelling upon, but it can lead observers of cultural exchange to focus instead on the ques-tions of assimilation, defamiliarization, or compatibility between Shake-spearean and Chinese representational practices. This tendency leads to somewhat predictable conclusions about what and how these new works contribute to the host culture and to Shakespeare's afterlife. A related difficulty is an urge to reconcile fundamental differences between the aesthetics named by Shakespeare and by Asia, and to use their philosophical and structural similarities to support claims of universality.

This is precisely what has occupied the rewriters' attention, as evidenced by their philosophical investments in authenticity claims and *conventions* of interpretive authenticity. For example, some early-twentieth-century Chinese polemicists used Shakespeare and the iconic proposal for a new China to construct nuanced cultural signifiers that were deployed to the exclusion of other competing reformist agendas. Authenticity became a trope that was manipulated to exercise authoritative claims over political and cultural reforms. In a different period, authenticating discourses played another role. In the global cultural marketplace of the late twentieth century, the notion of authenticity enabled marginalized artists to counter oppressive cultural practices such as certain forms of interculturalism that efface local traditions. While the arbitrariness of the conventions of authenticity has to be recognized, it is equally important to be cognizant of what ideological work authenticating discourse can perform. It builds bridges in some places but blocks avenues for exchange elsewhere.

The lack of theorization means that the topic of Shakespeare *and* China is usually met with surprise and suspicion.[19] Yet our reaction of surprise in relation to the subject is itself surprising. The ideas of Shakespeare and China add several levels of discordance to the fields of Shakespeare and Chinese studies and to the praxis of performance. As much as such discordance is challenging, it can also be the source of exciting and provocative intellectual and artistic works. Despite the increasing currency of transnational studies in the humanities, the politics of recognition has continued to operate not only in the study of minority cultures—as Françoise Lionnett, Shu-mei Shih, and Charles Taylor point out—but also in Shakespeare studies.[20] Selective attentiveness, if not valorization, has routinely been given to the most dominant and the most resistant readings of Shakespeare, highlighting a linear relationship of either assimilation or opposition between Shakespeare and world cultures.

Therefore, one of the first questions to be addressed in the study of Chinese Shakespeares is: Why should we concern ourselves with the place of "China" in Shakespearean criticism where non-European cultures do not seem to have a place? Why should Shakespeare be associated with China at all, since they appear to be antithetical to each other? The same question could be rephrased as one from the perspective of Asian studies: What can the presence and absence of Shakespeare in the Sinophone world tell us about Asian modernity and postmodernism? Scholars disagree on the theoretical implication of these questions. Jonathan Bate takes the middle ground and posits that Shakespeare's global appeal results neither from his linguistic virtuosity nor the power of the British Empire.[21] Dennis Kennedy, however, takes a more radical position and argues against the idea of cultural ownership and "the native familiarity that English-speakers assume for Shakespeare."[22] There are similar debates about essentialism and the hybridity of modern Chinese literary culture. One of the most contested notions is Chinese culture's purported independence from other cultures, or China's exclusivity. James Liu considers twentieth-century Chinese literature and theories too "Westernized" to merit serious study, while Rey Chow defends the necessity to read "modern Chinese literature other than as a kind of bastardized appendix to classical Chinese and a mediocre apprentice to Western literature."[23]

These initial points of contention have motivated my study, and cultural and performance theories inform the exploration of the shifting localities of the so-called unfaithful or self-syndicated authentic representations of Shakespeare and China. We should concern ourselves with foreign Shakespeares, because Shakespeare, for the past century, has been writ larger than his text. Specifically, artistic interpretations of Shakespeare and histories of the Sinophone world provide rich materials for locality criticism. The fact that this cultural phenomenon does not settle comfortably into the grammar of our current critical vocabulary can also initiate useful reflection on the critical enterprise itself. The task of cultural criticism in this context is not simply to evaluate how "successfully" a given work represents the source texts or symbols of the host culture, but to locate its logic of representation within the collective cultural memory, politics, and the personal dimension of history.

The Pleasures of (In)fidelity

The reception of both Anglophone and non-Anglophone performances of Shakespeare has been dominated by morally loaded discourses of fidelity and authenticity ("Did they get Shakespeare or Chinese opera right?"), informed by variations of such questions as "Is it still Shakespeare?" or "Is the performance 'Chinese' enough?"[24] Even a more established field, such as Shakespeare on film, is still grappling with similar issues.[25] Although debates still rage about the status of translated canonical literary works, at stake are such questions as how Shakespeare and China are connected, how the connections are celebrated or contested in different times and places, and what these interactions create (films, theater pieces, ideologies, literary works, and new visions). These two entities are also connected via the market law. Shakespeare's currency in the Anglophone world generally, and the revival of Shakespeare in England particularly, is connected to the demands of the international cultural markets. The Anglophone cultural globalization in turn complicates the vested interests in Shakespeare among writers and performers in the non-Anglophone world. These interests are frequently marked by signs of resistance, apologia, and many other agendas. The interplay between Shakespeare and China thus reveals the plurality and the referential instability of these discursive entities.

I would now like to think these issues through the rhetoric of fidelity. It bears reiterating that adaptation has to be considered on its own terms. Characterized by its nature of in-betweenness, adaptation is neither a simple rejection of the idea of the singular author—as some avant-garde artists believe—nor an unproblematic tool to unsettle the tyranny of the author—as Gilles Deleuze idealizes.[26] Recognizing the discourses about fidelity is the first step to treat rewriting as a site where citations, recitation, and echoes collide to form new meanings.[27]

The first obstacle to overcome is the assumption of an ethics of fidelity.[28] Recent work has shown an acute awareness of these perils, reorienting the relationship between text and performance. Rewriting is not an appendage that gives way to the literariness of Shakespeare's text, but an agent that participates in the play's signification process. Even though the word "localization" was not in use until the nineteenth century, resistance to various activities named by localization has created a major ideological force throughout Shakespeare's afterlife.

The widespread investment in the particularities of Shakespeare's text and non-Anglophone traditions cuts across a range of otherwise divergent artistic movements and critical schools, including—perhaps surprisingly—those that may be deemed radical and even iconoclastic. This dominant paradigm bears an ethical dimension. Despite the recent shift of the object of inquiry from Shakespeare the text to the cultural institution of "Shakespeare," many artists and critics continue to be preoccupied with the issue of fidelity, as evidenced by interpretive strategies that riff on authenticating marketing moves, by mutually implicating historicist and presentist claims, and by artistic and scholarly activities united by the name of appropriation—a problematic term.[29] Although there is greater latitude for parody in East Asia than in Anglophone culture, varying degrees of essentialist reverence of the local culture or Shakespeare dictate that many artists see themselves as speaking for Shakespearean or Chinese aesthetics, or both. Despite having translated and directed several of Shakespeare's plays in Mandarin and Cantonese (and staged *jingju* plays in English), Daniel Yang fundamentally rejects the notion of transcultural performance.[30] Ong Keng Sen's postmodern pronouncements in *LEAR*— despite his challenge of cultural essentialism—focused on the purported authenticity of cultural locations ("New Asia" or elsewhere). Another equally revealing example is Feng Xiaogang's *Hamlet*-inspired feature film. When the high-profile film *The Banquet* premiered at the Venice and Cannes film festivals and subsequently screened in the Chinese-speaking world in late 2006, it generated heated debates about the film's dual identity.[31] Is the film Shakespearean enough? Is it Chinese?[32] Critical discourses about this film demonstrate the needs of multiple interpretive communities, including two opposing forces: the tendencies to exalt the hybridity of postnational cultural spaces and to reinscribe the nation into cross-cultural dialogues.[33] Behind these forces is the common tendency to essentialize cultural difference and mistake rigidly defined equivalents for intertextual work.

Even as some artists strive to seek the real, authentic Shakespeare or China, they are able to create only a sense of fullness that satisfies the desires for particular types of experiences dictated by historical circumstances. Therefore, the relation between cultural texts and representations is not a mimetic one, but an enabling relation between two mutually imbricated subjects.[34] The ideas of Shakespeare and of China are informed by performances of all kinds. They are producing subjects in the sense that they do not provide those kinds of reliable and immutable points of reference that many artists and audiences aspire toward.

Ironically, the familiar news about Shakespeare's global and transhistorical appeal can sometimes dull the critical attention.[35] What is worthy of attention is the selective inattentiveness to the dynamics of "unfaithful" rewrites, or how the process of rewriting itself faithfully reproduces the economic and cultural dynamics of globalization. The distinctions between faithful and unfaithful break down where Shakespeare's afterlife is concerned, since the plays are so subject to multiple manifestations. In fact, a particularly compelling point of departure for exploring Shakespeare's afterlife is the ethical assumption at work in the seemingly commonsense distinction between normative and alternative interpretations (English versus foreign Shakespeares; faithful versus unfaithful adaptations; authentic versus inauthentic representations of China). The so-called alternatives are in fact central to our contemporary performance culture, in which classic plays can still be performed for entertainment and intellectual stimulation. Local Shakespeares are not a binary opposition to canonical metropolitan English-language representations that are perceived to be "licensed" and more faithful.

It is important to recognize that any system of performance, like any mode of cultural production (for example, *jingju*), is not an alternative to a legitimate, naturalized, mode of representation (for example, English-language or *huaju* "straight" performance).[36] There is nothing outside the very system of signification that is being constantly reconfigured by each instance of performance and by the cumulative history of these reconfigurations. Therefore, it is more fruitful to pursue the question of "alternative to what" than to substantiate authenticity claims. At the risk of appearing to fall back into the remedial mode that defines new theoretical models in negative terms, I would like to point out that theorizing from the margins carries its own rewards.[37] Rather than a revelation of the supposed fidelity or infidelity of rewrites, this study focuses on the development of varied and often paradoxical articulations of Shakespeare and China and the tensions between their varied localities, emphasizing the cultural space between Shakespeare and China that sustains a heavily trafficked two-way exchange.

By two-way transactions, I mean the processes that revise and enrich the repertoire of knowledge about Shakespeare and China, as exemplified by Jiao Juyin's *Hamlet* (1942), which transformed Hamlet's philosophy in part through the use of a specific performance venue—a Confucian temple in southwestern China during the second Sino-Japanese War. Interrelations between Shakespeare and China constitute networks of signifiers that are themselves reconfigurations of other cultural signs. Some works have expanded the repertoire of Shakespeareness and Asian performance idioms to create interconnecting Shakespeare traditions that are both Asian and Western. One example is Wu Hsing-kuo's *Kingdom of Desire* (1986), a play inspired as much by *Macbeth* as by *Throne of Blood* (1957) by Kurosawa Akira, who has been identified as an "intensely Japanese

[but] paradoxically not solely a Japanese film maker."[38] Two mainland Chinese feature films based on *Hamlet, The Banquet* (2006) and *The Prince of the Himalayas* (2006), further expanded the interpretive frameworks for both the Shakespearean and Chinese texts. *The Banquet* produced a highly elastic vision of ancient Chinese imperial court culture; at the same time, it reinterpreted the structure of emotions in *Hamlet* through the stylization enabled by the knight-errant (*wuxia*) film genre. *The Prince of the Himalayas* was so popular in China that Mandarin–Tibetan *huaju* (spoken drama) stage versions based on the film, with the same cast and director, have been mounted in Shanghai and Beijing. This was a case where the performance idioms of the screen and the stage converged to create a new space for ethnic minority performers.

These works, in turn, enriched the interpretive possibilities of Shakespeare, just as Sarah Bernhardt's and Asta Nielsen's female Hamlets at the beginning of the twentieth century expanded the traditions of cross-dressed performance in Europe and the United States.[39] The transformation of cultural forms and values operates in both directions, thus informing and giving voice to the individual interpretations.

Myth Making

Despite these rich critical possibilities, studies of Shakespeare in popular culture and performance still tend to concentrate on Anglophone examples, relegating Asian Shakespeares to cocktail-party definitions of exotic spectacles. Likewise, the topic continues to strive for legitimacy within Asian studies. This is due in part to the technological operations of globalization as they play themselves out across nation-state structures and value systems.

Marginalization and myth making are mutually constitutive processes. Three main factors contribute to the marginalization of non-Anglophone Shakespeares and the mystification of Shakespeare's and China's exclusivity in the pedagogical and research contexts. First, due to the ephemeral nature of live theater, even the most commercially successful and the most extensively toured productions can never be as accessible as feature films. The other two factors are closely connected to the politics of the field: the misconception of the referential stability of performances at familiar centers—the United Kingdom, Canada, and the United States—and the widespread journalistic mode in writings about non-Anglophone

Shakespearean performance that reduces its subject of study to fleeting news items.

The marginalization of the field is a result of not a lack of publications but, ironically, an overflow of "reports" without theoretical reflection ("This is how they do Shakespeare over there; how quaint").[40] The reportage mode is unfortunately lacking in ideological analysis. It can be valuable for new works to be made accessible through descriptive reviews, but that cannot constitute the sole model of inquiry in the field.[41] Ultimately, cultural criticism has a different mission than a documentary film about an exotic object. It takes readers into a cultural event or a play in performance within its historical contexts not by replicating a full visual record of it, but by analyzing the logic of vested interests in visual, verbal, and textual signs.

Paradoxically, as an increasing number of rewrites become "familiarly known," they also become ornamental and predictably exotic objects that are never positioned to be properly known.[42] Many books on Shakespearean appropriation have a "non-West" chapter, but that itself is the problem. The dominance of the British–American axis in scholarship also contributes to the disinterest in non-Anglophone Shakespeares. Editors would not think of including a token chapter on American or British productions. Even scholarly works that engage a globally articulated subject such as racial difference are engulfed by the American and British "obsessions with black and white."[43] The hierarchies of subject dictate that only selected examples are concentrated on. However, even when non-Anglophone Shakespeares are analyzed, there is a critical neglect of the appropriation of the local interpretive practices (performance, translation, rewriting, reception). A few new works have responded to this critical impasse by demonstrating that symbiotic negotiations over Shakespeare's works do not occur only in traditionally defined peripheral localities but also at the Anglophone centers of Shakespearean performance.[44] What is needed is a necessarily more capacious and polymorphous sense of China or Shakespeare as a continually evolving repository of meaning rather than a fixed textual corpus. Just as the field of cinematic Shakespeare has recently adopted new paradigms that challenge "the notion that Shakespeare film is only of interest for its immediacy," the assumption about the ephemeral value of Asian Shakespeares can be fully examined only when we shift the critical energy from documenting individual rewrites as pieces of exotica to historicizing and theorizing their interrelated trajectories.[45]

In the past few years, as the contingency of performance and the referential instability of Shakespeare are being reexamined,[46] Chineseness has been likewise reassessed as a theoretical problem.[47] One of the most contested notions is the purported exceptionality of China in both scholarly discourse and popular culture.[48] On the one hand, European Sinologists (such as François Jullien) and philosophers (such as Leibniz) have repeatedly used rhetorically constructed differences of China to form an antithesis to European philosophy.[49] On the other hand, intellectuals and directors in China, especially those who are actively engaged in cultural translation, often turn China into a repository of idealized cultural values. Subscribing to the idea of identifiable and fixed cultural boundaries, they have developed an obsession with "Chineseness" that contributes to the fantasy that everything Chinese is "somehow better—longer in existence, . . . more valuable, and ultimately beyond comparison."[50]

The habitual mystification of China is present in many other areas. Within the purview of theater studies in North America, Asian performance remains the ultimate Other, "unknowable, unlearnable, unfathomable, [because] the languages are imagined to be indecipherable, . . . names are backwards, . . . cultural values . . . totally alien, [and] performers are trained from birth."[51] Ironically, some scholars of Asian studies are willing to endorse this attitude, readily confirming the difficulty of their own specialty and the challenges of cross-cultural dialogues. As recent scholarship has recognized, Chinese institutions—cultural, social, political—are often imagined as though they "began in times immemorial."[52] On the one hand, contradictory images of China in the popular and academic discourses around the world repeatedly challenge Western conceptual frameworks. On the other hand, assumptions nourished by "an entrenched Eurocentric worldview prevalent in *both* China and the West" have hindered the development of more productive ways to think about China.[53] Michel Foucault articulates this problem when he writes in his comments on Jorge Luis Borges's imaginary "Chinese" encyclopedia: "In our dreamworld, is not China precisely this privileged *site* of *space*? In our traditional imagery, the Chinese culture is the most meticulous, the most rigidly ordered, the one most deaf to temporal events, most attached to the pure delineation of space."[54]

Such dreams abound. Early-twentieth-century Chinese writers have been said to harbor an "obsession with China,"[55] whereas contemporary Chinese writers, as David Der-wei Wang observes, have attempted to "break away from hard-core obsession with China" by engaging in a frivolous "flirtation with China," approaching the country—"the most serious serious subject"—from very different perspectives.[56] This detachment of political action from literature may be characteristic of cultural production of the postmodern era, but positivism and a redemptive discourse continue to haunt the production and reception of Chinese Shakespeares. Since the late nineteenth century, Chinese artists and intellectuals have repeatedly recast new ideas—local or foreign—in a remedial mode, failing to recognize the fictional space occupied by "China."[57]

I hasten to add that these obsessions with Chineseness that mystify China are as pervasive among the artists as among the critics, both in and beyond the Sinophone world, who participated in the production of China as a mythic Other in Shakespearean performances. In fact, the double logic of intercultural performance relies on both recognizable, knowable elements of otherness and irreconcilable outlandishness. Both global Shakespeare and Chinese performance operate on the basis of the contrast between a knowable component of the Western canon and an "unknowable" Other. Studies of the phenomenon also share a mystified and undefined vocabulary.[58] China has repeatedly been summoned to fill in for the role of the Other, while Shakespeare remains a constant, a set of texts with established meanings. In an increasingly globalized world where outlandishness becomes harder and harder to achieve, artists and writers resort to even more drastic tactics to produce this otherness to contrast the readily familiar (although not really properly known) canon—Chinese, English, or otherwise.

The history of Chinese-themed performances of Shakespeare in and beyond the Sinophone world is complicated by these stereotypes that sustain social and literary imaginaries about Shakespeare and China. However, the illusion of antithetical and isolated identities of local and global cultures leads to a tendency either to ignore the connections between Shakespeare and China, or to explain the "odd" presence of Shakespeare in the Sinophone world and "China" in Shakespearean performances by the absence of a linear teleological history.

Terms of Engagement

Shakespeare's impact on non-Anglophone cultures is a two-way process, but the complexity of the two-way transaction is often obscured by confusions about categories and the limits of such dated terminology as cross-cultural "filtering" that pushes the acts of reading and writing across time and media into a discourse of commensurabilities that simply reaffirms ideological formations of identities.[59] It is no more productive to propose an Asia-centered paradigm to counter the dominance of pre-established Western-centered rubrics, but it is important to be attentive to both what these cross-cultural exchanges enable us to see and what the process of rewriting obscures or denies.

To that end, I will now discuss the basic terms through which I examine Chinese Shakespeares. Much of the dispersion of Shakespeare has been triggered by the more familiar defining factors of diaspora culture, such as the demographic movement of people across different regions (hence the categories of "touring Shakespeare," "Shakespeare in North America," and "Shakespeare in colonial India").[60] However, the global movement of ideas has also played a key role in the course of the long and eventful history of Shakespeare's afterlife. For my purposes, the more commonly used means of reference, Shakespeare *in* China, or a brand-name writer *in* any given culture for that matter, is not a viable critical category.[61] Such categorization obscures the dialectics of exchange between different cultures and implies the imposition of one culture upon another, investing certain texts with a transhistorical status. As its title suggests, *Chinese Shakespeares* examines encounters of Shakespeare and China as a transformative process (for example, expanding the meaning of traditional China through Lin Shu's bold rewriting of Shakespeare), as a cultural practice (for example, reading Shakespeare during the Cultural Revolution or quoting Shakespeare to support the agendas of the nouveaux riches and political leaders), as texts (fiction and reviews), and as performances.

By the term "Chinese Shakespeares," I identify the theoretical problems and multiple cultural locations of the ideas associated with China and Shakespeare, rather than the audience simply by nationality. "China" refers to a number of ideological positions (for example, the imaginaries of China) as well as a range of geocultural locations and historical periods that encompass late imperial China (1839–1910), Republican China (1911–1949), Communist China (1949–present), post-1949 Taiwan, Hong Kong, and the Chinese diaspora.[62] As the multidirectional traffic among these richly diverse locations include touring performances and intraregional collaboration, it is important to consider the networks of cultural production within, on the margins of, and outside "China."[63] Registering these asymmetrical cultural flows enables us to chart new territories for

comparative studies of cultural phenomena that go beyond geopoliti-
cally defined "national Shakespeares" such as India's or the PRC's
Shakespeare.

Similarly, the West represented by Shakespeare is itself a complicated,
slippery category.[64] "Shakespeare" refers to not only the works but also
the reputation and values associated with William Shakespeare. Just as
China does not remain the same every time it encounters Shakespeare,
"Shakespeare" signifies anew its attendant values each time it encounters China. The artists who engaged with Shakespeare have taken that
name to mean a number of different, and at times contradictory, things,
including authorial fantasies, editorially mediated modern English editions or translations, updated film versions, influential touring stage
productions, Western (or even universal) humanistic values, a desirable
point of origin for authenticity claims, an icon of a social class, and a
cultural institution (Renaissance humanist, Marxist, postmodernist).[65]
The illusion that East and West are two self-contained sites recurs in the
works of writers, translators, filmmakers, and theater artists who engage
in differing discourses of representation that range from the iconoclasm
of early-twentieth-century China to the reinscription of the personal
into the political in the Chinese diaspora in the twenty-first century.
The contrasts between different localities hence inform the strategies of
interpretation.

My use of "China" and selection of works for analysis have probably
raised questions about the scope of my study: Shouldn't there be more
"representative" productions for each period from mainland China, for
example? Why not include more descriptions of the latest performances?
Beyond the obvious difference in terms of genre (scholarly monograph
versus encyclopedia, and critical analysis versus theater or film review),
these questions are in fact part of the ideology being analyzed. It is not
my intention to press the case of the writers and artists examined in this
study as representative individuals in an outdated area studies model.
Nor have I concerned myself with satisfying the appetite for reportage of
the latest performances. The tendency to look for signs of updatedness
merely in descriptions of exotic works reveals a bias about the type of
intellectual labor deemed worthwhile for the field.[66] Generations of writers, artists, and critics have spoken as if in possession of Shakespeare or
China.[67] In this context, we need to reexamine the perceived exclusivity of
local culture.[68]

"There is method in 't"

To pursue the alignments of ideologies at work, I concentrate on the dynamics of the claims, or self-serving apologia, that attempt to reify Shakespeare's works and Chinese culture. In an age when performances of Shakespeare, in English or otherwise, are becoming increasingly intercultural, oddity should lie not in the Shakespeare–China connections, but in the entrenched views of Chinese identities or Shakespearean authenticity. Through negligence and silence, some artists and their critics have failed to acknowledge how their rhetorical strategies about Shakespeare and China undermine or reinforce a perceived but unquestioned antithesis between different cultures. Recent scholarship has begun to raise and reassess some of these issues, including fundamental questions about interculturalism,[69] "[the obsession with] authenticity,"[70] and theater's capacity to work against various discourses of legitimation.[71]

Given Shakespeare's ubiquity, there is an infinite range of genres (translation, literature, theater, film, television) and sites (popular culture, commercial appropriation, the Internet) that would allow us to engage questions of cross-cultural epistemologies. However, the nature of Shakespeare and China as contesting entities emerges most clearly in performances that constitute both contingent sites and palpable sights of such encounters. Therefore, I focus here on rewrites for stage and screen but contextualize the performance culture within the networks of two related modes of cultural production: fiction and cultural translation (missionary writings and travel literature), since these genres are invariably cross-fertilizing. The range of genres illustrates how a transnational knowledge bank anchored in a literary culture might be formed.

More important, the current state of scholarship calls for a more productive conversation. Studies of East Asian Shakespeares often focus on traditional theaters, marginalizing the less "exotic" modes of film or *huaju* and reinforcing ideological investments in what Asian rewritings of Shakespeare should be. The Chinese silent-film and feature-film adaptations of world literature are rarely, if ever, explored. In the standard books on cinematic Shakespeare, it is the American, British, French, Italian, and occasionally Japanese (almost exclusively Kurosawa) traditions that are investigated, but never the Chinese filmmaking practice or the cultural underpinnings behind it.[72] In the other direction, Chinese film adaptation of world literature is also a topic that existing film studies and

Chinese studies scholarship has singularly failed to address.[73] To rectify this situation, selected cases of Shakespeare in Chinese fiction and cinema are taken into account in a comparative context.

Although some aspects of the history of Shakespeare in the People's Republic of China have been chronicled elsewhere, a critical history has thus far been eschewed. I juxtapose mainland Chinese works with contrasting case studies of works that originated elsewhere (post-1980s Taiwan, postmodern Hong Kong, and touring productions in Europe). Some of the most exciting interpretations of Shakespeare and China have appeared outside China proper. To fully appreciate the discursive richness of the encounters between the Chinese and Western conceptions of Shakespeare and China, we must consider the itinerant projections of Shakespeare and China in different periods, genres, and locations.

My case-study approach to these issues is informed by firsthand observations of performances, archival research, and a range of primary texts that may appear to be insignificant secondhand opinions, such as reviews, interviews, and rehearsal notes. The audience response, constituency of the audience, artists' second thoughts, and processes of experimentation are all subjects that demand critical analysis—along with what happened on stage or on screen. Much of the historical and theoretical work here is carried out in the conviction that textual traces of the production and reception of a work are as important as the visual clues in furthering our understanding of Chinese Shakespeares. Using multiple sources to reconstruct these cultural events enables a critically alert reflection on them, rather than descriptive reports of such elements as the casting, rehearsal, and acting style, commonly found in studies based solely on personal accounts of live performances.[74]

Although my analysis observes a chronological order even as it traces the nonlinear histories, and at times recursive patterns, of these encounters, this framework does not imply that Shakespeare–China relationships have unfolded in a teleological cultural history. Artists are aware of, or react against, past trends and may even advocate a false sense of progress. However, dominance of one mode of engagement or approach does not always signify an evolutionary progress, but points to changes of informing principles and historical exigencies. For example, in the rhetoric of globalization, hybridity is often celebrated as a progressive notion, because its political agency is believed to have activated cultural flows.[75] Whether this is true depends to a large extent on historical period. Only a location-specific decoding can tease out the links between hybridity and different modes of intercultural engagement. By necessity, the history of these exchanges remains fragmentary. It is both undesirable and impractical to seek a full inventory that runs the risk of replicating the problems of evolutionary cultural history. The weight of teleological history—coupled with nationalism that promotes necessary progress—often writes certain works and events out of the master narrative, denying them the serious consideration they deserve. As Prasenjit Duara writes in *Rescuing History from the Nation,* the mode of "Enlightenment" history assumes that "the Other in geographical space will, *in time,* come to look like earlier versions of us."[76] Both the nonlinear flow and arrest of the cultural processes that constitute Chinese Shakespeares have a great deal to teach us about the circuit of world literature.[77]

The rhetoric of localization and globalization obliges us to reassess existing narratives that tend to imply smooth progress and that push history into the realm of myth—Shakespearean, Chinese, or otherwise—or what David Lowenthal calls "heritage" in a different context (narratives that are closed to critical scrutiny).[78] While taking into account the historical experiences of performers, rewriters, readers, and audiences, I have avoided dividing the history of Shakespearean performance or cultural history along rigid geopolitical time lines and regions. For instance, the revival of Chinese-opera Shakespeare in the 1980s calls for an examination of the connections between works produced in different Chinese localities. While it may sometimes be necessary for historians or directors such as Herbert Blau or Richard Eyre to speak of the audience or readers as an imagined unified community, I have tried to retain a certain level of skepticism about the collective by attending to the subtle differences between individuals responding to the same play in the same historical period.[79]

The history of Shakespeare and China is a history of exchanges that have enabled reinterpretations, extensions, debates, and revisions of Shakespeare's cultural significance and Chinese politics of culture. The ethical is the subject of chapters 2 and 3, but this book also has an ethical dimension. It is necessary to reconstruct and critique the asymmetries between the ideas of Shakespeare and China so that we can better understand the various narratives about cultural difference in a broader context. Research on the different levels of discordance introduced by Chinese Shakespeares is also conducive to productive intra-Asian dialogues in today's increasingly English-speaking global culture. Let the conversation begin.

PART II

The Fiction of Moral Space

2 Shakespeare in Absentia:

The Genealogy of an Obsession

For a number of reasons, Shakespeare became all the talk in China before actual performances took place and before literary translations were available, thanks to several groups of intermediaries. Some of these intermediaries included Anglo-European missionaries, translators, and Chinese reformers, who attempted to popularize competing visions of modernity to the general public. The absence of Shakespeare's plays did not stop the Chinese from constructing a hypercanonical presence of Englishness. What did Shakespeare's name represent to this public? What exactly did they have in mind when Chinese intellectuals announced their determination to find or inspire a Chinese Shakespeare? Two theoretical questions emerge from this context: Why did the deferral to an absent authority occur? How does a writer get "read" *avant la lettre*, to evoke Jacques Derrida's metaphysics of presence and absence? Drawing on Martin Heidegger's critique of exteriority and interiority, Derrida used the notions of speech (as a form of presence) and writing (as a form of absence) to construct a metaphysics of presence motivated by a desire for a single origin of truth, a "transcendental signified." In China, this desire has created a hypercanonical presence of the author in the absence of Shakespeare's text.[1]

One of the most intriguing cases of nineteenth-century Asian encounters with Western culture is the Chinese reception of "Shakespeare" as an idea for half a century before he was a text or performance event. Driven by the Chinese intellectuals' desire to speak for the dead in moralizing terms, the uses and abuses of Shakespeare *without* Shakespeare rewrite the cultural essentialism in the grammar of the global. As mediators, nineteenth-century missionaries and Chinese intellectuals had to confront the complexities of the varying discursive modes of past and present speakers in different localities. This prehistory is an integral part of the complex and variously influenced local Shakespeare tradition from 1900 to the present.

Chinese Epistemologies of the European West

As systems for perceiving the world, nineteenth-century Chinese and Western epistemologies confront each other in their displaced localities. Until the fall of the Qing dynasty, the Chinese political consciousness operated on the assumptions of Chinese superiority to all outsiders. The situation changed dramatically in the nineteenth century. Commercial competition, along with cultural conflicts with the West, soon culminated in war. The first Opium War (1839–1842) and a series of diplomatic setbacks were a shock to the Chinese monarchy, which gave rise to self-doubt and led to what might be called a discourse of deficit. The discourse of deficit focused on what "old China" lacked in relation to industrialized Western nations and Japan. It defined the Chinese epistemologies of world cultures and was permeated by contradictory images of what constituted modernity. Defeat in the first Sino-Japanese War in 1895 and the failure of the Hundred Days' Reform in 1898 further shook the complacency of the Chinese intelligentsia. After centuries as a marginal island nation paying tribute to the Chinese Empire, Japan suddenly emerged as a palpable threat to China's national sovereignty. Understandably, the newly powerful neighbor attracted the attention of Chinese reformers, although they tended to regard Japan "as nothing more than a transparent window on the West."[2] It became clear that in order to strengthen itself, China had to follow in Japan's footsteps and appropriate a large amount of Western ideas and knowledge—not simply import Western technologies. This belief partially explains the emergence of urgent proposals to reform China not only from without (that is, importing military technologies) but also from within by reforming the Chinese worldview.

In relation to the Shakespeare in absentia, this period witnessed an epistemic break. Between 1839 and the 1930s, a discourse of modernity emerged through the self-strengthening and "foreign affairs" campaigns, which gave rise to urban exoticism.[3] Leading scholars like Liang Qichao, who coined the standard Chinese transliteration of Shakespeare's name (Shashibiya, still in use), argued in 1902 that the best way to educate "new citizens" with a modern outlook was to introduce European thought and literature to China.[4] By the late nineteenth century, treaty ports like Tianjin and Shanghai had large Anglo-European communities, foreign concessions, and Western schools.[5]

Because the fascination with new and foreign culture and consumer products had a long tradition in China before the nineteenth century, there was a preexisting framework within which modern Chinese writers and playwrights could rapidly appropriate non-Chinese cultural texts. The well-documented history of artistic exotica goes back several centuries.[6] In the late nineteenth century, the unfolding of Western exoticism in modern Chinese culture was tied to the presence of Chinese intellectuals returning from abroad and the rise of Western enclaves in Chinese urban centers. Thus the interest in exotic commodities was fraught with ambivalence.[7]

The late Qing (1839–1910) and early Republican (1911–1930) fascination with Anglo-European ideas and products can be seen as an extension of the earlier culture of curiosity, but this modern fascination with the exotic extended beyond the boundaries of material and visual culture. It also extended the range of interests to foreign ideas, rather than being limited simply to material culture. The period between 1840 and 1848, for instance, witnessed the publication of thirteen collections of Chinese and foreign works about world geography and "progressive" Western ideas, including one volume compiled by Lin Zexu (1785–1850), governor-general of Hubei and Hunan provinces.[8] In the 1860s, the imperial government established the first official institution and put Lin in charge of translating Anglo-European works and textbooks on geography, travel, political philosophy, literature, and general Western knowledge. The knowledge fermented among various social classes even without any programmatic effort in China to encourage the study of these translated texts.

Beginning in 1870, poems by Byron, Goethe, Shelley, and Heine started to appear in translation, followed by translations of works by Charles Dickens, Victor Hugo, Leo Tolstoy, Washington Irving, and Harriet

Beecher Stowe.[9] It was in this same decade that biographical sketches of Shakespeare started to appear, without interpretations of his plays. Shakespeare—although by now well known among the intellectuals—did not appear even in partial translation until 1904, when Lin Shu and Wei Yi published their collaborative classical Chinese translation of Charles and Mary Lamb's *Tales from Shakespeare*. The first complete translation of a Shakespearean play appeared in 1921 when Tian Han's *Hamlet* (*Hamengleite*) was published.[10] By the 1930s, the Chinese fascination with Europe gave rise to the intensive translation of Western dramas for their intellectual content.

The Making of an Icon

David Garrick, arguably the founding father of what would later be known as the Shakespeare industry and Bardolatry, staged a Shakespeare Jubilee in Stratford-upon-Avon in 1769, in which he hailed Shakespeare as "our Shakespeare" and "Avon's swan."[11] Missionaries and local intellectuals in fin-de-siècle China would agree with Garrick, but for very different reasons. Shakespeare's early presence in China was not the result of translation, teaching, performance, or any other form that would have entailed a substantial engagement with his texts, but took the form of informants' references and an abstract panegyric. Nineteenth-century Chinese reformers used Shakespeare's name for various agendas, which began with a reference by Lin Zexu in a rendition of Hugh Murray's *Cyclopedia of Geography*, entitled *Annals of the Four Continents* (*Sizhou zhi*, 1839), which was likely a group effort. It was a work that was conducted under his supervision by competent collaborators and in which, in addition to the translation and editing, Lin and his team added their views to the countries mentioned and compared them with China.[12]

Although it may seem accidental that Lin Zexu should be the first to introduce Shakespeare in Chinese, the historical condition suggests otherwise. He played a central role in the attempts to stop the opium trade. His failure is well known (through documentaries, television series, and feature films), but his engagement with Anglo-European culture is not. In his carefully phrased letter to Queen Victoria, he mobilized the "traditional forces and values of the Confucian state" and exerted moral coercion on the English.[13] His administrative position accounted for his interest in English history and culture.

Because Lin was more interested in informing his fellow officials about the English national character and likely behavior in time of war, he gave no concrete references to Shakespeare's plays. His only descriptive phrase for Shakespeare is "prolific," which is followed by a description of the British as "greedy, tough, alcoholic, yet skillful in handicraft."[14] There are strong parallels between these stereotypical and reductive comments and those made by seventeenth-century visitors to England.[15] Thus Shakespeare was introduced as part of the Western knowledge that Lin passed on to his countrymen to prepare them to resist the European powers.

The publication of Lin's text coincided with the beginning of the first Opium War between China and Britain, at the time the most important European power in China. With the establishment and rapid growth of the British East India Company, England became the most powerful capitalist country trading with China in the nineteenth century.[16] Lin's choice to introduce Shakespeare was hardly accidental.[17]

Although Lin had minimal knowledge of English, he worked with linguistically competent collaborators to determine the content of the foreign-language sources, which he used in the reference book. Lin was not the only translator at the time, Chinese or English, to have no knowledge of the source language and who consequently made no factual references to foreign texts.

In addition to Lin's "know thy enemy" narrative, Shakespeare appeared in other accounts written by either Chinese travelers or European missionaries to China. In 1856, William Muirhead mentioned Shakespeare (Shekesibi) in his translation of Thomas Milner's *The History of England: From the Invasions of Julius Caesar to the Year A.D. 1854*.[18] Other accounts also demonstrate that as much as Shakespeare can be used as a space for the interplay between national consciousness and international politics, he can also serve conservative purposes.

On August 11, 1877, a Chinese ambassador to England wrote: "The most famous [author] was Shakespeare, a talented playwright living in England about two hundred years ago. His stature is comparable to the Greek poet Homer."[19] In 1882, an American missionary described Shakespeare as "a poet known for plays that articulate man's joy and sorrows with unparalleled eloquence since Homer."[20] The preface to an anonymous 1903 translation of Charles and Mary Lamb's *Tales from Shakespeare* resorts to hyperbole, not for the first time: "Shakespeare is the finest poet in the world. His plays and fiction sweep the world like wind and are immensely popular."[21]

The uniformity of these references is striking. Almost all of them refer to Shakespeare as a symbol of the superiority of Anglo-European cultures. In short, during the second half of the nineteenth century, Shakespeare was known to a group of elite, privileged intellectuals as a colossal figure representing the "West." Superlatives seemed to be in order even when Chinese commentators mentioned Shakespeare in the Euro-American context at a later time when Shakespeare had a more substantial textual presence in China. In one of his eight "Collected Discussions of European and American Fiction" in *Short Story Magazine* (*Xiaoshuo yuebao*) in 1913, one Sun Yuxiu of Wuxi in Jiangsu Province compared Henry Fielding, Samuel Richardson, and Shakespeare, and concluded: "Fielding's works only had a few ardent admirers and Richardson was fashionable in a particular historical period, but Shakespeare alone is of all ages and of all nations." Sun qualified the statement by adding, with a certain national pride, that "even though it is not known how Shakespeare compared to [China's] Qu Yuan and Du Fu, in Europe and America alone there is no other writer who could compare with Shakespeare."[22]

What is even more striking is that these panegyric patterns have continued into the twenty-first century. Lang Lang, the twenty-five-year-old mainland Chinese pianist who played at the opening ceremonies of the Beijing Olympics in 2008, equated Shakespeare with Western modes of thinking.[23] Phrases such as "the greatest playwright" and "literary giant" are often used to describe Shakespeare in a marketing context in the Chinese-speaking world (stage productions, travel industry, English courses)—which is understandable, as it is generally the case everywhere else in the world too. Australian cricketer and coach Ric Charlesworth opens his motivational handbook *Shakespeare, the Coach* with an epigraph taken from Ben Jonson's dedication to the First Folio of Shakespeare. Charlesworth's book joins a long list of such manuals in English, Chinese, and other languages, many of which create a moral space around Shakespeare's stature.[24] However, it is surprising that such phrases also recur in contexts that do not call for such embellishment. Several recently published Chinese-language scholarly volumes on Shakespeare open with a striking uniformity—reaffirmations of Shakespeare's universality followed by a de rigueur quote from Jonson's dedication: Shakespeare is "not of an age, but for all time."[25] This is the case in China, Taiwan, and some English-language works. Some argued from unchecked assumptions and spoke of Shakespeare's universality in broad categories and in an unproblematic tone.[26] Numerous scholarly articles demonstrate the same penchant for justifying for writing about Shakespeare by reasserting Shakespeare's greatness.[27] In his preface to Liang Zongdai's translation of Shakespeare's sonnets, the celebrated poet Yu Kwang-chung (b. 1928) is compelled to remind his readers that Shakespeare is "England's greatest playwright and a saint of all times."[28]

Why would these scholars assume that their specialist readers need such justification or reminder? While these panegyric impulses—whether in 1882 or 2006—appear to fuel a similar rhetoric that harks back to Matthew Arnold's pronouncement in 1869 that great works of art constitute the "culture" that embodies "the best which has been thought and said in the world," their roots lie in different historical contexts: cultural engulfment in the nineteenth century and a renewed desire to defend high culture in the twenty-first century.[29] Douglas Lanier's observation of the rise of the genre of "Shakespeare corporate-management manual" in English provides some parallels to the situation in China and Taiwan: "[D]espite the concerted politicizing of Shakespeare in many quarters of the academy and theatre throughout the '80s and '90s, Shakespeare remains by and large an emblem of cultural legitimation for the existing social and economic order."[30] Shakespeare's status as an icon was shaped by the logic of the nation-state in nineteenth-century China and by an illusion of enlightenment in twenty-first-century China and Taiwan.

Whereas Lin Zexu was concerned with knowing more about the British, Yan Fu (1853–1921), a key reformer who studied in Britain and who had an excellent command of English, was more interested in how foreign models could serve to strengthen China by broadening the Chinese worldview. The Chinese reformers' focus soon shifted from the "know thy enemy" rhetoric to an interest in building a new Chinese identity. Yan commented on Shakespeare's literary fame in a comparative context: "Shakespeare was an English poet and dramatist who lived during the time of the Wanli reign of the Ming dynasty. His extant works have been translated and treasured by countries all over the world."[31] In the preface to his 1894 translation of Thomas Huxley's *Evolution and Ethics*, Yan emphasizes the universalism of Shakespeare's characters, pointing to the fact that the range of human emotions has not evolved or changed.[32] Yan's translation had a great influence because it was later adopted as a textbook for schools that taught Western affairs (*yangwu*). It is surprising that even Yan, a serious translator, did not see any point in translating

Shakespeare.[33] His emphasis was on what was deemed morally appropriate aspects of Anglo-European literature and philosophy. Not surprisingly, in 1896 we hear that Shakespeare "has such profound understanding of life that he is capable of portraying the human conditions, virtue, and vice in the most compelling way."[34]

These early Chinese references to Shakespeare bear dwelling on. They do not show any linear evolution of Shakespeare's fame. There are two issues: the historical significance of these texts and the appropriation of the national poet of an invading country. First, the fragmentary comments serve as a reminder that the history of literary reception rarely evolves in a linear fashion. The scholarship on the subject has regularly neglected this prehistory. Scholars have erroneously attributed Lin Shu as the first person to introduce Shakespeare to China. Take Meng Xianqiang, for example. With a vision of teleological history, he quickly dismissed these biographical references by Lin Zexu and other missionaries as insignificant, marginal steps in a "preparatory" evolutionary stage of the history of reception.[35]

Second, Shakespeare's perceived neutrality facilitated the contradiction between resisting British invasion and at the same time praising its iconic national poet. Underlying the references to Shakespeare was an implicit argument that Shakespeare was a universal genius who could provide an alternative mode of thinking and ethics for Chinese in search of a modern identity. The Chinese use of Shakespeare parallels the reception of Shakespeare in nineteenth-century America. Even though the United States owed its existence to a war against England, Shakespeare was widely appropriated to the cause of the American nation.[36]

The most obvious difference between nineteenth-century China and America was that English was the national language of the United States and educators knew that Shakespeare was a model for that language. The large number of Anglophiles in the educational establishment in the United States also accounted for the presence of Shakespeare, and the British heritage, in American culture. Modern China also owed its existence to wars, specifically the wars of resistance against Japanese and European encroachment. However, the Chinese reformers' appropriation of Shakespeare was informed by a different rhetoric. The emphasis on cultural alterity and an open-ended national identity dominated the translation and introduction of Western thinkers and literary figures, which explains why—in contrast to the United States—early Chinese appropriation of Shakespeare did not take root in the popular culture.

Theater-Going Accounts

Although unqualified and unsubstantiated "biographical" sketches are legion, there are also sporadic theater-going accounts that engage Shakespeare more substantively. A few privileged Chinese elites during this period saw Shakespeare's plays in performance. Their accounts demonstrate a fixation with the strange yet entertaining plot rather than the characters' psyches. There was a shared urge to censor and domesticate unfamiliar narratives on stage, often overriding the desire to actually see the visual representations of these narratives.

Guo Songtao (1818–1891), China's first minister to England (1877–1878) and France (1878), saw one of the most important productions of *Hamlet* of his time, starring Henry Irving in the leading role, at the Lyceum Theatre in London on January 18, 1879.[37] Guo's description is short and void of details of the performance, but it does give us a sense of what he *saw*: "In the evening, Margaret invited me to go to Lyceum Theatre in London to see a production of one of Shakespeare's plays. The emphasis was on decorating the plots and not on spectacles or oration."[38]

Guo, like his contemporaries, appears to have been more interested in Shakespeare's "attractive plot design" than in his language and style. What did he "miss"? English reviews and documents suggest that Henry Irving, a successful actor in Victorian England, gave a quite different performance from the one Guo described. Guo probably saw the rerun of Henry Irving's *Hamlet*. Irving persuaded the manager of the Lyceum Theatre to "let him essay the role of Hamlet" in November 1874 and staged an acclaimed production.[39] After having toured Edinburgh in 1877, Irving became the manager and reopened the Lyceum Theatre in London with *Hamlet*, now under his management, on December 30, 1878. The 1877 performance was warmly received. Irving's Hamlet was "meditative, intellectual, tender, . . . and colloquial."[40] Contrary to Guo's report, British reviews of the 1877 performance concentrated on Irving's performance, not Shakespeare's plot design: "We see Hamlet think. We do not merely hear him speak, we positively watch his mind. We feel and know the man overburdened with this crushing sorrow, with his mind unhinged."[41]

The rerun that Guo saw in January 1879 did not seem much different from the 1877 performance described in the review. However, for Guo, the "plot design" of *Hamlet* was far more intriguing. Early Chinese encounters with Shakespeare were informed by a similar attitude.

To understand Guo's reception of Irving's *Hamlet*, it is necessary to consider the British reception of the production. Irving's performance was a major national cultural event enthusiastically anticipated by all classes of English society. Irving's Shakespeare (at the Lyceum) dominated the English stage until 1895, and Irving, the fashionable tragedian, was the first actor to be knighted. In the nunnery scene, Henry Irving played against Isabel Bateman as Ophelia, and he held his first-night audiences in his power. Irving credited the success of his controversial Hamlet to the "excitability of [Hamlet's] temperament" and the ways in which he expressed "the motive and variety of passion" on "a forcible mind."[42] By all accounts, Irving's performance was not one that emphasized the "plot design." The able Chinese ambassador would certainly know the contexts of British theater and high culture, yet he chose to prioritize the novelty of the plotline in his observation.

Zeng Jize (Marquis Tseng), another Chinese ambassador to Britain, attended an unspecified London production of *Hamlet* in 1879, according to Bram Stoker's memoir. Zeng had not read the play, but Sir Halliday Macartney accompanied Zeng and helped him to "be absolutely correct on the human side."[43] Zeng recorded his experience in his diary.[44] Like Guo, Zeng finds neither the performing techniques nor the stage design nor Hamlet's soliloquies striking; instead, he remarks on the narrative structure: "On the seventh day (of the third month, the fifth year of Guangxu [1880]) . . . I went to the theater with Qingchen, Songsheng, Yizhai, Xiangpu, and Shengzhai after dinner. The play concerns a certain King of Denmark who murders his brother and marries his sister-in-law. His brother's son takes vengeance upon him. The performance was over at the beginning of *zishi* [11:00 P.M.]."[45]

Guo and Zeng's reactions were remarkably similar, emphasizing the plot. Extant documents suggest they probably attended the same production. These records call to mind Lord George Macartney's reaction to Chinese performances in the diary of his embassy to China in 1793 that demonstrate a similar focus on the plot.[46] The fixation on the plot seems to be symptomatic of preliminary stages of cross-cultural encounters, as evidenced by the cultural anthropologist Laura Bohannan's account of the African tribe Tiv's reception of *Hamlet* in the 1950s.[47] The elders disagreed with almost every turning point of the story. The chief's questions problematize the naturalized epistemological foundation on which modern Anglo-European culture interprets *Hamlet*. The Tiv took issue with seven aspects of the story, including the appearance of Hamlet's father's ghost,

Claudius's marriage to Gertrude, Hamlet's madness, and whom the poison is for in the last scene. Most striking is the attention given, on the part of the Tiv and Bohannan, to the "story." Both the Tiv and Bohannan improvised to come to terms with each other's visions of "Shakespeare."

Guo and Zeng's diary entries and their locality-specific epistemology are illuminating in a number of ways.[48] First, their emphatic interest in plot design is indicative of early Chinese reception of Shakespeare as an author of romantic stories and tales about gods and spirits. Second, when the diaries of Guo and Zeng were published in 1882, they were read as reportage of life abroad in England and France; hence the focus on exoticism.[49] Their diaries chronicled their detailed observations of English etiquette and banquets as well as their interactions with the English gentry. What Shakespeare meant to the Chinese between 1839 and 1900 was a fiction, a convenient Other that articulates China's relation to the rest of the world. The topicality of Shakespeare in the Chinese reformers' writings superseded any contextual understanding of the plays themselves. The Shakespearean difference provided convenient shorthand for the qualities the reformers were proposing for citizens of the new China.

Shakespeare as a Character on Stage

In Shakespeare's global career, there has never been a shortage of plays that feature the writer as a character. Amy Freed's *The Beard of Avon* and Zhu Shu's *Shakespeare* (*Shashibiya*)—focusing on the purported connection between *Richard II* and the Essex rebellion of 1601—are only two recent examples in English and Chinese.[50] However, not all such works focus on Shakespeare's biography. As Shakespeare gained currency in late-nineteenth-century China, different forms of appropriation emerged. Shakespeare appears as a character in the Kun opera (*kunju*) *New Rome* (*Xin Luoma*, 1898), written by Liang Qichao, whose numerous political treatises and science-fiction stories concentrate on the import of Western culture, carving a temporalized space for ideas about modernity.[51] This play seems to be a natural extension of the late-nineteenth-century Chinese fascination with Shakespeare's biographies. It reflects Liang's understanding of the link between the rise of nationalism and vernacular literature.

An allegory about the foundation of a modern nation, *New Rome* dramatizes the events of the unification of Italy, which lasted from the Congress of Vienna in 1814 to the annexation of Rome in 1870. The action of this unfinished drama, as described in the prologue, was to serve as a model for China in a similar crisis, although Liang certainly could not predict history (the Boxer Uprising and the invasion of the eight allied forces, including western European countries, Japan, and the United States, would occur shortly after Liang completed *New Rome*). Despite its innovations, *New Rome* was ignored by readers and scholars alike—including those on the lookout for Asian rewrites of Shakespeare—although it was translated into Italian by Giuliano Bertuccioli and partially into English by William Dolby.[52]

In the prologue, Dante appears as the narrator, explaining his motive for coming to China (to see *New Rome*) and outlining the synopsis of the play following the *chuanqi* (transmission of the marvelous; a genre of Chinese drama) convention:[53]

DANTE: Metternich wildly wields despotic power,
  Mazzini organizes the Party of Youth;
  General Garibaldi thrice leads forth his citizen army,
  Cavour brings unity to the whole of Italy.[54]

Liang deployed Shakespeare and other European masters as moral authorities. A voice backstage engages in a dialogue with Dante, who is dressed like a bearded Daoist immortal in the *fumo* (literati) role type. The voice backstage asks: "China is just a sick Oriental nation. Why do you want to go there, mighty immortal?"[55] Dante reasons that since *New Rome* dramatizes the founding of his native land, he is compelled to "watch and listen" to the new play being performed in the "patriotic theaters in Shanghai." He stresses that "every word of the forty acts of the play is golden, and the fifty years of Italian history dramatized in the play provide good medicine and advice [for the Chinese]." Dante then announces, "I have invited two old friends, Shakespeare and Voltaire, to go see this play together."[56] At the end of the prologue, Shakespeare and Voltaire enter riding on a cloud to join Dante. This allegorical structure parallels the establishment of national literature as an academic discipline and the rise of nationalism. The nineteenth century witnessed the emergence of national literature with strong connection to a national consciousness embedded in the first great writers in its language; hence Shakespeare (English), Dante (Italian), and Voltaire (French) in Liang's play. While English literature as a discipline emerged to serve the imperial "civilizing" mission in a colonial context, the study of Chinese belles lettres was established, in Euro-Japanese terms, in tandem with the new identity of a Chinese nation. National literature, in this context, is conceived as an enterprise to earn a nation respect.[57]

New Rome is designed to inspire patriotism and unite the Chinese people. Liang intended to use the propaganda play to show that even drama in traditional *zaju* and *chuanqi* forms can deal with Western and modern topics. He invoked the cultural authority of three "national poets," Shakespeare, Dante, and Voltaire, to support his agenda for cultural reform.

If *New Rome* were a complete play, it would make a thought-provoking intercultural theater piece. For unknown reasons, Liang managed to complete only the wedge act (equivalent to a prologue) and six of the planned forty acts, with the action going only as far as Mazzini's founding of the Young Italy society. Liang's choice of diction intentionally reflects the play's design and its status as an intercultural drama. The characters quote Confucius and Mencius rather than texts from their own traditions. Conventional metaphors and *kunju* lyrics mingle with contemporary slang such as *feipang* (fat) and newly coined Chinese phrases such as *ziyou* (freedom) and *pingdeng* (equality). In act 4, Mazzini welcomes his mother with a kiss on her forehead. Whereas the prologue and the overall structure of *New Rome* resemble those of Kong Shangren's seventeenth-century *kunju* play *Peach Blossom Fan* (*Taohua shan*), the language and stage directions contain more traces of a culture in a transitional time.

Liang's interpretation of modern Italian history constructs a "synchronic global consciousness" that connected fin-de-siècle China to the founding moments of other modern nations.[58] *New Rome*, minor as it may seem, is an integral part of Liang's political thinking. Liang's contemporaries, such as Wang Xiaonong (1858–1918) and Huang Jilian (1836–1924), also wedded *xiqu* (Chinese opera) with Western topics. No fewer than a dozen new Chinese operas dealing with Western subjects were written and staged during this time.[59] While the nascent Western-style spoken drama was limited to the elite urbanites, *xiqu* was a popular form of entertainment with a much larger audience and was often used for propagandistic purposes. Hong Bingwen's aptly titled play *Mirror of History* (*Gu yin jian*, 1906) made no effort to obscure its historical allegory of Cuba's civil wars and the revolution in China. Wang Xiaonong's *Planting the Melon, Cause of the Orchid* (*Guazhong lanyin*) dramatized the modern partition of Poland; it played to full houses in Shanghai in 1904.[60]

Wang's comment on theater in the same year seemed to mirror Jaques's remark that "all the world's a stage" (*As You Like It* 2.7.139): "The world is a theatre, but I suspect the stage might be too small."[61] Featured in these performances were such events as Cuba's rebellion against the Spanish, Napoleon's achievements, and the Greek revolution. Most appeared in the traditional *zaju* or *chuanqi* form with intermingling Western features. The emergence of this group of new Chinese operas was nurtured by an unprecedented artistic license and local urgency. To drive home the message, Liu Yazi (also known as Ya Lu), the founder of China's first drama periodical, *Great Twentieth-Century Stage* (*Ershi shiji da wutai*), wrote in the first issue's editorial in 1904, "What we must do now is press the blue eyes and purple beards [of Westerners] into the Chinese costumes, and set forth their history, so that the French Revolution, American Independence, the glorious revival of Italy and Greece, and the cruel destruction of India and Poland may all be imprinted on the minds of our compatriots."[62] The rise of nationalism was seen as a defining moment of modernity. In Liang's effort to connect foreign history with China's present, the performance of the nation—personified through the figures of national poets—was staged in synchronic terms. In this context, Shakespeare functions as a global presence that is rooted in a synchronic rather than diachronic reading of history.

In Search of a Chinese Shakespeare

For the Chinese, the name and works of Shakespeare have been neither an explicitly contested symbol of imperialism nor a figure for national reappropriation, as has been the case in India and the Caribbean. This is the case because the areas of China under direct British control were small, and the effects of English-language education were limited to a small population. Instead of appropriating Shakespeare for national ends, early-twentieth-century Chinese intellectuals were preoccupied with strengthening China, embracing, as Jing Tsu observes, "failure as a way of building cultural confidence."[63]

As part of this agenda, the Chinese intellectuals searched for a "Chinese Shakespeare," a Chinese author with equivalent cultural value who might symbolize the nation's ancient unity and "modern" identity. They were looking for a cultural authority from whom to derive a modernized identity. China is not alone. "Who is the Indian Shakespeare?" has been a contested question for artists and writers in India.[64]

The argument that Shakespeare was recognized as a cultural authority to be emulated in both China and India would certainly be greeted with enthusiasm by the most unflinching advocates of Shakespeare's universality, although the same argument would also certainly meet with a flood of counterexamples.[65] The deferral to authority and the practice of privileging certain Western thinkers and writers, including Shakespeare, comprised a critical stage in the history of Sino-European cultural exchanges. The discourse evolved from emphasizing Shakespeare's status in Anglophone and world cultures (such as Guo Songtao's diary entry in 1877) to urgent calls for the birth of a Chinese Shakespeare so that China could catch up with its Western counterparts (as in Lu Xun's essay "On the Power of Mara Poetry" [Moluo shi li shuo, 1908]).

More detailed biographical information about Shakespeare appeared beginning in 1903.[66] Entries for Shakespeare can be found in the many reference books that missionaries published in China between 1903 and 1908.[67] On January 4, 1907, *Northern China Herald*, an English-language paper in Shanghai, published a synopsis of *China Ten Years Hence*, performed by the World Chinese Students' Federation (Huanqiu Zhongguo xuesheng hui), and quoted the student organization's rationale that resorted to Shakespeare's iconic status to justify Chinese society's need of drama: "While Shakespeare has been worshipped as the 'king of Poets' in the West, in China, dramatic performers have been regarded as one of the four meanest classes."[68] Without any grasp of Shakespeare's plays or what was then loosely defined as the "West," most discussions of East–West literary relations in the late nineteenth and early twentieth centuries were polemical in purpose and built on assumptions of cultural relativism.

Specific Chinese literary figures have been compared with Shakespeare across a wide historical divide. Su Manshu, a poet and monk, equated Shakespeare and Du Fu in his autobiographical novel in 1912 and gave Shakespeare the honorific title *xiancai* (genius from heaven), reminiscent of the titles traditionally given to Li Bai (*shi xian* [poet-immoral]) and Du Fu (*shi sheng* [poet-sage]).[69] Lin Shu also equated Shakespeare with Du Fu in his preface (1904) to his Chinese translation of Charles and Mary Lamb's *Tales from Shakespeare*: "Is Shakespeare not a genius of a great civilized country? Shakespeare's poetry could truly match that of Du Fu of our country."[70] In his introduction to Du Fu in an anthology,

Stephen Owen wrote in 1996, "Like Shakespeare in the English tradition, Du Fu's poetry came to be so deeply bound up with the constitution of literary value that generation after generation of poets and critics rediscovered themselves . . . in some aspect of the poet's work."[71]

Scholars' obsession to connect Shakespeare and major Chinese literary figures continued well into the late twentieth century, forming a continuous quest for a "Chinese Shakespeare," a designation that occurred in the early twentieth century but is still in use. For example, the influential playwright Tang Xianzu (1550–1616) has often been considered the "Chinese Shakespeare."[72] The "comparative eulogy" of Tang and Shakespeare is based on the fact that Tang is a contemporary of Shakespeare and that they hold similar status in their traditions in terms of innovations in language, diction, and dramatic forms. The analogy between Tang's and Shakespeare's styles and status within their respective dramatic traditions was first put forward by the Japanese Sinologist Aoki Masaru in 1933, and was echoed by scholars like Zhao Jingshen in 1946 and Xu Shuofang in 1983.[73] Aoki comments that it is extraordinary that both Shakespeare and Tang, the two "literary monuments of the Occident and the Orient," lived in the same historical period.[74] Tang's romance drama, *The Peony Pavilion* (*Mudan ting*), is frequently referred to as a Chinese equivalent of *Romeo and Juliet*. Tian Han, the first Chinese who completed a full translation of a Shakespearean play, visited Tang Xianzu's hometown, Linchuan in Jiangxi Province, in 1959. Moved by the important literary heritage of the site, he composed a poem that passionately compared Tang's characters with those of Shakespeare:

> Du Liniang is like [Shakespeare's] Juliet,
> Her love is deeply woven into the root of the plum tree.
> Why should this beautiful poetry be locked in Tang's White
>   Camellia Hall?
> Shining in Tang's hometown is his poetry, an equal to that of
>   Shakespeare.[75]

The analogy between Shakespeare and Tang, and particularly between *Romeo and Juliet* and *The Peony Pavilion*, has become a standard feature in studies of Tang Xianzu in both China and the West. For example, in her 2002 study of the performance history of *The Peony Pavilion*, Catherine Swatek draws on the popularity of Shakespeare in nineteenth-century America as a parallel example to illustrate the status Tang enjoys in Chinese theater history.[76] Ian Bartholomew reports in 2004 that "the opera [*Peony Pavilion*] rings all the changes on the romantic theme and it is hardly surprising that it has been compared to *Romeo and Juliet*."[77] Pai Hsien-yung, a novelist from Taiwan now based in the United States and the producer of an abridged *Peony Pavilion* that premiered in Taipei in April 2004, even drew an analogy between his production and Baz Luhrmann's film *William Shakespeare's Romeo + Juliet*. Pai said: "As *The Peony Pavilion* is about young lovers, I wanted young people to perform the leading roles, rather in the spirit of Baz Luhrmann's film which used a seventeen-year-old Claire Danes and a twenty-two-year-old Leonardo DiCaprio in the title roles."[78]

Also in April 2004, Zheng Peikai, a respected scholar of premodern Chinese literature, wrote an article on Tang Xianzu and *The Peony Pavilion*, noting with even greater enthusiasm that "Tang Xianzu (1550–1616) is undoubtedly the greatest dramatist nourished by the Chinese culture, a dramatist that could be compared to Shakespeare of England (1564–1616)."

In the subsection "China's Shakespeare" in his article, Zheng summarized Chinese and Japanese scholarship on Tang Xianzu that regularly compared Tang with Shakespeare in the twentieth century. Zheng concluded that the comparison served at least two purposes: to "eulogize" Tang and to boost Chinese confidence in traditional literary values in the face of the globalization of Western cultural values.[79]

These cases epitomize the incredible investments that Chinese intellectuals have made in the search for a Chinese Shakespeare. Shakespeare was useful to the Chinese intellectuals precisely because he was foreign and had sufficient international status, not because any affinity existed between the works of Shakespeare and those of Du, Tang, or Guan. It is not surprising that in a perceived setting of cultural bankruptcy, Liang Qichao should lament in 1902: "Poets such as Shakespeare . . . wrote poems many tens of thousands of words long. How amazing! China lags behind other countries in every respect; only in literature might we appear to rival the Western countries. And yet when compared with the refinement, depth, complexity, grandeur and beauty [of writers like these], China is still inadequate, lagging behind."[80]

Likewise, Xu Zhimo, a Cambridge-educated poet and an admirer of the Romantics, described Shakespeare as an artist of "cosmic character" in his 1921 lecture "Art and Life" at Peking University. Xu extrapolated from Shakespeare a "consciousness of life" that he used to frame his revolt against specific elements of Chinese literary traditions and, by extension, traditional Chinese culture as a whole. Polarizing Shakespeare and the Western traditions he represented, Xu asked: "Isn't it striking that we look in vain in the scroll of our famous literary figures for even the least resemblance of a Goethe, a Shelley, a Wordsworth, not to say a Dante or a Shakespeare?"[81]

It is not surprising that Xu could not find even the least likeness of Shakespeare in Chinese literature—no doubt because he looked in the wrong place (a non-Anglophone, non-European culture) for the wrong person (a premodern Chinese author writing in both the literary and vernacular modes and capable of being turned into a national figure posthumously). Xu continued his thoughts on the topic, which were representative of the zeitgeist of his time, stating that cultural differences lie in not only disparate cultural practices but also differences in evaluative terms. According to Xu, "the difference [between China and Europe] is not so much of kind as of degree," because "[the Chinese] possess an artistic heritage essentially inferior to that of the West." The Chinese heritage "fails to comprehend life as a whole." Therefore, Xu worried that it is "inherent in [the Chinese] race's nature that, in art as in other things, [they] are to be always unlike the rest of the world [in a negative sense]."[82]

Also participating in the discourse about national character was Lu Xun, one of the most articulate critics of feudal China. In the essay "On the Power of Mara Poetry," after quoting a few passages from Thomas Carlyle's *On Heroes, Hero Worship, and the Heroic in History* (1840), he hailed Shakespeare as a cultural hero because of the connection between his poetry and the voice of a nation.[83] Having studied medicine in Japan, Lu Xun probably read Shakespeare and other Western writers in Japanese; he had some grounding in German and English as well. Lu Xun's views on Shakespeare were clearly influenced by Carlyle's pride in Shakespeare as "the greatest Englishman ever made."[84] Lu Xun's patriotism, formulated in his search for a Chinese Shakespeare, was also modeled on Carlyle's patriotic ideal. Like many Chinese intellectuals of the time, Lu Xun searched for a voice to unite and reform the nation. In "The History of Science," he even concluded that "what [the Chinese] society needs is not only Newton [for science] but also Shakespeare [for emotive poetry] who can give people a sound humanity."[85] Lu Xun's essay celebrated Shakespeare's ability to initiate national regeneration and bemoaned the absence of "warriors of the spirit" in China.[86] In a call-to-arms tone, Lu Xun even asked where China might find its own "warriors of the spirit," such as Shakespeare. The search continued into 1913 when Sun Yuxiu closed his "Collected Discussions of European and American Fiction" (in eight installments) in *Short Story Magazine* with the sentence: "I wish for China that a Shakespeare will be born in time to protect the country through literature." Sun noted that Shakespeare's widely revered plays had promoted patriotism not only in Britain but also in France and Germany. It is therefore crucial for a nation to discover its own "Shakespeare."[87]

The need to find a Chinese Shakespeare was as urgent in the past as today. Most recently, the Chinese People's Political Consultative Conference (March 4, 2002) made it a central part of the plan for the 2008 Olympics in Beijing, which was dubbed a "cultural Olympics," to commemorate Guan Hanqing (ca. 1229–ca. 1297). A prolific playwright who was also a theater manager and sometime actor, Guan has been regarded as another viable candidate for the coveted title of Chinese Shakespeare. The urge to create a national Shakespeare seems to be just as strong in the United States, which Frances Teague has called "Shakespeare's American figure."[88] A festival titled "Shakespeare in Washington" was held in Washington, D.C., from January to July 2007, complemented by a radio documentary featuring such episodes as "Shakespeare Becomes American."[89] On April 23, 2003, the National Endowment for the Arts (NEA) announced its Shakespeare in American Communities initiative and billed it as "a gift of immeasurable value to the American people." The announcement self-consciously connected Shakespeare's reputation to the idea of a gift to a collective, the American people. Jack Valenti, the president and CEO of the Motion Picture Association of America, enthused: "Unless you know, read and hear his magic stories there is a vacancy in your life," while NEA chairman Dana Gioia offered a national cause: "A great nation deserves great art. We are proud to present to America the greatest playwright in the English language."[90] These modern-day panegyrics call to mind Xu Zhimo's and Lu Xun's remarks on the necessity of a national poet nearly a century ago.

The search for a Chinese Shakespeare was informed by the nationalist economy of cultural exchange between the first Opium War and the May Fourth movements shaped by the interplay between the competing pull of "total Westernization" and rediscovery of traditional Chinese cultural values.[91] As Shakespeare evolved from a name on a banner held by Chinese reformers to a repository of plays of high production value, this inferiority complex gradually gave way to a heightened interest in forging new expressive modes such as tragedy and spoken drama through Shakespeare as a translated author.

Coda

As such, the interplay between Shakespeare and China was defined by an initial focus on identifying models for cultural reformation, not literary innovation, which partly explains why so much attention was directed to the name and biographical sketches of Shakespeare rather than to his language and poetry, and why his texts could remain completely "invisible" for half a century. Modes of cultural translation included such forms as praise and entries in reference books. This approach did not require literary translation of the works.

Between 1839 and 1900, "Shakespeare" was a fiction to the Chinese in which reformers found a ready home. The topicality of Shakespeare superseded any interest in, let alone understanding of, his plays. Specific aspects of Western works were frequently magnified as the outcome of national and historical exigencies. Other Western writers shared the same fate in China: for a long time, Henrik Ibsen's plays were considered a form of social criticism rather than representative works of symbolism and modernism.[92] During the first phase of the Chinese reception, Shakespeare's cultural function can be located only outside the texts: in his global stature and with the military prowess of the "West," he came to symbolize Great Britain and the United States. The search for a modern national identity via Shakespeare has created sets of texts that are central to the imagined communities of the traditionalists and reformists.[93]

As much as the nineteenth-century Chinese attempt to appropriate Shakespeare as a progressive "modern" author is ahistorical and present-ist in inclination, it is simultaneously energized by the future spaces that Shakespeare and China are yet to inhabit. This is the central paradox of a reception history of Shakespeare in absentia. Although the fascination with Shakespearean biography was not unique to China, the deferral to the cultural cache associated with Shakespeare was a distinctive product of a time that activated both Chinese and British nationalist imaginations. Shakespeare was useful to radical Chinese reformers because he had become an intercultural sign that could be read productively in a cultural space that existed outside Shakespeare and China.[94] Shakespeare's presence put selected Chinese values to question. The absence of Shakespeare's text—by historical accident—compelled the translators and rewriters of Shakespeare to speak *for* the dead through the unruly voices of the living. Treated as a heuristic document, Shakespeare was convenient shorthand for the promising future the reformers saw for their fellow citizens—and this they did without actually reading the Shakespearean texts. The textual space of these exchanges would soon emerge in the rewrites of Lin Shu and Lao She.

3 Rescripting Moral Criticism:

Charles and Mary Lamb, Lin Shu, and Lao She

I never may believe
These antic fables, nor these fairy toys.
—*A Midsummer Night's Dream*

Fueled by the intruding presence of Shakespeare and by new senses of self created by cross-cultural contacts, the Chinese fixation on Shakespeare's celebrity biography has developed into complex mechanisms of idealism. Both Shakespeare and China were used as alibis or the pretexts for aesthetic experiments. In the early twentieth century, Shakespeare and his plays had a more important and sustained role in the formation of Chinese literary culture. Various forms of rewriting, rather than reference books and expository essays, became the agent of mediation between Chinese and English cultural texts.

The production and reception of representations of Shakespeare and China is further regulated by persistent patterns of invocation of ethical concerns, which entails both an approach to literature that is based on an ethical agenda and the belief that literature is capable of fostering an ethical responsibility in the reader. The ethical discourse about appropriating foreign cultural capital remains active in different forms. To demonstrate how Shakespeare was made to relate to China and vice versa at a time of national crisis, I pursue the issue of moralist criticism in two landmark events: the rewriting of Charles and Mary Lamb's *Tales from Shakespeare* in classical Chinese prose by the prolific translator Lin Shu (who did not read English) and his collaborator Wei Yi; and the popular novelist Lao

She's short story "New Hamlet," written in the modern vernacular. Lin's filtration of Shakespeare and the Lambs operates on the cultural logic of authentication, an honorific approach to his sources. Lao She's novella is more iconoclastic in nature, pruning and "talking back" to Shakespeare and the Chinese popular discourse about Hamlet.[1] This chapter explores the myriad points of aesthetic, ethical, and political contact between Shakespeare and modern Chinese literary culture. As noteworthy cases in literary history, Lin Shu and Lao She are not representative of Chinese modernism in the context of interpretive and translation practices. Nor did they seek to approximate the truth of Shakespeare's plays. They demonstrate how rewriting Shakespeare became one of the prominent avenues for the Chinese writers to map their temporal and local coordinates.

Literature and Ethics

The first four decades of the twentieth century—when Lin Shu and Lao She penned their works—brought not only continual warfare (both foreign invasions and civil war) but also a series of controversial cultural reforms. Before 1900, Shakespeare was reproduced for and consumed by the elite, but by the early twentieth century his works were established as part of the foundation of Western-oriented education for young Chinese. A number of universities founded by Western missionaries, such as St. John's University in semicolonial Shanghai, were established in treaty ports. Translation of Shakespeare and the Western modes of thinking (including natural sciences and engineering) received so much attention in China's nascent Westernized higher education during this time that ironically "the principal form of Chinese-language instruction that received the blessing [of the university] was translation: Milton and Shakespeare into Chinese prose, and vice versa."[2] As a result, students of missionary colleges were encouraged to perform Shakespeare in English to improve their English skills and to celebrate special occasions. In 1896, the graduating class of St. John's performed the trial scene from *The Merchant of Venice* in English.[3] Another student performance of the same play took place in 1902.[4] In addition to student productions (a school tradition at St. John's), the Shakespeare Club was founded at the university in 1900, which met on weekend evenings to read Shakespeare's plays.[5] Society at large gave the performances and the play reading a great deal of attention.[6] Performing plays in a foreign language was a common pedagogical strategy that in itself may not have carried an imperialistic overtone, but the Shakespeare Club paralleled the nationalistic sentiments of such Victorian organizations as the New Shakespeare Society, founded in London in 1873.[7] A professional *huaju* (spoken-drama) performance in Chinese did not take place until 1913, when the National Renewal Society (Xinmin she) staged *A Pound of Flesh* (*Yi bang rou;* inspired by *The Merchant of Venice*). The performance was based on Lin Shu and Wei Yi's text and directed by Zheng Zhengqiu (1889–1935) in the semi-improvisational manner popular in Japan and China of the time.[8]

The introduction of Christianity and Western education (including English-language education) was conducted in a moral earnestness and the rhetoric of universalism.[9] This pattern may have affected Lin Shu's moralistic reading of Charles and Mary Lamb's *Tales from Shakespeare* when he rewrote the tales. The missionary Griffith John declared at the General Conference of the Protestant Missionaries of China in Shanghai in 1877 (the year St. John's University was founded): "We are here . . . not for the mere promotion of [Western] civilization; but to do battle with the powers of darkness, to save men from sin."[10] Reverend Francis Lister Hawks Pott, president of St. John's University from 1890 to 1938, advocated the teaching of English language and literature as a means to broaden "the mental horizon of [the Chinese] students," hoping to "earn respectability of the English language" through associating it with learning in a cultural renaissance of Christian character.[11] It is in such atmosphere that Shakespeare's plays entered the Chinese education system and intellectual life.

In addition to its status as a marker of moral value and social status, Shakespeare's texts were also made an integral part of the nascent literary utilitarianism. The concept of translation in this period referred to a broad range of practices, including "paraphrasing, rewriting, truncating, and restyling."[12] This was particularly true in the massive (re)production of Western knowledge, including Lin Shu's translations of hundreds of literary works.

Within a few decades, Confucian values and their expression in traditional literature and drama lost their status as irrevocable norms. While societies such as New Youth (Xin qingnian) and the Spring Willow Drama Society (Chunliu she) advocated a fundamental intellectual rejuvenation, there were counterforces, led by such thinkers as Liang Shuming, who strove to retain Confucian principles.[13] The reformers were seeking a new authority to provide a new unity. It was believed that this goal could be achieved by integrating literary universals that were not only alien but also antithetical to traditional Chinese literary forms and values.

Two intrinsically divisive camps participated in the cultural debates about the relative value of Western and Chinese traditions. One position championed local contexts and insisted on the significance of the nation—a crystallized Chinese tradition, as it were. The other emphasized the value of cultural hybridization and a transnational cultural space as sources of Chinese cultural renewal. Both approaches made China's self-strengthening and choice of cultural membership an ethical—rather than a political—question. This tendency manifests itself in fictions inspired by foreign sources and translations of foreign literature that freely adapt and rewrite the contents, making the source texts invisible, replacing the originals and even functioning as such in the target culture.[14] Such is the backdrop against which Lin Shu and Lao She wrote, but they responded differently to the ethical discourses about Chinese–Western cultural exchange.

The Tale of *Tales from Shakespeare*

In *Strange Stories from Overseas* (*Xiewai qitan*, 1903), an anonymous translation of Charles and Mary Lamb's *Tales from Shakespeare* (1807), the translator commented on the strange and eventful reception history of Shakespeare in China "without Shakespeare." The translator justified the need for his Chinese version, referring to the availability of Shakespeare's plays in other languages: "Shakespeare's works have been available in French, German, Russian, and Italian. Without even having read his works, Chinese intellectuals have praised him. It is my hope that my translation will remedy the unfortunate situation and enrich the world of fiction."[15]

But the translation of the Lambs' volume that made a crucial difference was the classical Chinese edition *An English Poet Reciting from Afar* (*Yingguo shiren yinbian yanyu*, 1904) by Lin Shu and Wei Yi. Not unlike Bertolt Brecht, who politicized Shakespeare in his German productions at a time of conflicting ideologies, Lin adapted the Lambs' text in the process of "translating" them.

In most cases, Shakespeare's plays found their way into different cultures through performances or translations of the plays. However, many readers in East Asia first encountered Shakespeare through the Lambs. Various translations of *Tales from Shakespeare* influenced a decade of performance and understanding of Shakespeare in both Japan and China. The first Japanese-language (1885) and Chinese-language (1903) performances of Shakespeare were both derived from these translations, and the performances were based on *The Merchant of Venice*. The Lambs' *Tales* was also widely read; between 1877 and 1928, it was translated and printed ninety-seven times in Japan, while over a dozen editions appeared in China between 1903 and 1915.[16]

The Lambs' Shakespeare was not Lin and Wei's first translation project. Their rendition of Alexandre Dumas *fils*'s *La Dame aux camélias* (*Chahua nü*, 1899) a few years earlier is a milestone in translated literature in China, and their translations of other canonical and (now) obscure works from the Anglo-European tradition captured the imagination of Chinese readers and audiences during the decades surrounding the establishment of the Chinese Republic in 1911. Lin and Wei's translation of the *Tales* was particularly popular and had an enormous impact on a large readership. It generated so much interest that it was reprinted eleven times between 1905 and 1935 in three editions. Since at least the 1890s, Lin had devoted a large part of his literary career to such "translation" projects. He recalled that his mother often lost herself listening to him reciting the novels he translated well into the wee hours of the night.[17]

According to most scholars, Lin's rendition of the Lambs' text was the only source for Chinese readers interested in Shakespeare before Tian Han's line-by-line translation of *Hamlet* in 1921. However, historical evidence suggests the contrary. *An English Poet* was far from an isolated case. Not only had Lin himself published rewritings of other Shakespearean plays as serialized novels and individual books, but other writers and commentators also produced various versions of Shakespeare's plays that were widely circulated. The Lambs' *Tales* was also available in the original English with a preface and notes in Chinese. Along with advertisements for Lin's works, Shanghai's popular monthly *Short Story Magazine* (*Xiaoshuo yuebao*) carried prominent announcements in 1910 and 1911 of the publication of Chinese-annotated editions of Shakespeare's *Macbeth* and *The Merchant of Venice*.[18] Such bilingual editions were promoted as tools for studying English, but they also played an important role in the broader historical context of reading English literature in early-twentieth-century China. One advertisement for *Macbeth*, annotated by Shen Baoshan, clearly distinguished rewrites (or plot outlines) from texts in the original languages.[19] Even though Lin's *An English Poet* was indeed popular and has remained influential, the historical evidence has made it sufficiently clear that multiple, and possibly competing, sources were available. *Short Story Magazine* was established to "translate famous works" and introduce new concepts, and its publisher, Commercial Press (Shangwu yinshuguan), was itself a major force behind the early-twentieth-century boom in the publications of works of fiction—translated, reworked, or original.[20]

Although Lin is widely known as the coauthor of *An English Poet,* his contributions go beyond that volume. In 1916, he went on to "translate" more Shakespearean plays—history and Roman plays that were not included in *An English Poet* in 1904—with Chen Jialin, who, like Wei Yi, orally rendered the plays into Chinese. Under transliterated titles, such as *Leichade ji,* Lin's renditions of *Richard II, Henry IV,* and *Julius Caesar* appeared in the *Short Story Magazine,* and *Henry VI* was published as a single volume with Commercial Press. These later works clearly identified William Shakespeare as the playwright, but it is not clear whether they were based on any specific edition. Lin's shift from Shakespeare's tragedies and comedies to history plays was not insignificant. Since *Short Story Magazine,* which churned out a great number of texts from Lin and his collaborators, had an editorial policy to discourage manuscripts that dealt with "ghosts and demons" (*shenguai*) and actively solicited works of fiction that focused on, among other things, national histories (figure 3), it stands to reason that the prospect of being well represented in a key venue with decent compensation would prompt Lin to turn to Shakespeare's history plays.[21] "Lin's Shakespeare" was a mainstay in Commercial Press's growing list of titles, as evidenced by the full-page advertisements for Lin's works, including *Henry IV,* which first appeared in installments in *Short Story Magazine.* The June 1916 issue, in which the second installment of Lin's rendition of *Julius Caesar* appeared (serialized May–July 1916), even carried a special photo section celebrating the tercentenary of Shakespeare's death that included a reprint of what has come to be known as the Flower portrait of Shakespeare (figure 4). Lin also worked with an anonymous translator on *Henry V,* publishing it in the *Story World* (*Xiaoshuo shijie*) in 1925.

The publication of these works in *Short Story Magazine* was a significant event, as the magazine was Commercial Press's longest-running (1910–1931) and most influential literary journal during this period. Partly due to a widespread negative view of the magazine as the purveyor of superficial popular entertainment, the work of Lin and his contemporaries—whether related to Shakespeare or not—has gone unnoticed.[22]

Of special note are two features of literary translation in this context. Lin was solely responsible for translating the Lambs' *Tales* into classical

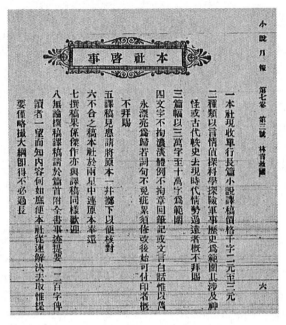

FIGURE 3   The editorial policy and submission guidelines of *Short Story Magazine*, March 1916.

Chinese prose, although he collaborated with Wei Yi, who orally rendered the English text into colloquial Chinese. They were not the only ones to use this method, as during this time translations of technical and religious texts also involved teamwork, and literary translation often operated outside the realm of belles lettres.[23] As a prose stylist, Lin was eminently qualified to render the result of the teamwork into classical Chinese. In their effort to simultaneously assimilate and differentiate different cultural perspectives, they were also translating the *Tales* against other texts, especially traditional Chinese narratives, reinventing some of the differences and connections along the way. In the case of the *Tales*, the distance between these texts and the elusive sense of Chineseness was articulated against English literature. Lin's readers, especially those who were among the sizable community of *Short Story Magazine*, would have been well informed about Lin's enterprise.

Lin and Wei's collection of twenty plays from Shakespeare (based on the Lambs' version) was a theatrical success story, even though the collection was not intended to be performed. In 1904, the National Renewal Society staged *A Bond of Flesh* (*Rou quan*), an adaptation of *The Merchant of Venice*. According to the director, Zheng Zhengqiu, this production—the

FIGURE 4   The Flower portrait of Shakespeare in *Short Story Magazine,* June 1916.

first professional performance of a Shakespeare play in China—was well received.[24] Its box-office success inspired a series of performances of Shakespeare's plays in 1914 and 1915, including *Othello, Hamlet,* and *The Taming of the Shrew.* Lin Shu's renditions were obviously very popular among readers and theater practitioners, as evidenced by the fact that all these performances were based on Lin's text.

There are two reasons for this popularity. First, Lin and Wei categorized Shakespeare under tales of ghosts and demons (*shenguai xiaoshuo*), a popular genre of traditional Chinese narratives with a ready audience, and second, Lin's reputation ensured wide circulation of his text. A full-page advertisement in *Short Story Magazine* for fifty novels (*xiaoshuo*) "translated" by Lin listed the titles on offer under separate categories (figures 5 and 6).[25] He was the most important translator of foreign literature who, in addition to translating Shakespeare, rendered more than 180 Japanese, German, French, Spanish, and English dramas and novels into classical Chinese.

Given the heavily coded ethical terms in which Chinese Shakespeares were initially constructed, one must wonder why translated canonical texts are often said to contain or authorize meanings that diverge from received interpretations of the original texts. Why do translations frequently operate as allegorical extensions of what the original literally says? Walter

FIGURE 5   The advertisement for Lin Shu's works, including his translation of *Henry VI*, in *Short Story Magazine*, October 1916.

Benjamin and Jacques Derrida discussed these questions through their ideas of translation as an "afterlife" or an integral part of the "original." Their theories have made all writing multilingual.[26] A translator's allegorical reading of an original work is hardly surprising, if, as Derrida suggests, all texts are translations or translations of translations.[27]

However, when a writer (such as Lin Shu) does not know a second language and yet purports to "translate" foreign materials, the roots of allegorical or emblematic readings become a different problem. These "translators" translate the invisible text with their collaborators and their imagination. Lin's works are not only informed by the historical exigencies but also dictated by the unique circumstances of mediated and collaborated translation.

Lin's case is not unprecedented in the history of world literature. There were quite a few writers in the West who "translated" from nonexistent "originals," such as Ezra Pound, Bertolt Brecht, Judith Gautier, Victor Segalen, and William Carlos Williams and David Rafael Wang's translation of thirty-eight Chinese poems. Part of the process of "translation" for these writers is analogous to Lin's case. They usually involve a collaborative

FIGURE 6   The advertisement for Lin Shu's works in *Short Story Magazine*, March 1916.

process (either with someone proficient in the foreign language or through materials available in a language the writer knows). It is a process of re-imagination and reinvention. But what is unique in Lin's case is that he never traveled outside China. In fact, in China, he was widely regarded a steadfast advocate of cultural conservatism. In contrast, some of the avant-garde Western poets who appropriated East Asian sensibilities were considered by their contemporaries as creators of new traditions.

Ironically, Lin was perhaps one of the most unlikely persons to engage in the translation of foreign literature, which was perceived in early-twentieth-century China as one of the most important tools to promote modernization—exactly what Lin was striving against. A holder of the *juren* degree, he was a traditional scholar of Chinese philology and Confucian texts. As a firm believer in the moral burden of intellectual practices (*wen*), Lin was especially familiar with such Confucian classics as the *Book of Poetry* and the *Book of Rites;* he took a deep interest in the Cheng-Zhu school of Neo-Confucianism.[28] The moralist vocabulary in Lin's many works reflects his unique, although futile, attempt to universalize particular Confucian values.

Lin had no knowledge of any foreign language or culture, nor did he feel the need for such knowledge.[29] In Lin and Wei's collaboration, Wei would therefore orally render the stories and the main plot into Chinese, which Lin would then adapt to the style of classical Chinese and, in the case of dramas, to the conventions of *chuanqi*.[30] According to Lin, while the two longtime collaborators sat leisurely at night, Wei "coincidentally mentioned a few entries from Shakespeare's notebooks," which prompted Lin to "rush to the light to draft a translation." It took him only twenty days to finish the book, which he identified as a collection of "chronicles by Shakespeare."[31] It is noteworthy that in Lin's preface, Shakespeare—not the Lambs—was identified as the author.[32]

Lin and Wei's choice to "translate" Shakespeare was perhaps not coincidental. They collaborated to translate a great number of Western writers, both prominent and obscure in Lin and Wei's time. However, their decision to translate Shakespeare from the Lambs' *Tales from Shakespeare* rather than directly from established late-nineteenth- and early-twentieth-century English editions (such as Edmund Malone, Samuel Weller Singer, or Clark and Wright's Cambridge editions) invites speculation. The availability and popularity of the Lambs' *Tales* in England may have played a role. Our next questions necessarily involve the process of collaboration among Shakespeare, the Lambs, and Lin and Wei.

How was the Lambs' text received in Britain? Even though the collection of tales seems like an infantalization project, it is useful to bear in mind that Charles Lamb was a respected Victorian essayist and Shakespearean critic. Coleridge praised Lamb's "exquisite criticisms on Shakespeare," and William Hazlitt even considered Lamb a "sounder authority than either Johnson or Schlegel on any subject in which poetry and feeling are concerned."[33] While the Lambs' text has faded from critical attention today, it has achieved an undeniable "children's classic" status, enjoying wide circulation as audiocassettes, compact discs, and illustrated books. Several editions were brought out between 1999 and 2007.[34] Late-twentieth-century scholarship has also acknowledged the Lambs' achievement in their *Tales*. Charles Marowitz, for example, writes of their rendition of Shakespeare's plays into "simple, unambiguous, and definitive narratives for 'children'": "It's quite an amazing feat, when you stop to think of it: a definitive rendition of what a play is actually about. I know few critics who are able to achieve such succinctness. But of course, apart from being impressive, it is also highly suspect, because the 'stories' of the plays need not at all be the tales the Lambs found in them."[35]

Charles and Mary Lamb adapted Shakespeare's plays into prose narrative intended for children and women who would otherwise not have the
opportunity to be exposed to Shakespeare's wit and language: "For young
ladies too, it has been the intention chiefly to write; because boys being
generally permitted the use of their fathers' libraries at a much earlier
age than girls are, they frequently have the best scenes of Shakespeare by
heart, before their sisters are permitted to look into this manly book."[36]

Not surprisingly, *Tales from Shakespeare* is heavily moralistic, censored
by Victorian politics of domesticity. Commenting on his experience attending performances of *Hamlet*, Charles Lamb wrote that it "abounds in
maxims and reflexions beyond any other, and therefore we consider it as
a proper vehicle for conveying moral instruction."[37] The widespread Victorian attitude toward Shakespeare may have influenced Lin's contemporaries (Western missionaries or the Chinese intellectuals who had contact
with them) who then supplied Lin with the raw materials for his creative
translation and rewriting. In 1897, Calvin Brown promoted Shakespeare
in a school curriculum but acknowledged the challenge that Shakespeare
posed for many students—thus the usefulness of *Tales from Shakespeare*. He
wrote in *Modern Language Notes*: "Let Shakespeare be assigned only for
reading and then only such plays as *The Merchant of Venice* and *As You
Like It* and not the mighty tragedies. In this connection Lamb's *Tales from
Shakespeare* might be found useful."[38]

The Lambs acknowledged that their text was gendered, classed, and
edited according to moralist principles, but they also stressed: "[Shake-
speare's] words are used whenever it seemed possible to bring them in."[39]
Indeed, many of the better-known phrases and passages—in excised,
edited prose—were preserved. The following passage illustrates how the
Lambs present Hamlet in unambiguous, moralistic terms:

> The young prince . . . loved and venerated the memory of his dead
> father almost to idolatry, and being of a nice sense of honour, and
> a most exquisite practiser of propriety himself, did sorely take to
> heart this unworthy conduct of his mother Gertrude: insomuch
> that, between grief for his father's death and shame for his mother's
> marriage, this young prince was overclouded with a deep melan-
> choly, and lost all his mirth and all his good looks.[40]

The difference between the Lambs' and Lin's texts compels us to ask:
What did Lin "inherit" from the Lambs? What did he change and why?

Lin clearly capitalized on Victorian critical ethics and exaggerated the potential for moral instruction in Shakespeare. However, he also made significant changes to the Lambs' text for his own agenda. Lin gave each play a *chuanqi*-style two-character title with an eye on rhyme and semantic balance. In general, there are four types of conventional *chuanqi* titles: name of the protagonist, name of the protagonist (or primary object or the protagonist's profession) plus the key plot element, name of the protagonist plus the key plot element and the word *ji* (story), and key plot element plus the word *ji*.[41] Lin adapted the second convention when renaming Shakespearean play titles. The titles and the order of the plays in Lin's text are different from those in the Lambs' *Tales from Shakespeare*, which begins with *The Tempest*, whereas Lin's version begins with *The Merchant of Venice*. He had given the plays new titles for the purpose of highlighting major themes of each play."[42] Overall, Lin's titles appealed to his target readers' love of the outlandish, and the tales showed that he was a moralist interpreter:

The Merchant of Venice	*A Bond of Flesh (Rou quan)*
The Taming of the Shrew	*Taming a Shrew (Xun han)*
The Comedy of Errors	*Twin Errors (Luan wu)*
Romeo and Juliet	*Committing the Crime of Passion (Zhu qing)*
Timon of Athens	*Enemies and Gold (Chou jin)*
Pericles	*Providential Reunion (Shen he)*
Macbeth	*Bewitched Omens (Gu zheng)*
All's Well That Ends Well	*Remedial Harmony (Yi xie)*
Measure for Measure	*Love Match in Prison (Yu pei)*
Hamlet	*A Ghost's Summons (Gui zhao)*
Cymbeline	*Ring Evidence (Huan zheng)*
King Lear	*The Daughter's Mutiny (Nü bian)*
As You Like It	*A Gathering in the Woods (Lin ji)*
Much Ado About Nothing	*Wedding Troubles (Li hong)*
A Midsummer Night's Dream	*Cunning Fairies (Xian kuai)*
The Winter's Tale	*Rediscovered Pearls (Zhu huan)*
Othello	*The Black General (Hei du)*
Twelfth Night	*Bewildered Wedding (Hun gui)*
Two Gentlemen of Verona	*Blunder of Emotions (Qing huo)*
The Tempest	*A Tempestuous Cause (Ju yin)*

These "major themes," which Lin mentioned in his preface, were obviously derived from moralist interpretations of the tales. Not unlike the early Japanese encounter with Shakespeare, when the Victorian moralist Samuel Smiles's *Self-Help; with Illustrations of Character and Conduct* (1859) was translated and published as the best-selling *Stories of Successful Lives in the West* (1871), Lin and Wei took it upon themselves to inform *and* instruct their Chinese readers.[43] While Lin's choice of titles for the stories may suggest a fixation on novel (Western) stories that focus on the strange and the unexpected, Lin made further changes to the Lambs' text in order to use Shakespeare against those of his radical contemporaries who were in favor of total Westernization.

It is useful to briefly consider the similarity between Lin's reading and later *xiqu* adaptations of Shakespeare. The requirements of stylization and the de facto framework of traditional China means the titles for the scenes in Chinese translation would bear an ethical imprint. Many *xiqu* adaptations contain two-character scene titles that focus on a lead character and the ethical underpinning of the main narrative. The Shanghai Kunju Company's 1986 *Macbeth* (titled *The Story of Bloody Hands* [*Xieshou ji*] in Chinese) is an illustrious example:[44]

Act 1: "The Emolument of Nobility" (*jin jue*), corresponding to act 1, scenes 1, 3, and 4
Act 2: "Conspiracy" (*mi mou*), corresponding to act 1, scene 5
Act 3: "Shifting the Blame" (*jia huo*)
Act 4: "Ruining a Banquet" (*nao yan*)
Act 5: "Seeking Advice from the Witches" (*wen wu*)
Act 6: "Madness in the Boudoir" (*gui feng*), corresponding to act 5, scene 1
Act 7: "Paying with Blood" (*xie chang*), corresponding to act 5, scene 7

As for the content and style, Lin opted for the sensational and moralizing principles, building on Charles and Mary Lamb's version, which added elements of the fairy tale to Shakespeare, but for very different purposes. Lin's text was not intended for children. Additionally, Lin omitted references to Christianity, whereas descriptions of the characters' appearance were given primacy. However, Lin did not excise the Lambs' representation of foreigners in Shakespeare's plays, inheriting their biased view of race and ethnicity. Comparing a section of Lin's text (*A Bond of Flesh*) and its corresponding section in the Lambs' text (*The Merchant of Venice*) demonstrates the point:

Lin's Text

Xieluoke is a big-bellied Jewish merchant. He always lent money and profited on the interest. He earned numerous sacks of gold, yet he exacted the payments of the money he lent with great severity. He never gave the borrowers a break. Therefore, everyone hated him. One of his enemies was named Antonio, a man from Rome.[45]

Lambs' Text

Shylock, the Jew, lived at Venice: he was an usurer, who had amassed an immense fortune by lending money at great interest to Christian merchants. Shylock, being a hard hearted man, exacted the payments of the money he lent with such severity that he was much disliked by all good men, and particularly by Antonio, a young merchant of Venice.[46]

As they sanitized Shakespeare for the Victorian family room, the Lambs demonstrated little sympathy for Shylock.[47] Shylock's view of the events, as presented in Shakespeare's play, has been left unrepresented, and Portia enters the courtroom to recognize immediately "the merciless Jew." Her question, "Which here is the merchant and which the Jew?" (4.1.169), has been excised even though the famous line does not contain grammatical or semantic elements that would present a challenge to the Lambs' intended readers. Lin's text builds on these images and adds visual details of the events and characters' appearance along the lines of *chuanqi* conventions.

Lin made more changes, notably in *A Ghost's Summons*, adapted from *Hamlet*, which he went to great lengths to reframe in a Confucian context. His *Hamlet* begins with an evaluative description of the members of the royal family and turns the play into a domestic tragedy, focusing on spousal devotion and filial loyalty rather than national politics. Claudius becomes Kelaodiu, which is a phonetic translation that carries a derogative connotation: *lao* means "old," and *diu* means "lost." This is perhaps no coincidence. Among the many possible homophonic characters that could have been used to transliterate these foreign names, Lin consciously opted for this set of characters. Similarly, Gertrude becomes Jiedelu, with *de* meaning "virtue."

Lin thus deviates substantially from the Lambs' version. Lin has it that Hamlet "is known throughout the country for his filial piety." The prince is not ambitious and "does not have his heart set on the crown."[48] Lin adds that "the filial nature of the prince is so deeply rooted in his character that he wears black all year long to mourn his father."[49] In contrast, the Lambs' Hamlet is "overclouded with a deep melancholy" because of his mother's hasty marriage, which he considers more damaging than "the loss of ten kingdoms." The Lambs have it: "Not that the prospect of exclusion from the throne, his lawful inheritance, weighed so much upon his spirits, though that to a young and high-minded prince was a bitter wound and a sore indignity; but what so galled him and took away all his cheerful spirits was that his mother had shown herself so forgetful to his father's memory."[50]

Continuing his revisions of the Lambs' text, Lin has Hamlet lock himself up in his room rather than attend Claudius and Gertrude's wedding.[51] Ophelia becomes Hamlet's wife but without any explanation of when and why they are married.[52] Laertes is referred to as Hamlet's "brother-in-law" (*qi di*).[53] After Hamlet kills Polonius, Lin has Hamlet cry "to mourn the death of Polonius" because he feels that he must apologize to Ophelia for killing her father.[54] Significantly, the character of Ophelia has also been adapted to conform to that of a young lady from an upper-class family informed by Confucian moralities. While Ophelia seems to have died of an accident by a stream in the Lambs' text, Lin has her commit suicide because of her grief over her father's death. Ophelia is torn between her obligations to her father, who is killed by her husband, Hamlet, and her love for Hamlet. Ophelia's madness does not receive as much emphasis in Lin's text as it does in twentieth-century *Hamlet* criticism or in the Lambs' text. Reading Lin's and the Lambs' texts side by side reveals how Lin's moralist interpretation operates:

Lin's Text

When Hamlet returned [from the trip to England], he ran into the funeral procession of his wife, Ophelia, who had taken her own life because of her grief over her father's death. Upon hearing the news that her father was killed by her husband who had lost his wits, Ophelia fainted and then lost her mind, singing all day without combing her hair. One day she came upon a willow brook. She plucked many flowers and clambered to hang these flowers on a bough, saying she was decorating the willow tree. The bough unexpectedly broke and she died [in the water].[55]

Lambs' Text

This was the funeral of the young and beautiful Ophelia, [Hamlet's] once dear mistress. . . . There was a willow which grew slanting over a brook, and reflected its leaves on the stream. To this brook she came one day when she was unwatched, with garlands she had been making, . . . and clambering up to hang her garland upon the boughs of the willow, a bough broke, and precipitated this fair young maid, garland, and all that she had gathered, into the water, where her clothes bore her up for a while, during which she chanted scraps of old tunes, like one insensible to her own distress, or as if she were a creature natural to that element: but long it was not before her garments, heavy with the wet, pulled her in from her melodious singing to a muddy and miserable death.[56]

Lin's moralist reading was intimately connected to the familial relation he invented, which complicates the ethical questions not found in the Lambs' text. Ophelia's death is mentioned only toward the end of Lin's text in a brief passage. Whereas the Lambs provide a detailed description of Ophelia's final moments in the water, Lin is more interested in Ophelia's urge to commit suicide and how she is torn between her husband and her father. Lin can be seen as a Confucian universalist, and the moral discourse here has far-reaching political and social implications beyond the façade of pseudo-translations.[57]

The Value of Fairies

Although he was a prolific translator, Lin Shu was a traditionalist who believed that Chinese culture and literature were valuable. It is clear from the analysis of his renditions of Shakespeare that Lin prioritizes cultural affinity in appropriating Charles and Mary Lamb's *Tales from Shakespeare*. In his *chuanqi*-style narrative, Lin brought Shakespeare

close to the Ming and Qing narrative tradition of love, filial piety, and exotic fairy stories. In Lin's traditionalist Confucian framework, the Lambs'
tales, intended for women and children, became stories for the predominantly male elite community in late Qing and early Republican China. In
the context of Chinese self-strengthening discourse, Lin's texts gave the
impression that Shakespeare concentrated on fairies and ghosts. Lin used
this strategic rewriting to counter the rhetoric deployed by those of his
contemporaries who were in favor of total Westernization and had been
influenced by the Enlightenment and rationalism:

> It is always said that the reason Europeans are superior to us is
> that . . . our outlook [is] old fashioned; that we prefer the old to the
> new and like talking about gods and spirits. . . . Those young people
> in our country, the reformers, thus try their utmost to seek the
> new. . . . If Westerners are really civilized, they should have already
> burnt [Shakespeare's] works and banned them. However, the fact
> is that the intellectual elite of the West is so fond of Shakespeare's
> poetry that every household in the country seems to be reading and
> reciting his lines all day long. . . . Nobody reproaches him for his
> antiquated thoughts, nor is anyone angry at his talk about gods and
> spirits.[58]

In line with his arguments about Shakespeare's greatness and the value
of traditional Chinese culture, Lin categorized his rewriting of the Lambs'
Tales as stories of gods and spirits. Lin was not assimilating Shakespeare
in order to introduce new expressive modes in the emerging modern
Chinese theater. He used rewriting, in the guise of translational Chinese
narrative styles, to make a case for the affinity between Shakespeare and
traditional Chinese modes of storytelling.

The radical reformers attacked all aspects of traditional Chinese culture, but Lin sought to counter their arguments by presenting a Shakespeare founded on ancient Chinese ideals. For the radicals, Shakespeare
was an icon of progressive Western culture. Lin tried to demonstrate that
Shakespeare upheld the same morality and value as those in traditional
China.

There is little evidence to suggest that Lin succeeded in persuading the
radical reformers. But his translations were immensely popular and successful with artists as well as the general public. Wang Xiaonong (1858–
1918), a famous Beijing-opera actor, read Lin's rendition of Shakespeare.

He wrote a set of twenty poems dedicated to Lin's translation and used Lin's titles as the titles of his own poems.[59] Cao Yu (1910–1996), one of the founders of modern Chinese drama, was fascinated by Lin and Wei's rendition of *Tales*.[60] Guo Moruo (1892–1978), an influential historian and playwright, was also "unconsciously influenced by and attracted to" it.[61] His *Ode of Thunders* (*Leidian song*) was inspired by Lin's rendition of Shakespeare's *King Lear*.[62] Lin's text not only was being read, but also was being staged. When Lin's versions of Shakespeare were performed they drew large audiences. Fu Sinian's (1896–1950) reaction to *The Merchant of Venice* in 1918 best sums up the reception of Shakespeare in this period. Like Lin, Fu emphasizes the moral lesson one could learn from the play, which he does not believe is possible with traditional Chinese drama: "The speech 'to bait fish withal . . .' from the *Merchant of Venice* so thoroughly expresses the view that men are born equal, that it is the *Doctrine of Social Contract* before Rousseau. In our classical Chinese drama and Beijing opera, there is nothing comparable to this."[63]

Fu's interpretation of the speech (3.1.53–73) is influenced by both the Lambs and Lin. The original Shakespearean text remains indivisible, but selected parts of Shakespeare's plays were highlighted. This expanded the currency of Shakespeare and Western learning in China in connection with very specific agendas. Lin and his precursors (who propagated Shakespeare's biographies) made desirable aspects of the biography and reputation of William Shakespeare highly visible. Lin justified his work by his well-intended fixation on his readers, not the foreign texts that remained inaccessible to the Chinese readers who needed the translations. Indeed, translation as an act of cultural negotiation has to be understood rather differently to make sense of this peculiar reception history of Shakespeare.

Despite its historically specific meanings, Lin's rewriting of the *Tales* has remained influential. In 2001, a new project was launched—in the footsteps of Charles and Mary Lamb and Lin Shu—to render all the Shakespearean plays into prose narratives. The preface duly acknowledges Lin's monumental work and argues that twenty-first-century readers need an updated prose version of Shakespeare—this time written in modern Chinese (*baihua*). Others followed suit.[64] Lin's legacy is visible in Taiwan as well. Multiple editions by different translators and publishers were brought out in consecutive years, attesting to the large market for the Lambs' text. Some editions even recycle the moral vocabulary of Lin and the Lambs. Liu Hongyan's 2005 translation includes the Lambs' preface, stressing the role of Shakespearean plays as "strengtheners of virtue," helping the readers to withdraw from "all selfish and mercenary thoughts" and cultivate "honorable thoughts and actions, . . . courtesy, benignity, generosity, humanity."[65]

If cultural translation is the reinvention of cultures, whether a translator is "trustworthy" in terms of his or her rendition of foreign texts is not an issue.[66] This tendency to make the original invisible is also evident in other early-twentieth-century Chinese writers, who in their rewrites or translations of foreign works reinvented the themes, moral frameworks, and contents of the original. Lin Shu's project provides interesting contrasts with later efforts to essentialize Confucianism negatively (May Fourth iconoclasm, Lao She's "New Hamlet") or positively (national essence [guocui]).

Lao She and Modern China's Hamlet Complex

Recognized in popular discourse as the core of the playwright's oeuvre, *Hamlet* has been not only frequently alluded to but also parodied.[67] Some of the best-known instances of the play's extensive literary afterlife include T. S. Eliot's J. Alfred Prufrock, who declares, "I am not Prince Hamlet, nor was meant to be," and commentary by Joyce's Stephen Daedalus. Shakespeare has also provided raw material for the themes and plots of various novels in English and German.[68] Farther afield, *Hamlet's* scenes with Gertrude and Ophelia are appropriated in the autobiographical writing of the Palestinian writers Ihsan Abbas (1920–2003) and Jabra Ibrahim Jabra (1919–1994). While there is a series of "Hamlet in literature" in English and European traditions, the majority of the creative interactions with *Hamlet* in East Asia remain performance based. In this context, Lao She's "New Hamlet" (Xin Hanmuliede, 1936), the earliest Chinese parody of Hamlet-like postures, is a milestone for East Asian interpretations of Shakespeare. (Dazai Osamu published *New Hamlet* [*Shin Hamuretto*], in July 1941, in the "I-novel" genre.) As Christopher Reed observes, "breaks with the most orthodox works of the past . . . often take the form of parody."[69] It is significant that "New Hamlet" parodies not only Hamlet's image in popular culture but also self-righteous moral criticism practiced by Chinese intellectuals of the time. What is "new" about "New Hamlet" is its protagonist's failure to confront anything tagged as "old."

Lao She's rewrite is based on the premise that modern China in a time of transition displays a Hamlet complex, partly inherited from the

Anglo-European discourses about the figure of Hamlet as a sign of the modern age.[70] One of the most significant historical events of Lao She's time was the May Fourth movement, which was marked by a pervasive pessimism and hesitation. Theodore Huters argues in *Bringing the World Home: Appropriating the West in Late Qing and Early Republican China* that "many, if not most, of the ideas that were brought forward in response to the national crisis were accompanied by a pervasive sense of impasse," which reflected "the fear that adapting too easily to alien ways would result in irreparable damage to the very set of [Chinese] institutions that reform was designed to save."[71] The Chinese tendency of inaction was certainly not new. In 1906, the missionary W. A. P. Martin (1827–1916) provided an account in the preface to *The Awakening of China:*

> Had the [Chinese] people continued to be as inert and immobile as they appeared to be half a century ago, I might have been tempted to despair of their future. But when I see them, as they are to-day, united in a firm resolve to break with the past, and to seek new life by adopting the essentials of Western civilization, I feel that my hopes as to their future are more than half realized.[72]

Whether Martin's account is a revealing observation of China's Hamlet complex or a manifestation of his own procolonialist bias fed by the promise of "Western civilization," it is evidence for the discourses about Hamlet-like characteristic that Lao She parodies. This was certainly not the first and will not be the last instance of reading *Hamlet* as political allegory. The connection between Hamlet as an idle dreamer and Chinese inaction in a time of transition calls to mind Ludwig Börne's 1828 essay in which he identifies Hamlet with Germany, "which can neither think nor act politically nor make up its mind to perform the deed of liberation."[73]

Lao She—one of modern Chinese literature's most well-traveled and articulate voices—wrote "New Hamlet" in the mid-1930s, some three decades after Lin Shu, facing similar social and historical conditions and questions of cultural affiliation. While Lin's generation witnessed the beginning of a series of conflicts between Chinese and western European values that eventually manifested themselves militaristically, Lao She's time saw much more intensified clashes not only between China and western Europe but also between China and Japan, a country that was once considered weak from the Chinese perspective. "New Hamlet" commented on what was perceived to be a problem of hesitation of a society caught between contending values; it also anticipated the anxiety of cultural engulfment of the next decade. Japan's invasion of China triggered the second Sino-Japanese War (1937–1945). Not only were the Chinese intellectuals and writers torn between the ideological choices of a Chinese or a Western worldview, but they were also caught between the emerging Communist causes (advocated by the CCP) and republicanism (promoted by the KMT, or Nationalists). The Nationalist–Communist civil war was fought intermittently over several decades from 1927 to 1949. Therefore, the wars of ideology shaped many writers' choices of subject matters and style.

Best known in the English-speaking world as the author of *Rickshaw Boy* (also known as *Camel Xiangzi,* 1936) and the *huaju* play *Teahouse* (*Chaguan,* 1957), Lao She wrote a great number of humorous, satirical works in a wide range of genres (short story, science fiction, exposé fiction, novel, stage play, essay) that remain popular to this day. Lao She's "comic talents" have attracted the attention of many generations of critics, including David Wang.[74] While Lin Shu wrote in classical Chinese, Lao She opted for the modern vernacular and helped—along with his contemporaries, such as Lu Xun—to make it not only an acceptable but also a desirable literary language.

However, what distinguishes Lao She from his predecessors (such as Lin Shu) and his contemporaries (such as Hu Shi) is that he does not subscribe to a polarized view of moralities and cultural values. Although Lao She shared with other May Fourth writers a commitment to the intellectual's social responsibility, he is primarily interested in the art of humor and storytelling. Many writers' concern with social issues has manifested itself in a nationalist overtone, leading some Western critics to read their works as a form of national allegory. Fredric Jameson has used Lu Xun as an example of "third world" writers whose texts can be read as national allegories.[75] Jameson's proposal of the third-worldness of modern Chinese literature is highly contested, but it is true that Lao She and his contemporaries are in search of not only a national identity but also a character that can effectively represent the symbolic weight of that quest. In contrast to Lu Xun, who created memorable characters such as Ah Q but is primarily interested in their utilitarian value (through symbolism), Lao She often has extended comic anecdotes that reveal his characters as individuals. Lu Xun's satires bear a distinctively intellectual overtone, while Lao She transformed the concept of humor in Chinese literature.

Written in the context of the nascent global economy in Chinese urban centers in the early twentieth century, Lao She's works reexamine May Fourth essentialism and the tropes of nationalism and cosmopolitanism. Lao She is often self-conscious about his ambiguous positionality because he has played many different roles in the East–West cultural exchange, including as a lecturer of Chinese at the University of London (where he collaborated with Clement Egerton on an English translation of *The Golden Lotus*), at a high school in Singapore, and at universities in Ji'nan and Qingdao. Before finally settling down in his native Beijing, he had traveled through Europe and lived in New York.[76] From his perspective, the challenge facing Hamlet at the crossroads of feudalism and modern consciousness was no different from the one confronting his generation. Hamlet's task involves battling a corrupt court *and* the pending invasion of a foreign military power. The Chinese society, as portrayed by Lao She and other May Fourth writers, was not unlike Hamlet in that the society is "so preoccupied with a philosophical posture *vis à vis* the immediate call for action that [it] is paralyzed by the posture."[77] Lao She's "New Hamlet" and other works explore the individual's struggle against society.

"New Hamlet" was not Lao She's only attempt at exploring the Hamlet complex and the unique challenges of modernization of China. The protagonist of his play *Homecoming (Guiqulaixi, 1942)*, which was originally titled *Hamlet*, was also based on the Shakespeare text. He seems to have been particularly attracted to an overrated characteristic of Hamlet: his idiosyncratic habit to pause, pose, and think rather than putting thoughts into action. Lao She's "New Hamlet" mocks the Chinese intellectuals' Hamlet-like habit to look backward rather than act. He also satirizes those who think that they know *Hamlet* and take the Hamlet-like posture to be fashionable. In Lao She's hands, Hamlet embodies the problems of a hesitating, modern China poised in search of new identities amid competing visions of modernity. Thanks to Lin Shu, Hamlet was now an exotic character of foreign origin who was oddly familiar as a filial son. The leftist literary theoretician Hu Feng's (1902–1985) comment on stereotypes illustrates the popularity of the image of Hamlet:

Another form of misrepresentation holds that a type embodies either eternal "human nature," as Hamlet represents a certain kind of human nature and Quixote another, or a "national character," as [Lu Xun's] Ah Q represents the Chinese people. This is a very harmful misinterpretation. . . . Still, we do often say that a certain person is a Hamlet, or that a certain person is an X.[78]

Lin Shu's engagement with Shakespeare through the Lambs' text can be seen as a Chinese intellectual's attempt to connect different literary traditions despite his pronounced interest in the politics rather than literariness of the text. In contrast, Lao She's Hamlet-like characters are clowns in what can be seen as parodies of *Hamlet*. In Lao She's novel *The Two Mas* (*Er Ma*), which closely parallels his London experience, Ma Wei and his father, Old Ma, struggle to survive racism and other hostilities in early-twentieth-century London. Ma Wei is a clown-like figure with a "sullen face and melancholy posture . . . who is vulnerable as he is laughable."[79] Ma Wei is often cynical of his bitter experience in England. The narrative revolves around his repeated, but failed, attempts to flee—to break away from his father's Chinese mannerism, to flee London, to escape that which is responsible for his nondecision: "Ma Wei is aware of his predicament; his heart is filled up with [indecisiveness and melancholy]. Not only does his heart leave no crack to let other things come in, his whole body has refused to be directed by it. . . . He wishes the world and himself would be destroyed at the same time."[80]

The Hamlet figure in "New Hamlet," an overly self-confident yet confused college student named Tian Liede, is no less a clown than Ma Wei. Both exhibit peculiar habits and idiosyncratic mannerism. Like Goethe's Wilhelm Meister, Tian identifies with Hamlet. Wilhelm interacts with Hamlet as a director and an actor and declares, in one instance, that he has "learned the part [of Hamlet] and tried it out, feeling that [he] was becoming more and more identified with [his] hero."[81] Tian is a caricature. He and his perceived noble parallels to Shakespeare's Hamlet dominate "New Hamlet." Tian returns home as a self-proclaimed revolutionary, but he becomes an utterly misplaced character, unable to do anything for his father's family business. "New Hamlet" opens with a comical recapitulation of what Lao She sees as Hamlet's problems: lack of self-knowledge, procrastination, and "self-torturing philosophical poses":[82]

Once, after having had too much to drink, Tian Liede said—with mixed self-mockery and self-esteem—to his friend: "I am Shakespeare's Hamlet. We share the same given name, more or less."

"Do you often see ghosts, too?" his friend asked laughingly.

"Surely more than once! But . . ." Tian replied. "But they don't all come out to patrol at night in white robes and red eyes."

"A new Hamlet!" his friend said casually.

Thus it became his nickname, one that makes him nod in satisfaction.

A third-year student in college, he is very proud, very serious. He plans everything thoroughly, and he ponders all the time.[83]

A narcissist, Tian obviously takes pride in his purported connection to a well-known literary character of European origin, but he—like many of Lao She's contemporary study-abroad returnees—is unable to fully incorporate Western modes of thinking.

It is significant that Lao She not only reinvented the modern vernacular by using Beijing dialects and slang (which existed exclusively in oral form) in his writing, but also reconfigured the relationship between literary humor and exposé fiction. Humor as a form of expression was highly suspect in the Confucian tradition, seen alternately as frivolous or facetious. Even the antitraditionalist May Fourth writers were skeptical of humor, denouncing it as unfit for their "serious" purposes in reforming Chinese cultural politics. Lao She's contribution lies in his humanizing caricature. Tian's narcissism translates into his interpretation of his "Western" facial features:

He felt he was extremely lovable and yet pitiable. He often looked into the mirror: a long, thin face, a long and extremely white forehead. His eyes appeared to be sleepy. His mouth was wide and his lips thin. He is able to form a long thin line between his lips. His long, thin black hairs were gathered in a bundle at the back. He believed his appearance and character was so handsome to have exceeded ordinary standards.[84]

These characteristics were commonly considered to be Caucasian features, and the size of one's forehead was in proportion to one's intellect. Tian feels he that is superior to his peers but that he is misunderstood by them. Although he becomes a "new Hamlet" almost by accident, as indicated by the opening of the story, Tian does insist on his new affiliation with all things Western, from Hamlet-like poses to clothing: "With this positive self-knowledge, Tian develops a discerning taste for Western clothes, with attention to the minutest details. . . . Only then can he ensure the agreement between his outward appearance and his inner nature. Only then can he uphold his superiority and solemnity."[85]

Tian's fixation on Western clothes and what he perceives to be the Western mode of thinking reminds us of Dr. Mao in Lao She's short story "Self-sacrifice" (Xisheng, 1934). The protagonist, Dr. Mao, who has returned to China after having studied, as he claims, at Harvard, displays a comical mannerism:

> There was something funny about this man. He was in the "full armor" of a Western suit [yangfu], with everything where it ought to be. For instance, a handkerchief was carefully stuck in the outside breast pocket, a tiepin in the tie, a length of watch chain dangling across the lower portion of his vest, the correct shine on the tip of his shoes. . . . He wasn't wearing foreign clothes; he looked more like he had committed himself, under oath, to foreign clothes—the handkerchief must be there, the tiepin goes there, they were all a kind of duty, one of those religious commandments followed on faith.[86]

As Lu Xun astutely observed, while urban residents "have changed into Western suits, deep down they are every inch their ancients."[87] Accounts by Western observers on the scene confirm the unfortunate truth of Lao She's caricature of his contemporaries. The Chinese insatiable appetite for things Western went beyond reason and was satirized by Lao She. In 1913, Goldsworthy Lowes Dickinson (1862–1932), a Cambridge-based historian who traveled to China, described in no ambiguous terms the overwhelming pro-American bias of radical revolutionaries in Canton (Guangzhou):

> They were exactly like American undergraduates. Their whole mentality . . . was American. . . . This conversion may, of course, be superficial. There may be underlying it an unchanged basis of Chinese character. It is these young men that have made the revolution and established the Republic [of China]; they are doing all they can to sweep away the old China, root and branch, and build up there a reproduction of America. There is nothing . . . which they would not alter if they could, from the streets of Canton to the family system, and the costume of a policeman to the national religion.[88]

In tandem with his distaste for anything old (associated with tradition or China), Tian also suffers from an identity crisis. He disdains his father's now-withering family business of selling dried fruits and his family's involvement in the futile effort. The irony is that Tian needs the money his father sends him periodically so that he can continue to philosophize as a college student. He disdains the ways in which his father and his entire family labor in exchange for money. Neither he nor other characters around him seem to have even the remotest solution to the problem his father's business faces:

> Tian has not returned home for two years. He does not dare go home. . . . He has become a stranger in his own home. . . . He is in pursuit of a greater ideal, . . . a scheme to completely readjust the entire culture. He is not only against his father. He is against the whole world. . . . He has to abandon all that which is corrupted. I am a white lotus in a clear pond [Tian thought to himself]. Yes, I have to become a literary giant . . . and give the world a new voice and hope.[89]

Tian refuses to accept any blame for his own weak will, and he rejects the cultural inheritance from which he cannot escape. It does not take a cynical reader of Lao She to detect that Tian's mockery and self-important tone contrast with his inaction and helplessness. Tian concludes that he must not allow his lofty philosophy to be tarnished by his emotions. He must "run away," and yet, because he needs his father's financial support, he is unable to. He thinks of himself as a prince. He "hates the world" and asks "why couldn't I be born into a world that can better support a royal person like me!?"[90]

There is an interesting twist at the end of "New Hamlet," which involves a painting of Ophelia. Lao She parodies both melodramatic representations of Ophelia in popular culture and Lin Shu's moralistic treatment of Ophelia's death. Tian recollects in great detail a painting he had seen:

> Tian thought back on a reprint of a famous painting he had seen in a magazine: a beautiful girl floating in sparkling, clear stream, the lower half of her body in the water, her sleeves spread out across the surface of the stream, her long hair following the ripples like golden algae. Her snow white forehead was tilted upward as if she was hoping for something. . . . Her bosom was scattered with petals.

Tian did not know why he was thinking of this particular paint-ing and he did not want to bother with the story in it. He just felt her long hair and her jade forehead were so lovable and pitiable. Those flower petals, though, were a bit redundant, like painting feet on a snake. This thought gave Tian pleasure. He felt by the end of the day he was still in possession of critical ability. . . . He was transfixed by this painting he had conjured in his mind, and he smiled.[91]

The image could well come from John Everett Millais's oil painting *Ophelia,* which Lao She may have seen at the Tate Gallery during his time in London.[92] The painting was part of the original donation in 1894 and remains one of the best-known Shakespeare-inspired paintings in the gal-lery. As in Millais's painting, Lao She casts Ophelia as an innocent victim. The story ends with Tian—walking and daydreaming—unwittingly ar-riving at the door of his family's house: "The red sign of 'Tian Residence' suddenly appeared before his eyes and startled him."[93] After so much philosophizing and thoughts, Tian returns, to his surprise, to the place from which he initially sets out to escape. This witty ending seems to be Lao She's way of critiquing his generation's ideological investments in China (its superiority, its inferiority, its decadence) and/or the West (again, its superiority, its difference, its weakness). The image of Tian forms a typology of some of Lao She's contemporaries who had suggested total Westernization and yet were unable to break away from that which they initially set out to change. More importantly, Lao She, writing in the modern vernacular, uses the ending to criticize Lin's traditionalist aes-thetics. In Lin's rendition, Ophelia dies a tragic death that follows both Confucian ethics and traditional Chinese storytelling. In Lao She's story, the Ophelia in the painting becomes another icon of Western culture that Tian wholeheartedly embraces. The painting, like what Tian sees in the mirror, becomes part of Tian's comical self-assurance and mannerism.

Perhaps nothing better summarizes Tian's escapism than the popular early-twentieth-century American comedian Eddie Foy's musings "on the life of a small-time actor" in his burlesque of *Hamlet:*

To flee, or not to flee, that is the question
Whether 'tis nobler in the sun to suffer
The slings and arrows of outrageous scorching
Or to fling his claims against a sea of critics
And, I suppose, offend them;

To fly, to sneak, to "blow" and by that sneak
To say, I end the headshakes and the thousand
Natural wrongs the profesh is heir to.[94]

Coda

Lin Shu and Wei Yi's *An English Poet Reciting from Afar* and Lao She's "New Hamlet" are at several removes from an original, which is informed by the contrasts between the two authors—the former a translator with no knowledge of a foreign language and no experience traveling abroad and the latter a writer who had spent a considerable period of time in London. The distancing of Shakespeare functions both to enable the local culture to get over Shakespeare and to acknowledge his ready availability. The distance, in this context, becomes ideologically freighted. Lao She mined *Hamlet*'s potential as a moral allegory, and Lin Shu turned the Lambs' fairy-tale renditions of Shakespeare into a version that demonstrated Shakespeare's manufactured Chinese affinity for the male elite class in China. Both operated on moralizing principles, albeit with highly divergent agendas. Chinese readers, regardless of whether or not they were familiar with Shakespeare's text, did not question the omission of the substantive content of Shakespeare's plays, or the translations' detachment from the invisible originals, because an inward gaze dominated the mode of reception of Western culture. Lin Shu may have cared to read Charles and Mary Lamb's *Tales from Shakespeare* in English, but he could not and was not expected to read the original materials. Like Pound, Brecht, and other Western "translators" of foreign (Chinese) cultural text, Lin cast gazes toward his own culture. Lin Shu's and Lao She's cultural locations in the global colonial order shaped their practices of cosmopolitanism. The attention is on the social exigencies of the rewriters' own locality, which either did not call for a placement of the original text or demanded parody as critical reflection of history.

The diverse translational practices demonstrated by these cases open the possibility that translational differences are not always given. Rather, they are the result of conscious and complex maneuvers to relocate and absorb (by way of citing and reframing) cultural texts. Therefore, the meanings of China and Shakespeare were constructed in several layers of cultural semantics. The transmission process is customarily thought of as a process of degradation. However, Lin Shu's and Lao She's rewrites suggest that what is lost is just as significant as what is gained. Shakespeare's text passed through Charles and Mary Lamb and acquired a new life in the hands of Lin Shu and Wei Yi, taking on the color of their Chinese-Victorian moral principles. From there, it entered the Chinese popular imagination, embraced by readers and theater audience alike. This process made it possible for Lao She to parody Shakespeare's *Hamlet*, Lin's *Hamlet*, and even Millais's *Ophelia*. As Shakespeare continued to gain local purchase, interpretations of Shakespeare and China extended from fiction to cinema.

PART III

Locality at Work

4 Silent Film and Early Theater:

Performing Womanhood and Cosmopolitanism

The acts of reading and writing in the broadest sense always involve relationships that are constantly refigured because of historical exigencies. As cultural life in China's coastal cities continued to gain momentum in urban cosmopolitanism and as new technologies were woven into the texture of daily life, Shakespearean drama shared a cultural space with forms of representation that were new to Chinese urbanites (silent film, proscenium indoor theater, Western stage technologies, illusionist performance). The reciprocal relationship of showing and gaze is rooted in and routed through the question of locality. In the strategic displacement of cultural tokens of Shakespeare and China, formal and ideological considerations are inseparable. In turn, Chinese reception of Shakespeare comes to be conditioned both from within the genres of cinema and theater and from without through the cultural and social institution. Similar to the nontheatrical genres of enacting Shakespeare examined so far, theatrical and cinematic performances in the 1930s and 1940s are made to occupy a multitude of localities through not just what is said but also where it is said. Shakespeare's plays defined the canonicity of Western classics for the Chinese, but they also constituted the site for artistic innovation for a generation of directors and performers seeking cultural renewal and modernization.

This chapter considers the articulation of cultural agency with a focus on the relationship between literary realism and illusionist staging in a *huaju* (spoken-drama) production of *Macbeth* (1945), and the notions of modern womanhood in silent-film adaptations of *The Merchant of Venice* (1927) and *The Two Gentlemen of Verona* (1931). The case studies of Shakespeare performances in Shanghai, mainland China's most cosmopolitan city of the time, situate these performances in the context of modern Chinese cultural reform and competing approaches to performing Shakespeare against the backdrop of changing ideologies.

Chinese interpretations of Shakespeare have oscillated between the two poles of exoticization and localization, emphasizing either distance or proximity between the Shakespearean and Chinese localities. What was claimed to be Shakespearean often turned out to be infused with local imaginaries of the West (that is, the gaudy features of Shakespeare's plays that attracted Chinese attention). Toward the end of the 1930s, many theater artists opted for topical presentations and social relevance in their work. While some topics are an extension of the self-strengthening campaign, the new woman's movement—part of the ideology of new urbanites—emerged in this period as a powerful force in literature and arts. Not only were women admitted to higher education, they also began to appear on stage and on screen as performers. A significant number of Western-style educational institutions—including women's schools and colleges—were set up in metropolitan areas, where female students frequently produced public performances of Shakespeare and other Western plays. These new cultural institutions thus helped to spread Shakespeare's works from small groups of elite promoters to local popular theaters.

The Theatrics of Cultural Reform

In the first few decades of the twentieth century, as the Chinese reformers were thwarted in their effort to instill new systems they believed would strengthen China, these reformers—many of whom were a cross-breed of intellectuals, writers, and theater artists—came to the conclusion that before any changes could be initiated, new ideas and progressive thinking had to be instilled in people's minds. Many intellectuals who were interested in political and social reforms concerned themselves with the social functions of new literature and theater. In 1904, Chen Duxiu (1879–1942), an important reformer of literature and drama who would later become one of the founders of the Chinese Communist Party, advanced a bold argument about the pedagogic and propagandistic values of this new theater in an influential article outlining the steps to reform Chinese theater.[1] He started by justifying his "lauding the importance of actors" by comparing the status of actors in China and in "the countries in the West":

> Theatre is a great school for all the people under heaven; theatre artists are in fact influential teachers. [In the past,] actors were considered no better than prostitutes, not permitted by the court to become government officials through civil exams. . . . In the West the situation is just the opposite: the actors are equals of the literary and the learned, because it is believed that theatre is extremely important in fostering morals and values.[2]

Chen connected this reform to a national salvation program, not to the entertainment value of the new techniques. Because "the manners and customs [of China] are uncivilized" and "[China] is in very real danger," Chen argued that it was not enough to popularize progressive ideas just through the newly established Western-style schools, novels in the vernacular language, and newspapers. He concluded by emphasizing the theater's social function: "Right now our country is facing serious crises. . . . Only the reformed theatre can change the whole society—the deaf can see it, and the blind can hear it."[3] Chen was not alone.

New theater, which was to be known under different names in its formative years, emerged as the clear choice for Chen and some of his contemporaries. Rival forms of cultural production competing with the new theater included the novel as popular vernacular literature, traditional stylized theater (a form of grassroots entertainment especially popular in rural areas), and the newspaper (a new medium at the time). The earliest productions in the form of new theater had all-male casts and were semi-improvised. They were also influenced by Japanese *shinpa* (new school) theater through Chinese artists who studied in Japan. In 1915, the Spring Willow Society (Chunliu she) staged *Spring Dream* (*Chun meng*), a play adapted by Lu Jingruo from Kawakami Otojirō's Japanese play *Othello* (1903).

Although the reformers participated in the discourse about theater's new social function, they showed great anxiety about finding an effective way to bring out that function. Among the features of Western theater, tragedy attracted the most attention, because Aristotelian and Shake-spearean tragedies were unknown to Chinese theater.[4] As early as 1904, Jiang Guanyun lamented the inadequacies of traditional Chinese drama and quoted Napoleon as saying, "Tragedy is good for rousing the spirit."[5] To his generation of dramatists, Western dramas provided not only in-spiration, new themes, and plots, but also new modes such as tragedy. Wang Guowei's influential *History of Song and Yuan Drama* (*Song Yuan xiqu kao,* 1912) is another prominent example of cultural criticism that revolves around various conceptions of tragedy; it has been described as "the first systematic Chinese-authored insertion of Chinese literature into the discourse of 'world literature.'"[6]

In the reformer's argument for importing tragedy, tragedy's social func-tion superseded its artistic implications. In an article published in 1918, Fu Sinian put forth a more radical argument that Western drama was the only legitimate form of theater. Fu's article anticipated the trend toward realism in the performances of Shakespeare and other *huaju* plays in the 1930s and 1940s. Fu set up Western drama as an antithesis to traditional Chinese theater. *Xiqu* theater (Chinese opera) was characterized by stylized movement, symbolic makeup and costumes, and flexible treatment of time and space. In contrast, the *"mofang* [mimesis; imitation]" in Western drama and theater used "acting" to imitate real gestures, movements, and events in daily life.[7] Fu's generalization is certainly problematic. Defenders of the values of traditional Chinese theater were understandably not involved in translating and staging foreign dramas. In contrast, the group of radical reformers was committed to the ideal of reforming the theater according to the model of Western realism. Since they privileged *huaju,* the Shakespeare performances naturally reflected that genre. The appeal of Anglo-European tragedies continued throughout the 1920s and 1930s, which explains the popularity of *Hamlet* and other Shakespearean tragedies in China.

It is worth noting that the term *huaju* was meant to be a translation of the concept of drama in European languages. It characterized Western-style theater as one emphasizing speech and dialogue—as opposed to mu-sical and gestural stylization in Chinese opera. Etymologically, *hua* means "speech," and *ju* means "drama." *Huaju* points to the obvious misconcep-tion of Western theater that resulted from a dichotomized perception of Asia and Europe. *Huaju* activists were unaware that Western-style theater did not always emphasize verbal elements over other elements, such as body movement and mise-en-scène. Translating drama as *huaju* (spoken drama), relative to traditional *xiqu* (stylized musical theater), also reveals early *huaju* promoters' preoccupation with creating an "intellectual" theater that aimed not only to entertain but also to educate through contending speeches and simulated public "debates" on stage. *Hua* (speech) was set up to challenge the *qu* ("song" or musical stylization) in *xiqu* theater. In the polemic view of the *huaju* advocates, spoken drama promoted intellectual reflection, while the traditional Chinese theater sought only to entertain and preach an outdated worldview.

After complete translations of Shakespeare's plays became available, two major approaches to Shakespearean performances emerged. The first attempted to preserve Shakespeare's foreignness by presenting the plays with spectacular scenery and costumes, following the Victorian tradition of staging Shakespeare and presumably legitimizing the performance by modeling itself on its English counterpart. Stemming from early localization projects, the second approach sought to smooth out the differences between the source and the target texts by reframing the plays in a local context. In these performances, the actions of Shakespeare's plays were unaltered, but characters, geocultural locations, and historical contexts were transplanted into their perceived Chinese counterparts. Both approaches were informed by May Fourth realism, a form of literary utilitarianism that emphasized literature's role in social transformation.[8]

Also prevalent in this period's performances was an appetite for exotic spectacles that approximated the "real" foreign country in the Chinese imaginary, which depended as much on the scenography as on the "authenticity" of the performance text. Under the influence of Japanese *shinpa* theater, *huaju* performances were considered so real by its early Chinese audience that they saw it "as real happenings, not theatre."[9]

The May Fourth vision of realism contained both a new aesthetic practice and a calculated cultural difference that undermined the stronghold of traditional Chinese social hierarchies. The imitation of Western reality in illusionist staging did not so much reflect a reality as create one, projecting a vision of life in a future China and its relationship with the changing world. The complimentary difference between Chinese illusionist staging and lived realities was used to create a new form of cultural identity.[10]

Macbeth in Wartime Shanghai

The Shanghai Amateur Experimental Theatre Company (an "amateur" designated noncommercial theater company) staged a production of

Romeo and Juliet based on Tian Han's translation in the Carlton Theatre in Shanghai in 1937, with an emphasis on visual effects and realism. Its goal was to smooth out cultural differences by making the play speak to and for the contemporary audience. The theater company selected a canonical English play for its first performance. The director, Zhang Min, employed an all-star cast, including film stars such as Zhao Dan (Romeo) and Yu Peishan (Juliet).[11] It is no coincidence that a theater company wishing to make a name for itself and attract younger audiences would choose a play dramatizing youthful exuberance. The potentially melodramatic love story forms a synergy with the star power of Zhao and Yu. However, the film actors, in this first attempt to employ realist acting techniques onstage, were not successful. Reviewers did not favor the acting style that was supposed to deliver psychological depth, since the actors appeared mechanical and void of emotion. Li Ming commented that the actors were unable to deliver Shakespeare's lines with persuasive force, and the dialogues were as dull as the recitation of "classical Chinese books." Li concluded that the director should have focused on defining and sharpening the "realistic" acting techniques rather than investing "arduous yet ineffective" effort in stage machinery and visual effects.[12]

Concentrating on visual effects and modern lighting facilities (projecting the rise and fall of the sun and the moon, for example), the production sought to delight the audience's senses. One gets the impression through its promotional leaflets and newspaper advertisements that the theater company was marketing new theatrical realism and an "authentic" foreign set. Tang Wen, a more sympathetic reviewer who saw the dress rehearsal, wrote that the production was "ten times truer than film," thanks to the magnificent stage set.[13] The actors were coached by a Russian fencing master. The fencing scenes were reported to be so true to life that actors were frequently injured.[14]

Along the same lines, advance advertisements featured production photos. A huge photo of the duel scene appeared in an ad in the *Shanghai Post*, accompanied by introductory texts that opted for the sensational: "On stage, there are a classical [*gudian*] Italian street and a romantic scene in the garden at night, . . . there is a gloomy crypt. [All this] comes with efficient lighting projecting the rise and fall of the sun, the moon, and the stars."[15] Among the many visual effects, the last scene in Juliet's tomb appeared to have been the most impressive. Tang Wen was struck by the scene's horror and pathos. Juliet's body was placed center stage on a high platform that was elevated to let the audience see Juliet. Moreover, the platform was connected to a flight of steps. The black velvet backdrop provided a sharp contrast with the light from the candles on the path entering the crypt.[16]

The high cost of elaborate sets and costumes posed a huge financial burden for theaters. Financial problems forced the Shanghai Drama Society into a three-year period of inactivity in the early 1930s. The Shanghai Drama Society was not alone, and Xiong Foxi articulated the need for "simplicity" (*danchun zhuyi*) in theater:

> We need to learn how to be economical in the theatre business. First, the play has to be shortened. Second, we should avoid frequent scene changes. Third, the number of characters should be minimized. . . . The reason that Shakespeare's plays are not suitable for our stage is not because the themes are outdated, but because these plays involve frequent scene changes and come with a long list of dramatis personae.[17]

Although the 1937 *Romeo and Juliet* was well received and lauded as visually stunning, it was also fiercely criticized by left-wing critics as a play of feudal hierarchies, unsuitable for the time. It was argued that *Romeo and Juliet* could not give the Chinese "enough nourishment."[18] But political commentary was far from the goal of Zhang Min's production. The cost of artistic innovation and the issue of political relevance continued to haunt performances of *Romeo and Juliet* and other plays in *huaju* and *jingju* styles during and after the second Sino-Japanese War in the subsequent decades. Chinese Shakespearean performances oscillated between the options for preserving the foreignness or highlighting contemporaneous social relevance. Toward the end of the 1930s—with the advent of the civil war between the Communists and the Nationalists, a full-scale Japanese invasion (launched on July 7, 1937), and World War II (1939–1945)—local calls for drama's relevance and theater's utilitarianism reemerged. Directors in the 1940s sought a different approach to staging Shakespeare, responding to both financial restrictions and new ideological needs.

One prominent example was Huang Zuolin's highly political 1945 production, *The Hero of a Tumultuous Time* (*Luanshi yingxiong*), based on Li Jianwu's (1906–1982) six-act tragedy, *Wang Deming* (1944), a play based on *Macbeth*. Huang's production was staged in Shanghai in April 1945, four months before the Japanese surrendered.[19] The focus shifted from outward spectacle on stage to the allegorical capacity of drama. Written a few years before the establishment of the People's Republic of China in 1949, Li's *Wang Deming* opted for social relevance. The new title *Hero of a Tumultuous Time* for the production connected *Macbeth* to the Chinese civil war. As the first performance of the newly founded Bitter Toilers Drama School in Shanghai's Lafei Grand Theatre, the production starred Shi Hui (as Wang Deming, the Chinese counterpart of Macbeth) and Dan Ni (as Dugu Xiu, the Chinese counterpart of Lady Macbeth).

The production was considered a somber reminder of the chaotic world the audience lived in. The audience, which had "experienced the tumult and war," could not help "following [Macbeth]" and fighting the enemies from without and within.[20] Interestingly, the audience willingly overlooked the darker side of Macbeth's character. Li Quan, an audience member, wrote in *Shanghai News:*

> The entire performance was so powerful that it could shake mountains. It enthralled us [the audience] from the beginning to the end. An aggressive and ambitious man assassinated the king . . . and destroyed himself. [Macbeth] was fighting [and defending himself from] enemies; he also battled with his own conscience. . . . We were out of breath throughout the performance.[21]

Of interest is the playwright's motive for writing *Wang Deming*. When the Japanese army took over Shanghai on November 12, 1937, all theaters and foreign-published newspapers were shut down. Li Jianwu and his fellow dramatists were unemployed and faced the difficult choice between "serving the enemy" to earn their personal livelihood and fulfilling their patriotic duty. After a few difficult years, Li refused the famous writer Zhou Zuoren's offer of an administrative position at the Japanese-controlled Peking University. Li also refused to work for any theater in Shanghai. However, he joined the Rongwei Theatre Company in 1942. Poshek Fu suspects that Li changed his mind because he was persuaded that the theater's profit-making orientation made it "the only cultural artifact independent of Japanese ideological control."[22] Although Li reiterated that he "joined the theatre [only] to earn a living," he was faced with the moral and practical question of how to turn theater into a force of resistance.[23] He started writing plays. In his Shakespeare-inspired plays such as *Ashina* (*Othello*, 1947) and *Wang Deming*, Li turned the imagined past into a metaphor for the present. To eradicate visible traces of the all-too-obvious political implications, Li transposed the original plays into a remote, unspecified point in ancient Chinese history.

In the character of Wang Deming, Macbeth acquires a frame of reference specific to the China of the 1940s. The play transposes *Macbeth* to the Five Dynasties period (907–960), when anarchy reigned and usurpations were frequent. The lead character's name, Wang Deming, sounds more natural than a mere transliteration of "Macbeth." Although *Wang Deming* is framed in a Chinese setting, there are close parallels with Shakespeare's text in several scenes that Li deemed crucial. For example, in act 3 of *Wang Deming* (which corresponds to act 2, scene 1, in *Macbeth*), before Wang enters to kill the king, he stares into the air and begins a soliloquy:

> WANG DEMING: . . . Is this a treasured sword [*baojian*] which I
> see before me? The handle toward my hand, inviting me to it?
> Come, let me clutch thee. I have thee not, yet I see thee still.[24]

However, beginning with the lines starting with "witchcraft celebrates Pale Hecate's offerings" in *Macbeth* (2.1.51–52), the play slides into substitutions and glosses:

> WANG DEMING: This pitch-black night is the ghosts' realm, and
> everyone is asleep. The universe is dizzy [quiet] as death. Only
> the hungry wolves, with sharp noses, pick up the smell of the
> dead from afar. [They] proceed like ox-headed and horse-faced
> demons from the Shadowy World [*yincao;* hell], with stealthy
> pace to the Sunlit World [*yangshi;* human world] to conduct a
> horrible business.[25]

The substitutions are particularly evident when compared with the original:

> MACBETH: . . . Now o'er the one half-world
> Nature seems dead, and wicked dreams abuse
> The curtain'd sleep; witchcraft celebrates
> Pale Hecat's off'rings; and wither'd Murther,
> Alarum'd by his sentinel, the wolf,
> Whose howl's his watch, thus with his stealthy pace,
> With Tarquin's ravishing [strides], toward his design
> Moves like a ghost. (2.1.49–56)

A crucial difference between Li and established translators such as Tian Han and Cao Yu is that Li considered himself to be writing a play inspired by *Macbeth* and not merely translating the play. From the passages quoted here, however, it is also clear that despite Li's intention to write a new play, he followed the original quite closely in some key scenes.

Interpersonal relationships and several layers of complexity in Macbeth himself have undergone considerable alterations in *Wang Deming*. The title character, originally named Zhang Wenli, is actually renamed after he is made the marquis of Changshan by Wang Rong (Duncan), his adopted father, whom he would eventually murder and usurp. This added layer of loyalty and filial duty in the relationship between an adopted father and son brings Macbeth's conflicted emotions to a different level. A sharpened focus on familial ties and duties overrides the Shakespearean questions about prophecy and destiny. The play also foregrounds Lady Macbeth's stubbornness and ambition. It is Dugu Xiu (Lady Macbeth) who first seeks prophecies from Jiutian Xuannü (Virgin Mother of the Ninth Heaven, a composite figure for the three witches) through a fortune-teller—a holy scribe at the ancestral temple of the Wang family. The dialogue exchanges between Lady Macbeth and the scribe, who receives prophecies from the goddess (and writes them on a plate of sand), are punctuated by pressing questions from Lady Macbeth. Such scenes not only point to Lady Macbeth as a dominating figure in the play, but also reflect traditional gender roles. Li gives Lady Macbeth more agency.

The mise-en-scène of *The Hero of a Tumultuous Time* provided a sharp contrast with the elaborate spectacle of the 1937 *Romeo and Juliet*. Throughout the play, the set itself did not change. Only the movement of props signaled a change of scene. There were only four spotlights, which used up the theater's electricity quota and left the company with only gasoline lamps. When Wang Deming reappeared on the stage after murdering the emperor, other actors (who were not due to appear) helped create sound effects from backstage as a chorus. The minimalist approach was adopted partly because of the financial restrictions and partly because of Huang's aesthetic preference. He championed simplicity as the key element in stage and costume design. Yet this preference did not turn the audience away. Obviously very popular among the Shanghai residents, the play was serialized in a literary journal the next year when the war ended.[26]

After *Wang Deming*, Li experimented with *Othello* in his *Ashina*. Although often characterized by directors as a superb mediator between Western drama and *huaju* theater, Li resisted that representation.[27] He claimed that his reinventions of Shakespeare are "one hundred percent Chinese" in terms of their language and structure.[28] He never thought of himself as adapting foreign plays, but as undergoing a creative process as painful and strenuous as "raising a child."[29] Li took pride in his transformation of "exotic moods into native Chinese contexts," while letting the "spirit" (*jingshen*) echo the original by Shakespeare.[30] As interesting as Li's approach is in theatrical terms, such discourses failed to acknowledge the fact that works such as *Wang Deming* always occupy a multitude of localities. What mattered was not just what is shown but also where it is presented.

Screening the New Woman

Chinese filmmakers shared some of the theater artists' concerns about politics and aesthetics. Shakespeare on film started in the late nineteenth century beginning with a silent film, Sir Herbert Beerbohm Tree's *King John* (1899). The film is a record of Tree's performance on stage. The short film, as its title suggests, was intended to promote Tree's production, which opened on September 20, 1899, in Her Majesty's Theatre in London.[31] The film's publicity pamphlets read "A scene—'King John, now playing at Her Majesty's Theatre,'" and "Beerbohm Tree, the great English actor, with leading members of his company in the death scene of 'King John.'"[32] Many other early silent films tended to replicate stage productions, and until recently most scholars did not treat them as standalone cinematic adaptations of Shakespeare, but as a means to preserve specific theater performances. In *Shakespeare on Silent Film*, the earliest and only book-length study of the subject, Robert Ball writes, "Though a record of a stage production can be valuable for an historian, early silent film Shakespeare cannot . . . be called properly cinematic."[33] Jack Jorgens is even more blunt: "[M]ercifully, most of them are lost, for those which survive are for the most part inadequate performances of Shakespeare and pale examples of film art."[34]

The beginnings of Shakespeare in Chinese cinema are a very different story, although that story also begins with silent film. Chinese silent-film adaptations of Shakespeare are significantly longer and serve a very different function without significant influence from the Anglo-European filmmaking tradition. Unlike their Western counterparts, Chinese silent-film Shakespeare productions do not attempt to replicate or promote specific stage productions, although the first silent film in 1905 was a video record of Tan Xinpei's *xiqu* stage performance of *Conquering Jun Mountain (Ding Junshan)*. The film, produced by Fengtai Photo Shop, initiated a genre known as theater-film (*xiren dianying*). Shakespeare on *huaju* and *xiqu* stages fostered the demand for theatricality among local audiences, who were drawn to the theater for the site-specific experience. In contrast, Shakespeare in Chinese silent film—with Chinese–English intertitles—was part of the studios' self-conscious attempt to market cinematic actuality to increasingly global communities located within and beyond China, including Shanghai's Chinese cosmopolitan urbanites, European expatriates, Hong Kong audiences, and Chinese immigrants in Southeast Asia and other parts of the world.

In the midst of a flurry of *huaju* performances of Shakespeare, several provocative silent-film adaptations of Western literary works demonstrated Chinese cinema's symbiotic yet tense relationship with *huaju* theater, *xiqu* theater, and literature in translation. The necessary absence of the aural dimension (*xiqu*'s music or *huaju*'s "spoken drama") and the abundant opportunities for visual experimentation shaped the production and reception of Chinese silent film. Although modest in number compared with films adapted from Chinese sources, the twenty silent-film adaptations of Western literary works between 1910 and the 1930s constituted constant patterns. These films include the Asia Company's *New Camellias (Xin chahua*, 1913), based on Lin Shu's translation of *La Dame aux camélias;* Zheng Zhengqiu's *Rediscovered Conscience (Liangxin de fuhuo*, 1926), adapted from Tolstoy's novel *Resurrection; Flying Boots (Feixingxue*, 1928), adapted from a German folktale; and *Detective Sherlock Holmes (Fu'ermosi zhentan an*, 1931).[35] Although most of these films no longer exist, the ones that do fall under the radar of many scholarly works on Chinese cinema because they defy categorization.[36] Similar to *huaju* Shakespeare, these films have a common ethical concern. Some adaptations added a moralist concept of redemption and retribution. Zheng Zhengqiu, frequently referred to as the father of Chinese cinema, added "conscience" (*liangxin*) to the title of his film adaptation of Tolstoy's novel.[37] Another overarching theme is how women characters (and actresses offscreen) deal with the tension between their different roles and their changing status in the social and familial structure.

While the aforementioned stage productions and social discourse about theater reform concentrated on the nation as a critical category, the nascent Chinese film industry engaged the concept of the modern girl and the new woman's movement. The cultural figure of the new woman is an integral part of the contested modern nation project, embodying an urban subjectivity in its new social image and performance on screen. Both male and female writers of this period (Ding Ling, Hu Shi, Mao Dun, and others) probe the shifting ideals of womanhood in their works, and "contending groups of Chinese intellectuals [also] used the 'woman question' as a keyhole through which to address issues of modernity and the nation."[38] The figure of the new woman evoked two contradictory images, both bearing traces of the changing gender hierarchy and the anxieties of Western influence: a modern woman with her own subjectivity and access to education and the legal profession formerly reserved for the male elite; and a femme fatale working against male cosmopolitan urbanites. Although the May Fourth writers, directors, and filmmakers tended to promote the connection between the new woman and Chinese modernity as uncontested, contemporary scholarship finds the connection paradoxical. In Rey Chow's words, "While it is by crushing . . . or neutralizing the many figures of femininity that are inextricable parts of an older order that the more heroic forms of Chinese modernity asserts themselves, Chinese modernism also consists in the conscientious inventions . . . of 'new' areas of interest, such as, precisely, women."[39]

Nowhere is this intense interest (often accompanied by voyeuristic impulses) in modern women as liberated individuals, characters, and movie stars more evident than in early Chinese cinema. In a telling statement about appropriate subjects for Chinese film in 1925, Zheng Zhengqiu emphasized the necessity of including women and love: "A film will not be well received by the spectators if it does not include women [in the story]. Therefore, nine out of ten Chinese films focus on love stories, especially foreign [European] ones."[40] The performance of European love stories rehearses new relations between men and women in Shanghai's urban culture. As much as the figure of the new woman is deployed to attack conservative traditionalism, it is also a channel through which the spectators' voyeuristic curiosity about the life of educated, professional women is satisfied.

The 1930s were also a time when women enthusiastically participated in the cosmopolitan performance culture, in school and beyond. Performance of Shakespeare's plays became a tradition at many Westernized schools and colleges. The history of missionary-founded colleges such as St. John's may suggest that only male students participated in *huaju* performances of Shakespeare, but women played an important role in shaping Chinese interpretations of Shakespeare and urban cosmopolitanism. Yuan Changying (1894–1973), who earned an M.A. in English literature at the University of Edinburgh in 1921, was probably the first Chinese woman to teach Shakespeare in China. She was a major advocate of Shakespeare in the college curriculum and of the value of student performance.[41] Of special interest here is the McTyeire School for Girls (Zhongxi nüshu, which literally means "Sino-Western Women's Academy") in Shanghai, founded by the Southern Methodist Mission. According to Yu Zhiping's memoir about her time there as a student in the 1930s, students performed in regular *huaju* productions, and Shakespeare was a mainstay of their repertoire.[42] Plays performed included *Twelfth Night* and *The Taming of the Shrew*. Like other girls' schools that flourished in this period (for example, St. Mary's Hall, founded by the American Episcopal Church Mission), the school provided an aristocratic education. As best-selling author Chen Danyan said, "Having a daughter who graduated from the McTyeire School was like having the finest dowry."[43]

Recent scholarship has focused on the concept of translated modernity. As Lydia Liu points out, the massive translation of foreign materials and borrowing and localization of foreign words and concepts have created new meanings rather than simply transplanting them.[44] The influence of Chinese translational practice is evident in the idea of modern womanhood, a product of China's translated modernity. Hu Ying believes that the new woman is a composite figure situated in a space between different cultural sources, neither original nor coherent.[45] Zhen Zhang regards the new woman in literature and film as a "translated cosmopolitan product, bearing resemblance to La Dame aux camélias, Sophia Perovskaia, and Madame Roland de la Platère, . . . yet tak[ing] on features and behaviors of her would-be literary ancestors and sisters in the Chinese literary tradition." It has therefore become not only plausible but also desirable for the new woman to have multiple identities: a filial daughter, a revolutionary, a modern military officer, a lover writing classical Chinese poems.[46] In many ways, the new woman in the film and drama of the 1930s represents the fear, promise, and perils of Chinese modernization and nation-building.

It comes as no surprise, then, that the earliest documented Chinese silent-film adaptation of Shakespeare, a film based on *The Merchant of*

Venice, should concentrate on Portia and the trial scene, dramatically emphasizing female agency throughout the story. Directed by Qiu Yixiang and premiering on May 29, 1927, in Shanghai, the film had a provocative and attractive title, *The Woman Lawyer.*[47] Portia is played by Hu Die, one of the most popular actresses of the time. The film reflects its contemporary society's anxiety and curiosity about the presence of women in the legal profession, which was itself just being established in Chinese urban centers. Using Chinese transliteration, the film keeps intact the setting and characters' names, such as Xue Luke (Shylock), Bao Qixia (Portia), and An Dongyi (Antonio). Extant historical documents show that the film is a full-length adaptation, and it concentrates on Portia's image as a new woman with a sharp mind and considerable wealth, rather than a woman impersonating a man (the court scene) or a prize in a ridiculous lottery (the caskets scene). As a woman exercising authority, she flaunts her male attire as she comes to Antonio's rescue in the court.[48] Bao Qixia volunteers her dowry (*zhuanglian*) to repay An Dongyi's debt in the court, but Xue Luke refuses it. Curiously, all references to Christianity and Shylock's Jewishness are excised, even though Shylock is explicitly referred to as a "Jewish merchant" in the most popular translation circulating in Chinese at the time, Lin Shu's *A Bond of Flesh.* The rest of the film script stays fairly close to Shakespeare's text but presents the play as an exposition of the concept of contract and legality.

While anti-Semitism is not the subject of this chapter, this film's emphasis on Portia and the bond must give us pause. *The Woman Lawyer* plays down the problematic status and fate of Shylock in order to assert a gender-conscious narrative that emphasizes social mobility and the role of the new woman. It is not insignificant that *The Merchant of Venice* is the first Shakespearean play to be staged in mainland China and Hong Kong, remaining popular since the late nineteenth century. Yet what is singular is the way in which the Chinese overlook the racial and religious tensions in the play despite changing historical circumstances. Rewrites and performances of the play continued to eschew racial and religious issues even after the Holocaust and after European Jews fled to Shanghai en masse. Much critical energy has been devoted to the legal debate and female agency in the play. In the 1930s, as in the new millennium, it is not uncommon for Chinese artists and critics to use the play as a pedagogic example about personal finance, highlighting the bond of flesh and the merchant. This is reflected in the most common Chinese translations of the play's title: *A Bond of Flesh* or *A Pound of Flesh.* The graphic and cautionary title remained in wide circulation until the 1980s. In 1999, Chinese premier Zhu Rongji quoted *The Merchant of Venice* to emphasize the value of market law for China. In Perng Ching-hsi's extended introduction to his 2006 translation of *The Merchant of Venice*, he focuses squarely on the questions of justice and Portia's character in the trial scene, sidestepping the religious discourse in the scene.[49] There is a similar tendency to overlook Othello's race.

Even in the new millennium, when Anglo-European interpretations of *The Merchant of Venice* are even more dominated by a post–September 11 awareness of racial and religious tensions, the Chinese reception of the play remains focused on the economy of exchange.[50] In a letter describing his impression of the Royal Shakespeare Company's (RSC) touring production of *The Merchant of Venice* in Beijing in 2002, an audience member from Anhui (a thousand miles away), Tian Chaoxu, wrote enthusiastically about the play's relevance to modern-day China: "China is developing so fast that 90 percent of the population want to make money. . . . *The Merchant of Venice* is a play that shows what happens to a society which places too great an emphasis on money. People should take notice of what Shakespeare has to say."[51] Shanghai Oriental Television's documentary about the RSC's visit to China aired the same year and followed the same direction in interpreting the play and the production. Indeed, the play can be read as a study of mercantile culture, but it is only one of its many themes. The production, directed by Loveday Ingram and starring Ian Bartholomew as Shylock, highlighted Shylock's struggles and conflicting religious values.[52] As Bartholomew stated in an interview, "This is a play that is really about what prejudice is [and] the terror of things that are different. . . . In the end I would like Shylock to be neither condoned nor condemned, but to be understood."[53] One must wonder what Tian and his fellow audience members saw in Shylock.[54] It is certainly possible, and sometimes even desirable, to differ in perspectives (the major theme of a literary work commonly shifts from culture to culture and from period to period), but it is striking that the same negligence of racial and religious differences has persisted throughout the history of Chinese Shakespeares. The selective attentiveness to positive and negative stereotypes about Portia is fashioned by local histories, but it also actively molds social trends. Thus adapted, *The Merchant of Venice*, as screened in China, becomes a pedagogic demonstration of the rise of new woman and the complex textures of modern life's legal and financial aspects.[55] Historical ruptures aside, the director and the audience's interest in the image of woman lawyer also contributed to the shift of thematic focus.

In addition to the star power of Hu Die, the lead actress, another important social factor contributed to the Chinese fascination with Portia. It is worth noting that Chinese and Western women lawyers held a special place in the public imagination in Shanghai. When Flora Rosenberg, a French lawyer, began practicing law in the foreign concessions in Shanghai in 1927, she received the kind of media attention accorded a celebrity. *Shen bao* and the *North-China Herald*, the most influential Chinese- and English-language newspapers in Shanghai, ran feature articles about Rosenberg.[56] The novelty of women lawyers drew the public's attention to women and legal education. In *Crystal (Jing bao)*, one of Shanghai's many tabloids (*xiaobao*) focused on entertainment news, Dan Weng published an article encouraging Chinese women to study law in the footsteps of their role model, Rosenberg.[57] In 1927, the Chinese government accorded women the right to practice law, and by 1936, the Shanghai Bar Association had some fifty women members.[58] A 1932 newspaper story about Zhou Wenji, a woman lawyer, reflects a fixation on the image of Portia in the film: "There was a woman lawyer named Zhou Wenji. A few days ago, she appeared in a court of law, speaking fluent and elegant Mandarin. She is well-organized, soft-spoken yet firm, relaxed and confident. Her sharp mind deeply impressed other lawyers in the court."[59] The popularity of *The Merchant in Venice* in Shanghai (in Lin Shu's text, on stage, and on screen) was clearly not an accident, but coincidental with the public interest in women professionals, especially actresses and female lawyers.[60] Another newspaper story implicitly compares another woman lawyer in Shanghai to the righteousness of Portia: "Tu Kunfan is in love with justice and righteousness. She often does not take fees from her clients. If she lost a case, she would refuse food and cry."[61] The anecdote highlights Tu's feminine quality and genuine concern for her clients, and draws attention to what distinguishes Tu from her male peers. A female lawyer's appearance was seen as an expression, if not guarantee, of her quality of mercy in a court of law where legality reigns supreme.

In fact, the fascination with Portia and women lawyers in both the film industry and the media can be traced back to Lin Shu's rendition of Charles and Mary Lamb's *Tales from Shakespeare*. Lin did not follow the original order of the plays, and *The Merchant of Venice* became the first story in his version. Lin refers to Portia (Bao Tixia) as "the most beautiful woman of the nation [*guo se*]" and as a woman whose beauty "is admired throughout her country [*ju guo yan qi se*]."[62] Lin devotes over half of his text to the trial scene, in which he adds a line not found in the Lambs' text, shifting the emphasis from Portia in male disguise to her femininity: "All at the court remained surprised and impressed by the beauty of the [woman] lawyer."[63]

Silent Knights: *The Two Gentlemen of Verona* on Screen

Shanghai was not the only center of cosmopolitan imagination. Another notable cinematic rewriting of Shakespeare from the silent-film era is *A Spray of Plum Blossom* (*Yi jian mei*, 1931), directed by Bu Wancang. Also known as *The Amorous Bandit*, the 110-minute silent film turned Shakespeare's *The Two Gentlemen of Verona* into a chivalric romance about two self-determined modern women traveling from Shanghai to Canton (Guangzhou). Canton, China's gateway to Hong Kong and Southeast Asia, stands in for Milan, where the men go to complete their education in male friendship and become knightly gentlemen. The "amorous bandit" refers to Hu Lunting (Valentine), an exile who leads a group of Robin Hood–style bandits who identify themselves as "A Spray of Plum Blossom." They vow to "help the weak and suppress the villains [in power]," as the plum-blossom-marked notes they leave at crime scenes reveal. Another source for the film's title is a classical Chinese poem composed by Hu Lunting (played by Jin Yan) and Shi Luohua (played by Lin Chuchu) on a rock in Shi's garden, which is filled with plum blossoms. The setting, the characters' names, and the codes governing social behaviors have been thoroughly localized.

The film boasts a stellar cast, including Ruan Lingyu (1910–1935), one of the most revered actresses of the 1930s. Her acclaimed roles and films include a patriot in *Three Modern Women* (*San ge modeng nüxing*, 1933), also directed by Bu Wancang, and a woman writer in *New Woman* (*Xin nüxing*, 1934), directed by Cai Chusheng. Before committing suicide at the age of twenty-four, she appeared in twenty-nine films. In the culture of stardom, Ruan's private life attracted as much media attention as her films. Her unhappy marriage, pending divorce, and affair with another man attracted vindictive coverage. Her extramarital romantic interest and defiance of normative social roles assigned to women in real life seems to parallel her role in *A Spray of Plum Blossom*.

Although the film was marketed as both a "domestic film" (*guopian*) and a "Great Picture of Knightly Love" (*Xiayi aiqing jupian*) one of its advertisements clearly demonstrates the paradoxical nature of China's cosmopolitan performance culture.[64] The two couplets that frame the ad read:

Resist Foreign Cultural and Economic Invasions;
Propagate the Essential Virtues of Our Nation.

Down with Films That Are Nonartistic and Harmful to Society;
Regain the International Status of Domestic Films.[65]

The couplets and essentialist discourse become self-contradictory when one considers the film's genre, style, and theme. Interestingly, the Lianhua Studio initially marketed the film as one of the "ten great [Chinese] works" with an "original screenplay by Huang Yicuo," rather than Shakespeare, although the film itself opens with a quotation in English from *As You Like It* (with modernized spelling) and attributes it to Shakespeare:[66]

All the world is a stage.
And men and women merely players.[67]

The film's title marks its distance from the Shakespearean point of origin, while the film's opening sequence lays claims to Shakespeare but references a completely different Shakespearean play. As such, the film seems to acknowledge local moviegoers' desire for Western novelty, and yet at the same time teasingly denies the validity of any sense of authenticity. *A Spray of Plum Blossom* opens up a new vista where citation and appropriation—rather than translation—creates and asserts the authority of a new "original" in the transnational circuit of literary texts.

The opening sequence is followed by a statement in English that establishes the film's mood: "Life's adventure commences as college session terminates." Hu Lunting (Valentine) and Bai Lede (Proteus) are recent graduates of a military academy ready to take on the world, although Bai Lede "knows more about girls than soldiers." The cast list, first appearing in traditional Chinese characters, then in English, also provides the original names of Shakespearean characters, making it clear that the localized Chinese names are partly based on Chinese transliteration of the foreign names (for example, Julia as Zhuli). The cast members' names are also listed in English, as they were known outside the Chinese-speaking community: Lily Yuen (Ruan Lingyu), Lim Chocho (Lin Chuchu), Raymond King (Jin Yan), and so forth. The Lianhu Studio had clearly hoped for a large market that extended beyond China.

Like *The Woman Lawyer,* the film displaced the themes of fidelity and betrayal in *The Two Gentlemen of Verona* into a female-centered frame of narration that was perceived by the filmmaker and the studio as more modern. Familial ties further complicate the gendered representation of Shakespeare's characters. Hu Lunting (Valentine) is the brother of Hu Zhuli (Julia), and Shi Luohua (Silvia) is the daughter of Governor Shi of Canton (the Duke of Milan in *The Two Gentlemen of Verona*) and the cousin of Bai Lede (Proteus). The Duke of Milan, who is unrelated to Proteus in Shakespeare, is now his uncle. The familial connections shift the audience's attention to domestic matters. The film thus turns Shakespeare's picaresque adventure into a bildungsroman about two modern women.

While the film retains Shakespeare's two pairs of troubled lovers, the emphasis has been shifted to the roles of Hu Zhuli (played by Ruan Lingyu) and Shi Luohua. Ruan Lingyu departs from her previous melodramatic roles (for example, a modern woman who is unable to resist her tragic fate) to play a witty and self-determined woman. In an early scene in which she sings and plays the song "I am Willing" on piano, the English intertitles introduce her as "Julia, sister of Valentine, a model of the modern maidens," and the Chinese intertitle describes her as "a modern woman ahead of her times." Throughout the film, she and Shi Luohua form a strong bond in sisterhood in masculine disguise or posture. The two "modern" women are often dressed in military costumes. Shakespeare's feisty Silvia becomes Shi Luohua, "a maiden with a spirit of masculinity" who often walks around with a horsewhip in hand and, in a prolonged scene, rides horses with her male peers. She also commands her male and female subordinates. After Hu Lunting is banished, Shi Luohua takes his position, showcasing "the way of a perfume general."[68] The scene highlights the theatricality of a woman playing the role of a general, which exists in fiction but not yet in real life. When Hu Zhuli arrives in Canton in search of Bai Lede, her fiancé, Shi Luohua has her dress as a man and serve as her protégé. In Shakespeare's play, Silvia disguises herself to serve as Proteus's page. In the film, played by Ruan, Hu Zhuli appears in masculine military uniform. To make her transformation in Canton more dramatic, the film shows Hu Zhuli arriving in Canton in extremely feminine clothes and in tears, alone.

Coupled with Ruan Lingyu's star power and the force of the market economy, the rhetoric of female agency helped to turn Shakespeare's *The Two Gentlemen of Verona*, "a shallow story of deep love" (1.1.21), into a bildungsroman for two "gentlewomen" of Shanghai and Canton. The film and its appropriation of the figure of the new woman was quite popular and well received. A reader of the *Film Magazine* wrote enthusiastically from Nanjing:

> I finally got a chance to see the long-awaited *A Spray of Plum Blossom*. . . . I want to inform you of the Chinese people's enthusiasm for Lianhua's productions. It was raining so hard that day. We arrived at the theatre two hours in advance but there were already many waiting for tickets. . . . From the beginning to the end, I watched contentedly with my mouth open.[69]

The image of these two women, accentuated by such epithets as "perfume general," fed into the dominant subgenre of the new martial-arts film commonly known as martial heroine (*nüxia*) film, which expanded both the domestic and foreign markets for Chinese cinema. Zhen Zhang's study discusses several salient features in the narrative pattern of these films. The protagonist, usually a "maiden turned knight-errant," rescues another maiden in distress and "initiates the other maiden into the world of martial arts and knightly grace." The heroine often becomes the arbiter of a community. The theatrics of female agency mean that other characters are relegated to the background. The men they "love to hate," in this case Bai Lede (Proteus) and Diao Li'ao (Thurio),[70] "serve as mere foils to the two 'gentlewomen.'"[71] Of special interest is a scene in *A Spray of Plum Blossom* where Shi Luohua takes over Hu Lunting's position as the chief of the military police squad (figures 7 and 8). As she takes command, she walks in military uniform, saber hanging from her waist, to the front of the squad in a courtyard as her squad salutes her. But she dons a striped skirt and wears her hair long instead of tucking it into the officer's cap. The androgynous quality underscores at once her femininity and her transformation. She appears in the same costume at the end of the film.

FIGURE 7   Lin Chuchu as Shi Luohua (Silvia) takes over Hu Lunting's (Valentine) position
as the chief of the military police squad in *A Spray of Plum Blossom*, directed by Bu Wancang,
Shanghai, 1931.

The film adds a twist to the popular female-knight genre by interrogating the gendered imagination of the figure of new woman as necessarily masculine in appearance and outlook. Hu Zhuli and Shi Luohua's androgynous quality also reflects the widespread anxiety about the hybrid identity of the new woman, which is located between tradition and modernity, and between variously defined gender roles.

Interestingly, the central position of the two women in the film anticipates the general sentiments of late-twentieth-century Shakespeare criticism. As one of the least-appreciated and performed Shakespearean plays, *The Two Gentlemen of Verona* has historically been either ignored or slighted. However, criticism of the recent past has commended Shakespeare's "tendency to hand over most of the initiative and just judgment to the women" in the play,[72] as well as Silvia and Julia's remarkable "constancy, devotion, and empathy."[73] Although at the end of the play Julia and Silvia are subjected to female identities defined by heterosexuality and marriage, their Chinese incarnations as martial heroines do not go through the same process. The play ends with a disturbing silence from Julia and Silvia, as the duke and Valentine sort out the entangled relationships and arrange the marriages (5.4.121–73). In the film, after Hu Lunting is reinstated to his previous position and the two couples (Hu Lunting and Shi Luohua, and Bai Lede and Hu Zhuli) are married, the four, now

FIGURE 8   The squad salutes Shi Luohua, who dons a striped skirt with a saber hanging from her waist, in *A Spray of Plum Blossom*.

with additional ties through marriage and service in the same squad as officers, are shown riding on horses to inspect the troops (figure 9).[74]

Coda

Chinese versions of Shakespeare are variously articulated in a presentation of lavish Westernized spectacles (Zhang Min's *Romeo and Juliet*), an exploration of local voices (Huang Zuolin's *The Hero of a Tumultuous Time*), and new gender identities (Qiu Yixiang's *The Woman Lawyer* and Bu Wancang's *A Spray of Plum Blossom*). These works oscillate between performative modes that engage the meanings typical in the local culture and the effects of a foreign cultural text.

The association between foreign scripts and local stagings was a reciprocal process of revision. China's new theater and cinema expanded the realm of signification of Shakespearean drama; Shakespeare and the new woman were deployed as universal figures of Chinese modernity. As rewrites ventured out between the two poles of localization and

FIGURE 9   Ruan Lingyu as Hu Zhuli (Julia) and Lin Chuchu as Shi Luohua (Silvia) in military uniform and skirt examine the military police squad in the final scene of *A Spray of Plum Blossom*.

exoticization in an attempt to be cosmopolitan, competing narratives about modernity in Chinese Shakespeares on stage and on screen simultaneously disrupted and reaffirmed the vernacular politics of new performance idioms (silent film, naturalist theater, spectatorial exoticism). The notions of modernity being explored ranged from political modernity (that is, where political exigencies reigned) to social modernity, as in the case of the new woman.

As China entered a new political era after the founding of the People's Republic of China in 1949, performances of Shakespeare were alternately repressed and encouraged, again for varying aesthetic rationales and political agendas. However, the two Chinese approaches to Shakespeare identified in this chapter—preserving the foreignness and smoothing out the differences—persisted in different forms in many later performances that presented new content and implications associated with "foreignness."

5   Site-Specific Readings:

Confucian Temple, Labor Camp,
and Soviet–Chinese Theater

Some of the most fruitful interactions between the "airy nothing" of a literary motif and its "local habitation"—a physical and felt presence in a local community—can be found in the radical adaptation of
Shakespeare to the local exigencies.[1] The power of political theater stands
out against Hamlet's casual comment that the poison in/of theatrical representation is but "false fire" (3.2.266), not to be feared. When theater-
making is caught up in ideological wars in a time of political crisis, it
becomes a matter of life and death. Although this phenomenon is not
exclusive to mid-twentieth-century China or to the history of Shakespearean performance, the questions of locality and site-specific interpretations
call for a reassessment of the relationship between politics and art. How
should the politicization of aesthetics be historicized in relation to an
academic culture that distrusts the notion of *l'art pour l'art* but insists on
reading literature politically?

At stake is not the validity of authenticity claims (as in the retrieval of
authorial intentions or reproduction of the "truth" about Shakespearean
plays) but the dynamics between the locality where various conventions of
authenticity is derived and the locality where the performance or reading
takes place. The unexpected twists and turns of history can give significant

meanings to these localities, including the site of the performance, the setting of the plays, and the audience's cultural locations. How do theater artists adapt the Shakespearean localities to enhance the perceived value of the performance and its venue? What do these aesthetic maneuvers tell us about Shakespearean appropriation? This chapter investigates three mid-twentieth-century site-specific readings: Jiao Juyin's production of *Hamlet* (1942) in a Confucian temple in wartime China before the Chinese Communist Party (CCP) gained power; Wu Ningkun's reading of *Hamlet* in a labor camp during the Cultural Revolution; and the politics of memory and "apolitical" interpretation in a Soviet–Chinese production of *Much Ado About Nothing* before and after the Cultural Revolution (it premiered in 1957 and was revived in 1961 and again as a "carbon copy" in 1979). These cases suggest that even though the Soviet interpretations of Shakespeare were influential in many socialist countries, Shakespeare's lengthy affiliation with Marxist ideology is much more unpredictable.[2] Figuring prominently in the Chinese cases are collective cultural memory, decidedly local readings of Shakespeare, and the particularities of the site of performance. While Shakespeare was turned into a site for political comment in the 1940s, Shakespeare performances from the 1950s to the 1970s did exactly the opposite and made every effort to produce ostensibly depoliticized interpretations.

Site-Specific Roles of Shakespeare

In the context of live theater, site-specific as a category might seem redundant. After all, local specificities are part of many live performances. Many theater scholars have maintained that live actors and audiences are always "site-specific."[3] The dynamics of a production differ from one evening to another, even with the same cast at the same venue. As opposed to cinema, theater has frequently been regarded as the site for unique economic events that are indigenous, place-bound, and highly dependent on the "repetitive labor of actors and technicians."[4] In addition to the economically determined site-specificity of theater, the intricate interactions between actors and audiences are transient and cannot be replicated. Site-specificity has thus been considered a staple of liveness.[5]

While these features of theater are true most of the time and have gone uncontested, a new internationalism has for years begun to make theater resemble mass-produced film and television. Since the mid-twentieth century, more and more productions have been locally conceived but globally marketed—they tour widely and are far from site-specific. In fact, much of their viability hinges on their transportability and global accessibility. The Royal Shakespeare Company's touring performances are some of the most prominent examples. Some Asian productions of Shakespeare are also designed with a wide range of nonhometown audiences in mind, including Ninagawa Yukio's and Suzuki Tadashi's transnational performances, although the directors themselves and their critics hold different views on this.

In contrast to productions that tour to multiple locations, the productions of *Hamlet* and *Much Ado About Nothing* under discussion here are defined by their local specificities, specificities that will be lost on a different audience in a different performance venue or context. When Shakespearean localities collide or merge with the localities of the performance, new stories are created to meet the challenge or to exploit the perceived connections and disjunctions. As a breed of uniquely local "international" Shakespeare, site-specific rewriting contrasts with more readily transferable performances that tour from city to city as well as with Hollywood Shakespearean films.

Shakespeare and his plays have frequently been given site-specific roles in theater and in reading communities either at times of crisis or when politically sensitive themes were evoked. Site-specific and political readings of Shakespeare are nothing new, if we accept that the staging of *Richard II* in 1601 was connected to Essex's rebellion and that *Macbeth* was written to please King James I of England (James VI of Scotland), who traced his lineage to Banquo.[6] Other Shakespearean plays entailed equally significant connections between fictional and historical localities at the time they were first staged, followed by a long history of political reading in Russia, the Eastern bloc, wartime and postwar Germany, postindependence India, and twentieth-century China.

What is unique with the Chinese cases of site-specific interpretations is that the subject matter of a play is not necessarily always the reason for the choice of the play. Israeli director Hanan Snir had every reason to choose *The Merchant of Venice* for his 1995 Weimar production and set it in a concentration camp, but topicality was exactly what some Chinese theater artists sought to avoid.[7] Several distinct and potentially unconnected localities are put to question in a single production.

Drama as Political Events and the Politics of Theater

When discussing "the distinction between pure and political knowledge" in *Orientalism*, Edward Said asserts: "it is very easy to argue that knowledge about Shakespeare . . . is not political whereas knowledge about contemporary China or the Soviet Union [in the 1970s] is."[8] As it turns out, the Chinese knowledge about Shakespeare and other local and foreign writers has always been political, including the Soviet–Chinese reading of *Much Ado About Nothing* that purported to be an apolitical exercise.

The aesthetic practices of mid-twentieth-century China were punctuated by a keen sense of the political, and Shakespeare performances were increasingly informed by local knowledge. This is a period when Chinese theater was in search of safe "apolitical texts," but this is also a period when the political turn in literary culture was alternately seen by different constituencies of the society as a left turn, a right turn, and a wrong turn, as Communist China began to lay claims of local "ownership" on select sets of foreign ideas, including Marxism, Stanislavskian acting method, and Soviet social and cultural institutions. The dual canonicity of Shakespeare as an author widely read and performed gained additional purchase through Karl Marx, who cites Shakespeare at length to support his arguments, and through the Russian and Soviet traditions of political Shakespeare.[9]

When history has been held hostage, theater artists found ways to speak through dramas disconnected from local circumstances. Theater speaks through its new locality in the play. Three factors have contributed to local readings of the ideas of China and Shakespeare during this period.

First, torn between a number of wars, mid-twentieth-century Chinese theater artists opted for topicality and social relevance in their work. While literary production and theater as public entertainment continued to thrive and acted as a depository for collective cultural memory, the preference for topicality came to define much of the artistic activity during this period. After two decades of improvisational performance, Shakespeare's plays were fast becoming part of the Chinese repertoire to train *huaju* (spoken drama) actors in the 1930s, hence their popularity in drama academies and conservatories. The founding principal of the National Drama School, Yu Shangyuan (1897–1970), included Shakespeare in the repertoire of his new school and theater, for he believed that "Shakespeare is the most important playwright in the history of drama, and we [Chinese theater artists] cannot ignore him."[10] Yu obviously followed his Anglo-European contemporaries in eulogizing Shakespeare. He maintained that the reason to stage Shakespeare in China was that "performance of Shakespeare has been an important criterion to measure success for theatres worldwide and not just in England"[11] and that "the most celebrated and achieved actors of our age [outside China] achieved fame through their performances of Shakespearean characters." One of the degree requirements at the National Drama School was a Shakespeare production. Each graduating class was required to stage a Shakespearean play. During wartime, the requirement was not enforced every year, but the first, second, fifth, and fourteenth graduating classes did perform Shakespearean plays at graduation, including *The Merchant of Venice* (1937), *Othello* (1938), and the *Hamlet* (1942) discussed in the next section.[12] Yu himself also codirected with Yan Zhewu a production of *The Merchant of Venice* on April 25, 1948, celebrating Shakespeare's birthday.

Second, an important mid-twentieth-century cultural phenomenon is modern China's political and cultural ties to the Soviet Union.[13] The 1950s saw a significant number of "Soviet experts" in all fields recruited by the Chinese government to transfer their knowledge to the Chinese as the CCP capitalized on the propagandistic, pedagogic, and political capital of theater. The artists, in response, found their way around the politicization of literary texts. Under extremely unusual historical circumstances before and after the Cultural Revolution (1966–1976), Chinese and Soviet artists worked closely with one another and created Shakespearean productions that made a difference. In many cases, the difference marked the line between life and death. One of China's most devoted and influential Soviet directors was Yevgeniya Konstantinovna Lipkovskaya (1902–1990), an experienced acting teacher at the A. N. Ostrovsky Drama Institute in Leningrad. Lipkovskaya's two-year residency at the Shanghai Theatre Academy culminated in two productions she directed: Shakespeare's *Much Ado About Nothing* and Boris Andreevich Lavrenyov's *Razlom* (*Break Up*).[14] Over a period of two years in the late 1950s, she worked with a group of students on *Much Ado About Nothing* (premiered in Shanghai in 1957).

Third, the most brutal force that reshaped the landscape of culture and theater is the ten-year Cultural Revolution, which, ironically, had more to do with censoring than revolutionizing performance culture; yet this is also one of the most intriguing periods for Shakespeare performance in

East Asia. The Cultural Revolution attacked bourgeois remnants, bureau-cracy, vested interests, and, above all, "foreignness" and antiquity. In this peasant-centered culture, there was no place for Shakespeare or any non-Chinese playwright. Shakespeare's perceived moral preoccupations (such as an antifeudalist tendency and humanism) are ironically not those of the Chinese Communist revolutionaries. The only plays performed on stage during the Cultural Revolution were state-endorsed model plays (*yangban xi*) that uniformly portrayed an imaginary bright future of Communist China. The power struggle and mass campaigns during this period were masked by ideological debates on the functions and values of literature and art, especially theater.[15]

Staging *Hamlet* in a Confucian Temple

As helping to educate vigilant and patriotic citizens (whatever ideology was current) became the dominant mission of theater, the local-ity of Chinese audiences was given primacy. A case in point is a produc-tion of *Hamlet* set in premodern Denmark and performed in a Confucian temple, directed by Jiao Juyin (1905–1975). First staged in Jiang'an in rural Sichuan for general audiences during the second Sino-Japanese War in June 1942, it was revived later in Chongqing, the provincial capital. The production married the foreign setting to local theatrical and allegorical spaces in a dialectical process that testified to the reciprocal impact on both the target and source cultures. The unique circumstances of this production may prompt one to ask: Why theater during the war, and why *Hamlet?* During a time when the theater was suspect, the Shakespearean canon was an obvious choice to avoid censorship by the Nationalist gov-ernment. Theater's function as a site for social education as well as its potential for propaganda were seen as compelling reasons to stage public performances. Performances provided entertaining relief, raised funds for military operations, and boosted the audience's morale. All these site-specific meanings derived from the performance venue and cultural loca-tion of the production were inaccessible to American critics of the time. When the *New York Times* reviewed Jiao's production in 1942, the feature that drew Brooks Atkinson's attention was the actors' Western makeup and prosthetic noses. The review states that the actors "have built up a series of proboscises fearful to behold. The king has a monstrous, pen-dulous nose that would serve valiantly in a burlesque show; Polonius has a pointed nose and sharply flaring mustache of the Hohenzollern type; Hamlet cuts his way through with a nose fashioned like a plowshare."[16]

In addition to the prestige of performance associated with Shakespeare's stature, the ability to stage and attend plays during a time of war was itself perceived as a victorious gesture. What was made propagandistic was not always only the play's allegorical dimension but the act of staging the play itself. As Fu Xiangmo, a Jiang'an native and a journalist for the *Citizen's Gazette* (*Guomin gongbao*) and *Social Welfare* (*Yishi bao*), pointed out in his review of the Jiang'an performance, although he was a *huaju* lover, he had not seen many recent productions because "nine out of ten amounted to nothing more than a piece of war propaganda." He noted what a precious opportunity it was to be able to see a nonpropaganda play during a time of war, and a good *huaju* production of Shakespeare in small-town Jiang'an "in a remote corner of China's hinterland."[17]

Jiao's *Hamlet* was staged in 1942, five years after the fall of Nanjing to the Japanese. Chiang Kai-shek (Jiang Jieshi, 1887–1975) and his Nationalist government moved the capital to Chongqing, which triggered a nationwide migration. Elites, bankers, scholars, artists, and members of other social classes who could afford to move all relocated to Sichuan Province, as did schools and universities. The realities of the new locality—backward economic conditions and frequent Japanese aerial attacks—only lowered the morale of these refugees, who were uprooted from their hometowns now in the Japanese occupation zone. Live theater became a symbol of cultural life, and the presence of cultural life helped to maintain the dignity of the Chinese refugees. Yu Shangyuan was invested in the symbolic value of wartime theater. At the revival of the Jiang'an *Hamlet*, Yu wanted the performance to achieve two goals:

[1.] The social significance of *Hamlet* [to us] is Hamlet's progressive and revolutionary [*geming jinqu*] spirit, which is what the Chinese people need during the Anti-Japanese War. . . . Prince Hamlet resisted the destiny arranged by Fate, countered feudal oppressions, and sought liberation from an environment filled with licentious and corrupt individuals.

[2.] Those countries that produce the most high-quality Shakespearean productions are the countries with the highest cultural prestige. . . . Performing Shakespeare is a crucial step for our country to catch up and to join the countries with world-class cultural achievements.[18]

It is striking how procolonialist the assumption of Yu's comments turns out to be. On the one hand, it demonstrates the imperatives of the cultural renewal project to establish Chinese self-esteem. On the other hand, the assumption about the prestige of any Shakespearean performance defeats its own purpose to celebrate indigenous Chinese values and exceptionalism. The competing pull of admiration of Western theater and Chinese nationalist sentiment constitute a uniquely local Shakespeare in the emerging postcolonial world. It is worth mentioning that this sentiment dominated mainland Chinese productions until as late as the 1980s. Zhang Qihong, director of the Chinese Youth Art Theatre's *The Merchant of Venice* (1980), made a similarly procolonialist comment at the first Shakespeare Society of China meeting in 1985. She invited Shakespeare, a "god" of England, to descend to China and display his "profound critique of feudalism, great realism, humanism, and moral power."[19]

Yu's comments invite further speculation. The many contradictions and ideological positions have made Yu's reading of *Hamlet* opaque. For example, the destiny that Hamlet resists is never made clear. Unlike Lin Shu's rewriting of *Hamlet*, which made the play conform to Confucian ethical codes, Jiao's performance generally followed Shakespeare's text. However, the mise-en-scène and the director's approach suggest that the production was informed by the pre-1940s Chinese critical tradition of a "Confucian Hamlet."[20] Theater artists and literary critics in mainland China have concentrated on selected themes in *Hamlet* that resonate with traditional Chinese literary culture and with Confucianism, such as usurpation, filial piety, and legitimacy of rulership. As Lu Gu-sun observed, "To some of the early Chinese readers and critics of *Hamlet*, the . . . theme of the play was . . . conveniently in compliance with the Confucian ethical code demanding filial piety, . . . and constant chastity, and with Buddhist tenets of karma."[21] For example, Tian Han associated Hamlet's melancholy and "patriotic" concerns—"The time is out of joint: O cursed spite / That ever I was born to set it right!" (1.5.188–89)—with *On Encountering Sorrow* (*Lisao*) by the Confucian poet Qu Yuan (ca. 339–ca. 278 B.C.E.) in his postscript to his translation.[22] Similar to English-language Shakespeare scholarship and editions in the 1960s, Chinese scholarship emphasized moral criticism, although the Chinese preoccupation with morality lasted nearly an entire century. As the first Shakespearean play to be translated into Chinese in its entirety, *Hamlet* holds a special place in Chinese visions of Shakespeare. There have been numerous Chinese adaptations and spin-offs of *Hamlet*, including Lao She's short story "New

Hamlet." There were also engagements with *Hamlet* that challenged the tradition of Confucian criticism of Chinese and Western literary works, such as Lee Kuo-hsiu's play *Shamlet*.[23]

This is not the first instance of a nation associating itself with the positive or negative traits of various characters in *Hamlet*. German poets and intellectuals have repeatedly identified Germany with Hamlet since the nineteenth century. In 1800, the Shakespeare translator Ludwig Tieck indicated that what was needed to begin Germany's own golden age of poetry (to follow in Shakespeare's footsteps) was a Fortinbras-like figure.[24] In Ferdinand Freiligrath's poem "Hamlet" (1844), the German dissident, poet, and Shakespeare translator declares, "Germany is Hamlet!"[25] The analogy became so widely accepted that Horace Furness was compelled to dedicate the *Hamlet* volume of his 1877 New Variorum Edition of Shakespeare to the Deutsche Shakespeare-Gesellschaft on behalf of "a people whose recent history has proven once and for all that Germany is not Hamlet," alluding to the rise of the German Empire under Bismarck as an indication that Germany was no longer hindered by self-doubt.[26]

This is where the similarity ends, however. Director Jiao also highlights procrastination as the most important aspect of Hamlet's character, but he explains the negative trait away by arguing that "Hamlet's hesitation is not caused by cowardice but his love for truth." Jiao then turns to China's Hamlet syndrome: "We Chinese people are often too cautious about everything, and as a result we lose courage. In the end we can do nothing."[27] As Hamlet was being held as a negative example in China, he was also being commended for his "patriotism" and filial piety. In Jiao's production, Hamlet fully accepts the revenge mission as his undeniable duty as a son. The competing interpretations in the Chinese case complicate the reading of Hamlet. For Jiao and his audience, the Danish prince was at once a positive and a negative example. On the one hand, Hamlet's patriotic concern about the corrupt court made him particularly at home in a culture of filial duties and political loyalty. On the other hand, his inaction and irresolution resonated in the Chinese psyche. Jiao gave his wartime *Hamlet* a call-to-arms tone, but did not resolve the essential paradox in these competing narratives. The pull of admiration for Hamlet as seeker of truth is countered by the production's local bias and contextual underpinnings.

In this context, this wartime performance was already loaded with decidedly local connotations. Yu remarked that even though *Hamlet* is a tragedy, its wartime production was actually an uplifting experience because the spirit was "exactly what the Chinese people needed to resist the Japanese invasion."[28] This attitude reminds us of another prominent wartime Shakespearean performance from the same period, Laurence Olivier's *Henry V* (1944). Compared with Olivier's jingoistic and nationalist film, which was dedicated to the "commandos and airborne troops of Great Britain," the choice of a hesitating Hamlet motivated by personal causes—instead of, say, a traditionally defined patriotic Shakespearean hero—may seem quite odd at a time when China, like Olivier's England, was at war. However, the production's ideological purposes—although at times self-contradictory—were to uphold Hamlet's moral integrity as a positive model and to use Hamlet's hesitation as a negative lesson. This is most evident in the director's statements.

The fortuitous site of performance added unexpected layers to the question of the politics. This production was first staged in the temple in Jiang'an rather than Chongqing because the school was located in Jiang'an. Tucked away from the metropolitan culture of the provincial capital, the small town was a pastoral other place where alternative political readings of *Hamlet* could find a ready home. The Confucian temple was chosen as the performance site not because that particular temple was attractive or more culturally significant than other temples or venues, but because, like many village temples in rural China, it functioned as a convenient and traditional gathering space in the town. It was financially unfeasible to construct a theater during the all-out war of resistance against the Japanese, and the Confucian temple was one of the readily available architectural spaces to be found in many Chinese towns. The temple's architectural structure and allegorical space provided a ready site for such a performance and was used as a makeshift stage. In other words, the choice of performance venue inherited the accidents of history. In historical hindsight, the temple bears the marks of wartime exigencies and limitations. While temples and teahouses, among other informal performance spaces outside playhouses, were regularly used for public performances in China up to this time, the courtyards and the central halls of Confucian temples were used almost exclusively for dedicatory ritual performance. Temples serve as sites for collective memories and gathering places, but the Confucian temple in particular has been regarded as a sacred site for Chinese intellectuals. Therefore, Jiao's *Hamlet* became a major public event not only because of its innovative stage design, but also because of its unconventional performance space for a Western-style spoken drama performance.

This is the historical context of Jiao's *Hamlet*. Accompanied by music (Handel's Largo and Beethoven's Minuet in G), the production ran for three performances in Jiang'an but left a lasting impression on the audience, many of whom came from nearby rural areas for their first *huaju* experience.[29]

Directed by Jiao Juyin, a French-trained Chinese director who would become one of the major figures in modern Chinese theater, the performance was based on a popular translation, with cuts, rather than a Sinicized rewriting. He worked closely with Cao Yu, Ouyang Shanzun, and Zhao Qiyang to create the aesthetic style of the Beijing People's Art Theatre. An influential director and drama theorist, Jiao is widely recognized for his productions of canonical modern Chinese plays such as Lao She's *Teahouse*, which was revived by the Beijing People's Art Theatre as part of the centennial celebration of Jiao's birthday in 2005.

Scripted and not improvised, as many early-twentieth-century Chinese performances had been, this production was one of the earliest complete performances of *Hamlet* in the *huaju* format.[30] The drama-school-initiated performance of *Hamlet* thus attracted both intellectuals and villagers. This performance led to its revival later that year in a formal indoor theatrical space in Chongqing, rather than in a temple in the rural area. The production was revived as part of the Ministry of Education's "[wartime] social education" campaign (Shehui jiaoyu kuoda xuanchuan zhou) in Chongqing, the provincial capital of Sichuan and the temporary capital of China during the war.[31] The "social education" in this context was a wartime patriotic campaign. The choice to perform *Hamlet*, a work thought to represent Anglophone cultures (including China's ally America), would certainly encourage support of China's Western allies. However, extant historical documents show that the director and promoters of this production were more interested in *Hamlet*'s symbolic capital and in the perceived prestige and significance of being able to stage Shakespeare under challenging wartime material conditions. They, and their audience, did not seem to be invested in *Hamlet*'s cultural connection with China's Western allies during the war, although the production, in the context of Yu's drama school, had a pronounced purpose to boost morale and confidence of the Chinese.

Much of the production's vitality lies in its ingenious use of the temple as an allegorical space under poor conditions, including frequent power outages. It was staged on the balcony in front of the shrine to Confucius, with seated audiences in the courtyard looking up to the balcony at the end of a stone staircase. The temple had two wings and a central hall. The stage design took advantage of the temple's preexisting structure, covering the red pillars with black cloth. The stage had a startling colossal depth of nearly two hundred feet, with twenty-four-foot curtains on each side hanging between the pillars as decoration. The curtains concealed or revealed a combination of pillars and scene depth to dramatize the twists and turns and haunted atmosphere in "the sinful and perilous Danish court."[32] For example, Polonius gave his blessing and his advice to Laertes—"Neither a borrower nor a lender [be]" (1.3.57–81)—as he followed Laertes back and forth around different pillars, moving toward the back of the hall, which, for lack of lighting, was dark. Similar movements around the pillars were used for Polonius's other speeches. The arrangement highlighted his ill-received lengthy speeches and the unseen twists and turns of court politics. The performance area thus acquired the depth of a proscenium stage. The ghost entered from the deep and dark end of the path lined with the pillars and curtains. The minimalist stage design—two chairs, a bed, and a table—worked well with the dim open space in creating a sense of mysteriousness.

The most striking instance when the localities of *Hamlet* and the performance venue are brought to confront each other is seen in the emotionally charged nunnery scene. Wen Xiying, playing Hamlet, was infuriated by the fact that Ophelia was sent by Polonius and that Polonius might be present. The scene culminated in Hamlet's passionate outburst and retreat into the backstage (3.1.142–49). He exited slowly toward the end of the hall, with the gradual drawing of the curtains following the rhythm of his heavy footsteps. Between the curtains was a two-foot gap through which audience members peered to view the lonely Hamlet moving in the dim two-hundred-foot corridor.[33] At the end of the corridor was the shrine of Confucius, which was not part of the set but was not removed for this performance. The local audience knew full well the location of the shrine, which intruded into the performance. The temple now existed simultaneously on different temporal and spatial dimensions in the fictional and real worlds, complicated by the desire to produce an "authentic" *Hamlet* in an authentic Confucian temple. Buried in his thoughts, Hamlet appeared to be heading toward the shrine—which existed outside both the Danish setting and the stage set—as if he now were seeking advice from the Chinese sage. It is not clear whether or how he found an answer, but the director and his audience have eagerly provided a number of inspiring but sometimes conflicting answers to the question of wartime theater.

Posed against the backdrop of the exigencies of this particular location, Hamlet's question—"To be, or not to be" (3.1.55)—acquired personal
and political urgencies for wartime Chinese audiences who rushed to
air-raid shelters on a daily basis, seeking refuge from Japanese aerial attacks. Attending theater in the temple, much like time spent in air-raid
shelters with neighbors and families, became a communal experience
that provided temporary relief through entertainment and at the same
time a sober moment of reflection in the chaos of war. The remote world
of Denmark, Fortinbras's resounding footsteps, and Hamlet's ontological question crossed the vast historical and cultural distance to form a
"patriotic" play. Performed against the backdrop of a Confucian temple,
the "foreignness" of Hamlet and his outlandish yet oddly familiar story,
for the Chinese audiences, became an apt expression of wartime anxieties
about losses. The ongoing Sino-Japanese War prompted Jiao to look for
moral messages in *Hamlet*. In an essay written on December 12, 1942,
before the revival of the production in Chongqing, Jiao directly related
Hamlet's problems to the Chinese situation, highlighting the lessons to
be learned from Hamlet's procrastination. He pointed out that in this
context the performance's aesthetics can be only secondary:

> The character of Hamlet [contains] a lesson for us who are living
> in the period of the Anti-Japanese War, an irony to undetermined
> people, and a stimulus to those who do not have faith in our ulti-
> mate victory. The Danish prince has seen clearly what he needs
> to do when confronted by political and familial crises; however,
> he hesitates and does not put his thought into action. This leads
> to . . . failure and destruction. The victory of the Anti-Japanese
> War hinges upon immediate and synchronized actions by all the
> [Chinese] people. This is why we introduce *Hamlet* to the Chong-
> qing audience. The success of [the troupe's] performing skills is
> secondary.[34]

This is intriguing, because the intellectuals' apparent sympathy for
Hamlet did not translate into admiration for his inaction. Hamlet's procrastination thus constituted negative lessons in moral behaviors. This
is a view shared by former U.S. secretary of state George Schulz, who
warned in the 1980s that the United States had become "the Hamlet of
nations, worrying endlessly over whether and how to respond" to terror-
ism.[35] This interpretation creates a negative image of a hesitating Hamlet.

There is another side of the coin. Although the director downplayed the importance of his actors' skills to accommodate the wartime propaganda, the audience responded enthusiastically and was mesmerized by the actors' performance, including Wen Xiying's Hamlet, Luo Shui's Ophelia, and Peng Houjun's Gertrude.[36]

Jiao seemed to contradict himself when he tried to explain Hamlet's hesitation. Recognizing procrastination as the most important characteristic of Hamlet, Jiao argued that Hamlet hesitated because of his "love for truth," not because of cowardice.[37] Yet, desperate to draw connections between the localities of *Hamlet* and his production, Jiao brushed aside Hamlet's "love for truth" and asked his audience to heed the moral of the performance: procrastination and inaction pave the road to failure.

The Confucian moral contexts became present in this particular production first by accident but were subsequently consciously deployed by the director and critics. But how could Hamlet be at once a Confucian hero, with an exemplary "spirit" fit for a time of war, and a negative example of procrastination, teaching the Chinese audience a good lesson for war? Much ink has been spilled in the history of Chinese Shakespearean criticism over Hamlet's character, and the qualities shared by Hamlet and the typical Confucian gentleman. Despite the popular belief in Confucian interpretations of *Hamlet,* Jiao's production was the first documented performance to take place in a Confucian temple. Up to the 1940s, before the CCP took over China and institutionalized Marxist-Leninism, most interpretations aligned Hamlet with historical and quasi-historical political figures who take it as their responsibility to set aright "the time out of joint" (1.5.189). Their frustration at not being able to communicate or realize their moral and political ideals led to their melancholic state. Unlike English-language criticism of the same period, mainland Chinese criticism did not give equal attention to the problem of Hamlet's procrastination. When it was mentioned at all, Hamlet's insistence on seeking truth was used to explain away the inconsistency. Performed against the backdrop of a Confucian temple and a tradition of "Confucian Hamlets," Jiao's production might have downplayed Hamlet's procrastination were it not for the demands of wartime theater. While Hamlet's sense of duty to the state was emphasized in the performance, the ending was not altered, because the performance was based on a translation.[38] The obvious contradiction in a truth-seeking noble Confucian Hamlet's untimely death prompted Jiao Juyin to extrapolate a moral lesson from Hamlet's negative example.[39]

Reading *Hamlet* in a Labor Camp

Responding to the Tiv's request for a story from her "tribe," Laura Bohannan, an anthropologist doing field research in Africa in the 1960s, chose *Hamlet* for its purported universal value. Hamlet's revenge tragedy has proved to be less than palatable; the elders countered Bohannan's interpretation and volunteered a better version of the story. Bohannan's candid account of her encounter with cultural others through "Shakespeare in the bush" has now become a story familiar to Shakespearean scholars. It serves as a reminder of the ongoing wrestling match between the global universals and local particulars. Jiao Juyin's production of *Hamlet* in a Confucian temple demonstrates an awareness of Shakespeare's transnational voice, as evidenced by Jiao's and Yu Shangyuan's references to the significance of their wartime project to stage Shakespeare. However, not unlike Bohannan and the Tivs, Jiao believed firmly in the singular truth of his interpretation of *Hamlet*.

Another example further illustrates the complex relationship between moralities and the cultural locations of Shakespeare's interlocutors. Chinese intellectuals, such as Wu Ningkun, continued to derive morals from *Hamlet* in tumultuous times. Wu's memoir, *A Single Tear*, chronicles his experience with detailed accounts of the ways in which he read Shakespeare in times of crisis.

While the actors and audiences of Jiao's *Hamlet* saw "China" on stage in the hall of a Confucian temple, Wu read himself into the characters in *Hamlet*. Wu had studied English literature at the University of Chicago. However, moved by patriotism, he left a potentially successful career and returned to Beijing to join the Communist "New China" in 1951. He took a teaching post at Yenching University (Peking University) and later moved to Nankai University in Tianjin, but soon found his optimism betrayed. The party suspected that he had been corrupted by capitalist modes of thinking while abroad. The literary tastes and collections of Wu Ningkun and his wife, Li Yikai, became questionable in the CCP's eyes, for they enjoyed especially "Western classics in English or in Chinese translation," and among their favorites were *Hamlet* and *Les Misérables*.[40] Throughout his autobiography, Wu repeatedly mentions *Hamlet*, which is his "favorite Shakespeare play":

At the end of my long day's work it was a joy for me to spend time talking with [my wife] about her reading. I would recite Hamlet's great soliloquies for her, especially the one that begins with "O! that this too too solid flesh would melt, . . . Or that the Everlasting had not fix'd / His canon 'against self-slaughter!" Or she would recite for me Ophelia's heartbreaking lament on Hamlet's derangement.[41]

For his alleged association with the capitalist West, Wu was persecuted and banished to a labor reform camp to be reeducated in northeastern China. Wu looked back on the bitter experience and wrote, "Apparently there was a lot I had yet to learn about what was new in the New China!"[42]

When he was to read *Hamlet* again, it was not in his faculty residence in Nankai University, but in a labor camp in the wilderness. Under close surveillance, Wu had still managed to smuggle in a copy of *Hamlet* to read whenever "the prisoners had to spend the day cooped up in a cell [when] a blinding blizzard blew from Siberia."[43] Of this experience, Wu later wrote:

> *Hamlet* was my favorite Shakespeare play. Read in a Chinese labor camp, however, the tragedy of the Danish prince took on unexpected dimensions. . . . The outcry "Denmark is a prison" echoed with a poignant immediacy, and Elsinore loomed like a haunting metaphor of a treacherous repressive state. The Ghost thundered with a terrible chorus of a million victims of proletarian dictatorship. Rosencrantz and Guildenstern would have felt like fish in water, had they found their way into a modern nation of hypocrites and informers. . . .
>
> I would say to myself, "I am not Prince Hamlet, nor was meant to be," echoing Eliot's Prufrock. Rather, I often felt like one of those fellows "crawling between earth and Heaven," scorned by Hamlet himself. But the real question I came to see was neither "to be, or not to be," nor whether "in the mind to suffer the slings and arrows of outrageous fortune," but how to be worthy of one's suffering.[44]

The nature of his tribulations explains the turn of the last phrase and highlights what Wu elides from speech: "or to take arms against a sea of troubles and by opposing end them." Such an oppositional stance may have been unimaginable for him, given his situation. Regardless of whether Wu thought there was a uniquely Chinese aspect to learning "to be worthy of one's suffering," his localism was achieved through analogous reading; hence his felt need to remind himself, "I am not Prince Hamlet, nor was meant to be." It is unclear what he means, because there are many possible interpretations of this echo of T. S. Eliot's Prufrock.

On the one hand, it could mean that he wishes to counter the unfortunate condition of Cultural Revolution by *not* taking on a Hamlet-like passivity. On the other hand, it could imply that Wu seeks justice on a more transcendent level and is not seeking revenge on those who unjustly imprisoned him. Wu seems to have likened himself to Hamlet:

> Hamlet suffered as an archetypal modern intellectual. Touched off by practical issues in the kingdom of Denmark, his anguish, emotional, moral, and metaphysical, took on cosmic dimensions and permeated the great soliloquies with an ever-haunting rhythm. When I recited them to myself on the lake shore, I felt this anguish was the substance of the tragedy.[45]

Valuably subjective, Wu's account resembles Primo Levi's account of his experience in a Nazi concentration camp.[46] Levi devoted an entire chapter to similar experiences with poetry under extreme conditions and in struggles with death.[47] Wu's case also parallels the practice of reading canonical literary works in political prison in a global context under varying circumstances. During the Irish Revolution (1916–1923), Irish Republicans rediscovered Shakespeare in prison. Ernie O'Malley wrote with excitement in a prison statement: "I like Shakespeare best." O'Malley's Irish Republican Army colleague Peadar O'Donnell went even further. His story bears striking resemblances to Wu's experience. He concluded: "Shakespeare was a great man, and I would suggest to the British ruling class that the least they can do when they jail folk like me is to present each of us with a copy of his works."[48] Time and again, humanist readings of Shakespeare have been recruited to the aid of dissident politics. In each case, Shakespeare's intellectual or political relevance was summoned to construct alternative realities for the readers. Wu's experience, in particular, demonstrates how the foreign identity of a text can be mined to liberate the reader from his locality.

Wu's reading of *Hamlet* emphasized the connection between particularities of his locality (suffering, injustice, politics) and those of Hamlet's, hence the motivation to continue to read it. During the Cultural Revolution, when no stage productions of foreign plays were allowed, reading Shakespeare in private became an alternative form of political intervention and emotional engagement.

Although a strong Confucian interpretive tradition existed to turn Hamlet into a melancholic but desirable gentleman, neither the audiences of Jiao's *Hamlet* nor Wu Ningkun wished to be Hamlet. In Jiao's *Hamlet,* the fictional inhabits the actual site of production. In turn, the performance site and its cultural location reconfigure the fictional. The situatedness of Jiao's production exemplifies a rooted configuration of localities in nationalistic terms. Jiao insisted on performative authority derived from cultural authenticity.

Jiao and Wu's politicization of literary texts unwittingly echoed the zeitgeist. The 1930s and the 1940s were marked by the subservience of art and literature to Communist and Nationalist propaganda. Both the CCP and the KMT cadres promoted with equal vigor the censorship of translated authors and native literature. Mao Zedong delivered two lectures to political cadres on May 2 and May 23, 1942. In the famous "Talks at the Yan'an Forum on Literature and Art," Mao reaffirmed the necessarily grassroots and political character of cultural production: "In our fight and struggle [*douzheng*] to liberate the Chinese people, there are two fronts: the cultural front and the military front. Since May Fourth, an army [metaphor taken in its literal sense] of cultural [figures] has been formed in support of the revolution in China."[49]

In this context, stage productions were designed to be not merely entertainment. Rather, they were designed to be important sites that served to educate the proletarian masses about the revolutionary cause *and* its future. When a theater group wished to concentrate on art for art's sake and avoid addressing the revolutionary cause, it would have to negotiate the associated risks. The director would have to find a safe text. *Much Ado About Nothing* emerged as a text that was safe for the actors and appropriate for the masses because it was perceived to be a romantic comedy of love, friendship, and trivial matters. It had much to do with "nothing."

Much Ado About Presentism?

As Stephen Orgel observes, it is a commonplace that readers and audiences find in Shakespeare what they wish to find, making Shakespearean drama a site of cultural memory, "where we acknowledge, fashion and perform the desire essential to the creation of our selves."[50] In the Asian context, the most dramatic transformation and urgent transmission of the Shakespearean valences (both positive and negative) occurred during revolutions. One such example is a Soviet–Chinese production of *Much Ado About Nothing*, first staged in Shanghai in 1957.[51] While the first three decades of the People's Republic of China (1949–1979) have typically been characterized by historians as "a barren age with little creativity . . . due to the Maoist politicization of literature and art [and] the subordination of aesthetic criteria to ideological doctrines," Haiyan Lee has noted that there are "stirring works that were enormously inspirational to the 50s–70s generations."[52] The 1957 production of *Much Ado* ranked among these works that provoked and inspired. One of its notable features is its insistence on interpreting *Much Ado* as an "apolitical" comedy portraying only "the bright aspect of life" in the new China. Its unusual claim to an "apolitical" representation of *Much Ado*, along with its historically conditioned motives for designating it as such, invited a reading of the play as a pastoral comedy. The way in which the production envisioned Shakespeare and China generated enough nostalgic sentiment to prompt later Chinese audiences to see a potentially dull reenactment of the event that had taken center stage almost two decades earlier.

Questions about the politicization of artistic works, historical accuracy, and authenticity, as well as ideological authority, revolve around the idea of rewriting as a venue where the present is seen in the art of the past and vice versa. Therefore, revisiting the politics of various claims about the political capital of appropriation (and lack thereof) would be a useful way to reenter the debate between historicism and presentism as critical approaches and appropriative strategies.

Walter Benjamin famously defined the work of art as possessing a unique "presence in time and space" and an "existence at the place where it happens to be."[53] In terms of drama, its unique presence in time and space would include its presence in textual forms and stage representations. Any performance would have to wrestle with three distinct times and spaces: those of the current stage performance, those of the *fabula* or story, and those of the playwright. The tensions and relationship among these entities inform most appropriative strategies and shape the outcome. Presentism, a critical operation that brings contemporary events to bear on premodern works, privileges the extended presence in time and space of artistic works and foregrounds the historicity of contemporary readers and critics.

Rewrites of canonical texts—a phenomenon that has existed for centuries—are often met with skepticism and historically conscious criticism, because these performances are perceived to be evading the historical specificity of the texts they seek to represent. However, the situatedness of the practice of literary interpretation and the reader's place and time should be acknowledged and confronted. The urge to privilege the present and to reinvent the repertoire of meanings is a response to the urge to re-store literary works to their earliest historical circumstances. As opposed to a historicizing way of reading Shakespeare according to an exclusive set of knowable "facts," presentism is invested in the validity and value of contemporary critical responses. It also brings to light the intricate rela-tionship between history and epistemology, past and present, and text and performance. History can never be reduced to a series of facts, preserved in a pristine state, as it were.[54]

The Soviet–Chinese *Much Ado About Nothing* espouses some of the cor-ollaries of presentism, but at the same time transcends the presentism–historicism dichotomy, because it is both a diachronic and a synchronic representation that simultaneously evokes historical authenticity and claims to deny the presence of any ideology—historical or present-time. The creation and reception of this supposedly apolitical Shakespeare are fraught with complications because at work are the politics of "apoliticiza-tion" in the advent of Maoism, filtered through Yevgeniya Lipkovskaya's theater philosophy. How can a performance and its carbon copy, run more than a decade later, be the site of collective memory about the revolution and, at the same time, be said to deny the presence of any ideology? Part of the answer lies in this particular production of *Much Ado*'s capacity to evoke an imagined Shakespearean history that is distant enough to appear politically "neutral" to the Chinese censors, which, in turn, creates a po-litically safe performance text for the actors and audiences to indulge in.

The distance of Shakespeare creates the opportunity to both make and avoid political comment. The 1957 *Much Ado* manufactured desirable his-tories and memories. As such, this work's trajectory over time contradicts the present understanding of historicist and presentist approaches to reading premodern texts. Under the historical circumstances of Soviet-Marxist-Maoism in the mid-twentieth century, China witnessed a Soviet–Chinese venture to appropriate *Much Ado About Nothing* for both practical and aesthetic purposes: to familiarize Chinese actors with the Stanislavsky method, to offer the Chinese audience a glimpse into what was perceived to be authentic theatrical realism and authentic Shakespeare, and finally to provide "apolitical" entertainment in a time when ideologies shifted as frequently as policies.

The same cast revived the production in 1961 and again after the Cul-tural Revolution in 1979, both revivals without Lipkovskaya. They were perceived to be apolitical and nontopical, and hence safe in revolutionary times. At the same time, the performances became the locus of nostalgic feelings motivated by the positive valence the actors and audiences conferred on absolute fidelity to the histories of *Much Ado*.

This fidelity is twofold. The actors and their audiences from the pre- and post-Cultural Revolution generations believed that this *Much Ado* was loyal to the "historical" Italy as recorded by Shakespeare and to an earlier, paradigmatic production in 1957. On the one hand, this production historicized *Much Ado* by resorting to realist representations with prosthetic noses, Italian wigs, and Stanislavskian psychological realism. On the other hand, every effort was made to avoid the slightest hint of any use of history to inform the present out of fear of political persecution. The directors and actors understood "history" in very particular ways—the imagined Shakespearean authenticity, the world Shakespeare conjures up in his plays, and the specific history of the 1957 Chinese *Much Ado*. Yet despite its reputation as being "apolitical," this production also claimed to present the bright aspect of the Chinese society under Communist reform, a Maoist requirement of arts and literature. Under unusual historical circumstances, the extreme version of historicism collided with the allegorical mode of presentist reading.

This contradiction is less frequently seen in performance practice, but a similar contradiction has emerged in academe's presentism-versus-historicism debate about meaning-making processes. Some scholars advocate a historicist mode of interpretation, while others seek to bridge the continuing divisions between textual scholarship and performance studies, arguing that to solve the problems associated with realizing Shakespeare's four-hundred-year-old texts in relevant modern performances, it is "not enough to read Shakespeare historically."[55] A dramaturgical analysis of the Chinese *Much Ado* will illustrate how it contradicts presentist and historicist modes of reading.

Soviet Shakespeare in China

Four years after Yevgeniya Lipkovskaya's production of *Much Ado About Nothing* in 1957, which was translated into Chinese as *Looking for Trouble in Trivial Matters* (*Wushi shengfei*), a group of Chinese actors, directed by Hu Dao, revived the earlier production on a summer night in Shenyang without changing even the smallest detail.

As the curtain rose, the audience saw a half-height wall set in a re-created medieval Italian city: Messina. A group of victorious warriors returning on horses from a battle appeared behind the wall. The audience saw the upper halves of their bodies as they rode across the stage. The actors wore period doublet-and-hose costumes with prosthetic noses, blue eyelids (replicating blue eyes), and wigs that imitated Caucasian hair colors and style. Thus opened the play, which critics described as "magnificent," realistic, and "grand."[56]

In April 1979, three years after the end of the Cultural Revolution and over two decades after the first performance, Hu Dao and the same cast (in the absence of Lipkovskaya) revived the production again (figures 10–15). Most of the original cast managed to return to the stage in the revival in Shanghai. This was possible partly because their involvement in the state-approved production in 1957 shielded them from political persecution.

In an interview, Hu proudly commented on two identical photos he had from the 1961 and 1979 performances.[57] In these two photos, the actress playing Beatrice and the actor playing Benedick—the same individuals in 1961 and 1979—were in identical poses and costumes in the same scene.[58] The 1979 performance preserved every detail of its predecessor. As act 1, scene 1, ended, on an empty stage with two curtains and an arch

FIGURE 10   Zhu Xijuan as Beatrice in Looking for Trouble (Much Ado About Nothing), directed by Hu Dao, Shanghai, 1961, the first revival of the production directed by Yevgeniya Lipkovskaya, Shanghai, 1957. (Courtesy of Shanghai Dramatic Arts Center)

FIGURE 11   *Looking for Trouble* (*Much Ado About Nothing*), directed by Hu Dao, Shanghai Youth Spoken Drama Theatre, 1979, the second revival of the production directed by Yevgeniya Lipkovskaya in 1957. (Courtesy of Shanghai Dramatic Arts Center)

reaching up to the proscenium, roughly twenty servants appeared in front of the closed inner golden curtain. They were preparing a feast. Each servant entered with her or his distinct step and pace, carrying wine barrels, a roast goose on a huge plate, and other dishes. Their action provided the backdrop for the scene that corresponded to *Much Ado About Nothing* 1.2.1–27. Leonato and Antonio carried on a conversation as the servants went on and off the stage. The servants crossed the stage with mouthwatering dishes in preparation for a feast. After a while, they returned to the stage with empty platters.[59] The stage soon returned to its previous state: empty and quiet. Then the inner curtain drew again to reveal Don John sitting in a chair, plotting with Conrade and Borachio against Claudio and Hero. The lighting for the conspiracy scene was changed to a cold tone, and the lively music immediately became more serious. Chinese critics were impressed by the new techniques. Cao Shujun and Sun Fuliang noted enthusiastically how the two curtains opened slowly to percussion beats to create the illusion of a wide-open stage.[60] Lu Hai was impressed by the verisimilitude of the "medieval castle" on stage.[61] Sun Yu lauded the 1961 production's achievement in "realism" and the power of the grand setting.[62]

There was much more to this production and its reruns than the "magnificent" stage set and the double curtains, however. It reflected a new

FIGURE 12   *Looking for Trouble* (1961). (Courtesy of Shanghai Dramatic Arts Center)

FIGURE 13   *Looking for Trouble* (1979). (Courtesy of Shanghai Dramatic Arts Center)

"Chinese Shakespeare" produced in a Sino-Soviet workshop of realism and Stanislavskianism. Having seen the 1957 *Much Ado*, Dong Youdao, a lecturer at the Shanghai Theatre Academy, noted that "Shakespeare's real home is in the Soviet Union. We found this statement to be true after having seen Lipkovskaya's *Much Ado*."[63]

FIGURE 14   Stage design of *Looking for Trouble* (1961). (Courtesy of Shanghai Dramatic Arts Center)

FIGURE 15   Stage design of *Looking for Trouble* (1979). (Courtesy of Shanghai Dramatic Arts Center)

The transplantation of Shakespeare from his "real home" in the So-viet Union to new China was a complicated process.[64] One of the most intriguing questions was why certain plays were chosen and others were not. Other than *The Merchant of Venice,* very few Shakespearean comedies were staged in China before the 1950s. However, in the period from 1956 to 1979, *Much Ado About Nothing* and *Twelfth Night* were two of the most frequently staged non-Chinese plays. Under similar conditions, the *Twelfth Night* staged by the Shanghai Film Actors' Theatre Company in 1957 was revived in 1958 and 1962, with the same translation and director.[65]

In Search of an Apolitical Fantasy World

Several factors contributed to the popularity of *Much Ado About Nothing* in this historical period, when Marxist-Maoism controlled all as-pects of public cultural life. First, the political upheavals and overt politici-zation of art sent theater practitioners and their audiences on a search for safe texts that did not contain any political messages that were in any way ambiguous.[66] *Much Ado* was turned into a comedy of lovers' wordplay. More importantly, the play was a safe text because it was chosen and de-signed as such by a respected Soviet expert recruited and approved by the state. Yevgeniya Lipkovskaya brought to the Shanghai Theatre Academy the prevalent interpretations of Shakespeare in the "model" Communist country—the Soviet Union, China's "Soviet Big Brother."

The second factor that contributed to the popularity of *Much Ado* was the actors' and their audiences' need to escape to a fantasy world removed from contemporary politics. The 1957 production of *Much Ado About Noth-ing* is a case in point. During the 1950s, theater companies were given the mission to propagandize the party ideology, to promote "progressive" ideas among the people, and to fight "class enemies." The monotonous practice of staging plays with the same theme ground down actors' enthu-siasm for the stage. *Much Ado* was a rare state-approved opportunity for the actors to try something different. The actors and the director were not at all interested in making the play relevant. Therefore, they did not mod-ernize or Sinicize the plot, costume, characters, or stage set. The 1957 pro-duction was approved before the Anti-Rightist Campaign; it was staged during the campaign without causing a stir. Only very few members of its cast were persecuted, not because these actors were involved in the production of *Much Ado* but because they had committed antirevolutionary "crimes" in the past.

Lipkovskaya gave the production a goal: to illustrate that a better life can be created through (class) struggles.[67] She also appropriated Stanislavsky's concept of dramatic action. For her, it always meant "fighting," because "without fighting, there is no action."[68] In an acting class, Lipkovskaya urged the actors to first "observe life" and understand "how people live."[69] Stanislavsky believed that "there is no such thing as actuality on stage"; therefore, "the aim of the actor should be to use his technique to turn the play into a theatrical reality."[70]

The level of attention the actors and audience paid to characterization and psychological realism drew them into the play's remote world and made the play appear irrelevant to contemporary China. In addition, after a series of incidents, *Much Ado* became a haven, sealing the actors off from the political persecution taking place outside the theater. The rehearsal room, "a sacred place" in Lipkovskaya's words, was a sharp contrast to the world outside.[71] The student cast members at the Shanghai Theatre Academy were eager to learn new acting techniques from the state-endorsed Soviet expert. They also received direct orders from the party committee of the Shanghai Theatre Academy, which prohibited them from engaging in anything other than their assigned task—rehearsing with Lipkovskaya. Outside the quiet rehearsal room, a new movement was feverishly under way. In May 1956, Mao encouraged people to voice their discontent and criticize any aspect of the new socialist society, because debates promoted progress and "even Marxism had to be developed through fight and struggle [*douzheng*]."[72] This incident, known as the Hundred Flowers Campaign, proved to be a short-lived period of free speech. In 1957, the political climate changed overnight. The first Anti-Rightist Campaign was launched, and those who had disagreed with Mao the previous year were persecuted. The group working with Lipkovskaya to stage *Much Ado* turned out to be extremely lucky, since they were prohibited from participating in any political activities in order to concentrate solely on perfecting their acting skills.

To protect herself and her students, Lipkovskaya was reported to have eulogized Friedrich Engels, quoting his canonized interpretation of Shakespeare.[73] She also quoted Mao's words in public. Lipkvoskaya's comments participated in the emerging discourse on Shakespeare's significance by the extreme Marxists (the Maoists) in China. Engels lauded the European

Renaissance as "the greatest progressive revolution that mankind has so far experienced, a time which called for giants and produced giants—giants in power of thought, passion, and character."[74] Marx and Engels also highlighted Shakespeare's vivacity and realism. In their letters, they criticized the German socialist Ferdinand Lassalle (1825–1864) for not using Shakespeare as a model for his historical drama, *Franz von Sickingen*. In a letter to Lassalle dated May 18, 1859, Engels championed Shakespeare:

> The realistic should not be neglected in favor of the intellectual elements, not Shakespeare in favor of Schiller. . . . What wonderfully distinctive character portraits are to be found during this period of the breakdown of feudalism—penniless ruling kings, impoverished hireling soldiers and adventurers of all sorts—a Falstaffian background that, in an historical play of *this* type, would be much more effective than in Shakespeare![75]

According to Marx and Engels, *Sickingen* was abstract and didactic, lacking the kind of convincing realistic representation of the action found in Shakespeare. They believed that Lassalle followed Johann Friedrich von Schiller (1759–1805) too closely and turned historical characters into mouthpieces of revolutionary causes.[76]

This rhetoric was appropriated by the Soviet critics and then replicated by the Chinese theater circle. Shakespeare became a realist writer of the Soviet people. Alexander Anikst, an important Russian Shakespearean translator, observed that Soviet criticism was based on "Marx's and Engels's letters to Lassalle." He repeated Marx and Engels's argument that "Shakespeare was no preacher, it was not in character for him to transform his heroes into 'mouthpieces' for his own views."[77] Anikst concluded that "Shakespeare the artist and Shakespeare the writer of the people are identical."[78] At about this time, Soviet interpretations of Shakespeare were translated and influenced Shakespeare reception in China. Among the standard Shakespeare criticism available were Chinese translations of Anikst's *Shakespeare and His Plays* (1957) and *Concise History of British Literature* (1959).[79]

The Soviet mode of performing and understanding Shakespeare was dominant in China. Works by leading Soviet Shakespeare scholars like Mikhail Mikhailovich Morozov and Alexander Anikst appeared in more than one version. Moreover, key texts of Stanislavsky's system were translated and widely circulated in China. *An Actor Prepares* was translated in 1956. One of the most important Soviet works translated into Chinese was Morozov's *Shakespeare in the Soviet Union* (*Shashibiya zai Sulian*, 1953).[80] Morozov's influence in China was visible from the 1950s through the 1980s, and his influential biography of Shakespeare was translated and widely read by students and scholars.[81]

Also of interest is the prevalent view that tragedy presents unique challenges for presentist artists. In the words of Anikst, "The complexity of interpreting [Shakespearean] tragedy is because it is unclear how the ideas of [his] work can be correlated to our present age."[82] Obviously, Anikst and other Soviet critics were unsure how to relate Shakespeare to their time because of the shifting political ideologies. This partially explains the Soviet–Chinese team's decision to stage a Shakespearean comedy.

The third factor contributing to the popularity of *Much Ado* was, surprisingly, its assumed political correctness. One might expect that when a safe performance text means an ideologically neutral play, very little room is left for political interpretation in its performance. But while a safe performance text does not transgress boundaries, it necessarily contains its own ideology—one that is *not* incompatible with the official discourse. Despite a conscious move to depoliticize the play, the theme of *Much Ado* was interpreted in a way that pretended to conform to Mao's other requirements for art. The thrust of Mao's argument in the "Talks at the Yan'an Forum" is that works of art and literature should only "portray the bright aspect of the society and the revolution" and that no emotion, including love, can transcend the division of social class.[83] Thus he argues, "The point of departure in literature and art is love, the love of mankind. Classes divide our society into antithetical entities . . . After the class [enemies] are destroyed, there will be wholesome love of mankind. We do not yet have it now."[84] *Much Ado* was presented as a play about country life, strife over trivial matters, and the merry wars between lovers. It also projected the bright aspect of social life, and thus by extension fulfilled the requirement that the theater serve an educational purpose. The moral lessons imbued in both literature and stage works during this period invariably held that brightness defeated darkness and that love and friendship could overcome all obstacles. Chen Shouzhu characterized Shakespearean comedies as "opposing the new capitalists' evil forces." More importantly, Shakespeare's comedies glorified "the victory of prevailing love and genuine friendship over all obstacles." They reaffirmed the positive, optimistic, and "happy aspects of life."[85]

Ironically, the predominant perception of Shakespearean romantic comedies as "celebrating love" failed to align itself with Mao's guidelines for art.[86] What Mao attacked in the "Talks at the Yan'an Forum" was in fact the bourgeois notion of universal love; neither love nor hate can transcend class division. In relation to the party line, Shakespeare's comedies projected the bright future of a new society, not necessarily a Communist one. Not surprisingly, the Soviet–Chinese *Much Ado About Nothing* was first staged before the most incapacitating imposition of Mao's doctrines. The popularity of the first production of this *Much Ado* may well have been sustained by a lingering desire for pre-1949 humanist sensibility. Its carbon-copy revival after the Cultural Revolution was enthusiastically supported by disillusioned intellectuals who had to mobilize humanism again as a counterdiscourse.

Utopia in a Dystopia

Yevgeniya Lipkovskaya introduced the metaphorical concept of "merry England," a theme she appropriated from Friedrich Engels. Around the 1840s, Engels invoked the idea of "merry England," the manners of the good old days, in "The Industrial Proletariat" in *The Conditions of the Working Class in England*.[87] The accounts of the working class in England in 1844 were written when Engels was living in Manchester. He used the idea of "merry England" as a contrast with the condition of the working class in urban centers, where the concentration of property reached its highest point. In his usual style of using literary works to support his argument, Engels linked the theme of "merry England" to Shakespeare's comedy:

> You who complain of the prosaic dullness of railways without ever having seen one should try traveling on the one from London to Liverpool. . . . It often seems as if one were still in the golden days of merry England and might see Shakespeare with his fowling-piece moving stealthily behind a hedge on a deer-poaching expedition, or you might wonder why not one of his divine comedies actually takes place on this green meadow.[88]

According to the *Oxford English Dictionary*, the idea of "merry England" originated in the Middle Ages. As shown by examples cited in the dictionary, the meaning of "merry" (or "merrie") in this phrase has evolved from the pleasant atmosphere of a place or country to an adjective "expressive of merriment, cheerfulness, or gaiety."[89] As Engels's appropriation shows, it refers to England "characterized by its pleasant landscape," a nostalgic picture drawn by Engels at the advent of the Industrial Revolution. In having "merry England" represent a nostalgic recourse to the idyllic past and pastoral life, Engels used the metaphor to extol the preindustrialized world. The ideological construct referred to a state of life and a state of mind that were utopian. Engels's "merry England" ultimately invoked a utopian vision of Communism.[90] The inhabitants of England allegedly enjoyed this way of life in a forgotten golden age. The proposal that people could live as contented peasants in an egalitarian society was not at all foreign to the Chinese Communists' idea of learning from the peasants, who were considered to be uncontaminated by the postindustrialized capitalists. For Lipkovskaya as well, "merry England" represented the central theme of *Much Ado About Nothing*. In the production, the theme was connected to the ideal of the socialist state.

While reluctant to specify the details, Marx famously proposed that in a Communist utopia, after the society transcends "the enslaving subordination of the individual to the division of labor," it will be possible for any person to "do one thing today and another tomorrow, to hunt in the morning, fish in the afternoon, rear cattle in the evening, criticize after dinner . . . without ever becoming hunter, fisherman, shepherd or critic."[91] Some of these utopian elements concerning the tension between town and countryside were reworked in Maoism during the Great Leap Forward and the Cultural Revolution.

The historical circumstances of Maoist China were conducive to the utopian vocabulary in the reception of Marxism and *Much Ado*—two sets of foreign ideas filtered by Soviet ideologies. As Maurice Meisner observes, "as Marxism moved eastward from its Western European homeland, . . . the doctrine tended to become increasingly infused with . . . utopian purpose." Mao Zedong shared Marx's "utopian goals" despite fundamental differences in their understanding of the gap between urban and rural conditions.[92]

Although the production itself did not conform to the Maoist ideology of love, Lipkovskaya invited her cast and audiences to indulge in the utopian vision of her interpretation of *Much Ado*, especially the idyllic and pastoral elements associated with Marxist-Maoism. In relation to the theme of "merry England," the structure of Lipkovskaya's adaptation is illuminating in several ways. Rather than following his usual comic formula, which begins with a journey from an urban to a rural setting and back to the urban with order restored, Shakespeare sets the action of *Much Ado* in a town that is conducive to carnival, eavesdropping, and courtship. Although all the actions of *Much Ado About Nothing* take place in the town of Messina, the town has a rural and pastoral character.

The pastoral setting was perceived by the director and actors to be conducive to escapism and socialist utopianism. To create this atmosphere according to the theme of "merry England," Lipkovskaya made the important decision to reorganize the structure of acts and scenes.[93] The scene transposition highlights the Beatrice–Benedick plot and marginalizes Don John. Beatrice is no longer compelled to ask Benedick to kill Claudio (4.1.289). The production, based on the widely circulated mid-twentieth-century translation by Zhu Shenghao, made changes to Zhu's text. This emphasis is not at all unfamiliar in the history of reception of *Much Ado* in Europe. King Charles I gave the play a new title, *Beatrice and Benedick,* and Hector Berlioz also titled his 1861 opera *Béatrice et Bénédict.* Don John was omitted in Berlioz's opera adaptation, and Charles I was more interested in the witty lovers than "their romantic opposites."[94] However, Lipkovskaya's emphasis on the Beatrice–Benedick plotline came at the expense of flattening darker aspects of the couple's journey in love. Without the deceit and misunderstanding that Don John contrives against the couple, Beatrice and Benedick's bond would be impoverished. Had Beatrice no need to ask Benedick to kill Claudio and thereby force him to choose between male friendship and heterosexual love, her nature and commitment would not be fully revealed.

Hu Dao, one of the assistants to Lipkovskaya in 1957 and the director who revived the production in 1961 and 1979, followed Lipkovskaya's conception of "merry England" and viewed *Much Ado* as a comedy that countered feudalism. For Hu, the play shows how people can "control their lives."[95] Lipkovskaya's structural reorganization suppressed the emphasis on Don John as an "evil force." Act 1 does not end with the conspiracy scene in which Don John plots against Claudio and Hero (act 1, scene 3, in the original). Instead, act 1, now entitled "The two arches of Cupid," ends with Don Pedro's words to Claudio and Leonato:

DON PEDRO: I will teach you how to humor your cousin, that [Beatrice] shall fall in love with Benedick, and I, with your two helps, will so practice on Benedick that . . . he shall fall in love with Beatrice. If we can do this, Cupid is no longer an archer; his glory shall be ours, for we are the only love-gods. (2.1.380–86)

In the play, two tricks are set up one after the other, one by Don John and the other by Don Pedro. However, the new act 1 ends with the more hopeful and brighter moment. The transposed scenes were very well received. Wang Qibang's review comments at length on the rearranged scenes, particularly act 1:

> Had they [the theater company] staged the play according to the original scene division, act 1 would have ended with Don John's con-spiracy and hatred. . . . It would have emphasized that plot line. . . . Now the performers reorganized the original five acts into four acts, the plot line of the love between Beatrice and Benedick was accentuated.[96]

Following the same guideline that no gloomy scene should end an act and therefore blemish the gaiety of the play, Lipkovskaya deleted the prison scene (act 5, scene 2). The transposition created a different flow of action, highlighting the positive and bright aspects. Don Pedro's line at the end of the new act 1 ("we are the only love-gods") echoed Hu and Lipkovskaya's interpretation of *Much Ado;* it was a comedy that worked against the idea that "everything is dominated and determined by God."[97] It also conformed to Stanislavsky's principle on how to end an act. Stanislavsky held that the change of scene should take place at a "moment of heightened impression," so the "interval produces not a minus leading to subsidence, but a plus." Consequently, the change of scene attempts to heighten "the spectator's interest."[98]

Memorialized Acting, Acting Memories

Chinese directors and actors were not only recycling the Shake-spearean classics as filtered through the Soviets, but also recycling pro-ductions that created collective cultural memory. The reception of the three productions of *Much Ado About Nothing* in 1957, 1961, and 1979 an-ticipates Anne Bogart's observation that "the act of memory is a physical act and lies at the heart of the art of theatre." Bogart proposes that "if the theatre were a verb, it would be 'to remember.'"[99] The cultural value of the 1957 Soviet–Chinese *Much Ado* was intimately connected to the poli-tics of memory and forgetting. Its unique circumstances of production memorialized the act of staging Shakespeare; in turn, the revivals served as sites where the audience's collective cultural memory of the revolution was reenacted.

The 1957 production marked the end of Yevgeniya Lipkovskaya's residency at the Shanghai Theatre Academy. She returned to the Soviet Union after the production, but the actors and students fondly remembered her as Madame Lipkovskaya, who taught them how to "live" on the stage. She never returned to China to direct other plays, however, because political conditions between the Chinese and the Soviets deteriorated rapidly. Due to a series of complex political circumstances, the relationship between China and its most important socialist ally declined in 1960, and the Soviet Union recalled some 1,400 scientists and experts from China.[100] Even though the Chinese government tried to gloss over the rift with such statements as "the imperialists will never succeed in their hopeless scheme to split the unity between the Chinese and the Soviet Parties and between the two countries," the situation did not improve.[101] In China, Mao's extremism created unprecedented famine and suffering during the Great Leap Forward (1958–1960), when some 20 to 30 million people died through malnutrition and famine.[102] There was no room for theater, not to mention Shakespeare or his comedies.

In 1961, the CCP adjusted its extremist policy after having witnessed its destructive force during the Great Leap Forward. The control over art and literature loosened briefly, and Hu Dao revived *Much Ado* with the same group. He preserved every detail of Lipkovskaya's mise-en-scène. There was certainly a degree of nostalgia involved; staging Lipkovskaya's *Much Ado* seemed to invoke memories of the relatively more peaceful time spent rehearsing with the Soviet director in the Shanghai Theatre Academy. The same nostalgic feelings could also be identified in the audience's response.[103] Several reviews mentioned the 1957 production, indicating that the audience was aware that this version reproduced the earlier production.

In 1979, three years after the end of the devastating Cultural Revolution, Hu revived Lipkovskaya's *Much Ado* again, with the same cast. After the torment of the previous decade, Zhu Xijuan (who played Beatrice), Jiao Huang (who played Benedick), and the other actors were old and out of shape. However, in the eyes of the audience, they looked beautiful. Li Ruru, then a first-year student who entered the Shanghai Theatre Academy in 1978 (when higher education was reestablished), saw the production with her cohort of students. She recalled that the performance was exciting and refreshing to them, particularly after ten years of being sealed off from anything outside China. For the generation emerging from the devastating Cultural Revolution, the Chinese title of *Much Ado* was an apt and "beautiful expression" of what they hoped for, that the nightmarish Cultural Revolution was much ado about nothing and China could be rehabilitated. They hoped *Much Ado About Nothing* would "excise [their] bitter experience with the easy and confident wisdom that the title implies."[104] For the audience in 1979, the point of reference departs from Shakespeare and becomes the "original" production in 1957.

While escapism accompanied by the rhetoric of art for art's sake ran rampant in the 1957 production, strong nostalgic sentiments defined the 1979 rerun. When the nightmarish Cultural Revolution ended in 1976, many people had a similar experience of waking up from slumber. They hastened to pick up what they had been forced to leave off ten years before. Therefore, Hu intentionally preserved the costumes, performing style, stage design, set, and all other details from Lipkovskaya's 1957 production, in which he had been involved. Reviving a production—preserved in a pristine state, as it were—that had had a decisive effect on their acting career seemed the most apt statement against politicization the actors could make. Zhu Xijuan wrote in reminiscence: "Eighteen years after the first performance [of *Much Ado*], I can finally understand the play better and know how to play Beatrice."[105] In a similarly excited tone, the director discussed the rerun in relation to the historical gap between the first production and its post–Cultural Revolution revival.

In addition to nostalgic sentiments, realism was also part of the discourse about these productions. The irony in this pursuit of Maoist "realism" is that Lipkovskaya's mise-en-scène actually deleted any connection with the contemporary world. That was probably the only safe way to respond to Mao's call for "socialist realism," a concept the Chinese Communists borrowed from the Soviet Union rather than May Fourth realism. Socialist realism limits the raison d'être of literary works to one and only one purpose: to "reflect [desirable] reality in its revolutionary development." There is an important difference between the assumption that arts can reflect daily life and the Western idea of mimesis. As Perry Link points out, during this time Chinese literature was intended to be a "mirror for life," but the mirror was made into an "inspired mirror, able to 'train the people in the spirit of socialism' by showcasing ideals."[106]

Interestingly, the "local" Chinese Communist ideologies that dictated this transformational process were themselves filtered by other discourses, including Marxism, Soviet Communism, and Maoism. Hu's

"real" realist Shakespeare in 1979 was very much a part of the postrevo-
lutionary Chinese imaginary of humanism and the Soviet version of
world culture. This Soviet–Chinese joint venture created a Marxist-Maoist
canon. The perceived use value of Shakespeare and the Chinese ideologies engendered a reality for the Chinese audience and authorities. That
reality proved to be so desirable and attractive that the production and its
revivals two decades later ceased to be theatrical events. They have come
to signify rites of passage. The unique case of this Soviet–Chinese *Much
Ado* testifies to the presence of multiple levels of political discourses embedded in theater works that challenge the presentism–historicism dichotomy. During this period, Shakespeare's plays were given several cultural functions: a state-approved ideological apparatus, a foreign—hence
safe—text filtered through the "Soviet experts" recruited by the Chinese
government, and a banned text during the tumultuous years of the Cultural Revolution.

Coda

Most theater historians agree that performance "deserves to be
judged by the impact it has in its own time, unaffected by changes in
fashion—in styles of costume and haircuts, of vocal and gestural techniques."[107] This is especially true with interpretations that engage at once
the fictional, cultural, and actual sites embedded within and beyond the
plays themselves. The audience can become so invested in nostalgic enthusiasm that they refuse to accept changes in fashion or gestural techniques. The site-specific meanings have come to be fully embedded within
the historical performance, which has been turned into an event itself.

Although certain meanings of the production will be associated with
the performance style and plot, other meanings are produced by the clash
of the associated cultural localities. In some cases (for example, Lipkovskaya and Hu), the choice of a nontraditional venue was intentional, with
well thought-out dramaturgical plans to incorporate the idiosyncrasies
of the site into the interpretations of China and Shakespeare. In other
cases (for example, Jiao and Wu), the choice was accidental, imposed by
historical exigencies or material conditions, gaining accidental additional
purchase on the production value.

Two questions remain: What does it entail to replicate a production?
Can site-specific readings be reproduced? One of Jorge Luis Borges's

intriguing short stories may help illustrate this problem. Borges's Pierre Menard sets out to appropriate Cervantes's *Don Quixote* but ends up composing another *Quixote*. Even though his *Quixote* coincides "word for word and line for line" with that of Cervantes, he confidently locates his *Quixote* within his locality and believes that these two texts can never read the same way, because they are composed in different contexts and constitute different localities—with the "history of Europe between the years 1602 and 1918" separating them.[108] The reason that Menard's and Cervantes's *Don Quixote,* although verbally identical, read differently is presented as self-evident, but the argument is provocative. If there are two identical stage productions of the same play, they could well "read" differently. The referential stability of drama is now recognized as a fiction, but less transparent is the intricate interplay between temporalities and localities. The 1957 production of *Much Ado About Nothing* and its revivals are gesturally identical twins (with the same cast, costume, set) but "read" differently. The audience, fully entrenched in what they chose to remember, refused to acknowledge this possibility.

Hamlet and *Much Ado About Nothing* continued to fascinate Chinese directors and audiences well into the late twentieth century. Another site-specific performance of *Much Ado* was staged under the Monument to the People's Heroes in Huangpu Park in Shanghai in November 1995. Titled *Looking for Trouble* in Chinese, the open-air production was set against the modern skyline of Pudong, across the Huangpu River.[109] The high-budget (RMB 500,000 or US$60,107) production was free and open to the public. Like *Hamlet* in the Confucian temple and the Soviet–Chinese *Much Ado,* this new production turned its performance site into a meaning-making agent. Despite low temperatures, an audience of thousands enthusiastically cheered the actors throughout the performance. The eighty-eight-foot-wide platform under the monument (where rock music concerts were regularly held) and its eighty stairs were incorporated into the set and became the courtyard of Leonato's house in Messina, Italy (figure 16). The performance began with four Chinese actors in generic seventeenth-century European court costumes entering on horses from the right of the platform. Wearing prosthetic noses and blond wigs, they followed the oval paths surrounding the monument toward two large Italian fountains.[110] In front of the stairs was a flower bed with a white marble statue of Cupid at the center. What looked like a naturalist *huaju* imitation of early modern Europe ended with a modern touch. As the performance proceeded, the costumes and props gradually "evolved" from early modern European

FIGURE 16   The Monument to the People's Heroes in Huangpu Park, Shanghai, forms the backdrop to *Looking for Trouble* (*Much Ado About Nothing*), directed by Yu Luosheng, Shanghai People's Art Theater, 1995. (Courtesy of Shanghai Dramatic Arts Center)

to Victorian English to contemporary Chinese (figure 17).[111] Don John fled on a motorcycle, a symbol of industrialization. Borachio fled on a bicycle, then the most common vehicle in Chinese cities, carrying a thousand U.S. dollars, a symbol of the global power of the capitalists. Before the play ended, Benedick said to Claudio: "Come! Come! We are old friends. Let us dance to our hearts' content before the wedding. Let our hearts dance and fly with our loving wives."[112]

Accompanying Benedick's announcement came a red Ferrari convertible. Beatrice entered in a white Western-style wedding gown and stood with Benedick, wearing a suit and tie, waving their hands to the audience from atop the convertible. Disco music and lighting accompanied the great wedding party. The smooth "evolution" of costumes and the sharp contrast between the early modern opening and the contemporary ending did not seem to bother the audience at all. Cao Shujun, a scholar actively promoting Shakespeare in China, considered this arrangement "brilliant," because it highlighted the "process of the spiritual regeneration of the protagonists." The modern, "liberating" suits and ties replaced the costumes from a feudal past. The flexible treatment of time and space in the production also signified "Shakespeare's charisma across national and historical boundaries."[113] Director Yu Luosheng made a similar comment

FIGURE 17   *Looking for Trouble.* (Courtesy of Shanghai Dramatic Arts Center)

during the rehearsal: "I intentionally made the historical setting vague by using both period and modern costumes. The passage of time is signified by the seemingly chaotic costume change."[114]

It appears that the differences between historical periods and between cultural locations are nothing more than the differences between costumes, and that the differences between contemporary China and Shakespeare's imagined Italy can be easily overcome by modernizing and changing the costumes. A metaphor for modernization staged against the rapidly changing skyline of Shanghai, the performance also signified the arrival of capitalism in China, or "capitalism with socialist characteristics," as the party puts it. As the immediate backdrop to the production, Shanghai's skyline and the park combined to form an ironic presence.

Rewrites of canonical works have frequently been seen as an act of political intervention in the postcolonial and global era. The vitality of the open-air *Much Ado* in 1995 was connected to its interpretive fluidity in relation to its site of performance and its historical implications. Ironic as it might seem, the popularity of the Soviet–Chinese *Much Ado* lied in its denial of any possible connection between the contemporaneity of the Chinese and the historicity of Shakespeare. It was precisely because there was no perceived connection—on personal or political levels—that it was a safe and desirable production in tumultuous times. Its curious insistence on interpreting *Much Ado* as an apolitical comedy that is irrelevant to the mid-twentieth-century Chinese realities conflicts with its other claims that this comedy portrays the "bright" and hopeful aspects of Communist China. This was not perceived to be a problem or a contradiction by the audiences, because the realities and histories were manufactured to frame the entire cultural event. Rich and diverse in dramaturgical concerns, Jiao Juyin's *Hamlet* and the Soviet–Chinese *Much Ado About Nothing* showcase how Shakespearean localities, performance venue, and the cultural location of the performance interact with one another fruitfully. Both productions translated the currency of locality through the site of performance, the perceived sites of origin of the performance idioms, as well as the allegorical settings that erase or accentuate, as the case may be, the presence of Shakespeare, the Soviet Union, and "China." In each of these cases, primacy was given to the performance venue and the "local habitation" of the play. These elements were configured to participate actively in the meaning-making processes.

As Clifford Geertz suggested, "The real is as imagined as the imaginary."[115] These instances are as much readings of Shakespeare's symbolic capital as they are rereadings of local histories, informed by the historical and imagined boundaries between each of these sites. These boundaries continue to be negotiated or reinforced in performance genres that fuse Chinese opera with *huaju* and other styles. And that is another story.

PART IV

Postmodern Shakespearean Orients

6   Why Does Everyone Need Chinese Opera?

I have thee not, and yet I see thee still.
—*Macbeth*

Chinese opera Shakespeares seem to cross national boundaries in the global marketplace with ever greater facility and an unprecedented degree of translatability. If film has become the "lingua franca of the twentieth century," the success of Chinese opera in recent decades is testimony to the rise of Asian visuality in the global scene.[1] David Henry Hwang's *M. Butterfly* (1988) is probably the best-known instance of the iconification of Chinese opera. As both a theater genre and a cultural symbol, *jingju* (Beijing opera) brought Giacomo Puccini's opera, Rene Gallimard, and Song Liling into a gripping narrative about the promise and peril of visual pleasures. One of the most intriguing questions about Chinese Shakespeares is the relationship between locally determined meanings and what has been perceived as a universal visual language in stylized performance. The visual history of foreign Shakespeare, especially Chinese-opera productions, presents unique challenges to directors, performers, spectators, and critics.[2] Why do artists and critics routinely give primacy to what is perceived to be a visual translation of Shakespeare despite the equally important roles of verse and arias in Chinese opera?

One quick answer is the global mass culture's penchant for images capable of crossing linguistic borders, as Stuart Hall and Fredric Jameson would have suggested.[3] In the late twentieth century, the assumption about the visual appeal of Chinese opera has become part of the cultural logic of touring Asian performances, creating a misleading division between *huaju* (spoken drama) for local, Chinese-speaking audiences and subtitled *xiqu* (Chinese opera) for international, festival audiences. Staging Shakespeare based on modern translations contemporizes and recontextualizes the meanings of the plays, granting the audience access to the plays through the modernity of translation, but the major differences between English- and foreign-language performances are usually most palpable and noticeable in their visual aspects.[4] What can the critics and artists' infatuation with visuality tell us about the uneasy coalition between classical text and traditional theater in modern times?

Just as *xiqu* performance idioms have expanded the possibility to play Shakespeare on both sides of the millennium, *xiqu* practices have also been altered dramatically. These changes actively participated in the defamiliarization process of both Shakespeare and *xiqu* in a global marketplace where newness frequently enters as a precious commodity. This chapter examines the critical inclination to essentialize *xiqu* and Shakespeare, beginning with a discussion of *xiqu* and visuality and concluding with a case study of a *jingju*-style *Othello*.

Shakespeare in Chinese opera has generated some of the most interesting and fruitful debates on intercultural performance over the past few decades. When they tour internationally, *xiqu* performances of Shakespeare are often shrouded in contested identities—definitely Chinese according to nearly all Western critics but decidedly un-Chinese according to many from the Sinophone world.[5] Like *huaju*, *xiqu* performances of Shakespeare go back several generations, but they remained sporadic until the 1980s when artists experimented with the visual aspects of Shakespeare's verbal metaphors. Although *xiqu* performances of Shakespeare have existed since 1914, the 1980s is a turning point. This period witnessed a revived interest in the spectral presence of intercultural Shakespeare—"ocular proof" of fruitful cultural exchange, as it were. Shakespeare became more regularly performed in more varied forms of stylization in China, Taiwan, Hong Kong, and other parts of the world in touring *xiqu* productions.

A number of events and historical reasons contributed to the rise and internationalization of *xiqu* Shakespeares in the 1980s, including Deng Xiaoping's Open Door Policy in China, the lifting of martial law in Taiwan in 1987, and the emergence of international Shakespeare festivals in mainland China. On a local level, *xiqu* performances have remained a must-see on most lists for cultural tourists—with special programs concentrating on a few scenes with strong martial-arts and acrobatic elements. Internationally, the rise of *xiqu* Shakespeare echoes what Dennis Kennedy calls neopictorialism in European theater of the same period, a movement to reinterpret Shakespeare by means of "ocular luxury."[6] It is not surprising, then, that *xiqu* productions of Shakespeare have toured more frequently and more extensively than *huaju* performances. Wu Hsing-kuo, one of the best-known names in *xiqu* performances of Shakespeare and other Western classics, has conceived, directed, and performed in some of the most widely toured *jingju* works. His Taiwan-based experimental *jingju* company, the Contemporary Legend Theatre, produced an adaptation of *Macbeth* titled *The Kingdom of Desire* that has been performed repeatedly around the world since the 1980s at premier performance venues and festivals: the National Theatre in London (1990); the Festival de Chateauvallon (1994); Aachen and Heerlen (1996); the Festival d'Avignon and the Millennium Festival in Santiago de Compostela (1998); Utrecht and Rotterdam (2001); the Spoleto Festival (2005); and elsewhere, including several hometown revivals in Taiwan.

Chinese Opera and Shakespeare to the Rescue?

As an art form caught between modernity and tradition, Chinese opera is already traversed by the demands of nonlocal spectators and the criteria of various interpretive constituencies. Shakespeare in Chinese opera as a new form of fusion theater has attracted both local audiences (*xiqu* devotees and the artistically adventurous) and what Kennedy calls global spectators.[7] Understandably, due to the extremely varied constituencies of the new audiences for *xiqu* Shakespeare, the reception of every performance is shaped by a wide spectrum of opinions. It is not unusual for *xiqu* aficionados to criticize the unconventional approaches of these performances, claiming that they damage an ancient form of art and have succumbed to the market law at the expense of Chinese traditions. Praises of *xiqu* Shakespeare's innovation often come from a second group, local audiences who are more adventurous in taste and not fully entrenched in the ideology of traditional repertoire and style of *xiqu*. For a third group—those who neither speak Chinese nor understand *xiqu*'s gestural codes—*xiqu* Shakespeare often appears "remarkably localized"[8] and "richer in sounds, music, and presentational support [compared with contemporary Anglophone theater]," and for good reasons.[9] For all three groups of audience, the currency of the specularity of stylization and Shakespeare is developed in the perceived otherness of the sights on stage, for better or for worse, depending on the audience's ideological positions. Despite dramatic changes in the styles of Chinese opera and in the definition of Chinese identities, Chinese opera has never failed to "be figured as a single, uncompromised lotus flower that resists all the temptations of hybridization . . . symbolizing a perfect Chineseness." After all, what could be more Chinese than Chinese opera?[10]

Accompanying the rapid internationalization of Chinese Shakespeares is a sustained interest in *xiqu*'s externalization of emotions and verbal narratives. Nearly a decade ago, John Russell Brown suggested that Asian theaters not only provide new sites for Shakespeare but also shed new light on the theater for which Shakespeare wrote.[11] We now need to ask: How do new sites of performance affect the traffic between different cultural identities? What roles do localization play in *xiqu* rewrites of Shakespeare? What are the theoretical and practical implications of *xiqu* theater's unique visual codes? If major venues and theater festivals in the West, such as the Lincoln Center, Edinburgh, Stratford-upon-Avon, and Paris, are no stranger to performances in full *xiqu* dress and makeup, why is there still an overwhelming emphasis on the exotic spectacle? Can the selective attentiveness to the intensified visual effects be justified? Throughout history, in both popular and critical discourses, there is a tendency to overlook the reciprocity of visual and verbal exchanges in Chinese-opera Shakespeares.

Huaju enactments of Shakespeare's plays often prioritize local aesthetic practices. The genre's conventions have created a hybrid identity, and *huaju* performances can be just as locally initiated as *xiqu*. And yet *huaju*'s Western motifs and the theater's purported affiliation with nineteenth-century Western realist theater have led some observers to believe that *huaju* productions (as "straight" translation) necessarily "perform according to, or close to, Western conventions," and, by implication, *xiqu* productions operate by "radically transforming the play" through adapting it to a decidedly local style.[12] To accommodate operatic arias, dance, combat, and acrobatics, Chinese opera, for practical and aesthetic reasons, has to condense the plot and be highly selective of dialogues and soliloquies to translate or represent. Parallel patterns of condensing can also be observed in other operatic and stylized adaptations of Shakespeare in Europe. However, there is a distinct investment in Chinese opera's "uniqueness." If the modernity of translation staged by *huaju* theater updates the range of meanings enabled by Shakespeare, *xiqu's* detached relationship with Shakespeare's text seems to invite the audience to *see* the text through visualization of metaphors, emotion, and motifs.

On the other side of the coin, the perceived affinity between Chinese opera and Shakespearean performative aesthetics has reoriented performers and audiences to focus on visuality and allegorical readings of the representations of China and Shakespeare. *Xiqu* directors often transform Shakespeare's archaism through stylization and allegory. While it is true that Shakespeare provides fresh ingredients and expands Chinese opera's repertoire, the remedial effect of Shakespeare and Chinese opera on each other has frequently been exaggerated, creating an epistemological veil. Reporting from the scene of a Chinese-opera production of *The Winter's Tale* at the state-endorsed and -sponsored Chinese Shakespeare Festival in Shanghai in April 1986, J. Philip Brockbank, late general editor of the *New Cambridge Shakespeare,* wrote, "While it was winter for [Shakespeare] in England it appeared to be spring in China." In his "revelatory discovery of new truths about Shakespeare's art" through Chinese opera, Brockbank applauded the advent of "a Shakespeare renaissance in China, remarkable for its scale, plenitude, and variety, distinctively Chinese and yet lucidly in touch with the England of Elizabeth and James." The powerful assumption behind this formulation relies on the notion that the best way to play Shakespeare is to present the plays as they are conceived—by the moderns—to have been played in Shakespeare's lifetime. This argument implies that the perceived parallels between Chinese-opera and Elizabethan-theater practices justify such rewritings. The most important task of a modern performance seems to be to resurrect Elizabethan or Jacobean England through the plays. He concluded that "conventional Chinese theatre was apparently in need of the intimate attentiveness to life to be found in Shakespeare's plays, while the plays themselves are clarified by the energies and styles of an exotic, simultaneously courtly and popular tradition."[13] Brockbank's observation, published in the *Shakespeare Quarterly,* sent a positive message about the possibilities of global Shakespeare to the Anglocentric communities of Shakespeare scholars located in China and the West. Dennis Bartholomeusz applauds how well Indian, Chinese, and Japanese productions of Shakespeare "touch[ed] the mythic dimensions of Shakespeare's art," uncovering hitherto forgotten elements in Shakespeare.[14] He reassures his readers that Beijing opera's "art of mime" is very convincing at "creating on a bare stage a river, rapids, a boat, with the aid of only a pole."[15]

Above all, audiences—Chinese or not—who do not know Chinese opera are usually uninterested in finding out what knowledge about the theater form is available, and are content with taking away from these performances what best suits their imagination.

Brockbank's widely cited comments encouraged many Chinese critics and artists who were exploring intercultural theater when China reopened its door to the world after the Cultural Revolution. Jang Tso Fang, a professor at Peking University, claimed that "Shakespeare is sick in the West, and much in need of traditional Chinese medicine."[16] In 2002, Cao Shujun, a respected Shakespeare scholar in mainland China, published a book with a title that paid tribute to Brockbank's comment: *It Is the Springtime for Shakespeare in China* (*Shashibiya de chuntian zai Zhongguo*). In his preface, Cao wrote, "Philip Brockbank, late president of the International Shakespeare Association, once said, 'it is the spring for Shakespeare in China.' The comment . . . vividly captured the boom of Shakespeare performance and criticism in China, hence the title of my book."[17] Brockbank's comment has been misappropriated to feed into the Chinese national pride and an unexamined assumption that the merit of intercultural performance can lie only in its remedial effect on the source or host culture.

Many critics and artists readily endorsed such a view. When interviewed by the *Wall Street Journal* about his solo *jingju* adaptation of *King Lear* (Lincoln Center, New York, 2007), the Taiwan-based performer Wu Hsing-kuo conceded, "Shakespeare is better known in China than Beijing opera." Wu ventured to compare *xiqu* and Elizabethan theater on the assumption that Elizabethan-theater practices remain normative for staging Shakespeare in English today:

> But in many ways, [Shakespeare's] plays and Beijing opera are very similar. In London 400 years ago, they played on an empty stage, just like in China. . . . In both traditions, there's great freedom in moving from scene to scene. Both are full of poetry. Characters in both traditions are given monologues to explain who they are. And they step outside the play to speak to the audience directly.[18]

Faye Chunfang Fei and William Huizhu Sun, both playwrights, directors, and theater scholars, came to a similar conclusion: "There seems to be a natural affinity between Shakespeare's plays and China's traditional theatre genres, such as *jingju* (Beijing opera), in terms of episodic structure and stylized theatrical performance, despite the differences in content."[19]

This popular view about Chinese-opera Shakespeare is not exempt from the pitfalls of interculturalism. The viability of intercultural performance does not necessarily rely on the compatibility of the traditions being appropriated. In fact, even if conceptions of how Shakespeare's plays were played in his lifetime were really identical to the practices of *xiqu* theater, that coveted historical connection would not in and of itself be sufficient to warrant box-office success or add artistic value to the production.[20] While Wu's solo *Lear* was performed on a bare stage with nothing but a few statues that doubled as rocks, his other works (*The Tempest* and *Macbeth*, for example) went against the grain of *xiqu* conventions by employing lavish sets and lighting effects to create visually stunning spectacles. The dichotomized view of *xiqu*'s remedial capacity for Shakespeare inaccurately casts *xiqu* and *huaju* (and *xiqu* and Shakespeare) as antithetical modes of expression, while the excessive emphasis on sameness shifts the critical attention away from the discursive richness of the dynamics of exchange.

The worthiness of a production was determined by its level of verisimilitude and its *textual* proximity to the psyche of Shakespeare's characters and narrative. However, the idea that stylization involves arbitrary codes of gesture and movement is problematic, for all signs on the stage can only mean by a process of deferral and referral to other signs and symbols. *Huaju* or Western theatrical realism is not any more natural than stylized theater. As Antony Tatlow rightly points out, in theater "signs are . . . polyfunctional, [and] everything is placed between quotation marks; all signs are denaturalized," because "everything is distanced by its representation."[21]

Paradoxically, despite its intercultural roots and modernization over the years, Chinese opera, rather than the modern *huaju* theater, is still regarded by both its practitioners and their Anglo-European audiences as the ultimate, quintessential representation of Chinese identity, thanks partly to the invention of Beijing opera as national opera (*guoju*) in the early twentieth century. Qi Rushan, Mei Lanfang, and their followers constructed the tradition of national opera, an ideology that posited *jingju* (rather than other regional Chinese opera forms) as the mirror image of Western illusionist theater.[22] Both Chinese and Western artists now deploy Chinese opera as a means to create and meet the demands of the cultural market for nontraditional Shakespeare. The powerful dichotomy between the traditional non-West, represented by *jingju*, and the global West, represented by Shakespeare, has allowed this oppositions to play out in the externalizing, defamiliarizing, and coded movements of the form. Enthusiasts for *xiqu* Shakespeare performances champion the "unfamiliar," differentiated dramaturgies' much coveted capacity to unseat conventionalized readings. This misperception operates in a way similar to that of the stylized Chinese-swordplay period films that Kwai-Cheung Lo has found to be reliant on cultural difference as a marketable feature "for the expansion of the commodification that is aesthetically consumed," turning ethnic difference into a "commodified spectacle."[23] Surely the importation of the foreign has contributions to make, such as liberating what has been repressed at home (that is, within Anglophone Shakespearean performance traditions and within Chinese-opera traditions), but Chinese opera's capacity to challenge the mimetic presuppositions of Shakespearean dramas needs to be reassessed.

Chinese opera across the Sinophone world, like many traditional Asian theater forms, faces fierce competition from television, film, and other forms of live theater (Broadway musicals, *huaju*, etc.). *Xiqu* theater companies are consequently witnessing a dwindling, aging audience. Chinese-opera companies rely on the paradoxical foreignness of Shakespeare and the perceived affinity between Elizabethan-theater and Chinese-opera conventions to repackage their arts for the new cultural market both at home and abroad. They have expanded their repertoire in order to attract younger audience who would otherwise never attend a *xiqu* performance, and secure touring invitations and increase international visibility.

The production and reception of *xiqu* Shakespeare is thus structured around a break with *huaju*-realism and an alternativeness defined by a departure from the "normative" performance styles in the West. The working of *xiqu* Shakespeare relies heavily on the perception of traditional China as an ultimate Other and Shakespeare's text as a constant. Chinese opera is not alone. Western audiences and critics regularly cast other genres of traditional Asian theater as rich in the visual but lacking in linguistic virtuosity, overlooking their arias and literary elements. When Oh Tae-suk's *Romeo and Juliet* (Mokhwa Repertory Company)—performed in *p'ansori* (one-person operetta) and other styles of traditional Korean theater—was staged at the Barbican Centre in London in 2006, the venue reassured its audience that the foreign production did not lose anything from its abandonment of Shakespeare's language: "The performer's physical vocabulary, heightened emotional state and comic timing create a sensual fusion that lacks nothing from the absence of the bard's language."[24] The British reviews also emphasized the sensory power of Asian performance and the pictorial perfection of every scene.

This tendency creates a positive stereotype about what *xiqu* should be and what *xiqu* Shakespeare does, exalting the remedial effect of Asian stylization and Shakespeare's complex characters on each other. The stereotype is not necessarily a simplification of sameness or difference, but a fixated representation of a dynamic exchange that rests on the high production value of the visual aspects of *xiqu*. This partially explains why *xiqu* Shakespeares sometimes receive negative reviews in hometown newspapers but more glowing reviews abroad. As Charles Spencer contends in his somewhat negative review of the 1990 staging of Wu Hsing-kuo's *Kingdom of Desire* in London, it has become almost de rigueur to endorse these unfamiliar spectacles—simply "because it is foreign and strange, . . . it must therefore be good."[25]

The reception of Huang Zuolin's *kunju* Macbeth, *The Story of Bloody Hands* (set in ancient China), is another telling example. Tatlow went to great lengths to make a case for the practical and aesthetic value of the opening scene, involving the transformation of the three witches into two dwarf specters and a taller ghost (all wearing grotesque masks on the back of their heads). While commenting on the 1987 European performance, he draws on Hong Kong and Chinese local specificities to argue for the potential incompatibility of direct translation of Shakespeare's text and *kunju* theater and to stress the practicality of Chinese-opera spectacles:

> I happily accept this spectacular visual effect [in the opening scene] in exchange for Shakespeare's witches' reptilian soup, which was intended, presumably, to invoke moral disgust over a black and fallen nature, . . . but which in fact almost sounds, at least up to "fillet of a fenny snake," or "toe of frog" and "tongue of dog," like a recipe for a style of Cantonese cooking. Here [in China and Hong Kong] nature is not a moral emetic but healthily edible. There is even a suggestion of shark's fin.[26]

His experience with the production leads him to conclude that "Western theatre verbalizes; East Asian theatre visualizes. The Western actor speaks the words; the East Asian actor embodies the codes."[27] Lois Potter's review echoes this general sentiment and what I have called positive stereotyping. Amazed by its "spectacular theatrical possibilities," she writes: "Whereas Shakespeare's play keeps most 'real' events offstage, [the *kunju Macbeth*] is almost pure spectacle. It shows everything except the murder of Duncan and even that is so audible that the royal physician rushes off to tell the heir-apparent to escape. . . . We are not asked to assume an ultimate reality behind what we see."[28] Part of that ultimate reality seems to be connected to Shakespeare's text that is invisible in the spectacle, making *kunju* a "fatal vision" in the international circulation of Shakespeare and Chinese opera, to borrow Macbeth's own words.[29]

The Chinese reception of the production is a different story. Conservative Chinese Shakespearean scholars at a forum held at the 1986 Shakespeare Festival in Shanghai questioned whether the spectacle in the ancient form of *kunju* could adequately represent the themes and contents of *Macbeth*. It was still widely held by Chinese critics that *huaju*—a form with closer affinity to the Western naturalistic theater—is a more effective and appropriate genre for performing Shakespeare. In the view of those who were against *xiqu* Shakespeare, this *kunju* performance had "devoured Shakespeare."[30]

Both the emphasis on the visual dimension of *kunju Macbeth* in Western reception and the ideology-driven reception in China seem to be controlled by notions derived from textual analysis (as in how closely the visual realizes Shakespeare's text). In recent studies, the relationship between Shakespeare's text and its stage representation has been connected to Shakespeare's viability. Some critics champion the adaptability of Shakespeare as evidence of Shakespeare's universality and supreme artistic achievement, limiting the performative possibilities of Shakespearean drama to "the delicacy of its texture," allusions, and metrical refinement.[31] Other critics theorize that this is the result of the penetrating power of alien signifying practices.[32] Printed text provides the illusion of a sense of closure, while visual clues sans text, as it were, tend to suggest open-ended questions.[33] It is unfortunate that the ideological investments in Chinese opera's visuality have turned *xiqu* into a system of signification antithetical to *huaju* and verbalization.

"Ocular Proof": A Black Chinese General in Beijing

While one may expect that most *xiqu* productions would not, or cannot, follow the *huaju* practice of doing "straight" performances of

Shakespeare in transplanted Western style (as in having Chinese actors wear wigs and prosthetic noses and retaining the character names and setting), some *xiqu* performers refused to localize Shakespeare. A representative *xiqu* production of this period is Ma Yong'an's *Aosailuo* (*Othello*, 1983), in which he blackened his face to play the title character.[34] The *jingju* production was aiming at racial impersonation, although it did not engage the Moorish subtext. Ma's black makeup was worn not as part of the convention in *jingju* but as a sign of racial difference. It is innovative not only because it is an entirely new facial pattern modeled on but not derived from *xiqu* aesthetics, but also because it is one of the earliest attempts for *jingju* practitioners to engage at length the notion of racial otherness through a black character.

Already an established *jingju* actor specializing in the "painted face" (*hualian*) role type, Ma was a household name throughout China.[35] He was widely known for his performance of the lead character, Lei Gang, in one of the revolutionary model plays, *Azalea Mountain* (*Dujuan shan*), during the Cultural Revolution. Flaunting his star power, Ma spearheaded the *Othello* project. Even though he and other actors of his fellow Cultural Revolution generation had played many unconventional *xiqu* roles in modern attire (without long opera sleeves or traditional makeup), his experiment with *Othello* still sent shockwaves through the *xiqu* and *huaju* scenes in China.[36]

Two factors contributed to Ma's fascination with *Othello*. When he was sixteen, he saw a Soviet film of *Othello* screened in Beijing and was intrigued by the complexities of the principal characters, especially Othello.[37] He saw Sergei Bondarchuk's performance of Othello in the film directed by Sergei Yutkevitch.[38] Ma was transfixed by the film's opening sequence of war on the high seas—with visualization of Othello's adventures as he tells Desdemona his stories—which concludes with Othello and Desdemona's wedding in a church. From that time onward, he developed a sustained interest in Shakespeare's plays. Second, Ma yearned to transcend his limits. As he put it,

> The biggest challenge to me, a person trained in the *hualian* role type, is to bring out the delicate emotions and sensitivity of a seemingly rough and masculine character like Othello. As an actor specializing in the *hualian* role type, I was used to enacting rough, militant, and quick-tempered characters such as generals, soldiers, or court officials. The love between Othello and Desdemona needs to

be carefully developed, so that the audience can relate to their situations later on in the tragedy.[39]

His performance did not disappoint the audience.

Before the curtain rose, music with a mixture of *jingju* and Western brass and wind resonance was heard. The music was familiar to the audience who saw the revolutionary model plays. *Jingju* percussion soon followed, announcing the arrival of eight soldiers each holding a tambourine. The martial dance consisted of somersaults, crouching steps, and other *jingju* martial movements. At the height of theatrical energy created by the music and the dance, the duke and his court officials arrived, discussing Othello's victory. Accompanied by Cassio and Iago, Othello entered in full medieval European armor with his face painted dark. He also wore a curled black wig, which was to be replaced by a gray wig at a later point. Iago (a *qiguan* [flag officer]) held a large flag as a visual representation of his rank and duty. In this rich landscape, Othello narrated a prologue following the traditional *jingju* practice known as *zibao jiamen* (reporting one's name and family origin). Thus opened the *jingju*-style *Othello* in Beijing to great acclaim.[40] Ma's production can be regarded as a new milestone for both Chinese Shakespeares and *xiqu* theater, because it is one of the few *xiqu* productions of Shakespeare that did not localize the setting, plot, or characters' names.

That said, Ma's decision to blacken his face to play Othello must give us pause (figure 18). His performance carries radically different meanings from those of an English-language production in which a white actor (most notably Laurence Olivier) blackens his face to play Othello. Star power and verisimilitude, among other factors, are at work in Ma's *Othello* to produce an exotic, or authentically fake, spectacle. His production handles the racial question rather differently from that of the National Asian-American Theatre (2000). In a literal sense, the spotlight has zoomed in on Ma's stylization and what happens when "Beijing opera meets Shakespeare" (a widely appropriated slogan in the publicity gimmicks and newspaper reviews) to such an extent that it sidestepped other questions such as racial difference that are usually associated with postcolonial productions of *Othello*. "Blacking up" may be uncommon in *xiqu* theater, but until the 1980s *huaju* actors frequently whitened up and wore prosthetic noses and wigs to play white roles in Shakespeare's plays. It should be noted that since black people have often been discriminated against in China, as studies of racial discourse have shown, it is one thing

FIGURE 18   Ma Yong'an as Othello in a *jingju* production of *Othello*, directed by Zheng Bixian, Beijing, 1983. (Courtesy of Ma Yong'an)

to play the part of a white character, and quite another to play a black person.[41] Chinese student actors blackened their faces to play "black slaves" in the Spring Willow Society's (Chunliu she) landmark *huaju* performance of *The Black Slave's Cry to Heaven* (*Heinu yu tian lu*, 1907), based on Lin Shu's popular translation of Harriet Beecher Stowe's *Uncle Tom's Cabin*.[42]

Unlike in China, where the artists and scholars take for granted the colorblind casting in Shakespearean performance, in the United States, where "the systematic practice of nontraditional or colorblind casting began with Joseph Papp's New York Shakespeare Festival in the 1950s," the practice has remained the center of fervent debates.[43] Whereas some actors and critics applaud the practice's potential to dismantle racial and cultural essentialism, the famous black playwright August Wilson condemns the practice for its blindness to inequality: "Colorblind casting is an aberrant idea that has never had any validity other than as a tool of the Cultural Imperialist."[44] Not so in China, at least in the eyes of the practitioners and the audience. Rather than highlighting racial issues (both in the plays and on stage where the Chinese played white roles), cross-racial casting in China was done in the spirit of transplanting imaginaries of Western realities—repetition with a difference. Colorblind casting refers to the practice of casting an actor in a role of any race. Far from being "blind" to racial difference, the practice often accentuates it, as evidenced by Ma's appearance on stage with full racial trappings, including a wig and blackened face, and by the early Hollywood practice of casting white actors in Chinese roles with slanted eyes and a braided queue. What motivated Ma's venture in theater? A quick answer might have to do with the unavailability of black *jingju* actors in mainland China. But Ma's ideological and aesthetic investments in the project invites speculation.

Mainland Chinese scholars Faye Fei and William Sun conjectured that what stood out in *Othello* as a more socially relevant topic in the early 1980s was perhaps "the issue of marriage between people of different social backgrounds." Othello's changing status "as a result of his extraordinary military merits, his marriage to a nobleman's daughter, and the insecurity and jealousy that emerge later were all situations that would resonate with Chinese theatregoers" as the society emerged from the Cultural Revolution, a time when the Communist Party closely guarded against social mobility.[45] However, the marriage dramatized in *Othello* is not between "people of different social backgrounds," but a radical one between people of different races. As evidenced by Ma's, Fei's, and Sun's reactions, mainland Chinese directors and critics tend to ignore the issue of race in performance. It was not until 1995 that foreign actors of the same race as the characters appeared on the Chinese stage, an unprecedented event in Chinese theater. In his *huaju* production of *Student Wife* (*Peidu furen*) in Shanghai, Yu Luosheng cast American actor Robert Daly in the role of Jordan and put Basia Wajs, a Polish exchange student in Shanghai, in the role of Lucia Speare.[46] Non-Chinese actors also appeared in Chinese television miniseries.

For Chinese artists and audiences of the 1980s, only a few short years after the end of the inward-looking Cultural Revolution, it was a different story. The racial difference between Othello and Desdemona did not seem so great; much energy was still directed toward the divide between China and the non-Chinese—a catch-all category for the foreign. As Ania Loomba notes in a different context, "the theatre is a place that allows— indeed, demands—the transformation of identities, but in actual practice such transformations have been carefully policed, especially with regard to Shakespeare's plays."[47] Loomba observes that in many non-Western countries, such as India, "a species of colorblind casting of Shakespearean plays is more in evidence, but casting practices are still shaped by social hierarchies."[48] Unlike theaters in India, the hierarchy at work in Ma's production was star power and the cultural capital of Shakespeare and *jingju*.

In Ma's performance, arias, stylized gestures, and foreign characters dominated the visible and palpable world of theater, while the racial and cultural identities of the Moor, Desdemona, and the Chinese actors embodying these characters were sidestepped. Ma remained undisturbed by the issues of racial conflict within and without Shakespeare's text. His *Aosailuo* stages cultural differences (although not necessarily racial difference) in physical terms, often in a hybrid form of *jingju* and *huaju* that "translates" poetic dialogues and complex verbal metaphors. The actors don semi-European costumes and walk the stage in coded steps and gestures. All characters and locales of the original play are presented in transliterations (for example, Aosailuo for Othello) without being localized into Chinese counterparts or consolidated into Asian equivalents.

Conceived, spearheaded, and performed by Ma, an already famous *jingju* actor, the *jingju Othello* inspired many directors and actors of traditional Chinese theater to recast Shakespeare's characters and stories, which led to a major revival of the playwright in the first Chinese Shakespeare Festival three years later, in 1986. Kuang Jianlian (stage name Hongxian Nü) of the Guangdong-based Yueju Theatre Company was one actor/director who was greatly inspired to begin working on her *yueju* (Cantonese-opera) *Merchant of Venice*. Ma was aware of the impact of his production. During my interview with him, he proudly referred to his *Othello* as "the first *jingju* Shakespeare since the establishment of the People's Republic of China in 1949."

Ma, although proud of the art to which he devoted his life until his retirement in 1996, has also been struck by theater's limitations and decadence. He began training in the *jingju* role type of *hualian* in 1952 under the tutelage of three masters: Hao Shouchen, Luan Xiaochen, and Hou Xirui. Accordingly, he is well versed and proficient at enacting villainous characters. The character of a general with ambiguous and controversial characteristics like Othello, according to Ma, is attractive to a seasoned actor proficient in an art form that requires delivery of psychological depth from outward gestures and codes rather than from inward drills of his psyche. Most importantly, it provided Ma the opportunity to break away from the tradition and discipline of his masters.

Aosailuo has a prologue and seven acts, with the main plotline focusing on the relationships among Othello, Iago, and Desdemona.[49] Ma exploited the color symbolism of white and black, the pure and the tainted. The backdrop was lit with blue light. The light and the wave patterns on the costumes conveyed a sense of the setting: Venice and Cyprus, two islands surrounded by the sea. However, in act 6, the backdrop turned red when Othello decided to kill Desdemona. Othello then compared the color of the sunset to the blood of Desdemona:

> OTHELLO: Iago, look, what is that?
> IAGO: The sunset.
> OTHELLO: No, it is not the sunset. It is blood, blood! It is Desde-
> mona's blood, Cassio's blood, and my enemies' blood! If you
> deceive me, it will be your blood, too. . . . By Heaven in great
> reverence, I swear, if I cannot revenge such great humilia-
> tion, I will no longer go on living in this world.[50]

This scene corresponds to act 3, scene 3, of *Othello*, where Othello re-veals his "bloody thoughts" (3.3.457) to Iago. Othello appeals to "black vengeance." He shouts frantically: "O blood, blood, blood!" (3.3.451). Ma's performance highlighted the physical dimension of color symbolism and metaphors.

Ma also explored the function of such tokens as the handkerchief, which was the primary symbol running throughout his production. In a scene that corresponded to act 3, scene 4, of the original, Othello asked Desdemona to "lend [him] [her] handkerchief" (3.4.52). Desdemona pro-duced a handkerchief, and Othello happily received it without even look-ing at it. He grasped Desdemona's hands, and then turned and walked away to smile to himself. As soon as Othello started fumbling with the handkerchief, he realized that the handkerchief was not the one he gave Desdemona. His facial expression was as dramatic as the heightened percussion beats, culminating in the strike of a gong. Othello threw the handkerchief away and shouted at Desdemona: "Where is the handker-chief?" The handkerchief as a physical token was featured prominently in this production. Every time it appeared, it developed the motif of love and jealousy. It also helped develop the plot. The physical presence of the handkerchief and the actors' interaction with it constituted a nonver-bal transformation, the "ocular proof" (3.3.360), of the theme of the play. *Othello* became as much a show for the eyes as a show for the ears. In-stead of hearing it reported, the audience saw Othello giving the handker-chief to Desdemona and vowing his love. Philip Brockbank recalled that "the tragedy of the handkerchief was rendered more poignant by Othello

FIGURE 19   Ma Yong'an as Othello in Western costume. (Courtesy of Ma Yong'an)

momentarily pausing in wonder and delight before breaking down on the line."[51]

A special feature of this *jingju*-style *Othello* was its use of pseudo-Western costume and nontraditional makeup (figure 19). Sporting a short curled wig, a blackened face cloaked in a black velvet mantle, and a pair of white *jingju* boots with thick soles, Ma made his first appearance on stage with operatic poses (*liangxiang*). The original opening scene, in which Iago and Roderigo wake Brabantio to the news that "an old black ram / is tupping [his] white ewe" (1.1.88–89), was replaced by Othello pronouncing a prologue that establishes his credentials. The prologue about Othello's military prowess was in keeping with the *xiqu* tradition of opening a play with a monologue. With a compelling delivery of his lines, stylized gestures, and eye movements, Ma gave a gripping and energetic performance as the tragic hero.

Ma's insistence on preserving both the local theater form and the narratives of Shakespeare's *Othello* may make one wonder whether he encountered any difficulty in the creative process. Ma used transliteration of names of characters (Othello as Aosailuo) and line-by-line translations of selected passages from *Othello,* so as to "be as close to the *original* as possible," because he believes that this is the only way to do Shakespeare in *jingju*. Otherwise, the play would be "merely adopting some Shakespearean plots," which is not compatible with his vision of a *jingju*-style *Othello*. Ma reasoned that if he were to rewrite *Othello* as a Chinese story and perform it in Chinese costume, he could simply stage a play from the traditional *jingju* repertoire. He said, "We often see foreign films with Chinese dubbing," which never come across as awkward, "so why can't I use *jingju* to 'dub' a Shakespearean play?"

Ma defended his choice of costume along with the decision to retain all foreign names in the play. As it turned out, for Ma, the preservation of foreign names or the invention of Chinese counterparts was not an issue at all. The curled wig and blackened face seemed more than sufficient to physically and visibly indicate cultural differences for him. The costumes took on a hybrid form of Chinese patterns set in a generic European medieval layout. The stage settings were simple and included a backdrop embroidered with the patterns of sun and moon and a line of rolling waves in shades of blue outlined by silver. Waves and patterns of whirling clouds connected the geocultural location of Venice and Othello's adventures. He found a functional similarity between Othello's supposedly military outfit and traditional *jingju* martial-arts costume. Othello's blue mantle, which resembled a style used in *jingju,* was useful when the scene called for swaying actions. Desdemona's white wedding gown was a strong visual contrast to the dark-complexioned Othello in silver armor. In Ma's color scheme, the white gown also implied death and bereavement. After Ma's *Othello* was staged, he won praise and recognition from Chen Haosu, the vice-mayor of Beijing. Chen's comment that Ma's *Othello* had enacted "a hero beguiled, a beauty victimized" with "exotic mood rendered in Chinese air" aptly summarized the reception of the production.

Presenting a Shakespearean play in the Western style dubbed by the *jingju* idioms involves a collaborative process. One of his most important collaborators, Sun Jiaxiu, a renowned senior professor of English literature based in Beijing, led numerous discussion sessions with Ma and his actors to prepare them for the "ultimate Shakespeare experience." Almost all Chinese-opera performances of Shakespeare are produced in this collaborative style. In such a format, the project is usually spearheaded by a devoted actor or director who aspires to cross generic and cultural boundaries. The Chinese translation, then, is chosen together with a senior Chinese Shakespeare scholar, and amended or complemented by an adaptor who is conversant in the particular performing style. The actors, sometimes even directors, rarely have access to the play in its English original, which sometimes forms an obstacle to their hope to present an "authentic" Shakespeare in its "original sauce and flavor." Their projects to stage Shakespeare in a stylized theater were a bilateral process that necessarily revised both Shakespeare's text and the *xiqu* conventions.

The *xiqu* and *huaju* genres converged in Ma's performance. Compared with the task of conveying psychological conflicts within each of the characters, keeping the plot and characters in their original setting was relatively simple. In the making of such a production involving a *huaju* director and a group of *jingju* actors, conflicts between representational practices occurred often. As *xiqu* traditionally does not have a director in the sense of a Western stage play but relies on the percussionist in the orchestra for rhythm and pace, it is not unusual to bring in a *huaju* director for a nonrepertoire *xiqu* play. While Ma conceived the project, he needed a director to give the performance a coherent style. The director, Zheng Bixian, was a graduate of the Central Academy of Drama in Beijing and was trained in the Stanislavskian system.[52] Naturally, she had a very different idea from Ma of presenting the scenes. The conflict between Zheng's and Ma's approaches is characteristic of performances of Shakespeare in the 1980s that attempted to blend *xiqu* and *huaju* conventions.

A case in point is the scene in which Othello sees and reacts to the "ocular proof" that Iago arranges for him. Being led on by Iago, Othello is prompted into believing that Desdemona is having an affair with his subordinate, Cassio. Zheng insisted that Cassio and Desdemona should be present in this scene and that Othello should wave a sword, for "how [else] could the audience know at whom Othello is 'thrusting his sword?'" However, Ma insisted on performing on a bare stage in accordance with *jingju* conventions. They agreed to not having Desdemona present and to use fake rocks instead. Ma was instructed by Zheng to hack at the stone as a physical expression of his anger. In rehearsal on an empty stage, Ma tried to project his illusions, doubt, and jealousy onto the stone. However, Ma found this style to be in conflict with the essential power of *jingju* to conjure up visions from the void.

Eventually, Ma got rid of the stone and acted on an empty stage. Supplemented by his expression in *jingju* gestures, Ma used a swaying dance in which he "saw" illusions from all directions in order to project his jealousy and anger in the scene. The mantle in this scene took on great effect, as did small movements and gestures that signified hesitation and uneasiness. Othello saw Cassio giving the handkerchief to a prostitute, a scene

arranged by Iago to persuade the already confounded Othello that Desdemona had been unfaithful. Appalled by the sight, Ma's Othello did not
express his extreme anger in grand movements, but froze on stage and
used silence and the absence of action to deliver the shock, which he took
as "most difficult *onstage*, since *actors* have been trained to *act*." Nonmove-
ment and the absence of lines effectively dominated the stage. Othello
then asked for poison but was discouraged by Iago, who encouraged
him instead to smother Desdemona in bed. At this suggestion, Othello
opened his eyes widely, staring into the void as if his mind itself had been
poisoned and possessed by Iago. Ma Yong'an used *jingju* conventions to
represent a character and dramatic situation unknown to the genre. This,
in turn, engendered new *jingju* performing idioms, especially nonmove-
ment, which Ma admitted was a very difficult choice. His training and the
conventions of *jingju* required him to sing and, most importantly, to *act*
according to specific sets of steps and gestures for specific *jingju* characters. The tensions in Othello's mind and between Othello and other characters became pretexts for innovations in an art form that traditionally
demands kinetic representation of the psyche of the characters.

Like most Chinese-opera performances of Shakespeare, Ma's *Othello*
assigned characters to the preexisting role types. While Othello was cast
in *hualian*, as expected, Iago was not cast in the *bailian* (white-face *jing*
role type), as is expected for crafty villains. Instead, he was cast in the
role type of *laosheng* (male character "generally over thirty and wearing
three-part beards"), since he was conceived of as a villain covering himself
up with moralizing language.[53] This made Iago a far more complicated
villain than he would have been as a *bailian*. As for Ma, he also blended a
difficult element into the Othello he portrayed in *hualian* onstage. In the
last scene, Ma sang Othello's lines to the "crying tune," which is such a
challenge for most *hualian* actors that most plays avoid incorporating it.
It is a challenge because *hualian* actors specialize in completely different
sets of arias that are more "heroic" and masculine. Before smothering
Desdemona as she lay sideways on a bed, Othello sang in this weeping
mode while looking toward an imaginary oil lamp:

OTHELLO (*sings*): Oh, your body is as white as snow, as pretty as a
    goddess.
  Let me extinguish this bright lamp.
  I will then extinguish the torch in your life.

. . .

I have plucked the rose, and it will only wither.

I can never restore your beauty.

Oh, I cannot restore your life.

I want to smell her sweet breath when she is still in blossom.

The fragrance and the sweet smell.

I will kill you.

Kill you first and then love you.[54]

Although this aria corresponds to Othello's soliloquy in act 5, scene 2 (lines 1–19), in the original version, only the metaphors of snow, rose, and "Desdemona's light," which translated into concrete images, were preserved, and allusive metaphors like "Promethean heat" (5.2.12) and "monumental alabaster" (5.2.5) were eliminated. Othello's aria was assisted by the music, percussion beats, and Ma's quick movement and rolling of his eyes.[55] The line "I will kill you" accentuated Othello's movement toward Desdemona.

The play ended with swaying physical actions on the part of Othello. The final confrontation between Othello and Iago was cut out, a choice that directed the focus toward the general. Ma stressed that "in *jingju* I could perform whatever my mind sees, not what my eyes see. That is drama, where we can do things that cannot be done in daily life."[56]

The *jingju*-style *Othello* was revived at the First International Chinese Shakespeare Festival in 1986, where twenty productions of fifteen Shakespearean tragedies and comedies were staged by a variety of theater companies ranging from *huaju* to Chinese-opera and puppet-theater companies. There, Ma Yong'an's *Othello* was in sharp contrast with Huang Zuolin's *kunju Macbeth*, which claimed to employ "authentic" *kunju* costumes and techniques.

Shifting Boundaries Between *Xiqu* and *Huaju*

Ma Yong'an's production counters the ideological take on traditional Chinese theater's cultural identity that defines what *xiqu* is or is not in relation to *huaju* and Western realist theater. Ma's performance also participated in the discourse of theater reform. The 1980s were an intriguing period in Chinese cultural history, as they were filled with

official political discourses on China's policy of openness and determination to rejoin the world, as well as a wide spectrum of unofficial
counter-discourses. The politics in the theater of this decade, also commonly known as the post-Mao era, have received greater attention than
the development of the new expressive modes, such as the combination
of traditional *jingju* movements, pseudo-European costumes, and the fusion of *chuanju* masks and *kunju* dance. No less important than the use
of the Western Other for political liberation is the use of the Western text
to liberate Chinese performing idioms from decades of suppression. The
meanings of Soviet-influenced Shakespeare performance in China, for
instance, were mediated by the political positions of its Chinese censors
and its audience.

As China entered a new era after Mao's death and the end of the Cultural Revolution, the 1980s witnessed a shift of emphasis from political
positioning to artistic innovation. Shakespeare was less frequently filtered
by local politics; instead, Shakespeare was filtered by the aesthetic principles of Chinese theater. Jiang Qing's "reformation" of *jingju* and her
creation of "revolutionary model theater" during the Cultural Revolution
had tyrannically suppressed the activities and development of many
forms of traditional theater for over a decade. Audiences and performers
yearned to expand the repertoire and performing genres beyond the limit
of model revolutionary plays and ballets. Theatrical experimentation and
the desire for artistic variety were officially encouraged by Deng Xiaoping, Mao Zedong's successor. Deng's program to modernize China re-
pudiated Jiang's rebuff of all things foreign. On October 30, 1979, Deng
championed such slogans as "Let foreign things serve China [*yang wei
Zhong yong*]" and "Let ancient things serve the moderns [*gu wei jin yong*]"
in his congratulatory remarks at the Fourth Chinese Literary and Artistic Workers' Congress in Beijing.[57] In addition to Deng's encouraging
message, the end of the ten years of repression of theater (1966–1976)
also contributed to the revival of all types of regional traditional theaters
in the 1980s. Performers were ready to take back the stage. After the
dominance of "revolutionary" nonrepertory plays for the Chinese-opera
stage during the Cultural Revolution, the traditional theater in post-
Mao China was more receptive to staging nonrepertory plays, including
contemporary plays and rewrites of Western classics. After all, if ballet,
symphonic music, and contemporary costumes have been widely used
in the revolutionary model theater—an amalgamated form of *jingju* and
other Western theatrical elements—then why couldn't regional stylized

theaters experiment with new role types, acting styles, and performance texts?[58]

In this new environment, one would have expected the theater business to thrive and have devoted audiences, when, in fact, most theater companies suffered from low attendance. Several factors—such as the sudden availability of color television sets, the popularity of new forms of entertainment such as disco music and ballroom dancing, and the lack of financial incentive among the actors—contributed to this "depression." As part of Deng's modernization project, the theater companies had to move toward commercialization and bear financial responsibilities. This modernization project generated its own difficulties, and it produced among theater circles a common saying: "Stage more, lose more; stage less, lose less; stage none, lose nothing."[59] While the theater companies of the 1950s had performed under strict political censorship but without financial pressure, in the 1980s they had to bear financial responsibilities and live up to the challenge of the new decade: finding their audiences. The relatively "liberated" ideologies in the post-Mao era did not translate into financial stability for theaters. The system of compensation, in particular, did not work well with the move toward commercialization. Actors of similar age, background, and rank were paid on the same scale regardless of talent and achievement. There was no incentive for actors to improve their skills. An actor who did not perform in the entire month would get paid the same salary as a more talented and devoted actor who acted every night if they belonged to the same rank.[60]

A new wave of reformation of the traditional theater emerged to answer this crisis. Many directors resorted to foreign plays and combinations of performing styles in the hope of attracting audiences. The motivations for theatrical reform gradually shifted from political to artistic and commercial ones. As a result, *huaju* was no longer the only "legitimate" and privileged genre in which to perform Shakespeare.[61] Theater tickets were affordable, and most productions appealed to a wider range of audience than students of Western literature or intellectuals.[62] Moreover, Shakespeare's plays were no longer confined to Mandarin *huaju* productions in large cities like Beijing and Shanghai. In the late 1970s and early 1980s, a volume of Shakespeare's plays sold over 720,000 copies, more than such popular traditional Chinese novels as *Journey to the West (Xiyou ji)*.[63]

As the division between the *huaju* and *xiqu* modes became less rigid, many *huaju* and *xiqu* directors collaborated, which proved to be another crucial step in artistic development during this period. Huang Zuolin, an important *huaju* director, used a minimalist stage set in a rendition of *Romeo and Juliet* that he codirected with Zhuang Zejing and Ji Qiming in 1980.[64] Interestingly, no scene changes occurred, and the curtain was never used in this *huaju* production. Huang turned away from the elaborate, realistic scenography prevalent in *huaju* performances and used lighting to signal scene changes. Time and space were treated flexibly, and actors performed on an almost empty stage,[65] elements that are more typically features of *xiqu* performances. Huang's *kunju*-style *Macbeth* (*The Story of the Bloody Hands* [*Xieshou ji*], 1986) was an experiment of what he called *"xieyi"* (imagistic or ideographic) theater, incorporating principles from Stanislavsky and Mei Lanfang.[66]

Another example of the fusion of *huaju* and *xiqu* modes is a 1981 production of *Romeo and Juliet*. The Shanghai Theatre Academy produced a Tibetan-language *Romeo and Juliet* with nine performances in Shanghai and Lhasa.[67] This *huaju* production incorporated stylized movements from *xiqu*. It did not emphasize the dialogue, as the name of its genre suggests; rather, the director deployed devices commonly used in *xiqu* to convey tensions. Nonverbal representations of the psyche of the characters are worked into a prolonged dancing scene (the ball scene, 1.5) where Romeo met Juliet for the first time. When Romeo discovered the presence of Juliet, the actors on stage stopped dancing abruptly and formed a *tableau vivant*. Critics regularly compared this device to a snapshot in film, although this practice is also found in *xiqu*. The only actor moving at this point was the actor playing Romeo. He knelt before Juliet and said: "How beautiful! . . . She is charming even standing among the goddesses." Romeo roamed the stage, looked at the frozen dancers, and compared Juliet with other characters by walking up and taking a close look at each of them. Then the music came on, and the dancing scene came back alive. When Juliet saw Romeo, the same device was used again, and Juliet danced alone in front of the *tableau vivant* to express the theme of "love at first sight."[68] Such a concept of visual realism changes dramatically in *xiqu* performances that aim at a different type of verisimilitude.

Chinese-opera productions of Shakespeare went on to fascinate with ever more diverse faces and forms. A striking example was a solo performance of *Macbeth* that was presented solely from the perspective of Lady Macbeth and through her recollection of past events, including the murders. Tian Mansha's solo Sichuan-opera (*chuanju*) *Who's Knocking* adopted a visual approach to translate inner tensions. Tian later developed this short sequence into *Lady Macbeth*, which is also a solo performance.[69] The production toured Bremen (2001), Berlin (2006), and else-where. Tian's *Macbeth* could not be said to be a solo performance in the strict sense of the genre, because Lady Macbeth was not the only character on stage. Zhao Wenxue played a dumb Macbeth, functioning as a prop onto which Lady Macbeth projected her thoughts, anger, fear, and anxiety. There were also other actors on stage. All of them played nonspeaking parts, forming *tableaux vivants* in some scenes but "props" in others. In the sleepwalking scene, some fifteen women in white robes joined hands in circles to form huge tubs on stage. Some tubs were formed by three actresses, while others were formed by five. Lady Macbeth moved from one tub to another, frantically washing her hands in these tubs. The stage was dark, but a cold blue light illuminated Lady Macbeth and the human tubs. Throughout this scene, codified movements transformed the water sleeves (*shuixiu;* long, flimsy silken sleeves stitched to each of the cuffs) of the women into water and ghosts. Lady Macbeth conveyed her fear of the ghosts of people she had murdered through the movements of her water sleeves and eyes in the dreamy landscape of human tubs that seemed to be ready to devour her. To create this solo performance, Tian had to incorporate elements from different theatrical genres, such as *huaju* lighting and narrating techniques that depend on the presence of props or *tableaux vivants*. Tian jumped at the opportunity to "bring Sichuan opera to the world through Shakespeare" and to reinvent the genre she professed.[70] Her motive to put Shakespeare to work for Chinese opera was shared by many Chinese directors and actors.

While the lure of the global cultural marketplace looms large, *xiqu*'s local audience—old and new—has not been forgotten. Several months before Wu Hsing-kuo and his Contemporary Legend Theatre staged their fourth adaptation of Shakespeare, *The Tempest* (December 30, 2004), they devised a series of visually oriented interactive activities for potential audiences to increase exposure.[71] One of the salient features of this production is its involvement of potential audiences at an early planning stage. Four different stories were published on the Web site of the Contemporary Legend Theatre, where audiences were able to cast votes for their favorite version until June 10, 2004. The four versions were "Twelve Chapters of Prospero's Magic," narrated from Prospero's perspective; "The Uninhabited Island of Caliban," with the half-human, half-beast "aboriginal" as the protagonist; "A Marvelous Voyage," narrated by King Alonso; and "The Mythical Magician," which focuses on the idea that "the world is a stage."[72] The version that received the most votes was staged (figure

FIGURE 20   Zhu Anli as Ariel in *The Tempest*, directed by Tsui Hark, Contemporary Legend Theatre, 2004. (Courtesy of Contemporary Legend Theatre, Taipei)

20). The tensions between the aboriginals and Taiwanese as well as the post-1949 immigrants in Taiwan—that is, the "present" of the audience's world—became the "stage" that framed the world of *The Tempest*. Through the interaction with the audience prior to the performance, "Shakespeare" was no longer a "Western" cultural icon but a provider of "outsourced" raw materials for an evening of visual adventure in *jingju*.

Coda

As more and more *xiqu* productions emerged, a fruitful conversation also began to take place between *xiqu* and *huaju*. To the global spectator, *xiqu* performances of Shakespeare radically defamiliarize what may have been held as the core idea of a particular Shakespeare play. A group of American student-actors responded enthusiastically to Ma Yong'an's *Othello* when they were shown its video during a performance workshop at Tufts University in 1994. The workshop director, William Sun, reported that the participants believed the production "was more effective in expressing certain characters' emotions than the naturalist [*huaju*] mode."[73] To the audience versed in traditional *xiqu* practices, such theater works destablize their fixated notion of what stylization can achieve. Reflecting on the boom of *xiqu* Shakespeares in the 1980s, Yi Kai, a Chinese theater critic, wrote:

> Since the opening up of our closed social and economic structure, our national spirit has changed from static to fluid, people's aesthetic concerns . . . and theatre-going habits changed from the collective to the individualized. . . . A profound, all-around reform has been going on slowly but surely within the traditional Chinese theatre circles. It is no coincidence that traditional Chinese theatre productions of Shakespeare have come along.[74]

Although the psychological dimension of dramatic conflicts is represented on stage by stylized expressions that are not normally associated with the speeches, the relationship between text and performance is not a linear one. While linguistic codes communicate "meanings" faster and gestural codes move more slowly between the sender and the receiver of the message, the physical realization of metaphors is more memorable and impressive. One might expect the linguistic codes to be more precise and gestural codes open to a wider range of interpretations. However, Ma's *Othello* shows that stylized Shakespeares can precisely define and express the range of emotions.

These brief recapitulations of key moments on the *xiqu* stage show how Shakespeare's plays functioned in Chinese opera and how Chinese opera has been transformed through its encounters with *huaju* and Shakespeare. The monopolizing political ideologies and dominating agenda to "strengthen China" in the former decades had faded. Shakespeare continues to be the most popular foreign playwright on the twenty-first-century Chinese stage. As China occupies a transitional, multiply determined space, the differing faces of Chinese Shakespeare signal the arrival of multiple forms to engage a global text and local consciousness in the new Asia that is in formation.

Xiqu Shakespeares consciously mobilize cultural differences to create new performing styles. Both Ma Yong'an and Huang Zuolin lay claims on authenticity. They claim that they have created the most authentic Shakespeare and the most authentic *kunju,* respectively. But it remains clear that what they created are new *jingju* and *kunju* bearing their individual marks as artists, not duplicates of authentic texts or a priori forms of Chinese opera. In the new millennium, the shift from seeking authenticity to privileging artistic subjectivity becomes more evident.

The fusion of *xiqu* and *huaju* elements and the confrontation between Shakespeare and *xiqu* force us to reexamine the connections and disjunctions between visual and verbal signs, and between Western and Chinese theaters. On the one hand, as Shu-mei Shih observes, "[the subtitled, annotated, translinguistic] visual work seems to have a lower linguistic threshold and hence is more easily decipherable and consumable across geocultural spaces."[75] On the other hand, the international interest in Chinese-opera Shakespeares is symptomatic of what W. J. T. Mitchell calls the "pictorial turn" in postmodern, spectatorial culture.[76] While, as Stuart Hall theorizes, the global mass culture "remains centered in the West" and always speaks English, Chinese Shakespeares in the global cultural marketplace appropriate the currency of Asian visuality to various ends— textual, theatrical, and cultural.[77]

The fusion of Chinese opera and Shakespeare compels us to question what we assume to be the metaphysical dimension of text, a print-derived ideology, and the kinetic energy of the visual. This reorientation illuminates the politics of aesthetic forms that initiated distinctively personal engagements with Shakespeare in the 1990s.

7 Disowning Shakespeare and China

At center stage stands a dispirited King Lear, who has just taken off his *jingju* (Beijing-opera) headdress and armor costume in full view of a packed audience. Following his powerful presentation of the scene of the mad Lear in the storm and on-stage costume change, the actor—now dressed as if he were backstage—interrogates himself and the eyeless headdress in a somber moment while touching his own eyes, evoking Gloucester's blinding and the Lacanian gaze in a play about sight and truth.[1] "Who am I?" he asks. "Doth any here know me? This is not Lear. / Doth Lear walk thus? speak thus? Where are his eyes?" (1.4.226–27). Here, the performer is self-conscious of the ways in which his own eyes become Lear's eyes.[2]

These two pairs of eyes represent the necessary split many performers experience on stage, a process of making null the performer's self-identity so that he or she becomes the part being performed. This scene complicates the popular understanding of acting in traditional Chinese theater. Innovative interpretations of himself as a character, a dog, and other *King Lear* characters ensues onstage—ten, to be exact. But what is singular about this performance is the presence of Wu Hsing-kuo, his production's cast of one.[3]

Presented by the Lincoln Center Festival and produced by Taiwan's Contemporary Legend Theatre (founded by Wu in 1986), this perfor- mance—titled *Lear Is Here*—took place at the Rose Theatre in New York on the evening of July 12, 2007, with revisions of its earlier incarnations.[4] As a performance where the intellectual met the corporeal, the produc- tion concluded with a meditative scene with Wu in a Buddhist monastic robe, playing an ambiguous role (as himself, as Lear's ghost, as a tran- scendent being, or as a personification of the *jingju* tradition in crisis), evoking again the discursive richness between the performer's conflict- ing identities on- and offstage. Wu's gesture called to mind Gloucester in an earlier scene set in Dover. Wu played the blind Gloucester, who "looked" to Dover as a site for his redemption. In a slip of the tongue in his continuous chanting of Duofo, the Chinese transliteration of Dover (which rhymes with "many Buddhas"), Gloucester conflates Duofo with Amituofo (Amitaba Buddha). In the final scene, Wu asks: "Who am I? I am me. And I am looking for me! I think of me; I look at me; I know me. . . . I kill me. I forget me! I dream about me again," laying a strong claim to the centrality of the artist's self.

The Buddhist-themed final scene in Wu's production is a fitting con- clusion to a new play that explores, if not heals, Wu's identity crises (his two irreconcilable strivings as a Taiwanese actor and a *jingju* performer) and the tension between the cultural identity of a Taiwan-based performer and an art form commonly seen as an embodiment of the Chinese na- tion.[5] The production seems to have disowned imaginaries of Shake- speare and China that are inspired by authenticity discourses, or what Barbara Hodgdon has called "fantasies of origin."[6] At center stage stands a performer who gives primacy to his personal life stories and the interac- tion between his personas and his audience, rather than attempting to authenticate representations of Chinese or Shakespeare's cultural texts.

Wu's incorporation of Buddhist motifs *and* his private self as heuristic auteur-performer in this production is not an isolated case. Serendipitous deployment of Buddhist readings of Shakespeare and variously defined personal scripts can also be found in other contemporary Chinese and Western directors' works, such as Michael Almereyda's film *Hamlet* (for example, Thich Nhat Hanh's scene),[7] Jean-Luc Godard's film *King Lear* (a metacinematic work in which Godard "addresses the limits of his control over his work"),[8] and Stan Lai's (Lai Sheng-chuan) three-man *huaju* (spo- ken drama) production, *Lear and the Thirty-seven-fold Practice of a Bodhi- sattva* (for example, Jigme Khyentse Rinpoche's recitation of a fourteenth-century Tibetan Buddhist scripture).⁹ Although many artists possess distinctive styles, these engagements with Shakespeare stand out in their championing of personal voices and individual empowerment.

This chapter addresses itself broadly to the logics of exchange between local and global "cultural prestige" and the artist's personal stake in the cultural market.¹⁰ I pursue these questions in two works from the new millennium. Lai's and Wu's rewritings of *King Lear* are two instances where performative conversations surrounding religious discourses and personal identities take place. Although premiered in Hong Kong and Paris, respectively, these two different stage interpretations of *King Lear* were both initiated by Taiwan-based artists, hence the focus on the island in the following pages. The two productions are selected for their contrast in diverse approaches and audiences. They demonstrate unique ways in which Buddhist motifs are used as interpretive frameworks to read both Shakespeare and Taiwanese directors and playwrights' personal stories. As a play about dispossession, ownership, dis/embodiment of the subject, and the search for identity, *King Lear* has become a central text for theater artists in the Chinese and Asian diaspora.

At the turn of the twentieth century, Chinese intellectuals rewrote Shakespeare as a symbol of "contemporary" Western culture to varying ends. With this in mind, the question becomes: At the turn of the twenty-first century, is Shakespeare still a contemporary for Chinese artists and their global audiences? What kind of "contemporary" has he become, or is he becoming? We may also ask whether the question of contemporaneity is still relevant when the familiarity and strangeness of different cultural texts are constantly being reconfigured. This study began with the question of owning Shakespeare and China in an expanding world of letters. The crux of this chapter stems from a different question: What difference would it make for artists to focus on the personal, if not autobiographical, mode of interpretation, rather than on national politics? Although the question of cultural ownership (differentiated access to authenticity) remains relevant, after the 1990s a new pattern of engagement affected individual and collective investments in competing conventions of authenticity. The new tendency is symptomatic of what I will call a personal turn, or "small-time Shakespeare," that has turned public performance and the international cultural space into a forum for personal script.

Small-time Shakespeare is a mode of interpretation that is best defined relative to big-time Shakespeare. Michael Bristol has used the concept of "big-time Shakespeare" to theorize the institutionalization and

appropriation of Shakespeare by large corporations and cultural institutions in the English-speaking world, such as David Garrick's famous
project in 1769, the Shakespeare Jubilee, which jump-started the Shakespeare industry. The twentieth century has witnessed diverse corporate
uses of Shakespeare's name and journalistic promotions of Shakespeare's
celebrity. In England, "Shakespeare" has sold diverse merchandise, ranging from cigars to sports news.[11]

In Taiwan, big-time Shakespeare can be found in sites similar to those
in the West, ranging from a Shakespeare Mansion (the name of an apart-
ment complex) and a Shakespeare Bridal Shop to an advertisement in
2003 of Dawei (David) Wang's English classes, which featured one of
the best-known Shakespearean lines: "To be, or not to be."[12] In China,
analogous "big-time" enterprises might be seen in the work of late Qing
and May Fourth reformers, who read Shakespeare in ethical and political
registers, among other instances.[13] This tendency bears out Red Buttons's
formulation that "the good time is the small time, the big time is the hard
time."[14]

In contrast to these endeavors, small-time Shakespeare is characterized by its personal touch. The trend reflects the artist's individual engagements with or reframings of Shakespeare's plays, reframings that
reaffirm local reading positions. These rewrites often have a personal
urgency for their creators. Far from confirming a retrograde notion, such
as the claim of literary universality, this recent wave of dazzlingly fresh
interpretations for the stage attest to the creativity of imaginative directors
willing to create hybrids of dramatic spectacle by combining the personal
with the fictional. The creators of small-time Shakespeare have superimposed their autobiographies onto Shakespeare's characters to construct
highly personal narratives.

These productions and their various incarnations in different locations testify to the vitality of Chinese Shakespeares in the past decade.
To the extent that personal identities articulate local concerns, the production and reception of these two *Lears* offer rich opportunities for the
exploration of Chinese Shakespeares from the margins of the Sinophone
world. They also provide useful contrasts to the history of Shakespeare in
mainland China. Since the 1990s, both Taiwan and Hong Kong theaters
have produced non-state-sponsored Shakespearean performances that
followed the logics of late capitalism and global cultural tourism. At the
same time, although bearing the mark of a double loyalty to alternative visions of Shakespeare and China, these productions contain self-conscious

repositionings of Taiwan and Hong Kong in relation to both their Chinese origins and Western connections. As images of Shakespeare and China become ever more globalized, theater artists deploy religious rhetoric and personal causes, if not obsessions, as means to personalize their works.

Making Theater in China's "Borderland"

Nearly a century of Chinese engagements with Shakespeare laid the groundwork for the personal turn in performance culture in the 1990s and the new millennium. Probably no other non-Chinese dramatist was as familiar to the Chinese audience by this time. This familiarity led to two new challenges for theater artists. On the one hand, the audience's familiarity with Shakespeare became a de rigueur foil against which the novelty and creativity associated with artistic experiments can be set off, providing a ready point of reference. Shakespeare has become a platform for directorial bravura, because most of the Chinese-language audience—the educated middle class—know their Shakespeare. Directors use Shakespeare to "redouble [their] efforts on the how" in theatrical experimentalism.[15] Although such a sweeping statement has to be qualified—only some Shakespearean plays are overly familiar to the Chinese audience—many directors have indeed exploited the purported familiarity to create new plays or new performance styles. On the other hand, such overfamiliarity breeds boredom, as Peter Brook candidly concedes: "I am more easily bored by Shakespeare and have suffered more ghastly evenings with Shakespeare than with any other dramatist I know."[16] Staging Shakespeare or Shakespeare-inspired plays in Chinese has now become a delicate task of balancing between these two poles.

By the 1990s, "Shakespeare" had become a familiar text and an appealing cultural commodity to audiences in Chinese theaters, whether they were Chinese, Taiwanese, international cultural tourists, or any combination of these. This familiarity with Shakespeare and the diversification of interpretive perspectives made it possible for new works that were no longer merely concerned with telling Shakespeare's tales. The question of "China," however, has been the central concern for *xiqu* (Chinese opera) and *huaju* theaters for so long that some artists have begun to avoid fashioning a core narrative built around Chinese politics and aesthetics. Alternative theatrical visions that put the notions of Shakespeare and China to question have emerged, even though there is still a strong tradition of performing straightforward translations of Shakespeare (such as the Hong Kong Repertory Theatre's *King Lear* in 1993 and *A Midsummer Night's Dream* in 1997 and 2000, all directed by Daniel Yang, former artistic director of the Colorado Shakespeare Festival).

In the recent past, however, directors have produced more radically "localized" Shakespeare with a distinct flavor of personal engagement. Rather than staging a "straight" performance or repositioning the plot-lines in a distinctively Chinese framework that supplies Chinese counterparts to the characters and geocultural locations of the play, many Chinese-language directors since the 1990s have been preoccupied with staging free-associative rewritings that were *inspired*, rather than reined in, by Shakespeare's themes; hence the rise of autobiographical narratives. New forms of performances include parody or scripted "improvisation," including Stan Lai's *Lear and the Thirty-seven-fold Practice of a Bodhisattva* (*Pusa zhi sanshiqi zhong xiuxing zhi Li'er wang*, 2000 and 2001); Lee Kuo-hsiu's *Shamlet* (1992; revived in 1994, 1995, 1996, 2000, 2006, and 2007);[17] the major musical-theater company Godot Theatre's (Guotuo juchang) *Kiss Me Nana* (*Wenwo ba Nana*, 1995), based on *The Taming of the Shrew*; fragmentary "remixes" of Shakespeare, such as the Shakespeare's Wild Sisters Company's *Crazy Scenes* (2002), based on scenes about madness in *Hamlet, Macbeth, King Lear*, and *Othello*; and solo performance, such as Tian Mansha's *Lady Macbeth* (2001, 2002, 2006) and Wu Hsing-kuo's *Lear Is Here*. Other examples include the Golden Bough Theatre's (Jinzhi yanshe) Taiwanese-language *Yumei and Tianlai* (2004), based on *Romeo and Juliet*.[18] These works emphasize the contemporaneity of audience and actors, and creative use of the stage and theatricalization of public spaces. Interestingly, these experimental works were not confined to small audiences, as many experimental works are; instead, they were immensely popular, had several reruns, and toured internationally.

It is no coincidence that such a trend emerged not only in Taiwan but also in other "marginal" localities such as Hong Kong and Singapore in the years after 1990. These immigrant societies have undergone several identity crises in recent years because they are contact zones of contested cultural values. Many such performances feature personal interpretations that focus on identity issues and metatheatrical reflections of the nature of acting. Ong Keng Sen's pan-Asian *LEAR* (1997), similar to Wu's *Lear*, engaged the same central question: "Who am I?" As a question being asked with increasing force by theater artists such as Ong, Wu, and Lai, it gains personal and political resonance. Among the multiple iterations of the personal in unexpected places is a *huaju* production in Hong Kong, titled *Hamlet / Hamlet* (2000) and directed by Xiong Yuanwei.[19] The production was so named because it staged the contestatory relationship between the actor's personal interpretation of the play on stage and Laurence Olivier's now-classic film *Hamlet*, projected onto a video screen. The film and the live performance turned each other into a play-within-a-play in different scenes. The production opened and ended with Yu Shiteng (Yu Sai-tang), who played Hamlet, watching Olivier's *Hamlet* on the screen along with his audience. In a scene in *Hamlet / Hamlet* where Hamlet and Ophelia watched the wedding banquet scene of Olivier's film, they engaged in a metatheatrical discussion of the play and their performance:

> OPHELIA: You have seen this scene in [Olivier's] *Hamlet* eight times.
> HAMLET (*sighs*): What can be more frustrating than having verified that which you do not want to verify! Don't you feel that what is happening on the screen is happening around us?
> OPHELIA: Let us hope nothing like that happens.
> HAMLET: God damn it! *Hamlet*, written by Shakespeare four hundred years ago, is already being staged right here around us.[20]

The production negotiated the performer's and director's claim to be an auteur and the processes of mediation and mediatization. As such, Xiong's production demonstrates interesting parallels to Godard's probing question about the filmmaking process in his *King Lear* and Almereyda's metaphor of personalized media technology in his *Hamlet*. In a sense, the small-time Shakespeare performance is always already a play-within-a-play in the life of its creator.

It is fitting that the new trend in performance culture to depart from Shakespeare and China in order to explore more personal concerns is energetically pursued in Taiwan, a locality that has historically defined its own identity in opposition, or in relation, to China, Japan, and the West. A country with a distinct blend of Chinese heritage and Western influence, Taiwan—a "contact zone" and an immigrant society—has become one of the most interesting sites of postmodern cultural formation.[21] Taiwan was officially incorporated into China in the seventeenth century, and from the 1960s to the 1980s, it referred to itself as a "free China" where authentic Chinese culture was preserved.[22] Throughout its history, Taiwan has experienced a paradox central to many other island nations: its geography simultaneously isolates it and opens it to the rich opportunities of cross-cultural exchange.[23]

Political tensions (Communism versus democracy) and cultural differences (due to over half a century of noncommunication between mainland Chinese and Taiwan residents) have come to define the cultural identities of Taiwan, where Taiwanese and Hakka dialects are widely spoken along with the official language, Mandarin Chinese. Taiwan's recent history and hybrid cultural landscape determine the metamorphoses of Chinese Shakespeares on the island. Michelle Yeh's characterization of the distinct identity of Taiwanese poetry rings true for contemporary Taiwanese theater as well—a synthesis of heterogeneous origins and "contending visions: traditional and modern, local and global."[24] Taiwan's indeterminable and uncertain status throughout history has given rise to a series of identity crises. Hybrid culture complicates the liminal space occupied by the idea of "Taiwan," producing forms of representation that engage with spatial and temporal ambiguities. Taiwan's theater actively participates in these processes and vividly reflects the discords arising from this liminal space, which gives it a unique dynamic. Rewrites of Western classics figure prominently in the formation of the identity of postmodern theater. Since the 1960s, Western influence has been felt in both the content of dramatic literature and the style of performance. Playwrights and directors not only have fused preexisting traditions with Western performance idioms (such as environmental theater, *huanjing juchang*), but also have adapted works by Bertolt Brecht, Luigi Pirandello, and Shakespeare, among others.

Taiwan's theater articulates competing visions of local identities, including but not limited to the three major viewpoints: a nativist campaign seeking to establish a Taiwanese republic, a proposal to reunite with mainland China, and the inclination to maintain the current situation. However, some theater artists have sought innovative ways to shun the political. Contributing to the rise of this trend are the economy of cultural prestige surrounding the star power of the performer, director, or playwright, and the infrastructure of Taiwan's performing arts industry. Many theater companies rely on strong ties to their founders: Stan Lai is to the Performance Workshop (Biaoyan gongzuofang) as Richard Burbage or Shakespeare was to the Lord Chamberlain's Men. Likewise, Wu Hsing-kuo's *jingju* career is inseparable from the company he cofounded, the Contemporary Legend Theatre. The personal appeal and unique styles of many Taiwanese playwrights and directors have been branded and become important marketing tools. The personal charisma of the founders has been crucial to these companies' success, because a majority of plays staged were written in-house, as is the case with Lai's *Lear* and Wu's *Lear*. In short, whereas mainland Chinese theater has had a longer history of state control and subsidy, contemporary Taiwanese theater has developed along a self-sustaining route of commercialization and internationalization since the 1980s. It is in this context that Lai and Wu began directing and writing plays. This was an era often characterized as the golden age of Taiwanese theater when today's major theater companies were established or first flourished.

Taiwan's performance culture thus reflects the vibrant mosaic of Chinese, indigenous (aboriginal), Japanese, and Western traditions. The previously analyzed narratives in fiction, cinema, and theater tend to be informed by collective national consciousness, whereas Lai's and Wu's *Lear*s share an urge to turn live theater events—a public form of entertainment that encourages communal experience and instant feedback—into a forum for personal scripts. However, it bears pointing out that while the Taiwanese artists' autobiographical approach contrasts with mainland Chinese intellectuals' reluctance to distinguish the national collective from the consciousness of the individual self, the difference should not be regarded as a liability to be overcome in teleological history. Articulated differently, the idea of "China" is as relevant to diasporic Chinese artists as it is to those in mainland China.

Fullness in Emptiness: Stan Lai's *Lear*

The place of Lai's work in a global context provides some clues to how his *Lear* project operates as small-time Shakespeare. One of Taiwan's most prolific and influential playwrights and directors (stage play, television series, opera, film), Stan Lai (also known as Lai Sheng-chuan) has been called an "American Asian," because he was born and raised by Taiwanese parents in the United States until the age of twelve before continuing his education in Taiwan.[25] He has had a distinguished career in theater, and his plays (twenty-seven to date) have been performed widely in Taiwan, mainland China, and Hong Kong, as well as in the United States. Commonly associated with the mainlanders (*waisheng ren*) because of his family background, Lai has identified himself and his theater works as deeply Taiwanese, inspired by the diasporic experience of Taiwan.

Japan's NHK Television once described Stan Lai as an artist whose theater was considered "outrageous and experimental" outside Taiwan, but
mainstream in his homeland. In fact, Lai's theater has been so successful
that "it has become Taiwan's theatre establishment."[26] Plays such as *Secret
Love in Peach Blossom Land* (also staged in English in Berkeley, California,
in 2007) have made Lai a household name in mainland China, Hong
Kong, and Taiwan, as attested by the sheer number of bootlegged copies
of live performances circulating on the market today—considering the
fact that the majority of Chinese-language audiences do not care to watch
videotaped stage productions. Lai's plays have drawn comparisons with
the works of Robert Lepage and Peter Brook. He has received Taiwan's
highest award for the arts, the National Arts Award, an unprecedented
two times (1988 and 2001).

Contradictions have shaped the styles and narratives of many of Lai's
works and have defined their success, including *The Night We Became
Crosstalk Comedians* (1985), *Secret Love in the Peach Blossom Land* (1986),
and *A Dream Like a Dream* (2000).[27] However, I would like to recast these
accounts of contradictions in a more enabling turn. Lai and his Performance Workshop have created a theater that is as intercultural as it is
local. Lai's works are at once experimental and commercially viable; they
espouse universal themes, yet are privy to the interplay between personal
pasts and presents; they are topical and deeply Taiwanese, yet are also
informed by Lai's cross-cultural experiences; last, but not least, although
they bear the unmistakable imprint of Lai's personal charisma, they are
products of a fluid and highly collaborative process, foregrounding the
subjectivities of all the participating actors. The hybrid nature of Lai's theater reflects not only his preference for pastiche, but his own hybrid identity as well. In Lai's own words, the raison d'être of his theater is to "specify the universal" by channeling "the Taiwan experience and the Chinese
experience as a whole," thus "revealing the human conditions on a universal level."[28] As suspect as this universalist claim may seem to critical
theory, it cannot be taken seriously as a representation of Lai's aesthetic
principles. Over the past two decades, he has worked almost exclusively
with themes that were decidedly local.

Even though rewrites of Western classics are not among Lai's best-
known works, he did acknowledge the important influence of Samuel
Beckett and William Shakespeare: "Some authors would allow you to
repeatedly return to their works at different stages in your life. You will
gain a different understanding . . . of their art and our life. There aren't

many, but Beckett and Shakespeare are definitely among their ranks. Both Beckett and Shakespeare are my best mentors."[29] These remarks come as no surprise, for Lai directed a production of *Waiting for Godot* as a doctoral student at Berkeley in 1982, a production that won the Eisner Prize. More recently, in 2001, Lai staged another production of the same play in Taipei, wittily titled *Waiting for the Dog-headed,* punning on the Chinese transliteration of Godot (Guotuo) and the pronunciation of "dog's head" (*gou tou*).

Taiwanese playwright and theater scholar Ma Sen argues that two waves of "Western tides" have shaped the landscape of modern Chinese drama, one in the early twentieth century, known as European realism (which Taiwan missed), and the other beginning in the 1960s, known as modernism and postmodernism.[30] Stan Lai's career coincided with the arrival of the second wave of "Western tides." Lai frequently moves between different notions of "homeland" and temporalities, as exemplified by his latest epic drama, *A Dream Like a Dream,* a twelve-act, ninety-scene, seven-and-a-half-hour performance that traces the life stories of four characters through their temporal and spatial movements (dating from 1928 to 2000 and moving from Taipei to Paris to Shanghai).

Lai, unlike his mainland Chinese counterparts, is less concerned with grand nationalist narratives and has responded differently to Western performance idioms and canons. His work addresses the politics of identity and problematizes the idea of "homeland," and he has focused for nearly two decades on developing and fine-tuning a unique method of collective playwrighting. The creative process involves scenes created collectively by Lai and the majority of the cast, although Lai, as the director, plays a stronger role in collating and revising the script. Therefore, many plays bear the distinctive trait of small-time theater and reflect the personal obsessions and life stories of the plays' collective creators. The theater created by Lai and his collaborators also consistently expresses Lai's preference for pastiche. Despite the experimental nature of many of his productions, they are commercially successful and touch their audiences by the performances' personalized and localized interplay between past and present.

But why would the theatricalization of religion be attractive to a secular transnational artist flirting with postmodernism? What emerges as "the universal" in Lai's works is the particular—a distinct version of Buddhism that Lai himself practices. Religious rhetoric thus becomes a heterocultural sign. His Tibetan Buddhist–themed rewrite of *King Lear* is a case in point. In *Lear,* Lai appropriates the fourteenth-century Tibetan Buddhist scripture, the *Thirty-seven-fold Practice of a Bodhisattva*, and explores a range of spectatorial possibilities that are complicated by the vocal textures of sounds and music from various localities. Lai resorts to pastiche to restructure fragmented emotions extrapolated from *King Lear* into an engagement of the individual beyond politics, a personal statement that dramatizes the artist's interpretation of Buddhism and *Lear*.

It is important to note that Lai, much like Gao Xingjian (Nobel laureate in literature, b. 1940), has developed religious rhetoric in his works over the past decades. Lai's *Lear* is the work with the most prominent religious motifs. However, Lai is by no means the first Chinese-language playwright to explore the relationship between art and religion. Chang Hsiao-feng (b. 1941), active in the 1970s, was known for an abundance of Christian-themed scenes, such as a prophet preaching directly to the audience in *The Fifth Wall* (*Diwu qiang*, 1971) and a missionary character in *Jade of Bian He* (*Heshi bi*, 1974). Her nine plays, completed between 1968 and 1978, were all staged by Christian fellowship troupes.[31] She combined motifs from the Bible and traditional Chinese stories. Chang's use of religion turned the theater into a church, and she used religious themes to initiate debates about art and religion that helped to resist the anti-Communist propaganda plays of the 1970s. Liu Ching-min's (b. 1956) works also have local Daoist connotations and ritualistic overtones (such as the use of ceremonial striding). The presentation of personal voices in the Chinese-French playwright Gao Xingjian's *Snow in August* (*La Neige en août* or *Bayue xue*), a play about the life of the sixth patriarch of Zen (Chan) Buddhism, demonstrates Gao's individualism and lifelong fascination with the artistic dimension of Zen motifs.[32] Although Lai is not the first to use religion strategically in performance art, he has made a unique contribution to postmodern theater by combining religious themes and collective improvisation, the method he has been using in playwrighting, rehearsal, and performance since the 1980s.

In these contexts, the significance of Lai's *Lear* is threefold. First, within Lai's oeuvre, this *Lear* project is the most articulate of his Tibetan Buddhist themes, bringing Buddhist scriptures and Shakespeare's texts together. While plays with religious themes are not new in Taiwan, Lai can be considered a pioneer in framing a globally circulated text, Shakespeare's *King Lear*, in another foreign but partially localized signifier, Tibetan Buddhism.

None of Lai's other works have such a pronounced Buddhist motif, but his choice of the scripture was not coincidental. The *Lear* project illuminates his close relationship with Tibetan Buddhism, promoting it both off- and onstage since his return to Taiwan from the University of California, Berkeley, in 1984. Offstage, in 1999, he published a Chinese translation of *Le Moine et le philosophe* (*The Monk and the Philosopher*), a book-long dialogue between the French philosopher Jean-François Revel (1924–2006) and his son, Matthieu Ricard (b. 1946), who left a career in biochemistry in 1972 to become a Buddhist monk in Nepal. The dramatic exchange and often-pointed contentions are embodied by the secular and sacred realms represented by the identities of the father and son. One year after the Hong Kong premiere of his *Lear,* Lai published a translation of Ricard's memoirs entitled *Journey to Enlightenment: The Life and World of Khyentse Rinpoche, Spiritual Teacher from Tibet.*[33]

While Lai has a long-standing interest in incorporating Buddhist motifs into his work, the span between 1999 and 2001 constituted the period when Lai was most articulate about his faith and its connection to his art. During his tenure as a Regents' Lecturer (1999–2000) at the University of California, Berkeley, Lai began to develop his next project, *A Dream Like a Dream,* with students. Onstage, however, his relationship with Buddhism was less one of direct promotion. He clarifies the place of religious rhetoric in his *Lear* in the program for the Hong Kong performance: "Art to me cannot be a religion in itself, but rather a window through which one can show one's 'religion.' Theatre . . . would be hard pressed to become a spiritual practice in itself, but rather a natural showcase to share and display the fruits of one's [religious] practice *outside* the theatre."[34]

In this respect, Lai's approach to religious rhetoric and theater differs markedly from that of the Taiwan playwright Lee Man-kuei (1907–1975), whose plays, like those of Chang Hsiao-feng, also thematize Lee's own religious experience. Lee was a practicing Christian. Lai is equally interested in creating a synergy between art and religion, but he gives primacy to artistic innovation, not proselytization through art. Conscious of the place of religion in his art, Lai seems to be more interested in redeeming Lear from oblivion, although he is cautious not to turn the theater into a place of worship or a religious establishment. While Lee openly preaches through her theater, Lai's theater is framed by the space between Eastern spirituality and new theatrical forms. *King Lear* becomes an exemplary drama about "the workings of *karma*" and self-sacrifice.[35]

Second, Lai's *Lear* brings Taiwanese experimental theater to a different level by infusing a religious rhetoric with a deep personal significance for him into formalistic experiments. The emergence of Taiwanese experimental theater in the 1960s was a reaction against the government's anti-Communist and anti-Soviet cultural policy. It was initiated and advocated by scholars and directors who had returned from the United States and Europe in the 1970s. Like its Western counterpart, Taiwanese experimental theater often bills itself as politically subversive and artistically innovative. However, even though Lai recognizes the necessarily political nature of religion and live performance, he also stresses its personal dimension, as evidenced by the emphasis on selfhood and subjectivity in his rendition of *Lear*.[36] This echoes Lai's observation in 1994: "I feel that in a given society, political events are often the gross-externalized manifestation of issues that have been internalized on an individual level."[37] The big time, for Lai, is indeed the hard time. Lai's personal religious experience decisively shapes this small-time Shakespeare production.

Third, in terms of its stylistic innovation and thematic concerns, Lai's *Lear* is unique even in the history of copious and diverse Asian rewrites of Shakespeare, which includes numerous internationally known *Lear* performances, such as Kurosawa Akira's film *Ran* (1985) and Annette Leday's *Kathakali King Lear* (1999) at London's Globe Theatre.[38] Many performances have focused on the familial dimension of the tragedy, highlighting either Lear or his daughters as the central characters. In contrast, Lai's *Lear* focuses on the actions of the characters and the tense space between what Lai understands as the "causes" and "effects" of these actions. The play does not set out to challenge the commonly perceived, weighted authority of Shakespeare, which has never been an issue for Lai. Rather, the alternativeness of Lai's *Lear* challenges the "cumulative power of mainstream production," both in Asia and elsewhere.[39] Its alternativeness, its small-time character, lies in its interpretive perspective, rather than in its deconstruction of an imagined original text of a higher order.

Lai's *Lear* began as a formal and stylistic experiment commissioned by Danny Yung in Hong Kong in March 2000. It appeared as the last of the four performances of the evening. A year after its premiere in Hong Kong, the play was brought back to Taipei with slight revisions. Lai's *Lear* conformed to the formalistic requirements imposed by the context of the Hong Kong Experimental Shakespeare Festival, a multimedia theater event organized by the Zuni Icosahedron, a membership-supported avant-garde theater collective founded by Yung in 1982. Four theater and film directors—Danny Yung (Hong Kong), Edward Yang (Yang Dechang, Taipei), Meng Jinghui (Beijing), and Stan Lai (Taipei)—were each invited to stage a thirty-minute performance based on *King Lear* under the same circumstances. The directors' works guaranteed disparate representations of China, while their training and cosmopolitan backgrounds solicited a Western viewpoint as well. Each worked with three performers, performing in hybrid styles with multimedia components and a transnational language of pastiche; each was given a video projector, a slide projector, a table, and two chairs (one of the most common *xiqu* stage setups). Lai's production experimented with the form of *huaju* and parallel interpretations of secular and religious texts. It was performed on a bare stage with eclectic stage properties that struck an air of amateur experiment (an inflatable kiddy pool, a crude dummy, and others). The result was an evening of innovative multimedia engagements portraying different aspects of *King Lear*. While Shakespeare's characters loosely connected these four disparate pieces on stage, their difference makes each of them individual theater works that can be discussed independently.

The 2001 Taipei performance was the second stage work of Off-PW, a subsidiary of Lai's Performance Workshop. It was slightly revised from the Hong Kong version and was given a different title, *Lear-ing* (*Li'er san ge wang*, which means literally "three King Lears"). The title pays tribute to the three performers. Li Jianchang (who was one of the actors for the Hong Kong version), Fu Hungzhen, and Stan Lai each directed thirty-minute pieces entitled *When They Play the Drums, Dance Lear,* and *Lear and the Thirty-seven-fold Practice of a Bodhisattva,* respectively. They still kept to the rule of one table and two chairs that Yung had established for the Hong Kong festival. However, the three-minute video footage shown during the Hong Kong production was cut in this version. Despite the significance of this production, both the Hong Kong and Taipei productions did not receive much critical or media attention, due partly to several political crises that relegated news about the arts to the back pages.

Lai's *Lear* is a Brechtian episodic drama without a linear narrative and without closure. The question of redemption remains open-ended. Lai is no stranger to limitations, and he has excelled at fragmentation and the restriction of material conditions. At the risk of imposing coherence on a performance that flaunts its lack thereof, I will attempt to analyze a number of themes that unite the production's dispersed metaphors, demonstrating that the play has more unity than the performance style. The production's most clever commentary appears in those moments where disjointed narratives meet.

Li Jianchang, Liu Liangzuo, and Na Weixun—the three actors in Lai's play—engaged in multirole acting, including King Lear, Goneril,

FIGURE 21   Li Jianchang, Liu Liangzuo, and Na Weixun in *Lear and the Thirty-seven-fold Practice of a Bodhisattva,* directed by Stan Lai, Hong Kong, 2000. (Courtesy of Performance Workshop, Taipei)

Cordelia, Gloucester, Edgar, a judge, and an echo, among others, and produced a surprisingly coherent presentation of fragmented narratives and emotions derived from the kingdom-division plotline of *King Lear.* Jigme Khyentse Rinpoche's prerecorded voice-over in English provided a strong Buddhist motif, while Na Weixun's live solo violin performance of Bach's Sonata for Solo Violin in G-Minor enriched the vocal dimension of the production (figure 21). It is noteworthy that throughout the performance, Na appeared to struggle to remember this piece as he played fragments and variations of the main theme on his violin. Toward the end of the play, as a white dummy body of a woman representing Cordelia was thrown into the kiddy pool at center stage, Na suddenly remembered the tune and was finally able to play the complete sonata. The musical twists and turns highlight Lear's struggles and transformation. In addition to its exploration of Tibetan Buddhism and sound, this play redefines the relationships between the individual and the collective and between dramatic and religious texts.

Lear and the Thirty-seven-fold Practice of a Bodhisattva is indeed a meditation on the redemptive quality of a disturbing tragedy that forecloses all hope. This meditative quality can be found in many of its juxtaposed

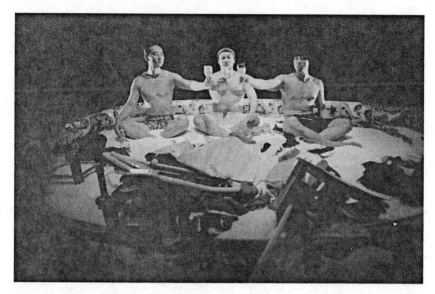

FIGURE 22   *Lear and the Thirty-seven-fold Practice of a Bodhisattva.* (Courtesy of Performance Workshop, Taipei)

passages from *Thirty-seven-fold Practice of a Bodhisattva* by Gyelse Togme, and a number of unidentifiable twentieth-century Chinese translations of Shakespeare's *King Lear*.[40] The performance consists of alternating symbolic scenes in which the actors recite the scripture, play the violin, and act as one another's echoes and more descriptive scenes in which the actors perform selected scenes from *King Lear*, such as the division of the kingdom and Lear in the storm (figure 22). These contradictions produced a performance akin to the Theatre of the Absurd and even the works of Beckett, as anticipated by Jan Kott in *Shakespeare Our Contemporary*.[41]

Why a Buddhist interpretation of *King Lear*? The play lends itself to a Buddhist interpretation, as recognized by some twentieth-century artists and scholars. James Howe argues that Lear's mental frame of reference in act 4, scene 6, "seems very like a Buddhist's" because the "new Lear, though still mad," reaches catharsis, turning the absurdity and cruelty of life into a game.[42] Lai's play proposes a similar reading, framing key moments in *King Lear* within the *Thirty-seven-fold Practice of a Bodhisattva*. Among the most popular bodhisattvas is Guanyin, who is known as the goddess of compassion and mercy. Despite the lure of political interpretations of *King Lear* (division of the kingdom) concurrent with a presidential election in Taiwan and the looming question of succession, Lai insisted that he "never thought *Lear* was primarily a play about politics." Rather, the quick turn of events in *King Lear* is presented by Lai's three actors in personal terms, as "the workings of *karma*, and how cause . . . creates effect," which is itself "a lesson greater than, and encompassing, politics."[43] Highlighted in this Buddhist recasting of *King Lear* are folly, human frailty, blind Gloucester's hallowed moralistic response to a world where evil befalls men randomly, Lear's futile attempts to bring justice to that world, and especially his hallucinatory trial of Goneril and Regan in the farmhouse (playfully reenacted in scene 8 of Lai's play).

The self-problematizing nature of Lai's *Lear* allowed space for the Buddhist alternative of not imposing meaning on our projections. The performance was divided into three scenes characterized by more symbolic language and movement ("Sound of the Waves," "The Thirty-seven-fold Practice of a Bodhisattva," and "Testing the Wind") and six scenes characterized by language and action that closely parallel key scenes from *King Lear* ("Division of the Kingdom," "Lear in the Storm," "Plucking Out the Eyes," "The Cliff," "Plastic Swimming Pool—The [Hallucinatory] Trial," and "Division of the Kingdom" again). Even though Lai's *Lear* opens and closes with one of the most familiar scenes of *King Lear*, the division of the kingdom and the challenge of Cordelia's truthful silence, this production has included other fragmented narratives that could be digested coherently only by an audience sufficiently familiar with Shakespeare. Several decades of theoretical reflection and Shakespearean performance practice in the Chinese-speaking world have provided a fertile ground for such experimental work. The fragmentation was further enhanced by the context of an experimental *King Lear* series in trilingual Hong Kong.

Audience members familiar with other versions and the performance history of *King Lear* would recall that *King Lear* has been a difficult play to perform and usually an uncomfortable experience for the audience, especially the play's bleak ending. This unease, among other factors, caused Nahum Tate's famously "updated" 1681 adaptation with a happy ending to dominate the English stage for nearly 150 years, until 1838. Contrary to most stage and screen interpretations, Lai's *Lear* concentrates on the dramatic opening scene rather than the ending. As has been noted by modern critics, including Peggy Phelan, the division of the kingdom constitutes a ceremonial "political theatre" that stages a love test and a test of allegiance.[44] Lai taps into the potential of this scene and the effect of having three male performers play the parts of the three daughters and Lear.

Lai's *Lear* opens with a scene derived from this staged love test, cutting the role of Cordelia and effectively silencing her. The play closes with a reenactment of the same scene, but the lines are spoken with a greater speed and with less angst. Before lighting the stage, a three-minute video of violent waves is projected onto a screen above the stage. Jigme Khyentse Rinpoche's prerecorded English voice-over is played back, and an actor's "simultaneous interpretation" in Chinese of lines from the scripture is heard:

Although he sees that in all phenomena there's no coming or
    going,
[Bodhisattva] strives solely for the sake of beings . . .
In one's homeland, waves of attachment to friends and kin surge,
Hatred for enemies rages like fire,
The darkness of stupidity prevails,
Oblivious of right and wrong.
Abandonment of his homeland is the practice of a Bodhisattva.[45]

These lines provide a pretext that problematizes the nature of Lear's love in general, not merely his love for Cordelia or his initial affection for Goneril and Regan. Lai thus frames *King Lear* in a moralistic religious text. To him, "each line of *The Thirty-seven-fold Practice of a Bodhisattva* seemed . . . to be speaking to Mr. Lear," particularly in these lines projected on the screen to accompany the video footage of ocean waves.

The chanting is heard throughout scene 1, "Sound of the Waves," and scene 2, "The Thirty-seven-fold Practice of a Bodhisattva." In scene 3, "Division of the Kingdom," the three actors sit down on center stage, with Goneril to the left, Lear in the middle, and Regan to the right. They deliver simultaneous selected lines from act 1, scene 1, beginning with Lear's "Mean time we shall express our darker purpose" (1.1.35–76). The simultaneous delivery of these lines makes it impossible to make out the details of Lear's announcement and Goneril's and Regan's responses. After Goneril and Regan finish, Lear delivers his repositioned lines to be greeted with silence and a dimming light:

LEAR: Tell me, my daughters . . .
    Which of you shall we say doth love us most,
    That we our largest bounty may extend

Where nature doth with merit challenge? Goneril,
Our eldest-born, speak first. (1.1.48–53)

The production quickly moves from the division of the kingdom to the scene with Lear in the storm, preceded by a short scene in which the three actors, without identifiable roles, withstand an imagined strong wind. Continuous English and Chinese chanting of the scripture gives separation to the actions, providing opportunities for reflection. Stanley Cavell rightly points out that Lear feels the need to stage a love test not because he wishes to reward political allies, but because he needs reassurance that he is worthy of his daughters' love: Cordelia's silence "is alarming precisely because [Lear] knows she is offering the real thing, something a more opulent third of his kingdom cannot, must not, repay."[46] Lai's rewrite features a Lear who does not (or is not able to) love Cordelia enough to be willing to ask for nothing in return, which makes him vulnerable and eventually leads to his death. This becomes especially evident in scene 8, when the mad Lear engages in a hallucinatory trial of Goneril and Regan. Again, Jigme Khyentse Rinpoche's prerecorded recitation of the scripture is played back, sometimes loud enough to drown out the actors' lines and other times as no more than a background drone. As Lear recounts the events and accuses Goneril and Regan of cruelty, the audience experiences different practices of a bodhisattva that obviously contradict the action unfolding before their eyes:

To avoid attachment to friends and benefactors
And their homes is the practice of a Bodhisattva.
Rude and biting remarks disturb others' minds
And spoil one's own Bodhisattva practice.
Therefore, to give up abusive talk
That others find unpleasant is the practice of a Bodhisattva.[47]

And these lines cannot be heard without a deep sense of irony as Lear loses his mind:

LEAR: Wherever I am, whatever I do,
    To be continually mindful and alert,
    Asking, "What is the state of my mind?"
    And thus to accomplish the good of others is the practice of a
        Bodhisattva.[48]

The performance is saturated with multiple voices in both the literal and metaphorical senses, challenging the audience to select a voice to follow. Even in those scenes where the recitation of the scripture is temporarily absent (such as scene 5, "Lear in the Storm"), the three actors struggle with one another vocally by repeating one another or by producing "echoes" that disturb or cancel out one another's lines. With a complex and rich vocal landscape, Lai's *Lear* explores both the psychological and religious dimensions of *King Lear,* but also memories inscribed in sound, or "sound as experienced through the well of time."[49]

Lai uses highly distilled passages in *King Lear* to explore the possibility of bringing what he calls the "medicine" (in Buddhist scripture) to the "disease" (represented in Shakespeare's drama). He found *King Lear* to be a masterpiece that displays "the myriad diseases of humanity," but that relentlessly refuses "the possibility of healing."[50] The diseases are not explicitly evoked in Shakespeare's text, but the transmutation of the Buddhist metaphor of medicine and disease usefully reframes some Shakespearean lines not translated and unspoken in *Lear and the Thirty-seven-fold Practice of a Bodhisattva.* In act 2, Shakespeare's Lear laments that he suffers from hysteria,

> LEAR: O how this mother swells up toward my heart!
> *Hysteria passio,* down, though climbing sorrow,
> Thy element's below! (2.4.56–58)

a disease that was loosely constructed in early modern pathology and literary imagination as a failure of speech associated with uterine dysfunction (hence gendered female). Unlike Shakespearean critics such as Richard Halpern, who asks "What [disease] does Lear suffer from?" Lai is more interested in the extent to which "disease" can be understood metaphorically, as evil that befalls the world and as the darkness of the unenlightened mind.

Disease in *King Lear* has remained a thorny and complex issue throughout several centuries of criticism, complicated by twentieth-century feminism and psychoanalysis. For example, Lear's "hysteria" and the stage direction "Enter Lear mad" (with several textual and editorial variants involving Lear dressed or crowned with wild flowers) in act 4, scene 6, rank among the most notorious points of contention in the play.[51] Interestingly, although Lai does not directly engage any previous stage or critical interpretations of Lear's disease as such, his rewrite demonstrates a fixation on the transcendental aspect of the experience of illness, and religion as a method of cure and prophylaxis for the society.

Bringing religion and the arts together proves to be a challenging task in secular enterprise. Lai has observed: "'Disease' seems to be a natural fit in the theatrical habitat, living and thriving in the great 'wooden O's' of the world such as Shakespeare's Globe. The natural habitat of 'medicine,' on the contrary, is religion, not art." He insists that it is more desirable to explore religious contentions in one's art: "That art has become a religion in itself . . . reflect[s] a latent disease in modern society."[52] The metaphor of medicine and the ideal world constructed by religious rhetoric seem to represent a nostalgic past for Lai. These points of origin are clearly separate from China as a political entity, but the religious discourses constructed by Stan Lai become venues where heterogeneous values are negotiated in the arena provided by small-time theater.

From Division of the Kingdom to Division of the Self

It is noteworthy that *King Lear* is one of the most frequently performed Shakespeare plays in contemporary Asia. *King Lear* holds a special place for both Chinese and Western postmodern theater. The play is to postmodernism what *Hamlet* was to Romanticism: "the icon of an age."[53] While the religious rhetoric in Stan Lai's *Lear* is an exercise in fusing Buddhist text with Lear's story and with the intellectualism of Lai's postmodern theater, Wu Hsing-kuo's *Lear Is Here* (*Li'er zaici*) is a metatheatrical venture that seeks to personalize the familiar story of *King Lear* and the texture of *jingju* culture. Each of the two productions of *Lear* demonstrates a different dimension of small-time Shakespeare. Wu's *Lear* relies on his autobiographical performance to defamiliarize the images of Shakespeare and China that have become iconic (for Shakespeare enthusiasts and *jingju* fans). As it turns out, Wu's struggle with multiple cultural identities echoes American civil-rights leader W. E. B. Du Bois's compelling question in 1903: "How does it feel to be a problem . . . of two souls, two thoughts, two irreconciled strivings?"[54]

Among the many innovations of Wu's production, I will pursue Wu's role as the heuristic auteur in his solo performances. To that end, I begin with two questions about the cultural background and the new genre of solo performance: What does it mean to be a *jingju* performer in Taiwan, a society that has increasingly distanced itself from all things Chinese? What is at stake in a solo performance like Wu's?

For political reasons, *xiqu* in Taiwan, especially *jingju* theater, has always formed an uneasy coalition with different advocacy groups. For historical reasons, Taiwan's cultural identity has been articulated in opposition to its Others, including the Dutch, the Japanese, and now the Chinese. In the mid-twentieth century, the KMT used *jingju* (known as *guoju* [national theater]) to promote appreciation of Chinese culture among the locals who had just been "liberated" from the Japanese colonial rule and to recruit the Japanese-speaking Taiwan residents into the "Chinese nation." Prominently featured in the culture war to reinscribe Chineseness into Taiwan's cultural identity was *jingju*'s association with Beijing, the perceived cultural capital of an imaginary China for the KMT, which had just lost mainland China to the CCP. After martial law was lifted in the 1980s, *jingju*'s association with China became its "original sin," as it were. *Jingju* thus evolved from a state-endorsed and well-funded theater genre to one that was rejected by the majority of the Taiwanese audience. Even without the new ideology, *jingju* already suffered from a dwindling, aging audience that consisted mainly of mainlanders who had followed the Nationalists to Taiwan in the 1940s. Nancy Guy notes that *jingju* in post-1980s Taiwan has been "an art caught up in a whirlwind of ideologies" and an art that is "in a state of limbo."[55] Taiwanese nativist campaigns and continual political tensions between China and Taiwan exacerbated the situation. *Jingju* became a scapegoat in the identity crisis, and support from the public and private sectors dwindled.

Wu Hsing-kuo emerged as a rebel in this environment, vowing to save *jingju* from its demise. He is noted for his controversial and bold reimaginings of Western classics and *jingju* theater. In terms of performing styles, since the 1980s there no longer has been a clear-cut distinction between *xiqu* and *huaju* theaters. This is especially evident in the works of the Contemporary Legend Theatre, which Wu founded in 1986. The company, under the leadership of Wu Hsing-kuo and his wife, Lin Hsiu-wei, experimented with *jingju* performing idioms, Western and Chinese music, and semi-illusionist sets. The company is widely known for its adaptations of *Hamlet*, *Macbeth*, *The Tempest*, and the Greek dramas *Oresteia* and *Medea*, many of which have become new classics for Chinese theater. In Wu's vision, the mission of his company in the twenty-first century is "not only to safeguard tradition but also to allow it to confront modernity, thereby giving birth to a third approach that will extend the future of Beijing opera."[56] Lee Kuo-hsiu's *Jingju Revelation* (*Jingxi qishilu,* Taiwan, 1996), a semiautobiographical play, uses the metatheatrical mode to present and comment on the convolutions of *jingju* and *huaju* theaters. Other *huaju* playwrights and directors have also been influenced by *xiqu* to various extents and, in turn, have changed *xiqu* theater.

It is in this context that Wu, by superimposing his autobiography onto Shakespeare's characters to produce a small-time, solo performance, has created a new theatrical genre. While solo *xiqu* performances—in a form that resembles concerts featuring one star singer and famous arias from European opera—have existed in China for many centuries, there were no complete plays written for and performed by any single actor. Now, however, autobiographical engagement with Shakespeare and the Western canon is a growing phenomenon. Since 2000, several notable Chinese solo performance productions that capitalized on the performers' celebrity biographies have toured Asia, Australia, Europe, and the United States. Among these plays are Zhao Zhigang's *yueju* (Shaoxing-opera) solo performance of *Hamlet in the Graveyard,* Huang Hsiang-lian's *gezaixi* (Taiwanese-opera) solo performance of *Romeo and Juliet,* Li Xiaofeng's *qinqiang* (Shaanxi-opera) solo performance of Goethe's *Faust,* Tian Mansha's *chuanju* (Sichuan-opera) solo performance of *Lady Macbeth,* and Wu's solo *Lear Is Here,* which is by far the most innovative and most widely toured among this group. The success of the recent Experimental Solo Chinese Opera Festivals in Hong Kong (2001 and 2002) and Taipei (March 2004), where several Shakespearean plays were presented as solo performances, including Wu's *King Lear,* is testament to the significance and increasing popularity of the emerging genre of solo Shakespeare. Central to the Chinese solo performance is the star actor's autobiographical intervention.

In recent years, this autobiographical strategy, one that eschews the national in favor of the marginal, has been employed by other Asian and, sporadically, Western performers in their engagements with Shakespeare.[57] Gareth Armstrong, for example, explores anti-Semitism and the splitting of selves when he performs many characters in his solo performance *Shylock* (directed by Frank Barrie). The production received rave reviews at the Edinburgh Festival (1998–1999), and has toured Washington, D.C., and San Francisco, among other cities. While Wu's and Armstrong's solo performances employ nonmainstream strategies, they have remained very popular and are still touring. The Japanese star actor Nomura Mansai's performance of Hamlet is another example of the visible intersection of the actor's persona and his assigned character. Lee Kuo-hsiu's *Shamlet,* an autobiographical parody of *Hamlet,* is a similarly prominent example. Ong Keng Sen's Shakespeare trilogy, composed of *LEAR* (1997), *Desdemona* (2000), and *Search: Hamlet* (2002), also demonstrates autobiographical traces and has been used by Ong to substantiate his claims to transcend both Occidentalism and the common self-Orientalizing tendency among Asian productions touring internationally.

Against this backdrop, Wu's solo performance addresses itself broadly to the filial sentiment in Shakespeare's text, to Wu's conflicting self-identities, and to the impasse between reviving *jingju* by infusing new performance idioms and preserving the "authentic" *jingju* tradition. Premiered in the Théâtre de l'Odéon and the Théâtre du Soleil in Paris in 2000, this one-man show has treated audiences in New York, London, Taipei, Berlin, Singapore, Macao, Seoul, Hong Kong, Tokyo, Prague, Shanghai, and elsewhere to differing layers of riveting narratives surrounding an extremely personal reading of the life stories of Wu and his characters. Ariane Mnouchkine, founder and artistic director of Théâtre du Soleil, invited Wu to conduct a performance workshop for actors in Paris in 2000, where Wu performed the first version of *Lear Is Here.* Using these fragmented scenes and encouraged by Mnouchkine, Wu developed the play into a full-fledged solo performance. The stage bill of its Lincoln Center performance dedicates the production to Mnouchkine: "This solo performance . . . was made possible by the encouragement of Ariane Mnouchkine. Without her, there will be no Wu Hsing-kuo's *King Lear.*"[58]

Informed by its author's personal urgency, Wu's solo *jingju* performance of *Lear Is Here* transforms Shakespeare into dramatizations of intersecting identities that matter to Wu, and to his audiences, by fostering interconnections between modern performers and early modern texts and between the personal and the fictional. *Lear Is Here* is a three-act, solo tour de force in the style of experimental *jingju.* Wu plays nine characters from *King Lear* in different *jingju* role types through a variety of acting techniques, including cross-dressing.[59]

This production does not follow the original plot of *King Lear,* but it renders the play's preoccupation with fatherhood in expressly autobiographical terms. As its full title *Lear Is Here, Wu Hsing-kuo Meets Shakespeare* suggests, this play is Wu's autobiographical rendition of Shakespeare's dramatization of a troubled relationship between father and child. The second part of the title should be accorded primacy. It is Wu who meets Shakespeare, and it is through such an encounter that Wu is able to negotiate multiple identities, especially that of Wu as a performer and that of his dead master. Act 1, "The Play," features the lonely Lear in the storm; act 2, "Playing," features the Fool, the Earl of Kent, Lear, Goneril, Regan, Cordelia, the blinded Earl of Gloucester, Edmund, and the "mad" Edgar; act 3, "A Player," features Wu himself as a character. The play is a journey from the inner world of the lonely Lear, through a burst of multiple identities and characters, to the autobiographical, manifested by the lonely Wu Hsing-Kuo.

The tension between father and child in *King Lear* is turned into an allegory about Wu's uneasy relationship with his *jingju* master. The performance of *Lear Is Here* can thus be regarded as a ritual that redeems Wu through a public performance of a private, personal experience (filial piety and his relationship with his teacher, among others). Wu's resistance to his dead master takes several forms. In the solo performance, Wu not only plays Lear, the wronged father, but also plays Regan, the unruly daughter; Edgar, the wronged son; and the blinded Gloucester (yet another father struggling with a troubled relationship with his son). In shifting between the characters of the daughter and the father, Wu dramatizes his resistance to the dominating father figure while imagining his master's response by impersonating the father. Understated at times, the production is designed by Wu as a commentary on his apprenticeship and career in *jingju*.

Stylistically speaking, through cross-dressing and playing multiple characters in different role types, Wu reacts against his master's classical training. Thematically, *Lear Is Here* dramatizes the confrontation between actors and Shakespeare's characters. It does not mimic or deconstruct Shakespeare's text, nor does it seek to represent that text onstage. The presence of the actor and his contemporary playwright—the same person, in the case of this *Lear*—are accorded primacy. The repositioning of Shakespeare's plays in autobiographical solo performances reasserts the value and authority of the local readers of a globally circulating text.

Lear Is Here is representative of "small-time Shakespeare" because staging the play had a personal urgency for Wu, who was struggling with a multiplicity of theatrical, personal, cultural, and national identities. Unlike most directors at the landmark Shakespeare festivals in China (1986 and 1994), Wu conceived and spearheaded his project with very strong personal motives. Unlike Wu's previous adaptations of *Macbeth* and *Hamlet, Lear Is Here* turns *Lear* into a healing site through which Wu channels his anxieties about a dominating master/father figure in his career. By performing the ten characters, Wu is able to reconcile a range of conflicting identities. The play is a montage of significant moments from *King Lear*, in fragmentary narratives, which revolves around a key passage in Shakespeare's play to create an amalgam of its characters, including the actor himself.

The struggle among the actor's many identities is condensed into a fundamental question posed by Wu and by King Lear: "Who am I?" The question is centrally represented in act 3, in which Wu as a character circles the stage and asks repeatedly: "Who am I?" Act 1 even retains a line-by-line translation of the following passage from act 1, scene 4, of *King Lear*:

LEAR: Doth any here know me? This is not Lear.
Doth Lear walk thus? speak thus? Where are his eyes?
Either his notion weakens, his discernings
Are lethargied—Ha! Waking? 'tis not so.
Who is it that can tell me who I am? (1.4.226–30)

In this postmodern pastiche, the sudden appearance of a line-by-line translated section indicates the importance of such a passage to the adaptation. Wu's strategy for negotiating multiple identities is to blur the lines among them, especially those of the characters in the play, with those of the performer on the stage.

Act 1 of *Lear Is Here*—the mad Lear in the storm—lasts nearly thirty minutes. Wu combines the choreographed steps of modern dance and the rhythm of postmodern theater to represent a range of emotions from act 3, scene 2, of *King Lear*. While in other acts of *Lear Is Here* Wu combines monologues with stylized movements, in act 1 he relies solely on coded gestures and dance to "translate" the storm scene and Lear's remorse, accentuated by *jingju* percussion. The howling hurricane, rumbling thunder, and rage are represented by Wu through strides, minced steps, somersaults, and, most strikingly, movement of the long *jingju* beard and sleeves.

Toward the end of act 1, Wu begins to bring his perceptions about his career and apprenticeship to bear on what he perceives as comparable emotions and conditions represented in *King Lear*. In full view of

FIGURE 23   Wu Hsing-kuo transforming from King Lear into himself in his solo *jingju* production of *Lear Is Here*, at the premiere of the new version with the orchestra of the Shanghai Theatre Academy, Berlin, March 24, 2006. (Photograph by Dirk Bleicker, courtesy of Contemporary Legend Theatre, Taipei)

the audience, Wu transforms himself from the old Lear into a Taiwanese *jingju* actor, removing his headdress and opera beard to reveal the painted face pattern denoting a *jingju* combatant male role (figure 23). He also takes off his costume to reveal his undercoat. While this undercoat is part of the costume, it is never revealed onstage. It supports the heavy costume of a combatant male role. By removing the headdress and revealing what is underneath the costume, Wu stages the theater-making process in reverse. Playing with the costumes, Wu speaks to the audience as himself, not as Lear:

> wu: I am back!
> (*Looking at the beard in his hand*) Who is he?
> (*To audience*) Does any one here know him?
> (*Looking at the beard again*) This is not Lear.
> (*Standing up*) Where is Lear?
> (*Strolling*) Is this Lear walking? Is this Lear speaking?
> (*Touching his own eyes*) Where are his eyes?

The speech here parallels Lear's comments, triggered by Goneril's cruelty, that were translated from act 1, scene 4, of *King Lear*. As he speaks, Wu smears the *jingju* paint from his face, thus destroying both makeup and theatrical illusion in this onstage costume change. The audience is struck by the contrast between the king and the ordinary human being behind the characterization of a king. By addressing the costumes of Lear, Wu stages the king as two bodies, that of a fictional character and that of a human performer representing that character, juxtaposed to reveal the performer in search of an identity. This is of course a major topos of European political theory. As a human being, the king is mortal, but as sovereignty, the king is immortal. Wu may be alluding to this issue, which has a direct bearing on his vexed relations with a master.

Wu continues to explore the confusion. While still smearing the paint on his face, he asks a series of questions:

WU: Is he confused?
  Is he insensitive?
  Is he conscious?
  Who can tell me who I am?
  I want to find out who I am.

Kneeling down and folding his costume in a reverential manner as if offering to gods in a ritual of sacrifice, he breaks away from Lear and assumes his own identity. Picking up the folded armor from the stage, he announces: "I'm back! . . . I have returned to my profession." The return Wu mentions here is an event with much symbolic weight. In 2001, two years after the disbanding of his Contemporary Legend Theatre, Wu returned to the stage with the highly experimental production, *Lear Is Here*. It signifies Wu's and the company's triumph over difficulties in finance and human resources.

In the prologue, Wu asked, not without a sense of humor, "Am I the only one left on stage?" As he writes in the stage bill, this production began its life in the most difficult time in his career: he had to close the company he had founded twelve years before, because "externally [he] had been rejected by many theatres [and Taiwan's funding agencies because of the negative association of *jingju* with China]; internally some members of the company could not understand [his] ideals." Wu thus sees himself in Lear, who "curs[es] heaven and earth," furious at "being rejected and betrayed." In the end, Wu feels he is not solitary in the solo performance, because "with me were those characters that were embodied in the *jingju* roles of *sheng* (male), *dan* (female), *jing* (strong characters), and *chou* (clowns)."[60]

But one may be tempted to ask: Why Shakespeare? Why *King Lear*? Why did Wu use a foreign play to initiate his reappearance on the Taiwanese stage? Wu chose *Lear* because the play coincidentally manifests a psychological process with autobiographical resonances. However, one has to wonder why Wu did not choose a Chinese play or simply write a new one. Clearly, Wu cannot completely avoid the charge that he is capitalizing on Shakespeare's global stature. Beijing opera, in Taiwan as well as in mainland China, has suffered from the serious problem of an aging and shrinking audience. Wu believed that a Chinese play would not draw as much media attention and as large an audience, let alone touring opportunities. As a theater artist, Wu was keenly aware of the economic burden of his (and his company's) return to the stage. Box-office success or alternative forms of financial support had to be secured, and Wu knew that an innovative Chinese operatic Shakespeare would draw more diverse audiences.

Experimental directors such as Wu may face the charge that they are playing up to the English-speaking global hegemony. But practical considerations aside, the autobiographical notes in the program *Lear Is Here* offer an interesting answer as to why Wu chose to adapt *King Lear*. In a section titled "I have no father, but masters," Wu recalls the formative years of his training. The title is indeed an apt description of his career in *jingju*. He was trained in the combatant male role type (*wusheng*) under the tutelage of Master Zhou Zhengrong. Wu lost his father in the Chinese civil war, and thus his master in the Taipei Fuxing Conservatory taught and disciplined him as a surrogate father figure. Before the formal master–disciple relationship could be acknowledged, Wu kowtowed, kneeling in front of Master Zhou in accordance with the traditional ceremony of a master accepting a disciple. Service and piety are part of what makes a traditional *jingju* apprentice's relationship to his master parallel that between a son and his father. Wu served tea and brought hot towels to his master during rehearsals, and he knelt to pay respect to him on important occasions, such as the master's birthday. He even had his name changed. One of his teachers in the conservatory thought his original name, Hsing-chiu (the last character means "autumn"), was too feminine and changed his name to Hsing-kuo (the last character means "nation") for him.[61]

However, as Wu became an established performer and began to foster his own aesthetic program, conflicts with Master Zhou ensued. One day, when Master Zhou beat him again during a training session, Wu grabbed

FIGURE 24 Wu Hsing-kuo cross-dressed as Regan in *Lear Is Here,* Contemporary Legend Theatre, 2004. (Photograph by Jens Bygholm, courtesy of Contemporary Legend Theatre, Taipei)

the stick and said reproachfully: "Master, I am already thirty years old, and I have enough motivation to perfect my skills. Is it really necessary to beat an apprentice when teaching acting techniques?" Master Zhou then refused to acknowledge Wu as his disciple, even upon his death in June 2000, the same month that Wu staged *Lear Is Here.* A few days before Master Zhou's death, Wu dreamed of fighting his master and killing him with his bare hands.[62] Believing that he shares many of Lear's characteristics—rage, madness, arrogance, and capriciousness—Wu declares that a solo performance of an arrogant and self-centered Lear would be the most apt announcement of Wu's return to the *jingju* stage and to help him "rediscover [his] identity."[63]

It is not difficult, then, to see why Wu picked *King Lear,* although his reaction to his master takes several forms. Shifting between the characters of daughter and father, Wu dramatized his resistance to the dominating father figure and, at the same time, imagined his master's response by impersonating the father. Through cross-dressing and playing multiple characters in different role types, Wu issued a statement against his master's training (figures 24 and 25). He is no longer a performer confined to

FIGURE 25   Wu Hsing-kuo as the "mad" Edgar in *Lear Is Here*, Contemporary Legend Theatre, 2004. (Photograph by Jens Bygholm, courtesy of Contemporary Legend Theatre, Taipei)

the combatant male role type, but a versatile actor who is able and willing to cross cultural and gender borders. Versatility and amalgamation are artistic breakthroughs and have become signs of resistance themselves.

Lear Is Here consciously mobilizes cultural differences, not to serve larger national politics, but to reconcile personal identity crises. It epitomizes a paradigm shift within the Asian tradition of adapting Western works, from seeking authenticity to foregrounding artistic subjectivity in modes of cultural production that rewrite global texts. Understandably, scholarly attention has been directed toward Wu's mastery of different expressive modes and his authority over Shakespeare's foreign text. The issues of Shakespeare's universality and cultural authenticity still dominate the critical discourses of intercultural performance—arguing for or against these categories. For example, Yong Li Lan acknowledges that "in juxtaposing Lear and Wu, the performative fictions of the iconic universal character [Lear] and the . . . actor were re-framed against each other." She is quick to point out that at stake in this "double enactment" is not Wu's "cultural identity," but his "cultural authority."[64] I believe that equally important is the relationship between Shakespeare's characters and modern actors enacting these characters, the autobiographical moments in Wu's performance exemplifying the cross-fertilization brought forth by this relationship dynamically reconceived in personal terms.

Let me return to the divergent agenda of big-time and small-time Shakespeares. Michael Bristol critiques the impersonal transactions in contemporary uses of Shakespeare that turn Shakespeare into "an article of commerce," exchanged among people "who remain strangers to each other."[65] Small-time Shakespearean appropriations contain a very different dimension. In the performances of *Lear Is Here*, Shakespeare's characters, the actors, and the audiences are no strangers to one another. In Wu's hometown performance of *Lear Is Here*, for example, a majority of the audience knew about Wu's identity crisis and cheered him throughout the performance as he announced, "I am back! I have returned to my profession!"[66] Informed international audiences, including Ariane Mnouchkine, were also able to link Wu's theatrical experiment to his life and his personal motives.[67] In a sense, audiences came for the transformation of Wu, not just the representation of Lear.

By using his own persona as one of the ten characters he performs and by superimposing the autobiography of his performing self onto the fictive biography of King Lear, Wu lays bare the tripartite composition of stage representations of characters, from the self to the actor's persona onstage to the character's psyche. *Lear Is Here* is a diachronic adaptation of Shakespeare that underlines the fact that the performer and his audiences exist in the present. The "past" represented by Shakespearean plays becomes an allegorical frame of reference for the "present" of the realities surrounding modern audiences. However, unlike institutional or political Shakespearean productions, "small-time" Shakespearean performances concentrate on the personal urgency of their creators, rather than on political exigencies. Most certainly, these personal motivations can be political, but they shape the performances in different ways. *Lear Is Here* fuses the biographies of fictional characters and the performer.

Throughout its years of worldwide performances following its Paris premiere in 2000, Wu's *Lear* has attracted audiences who have come to see Wu's most religious and autobiographical play, rather than simply yet another "Shakespeare in Chinese dress" or "Chinese theatre piece marketed through Shakespeare's currency." The production has been very well received by leading writers, scholars, and theater practitioners in both China and the West, including Ariane Mnouchkine, Eugenio Barba, Tan Dun (a New York–based Chinese composer), and Mo Yan (a best-selling Chinese novelist).[68] Wu's *Lear* is now one of an increasing number of Chinese Shakespeare productions initiated or commissioned by European theaters and festivals, including mainland Chinese director Lin Zhaohua's *huaju Richard III*, commissioned by the 2001 Berlin Asia Pacific Cultural Festival.

While Lai's *Lear* focuses on the division of the kingdom and offers a Buddhist reading of it, the aesthetic focal point of Wu's *Lear* is the division of the artist's self. Wu's take on the tension between the actor and his roles is analogous to that of William Shakespeare Jr., the Fifth's comments in Jean-Luc Godard's *King Lear*: "I've reinvented the lines. I've reinvented the plot. Now it's up to the characters. Or maybe it's the actors." Wu's *Lear* shares with Godard's film an attempt at self-understanding through restaging the creative process. As Peter Donaldson observes, "As the film opens itself . . . to the posthumous mess of the editing room, . . . Godard embraces one version of *King Lear*'s teaching, accepting limitations on his control and acknowledging the dangerous, chaotic, and contingent future that attends his (and our own) attempts at self understanding and creation."[69] The film bears the autobiographical trace of Godard's struggle with the Cannon production company.[70] One of the many narrative levels of Wu's *Lear* is the actor's struggle with the cultural institution known as Taiwan's *jingju*—a hybrid genre alternately seen as an oxymoron and an exciting new spectacle.

Coda

The post-1990s era has witnessed more internationally touring productions. Within the Sinophone world, there is a new focus on identity issues and their relationships to Shakespeare's individual characters. Stan Lai's contribution to Chinese-language theater and Shakespeare performance lies in his theatricalization of power and religion, as well as his articulation of Buddhist discourse in an increasingly politicized, secular world. Wu Hsing-kuo's production provides a radically personalized *local* Shakespeare. Their projects reveal that local readings of Shakespeare are not mimicry of originals of a higher order, but new epistemologies that actively participate in the formation of knowledge about China and Shakespeare and, in Wu's case, self-knowledge. While cultural translation is still inevitably allegorical, more artists are asking the question: Can engagements with canonical literature also be personal? And they are asking such questions with growing force.

Epilogue

In this study's conclusion lies its beginning. The epigraph to chapter 1, ". . . for the eye sees not itself / But by reflection, by some other things," bears dwelling upon. It is a useful allegorical resource to further our understanding of the rhetorical and critical construction of Chinese Shakespeares. Shakespeare's plays have allowed the writers, performers, readers, and audiences to see China through the eye of the Other, but this vision also becomes a projection of the gaze of Shakespeare's Other. The simultaneous dissociation of Shakespeare from the English Renaissance culture and association of unexpected texts create a new space of fiction—a postnational public sphere of diverse forms of multiculturalism in which the figures of Shakespeare and China operate.[1]

The heterogeneity and heteroglossia of Chinese Shakespeares frustrate intellectual tokenism and monolithic stereotypes. As the accents and visual signs of cultural production are fluidly shifted and reconfigured, they not only reflect changing historical exigencies but also register the artists' and readers' personal histories and localities. An experimental director may activate a series of Asian cultural markers but refuse to affiliate herself or himself with any of them (Ariane Mnouchkine and Ong Keng Sen); a writer may lay claim to both Beijing localism and cosmopolitan visions (Lao She); at international festivals, a Beijing-based director may prefer to be recognized for his personal style rather than his Chinese roots (Lin Zhaohua); a Taiwan playwright can belong at the same time to the communities of Taiwanese Americans and mainland Chinese emigrants to Taiwan (Stan Lai); in cyberspace, a Beijing-opera theater company can create new local connections with its potential patrons via interactive media (Wu Hsing-kuo's Contemporary Legend Theatre); and an immigrant director may identify simultaneously with London and Hong Kong (David Tse). An English actor may have an epiphany on a Chinese stage. Reflecting on the Royal Shakespeare Company's (RSC) first touring production in China (*Merchant of Venice*, 2002), Ian Bartholomew commented: "I have never encountered such sympathy playing Shylock before. Maybe performing the play in a non-Christian country creates a more even-handed response."[2]

The articulation of these wide-ranging localities is dictated by the roles of local and international cultural markets in the distinction between indigenous Shakespeares and those productions with less explicitly local association. As Chinese Shakespeares emerge in the international scenes, in addition to the thorny questions of authenticity and authority, one of the new artistic concerns is the pursuit of what can be called a global vernacular. The infatuation with Asian visuality examined in chapter 6 and elsewhere returns to haunt filmmakers and theater directors as they search for new vehicles to carry new artistic ideas across different cultural locations. These maneuvers are especially evident in films aiming at international markets and theater works commissioned by festivals. To tease out the practical and critical issues at stake behind the question of visuality, I would like to conclude with brief examinations of the uses of masks in Feng Xiaogang's film *The Banquet* and live video and children's games in Lin Zhaohua's stage production of *Richard III*.

The Banquet (*Yeyan*, 2006), with an all-star cast, emerged from a wave of period films and romantic epics that evoked internationally transferable and marketable conventions of cultural authenticity, ranging from John Madden's *Shakespeare in Love* (1998) to Zhang Yimou's *Hero* (2002) and *House of Flying Daggers* (2005) at the turn of the century.[3] Feng's film relies on transnational collaboration and symbolic geographies. Like a number of Chinese films that cater to transnational audiences, *The Banquet* exhibits a harmonious coexistence of grave subject matter and visual beauty, or what Rey Chow calls "a conjoined subalternization and commodification" in a different context.[4] Multiple slow-motion shots and fight sequences presented as stylized dance movements suggest a close affinity with other Chinese martial-arts films that have enjoyed popularity in the West but have been harshly criticized in the Chinese-speaking world, such as Ang Lee's *Crouching Tiger, Hidden Dragon* (2000). What distinguishes Feng's film from this group of films is its uses of masks as motifs and narrative devices. *The Banquet* incorporates some features of the sword-fighting knight-errant (*wuxia*) genre into a mask theater infused with the supernatural; a type of martial-arts performance that gives primacy to visual articulation but does not rely on, as is the case with *nō* theater, demonstration of the spiritual states of the characters through subtle shadings of the masks.[5]

The Banquet opens and closes with bold sequences involving masked figures engaged in a sword fight. The long opening sequence establishes a hierarchical order in which the visual dominates the verbal. In self-exile, the melancholic Prince Wu Luan is studying singing and mask dancing in a bamboo compound in the remote Yue region of southern China, when the messengers sent by his stepmother, Empress Wan (the Gertrude figure, played by Zhang Ziyi), arrive with the news of the death of his father and his uncle's ascension to the throne. Following the footsteps of the messengers, a group of assassins sent by the new emperor soon arrive at the compound. The prince wears a white mask without any patterns. Several shots focus on his eyes. It is notable that other than the opening narration and the imperial decree read by the messenger, no verbal exchange takes place in the prolonged scene, which is a study in color symbolism and nonverbal representations of emotion. In contrast to the prince and his companions' white masks and robes, symbolizing purity, the assassins wear black iron masks with bold patterns and are clad in black armor. An unnecessarily long and brutal fight sequence soon follows.

The masks serve several functions. As identity markers, they also conceal emotions. Prince Wu Luan wears the same mask and robe as his companions, and is thus able to escape the massacre. The ways the actors perform with the masks deny the audience access to their emotions throughout the fight. Very little eye contact between the characters is shown in this scene, which distinguishes it from the martial-arts-film convention it appropriates.

The film spells out the theme of surveillance in *Hamlet* through watchful eyes behind the masks. The camera movements frequently signal that the audience and the characters are gazing at a spectacle from a privileged position of invisibility. We see more varied uses of masks as the scene switches from the massacre at the bamboo compound to the imperial

FIGURE 26   Daniel Wu as Prince Wu Luan touching the mask and helmet of his dead father in *The Banquet*, directed by Feng Xiaogang, 2006. (Courtesy of Media Asia Distribution)

court, which is inhabited by more masked imperial guards who display no body language to indicate humanity or emotions. The camera follows Empress Wan through several corridors filled with guards. She finally stops in front of the dead emperor's armor, helmet, and dark mask. It is only when the camera zooms in that viewers see the new emperor's eyes behind the mask and recognize his presence. Empress Wan's first words to him touch on the mask's commemorative value and the theme of reality and representation: "The mask does not sit well on you." Her comments highlight the theme of conceit, to which Emperor Li replies candidly, "Indeed, this is not a good fit. I shall have a new one made." Dialogues and movement are kept to a minimum, as the contentions over identities—old and new—are conveyed through eye-line shots.

The same mask attracts the prince's attention, too, upon his return to the court (figure 26). The scene of Prince Wu Luan standing in front of his dead father's mask and armor is interpolated with an intimate scene between Emperor Li and Empress Wan. The presence of the ghost of Old Hamlet is indicated at this moment by a stream of bloody tears flowing from the hollow eyes of the mask. The camera moves to the back of the mask and shows the prince looking into its eyes. Again, the mise-en-scène prioritizes the visual over the verbal. The verbal exchanges between Hamlet and the ghost in the rampart scene are presented as a confrontation and alignment of the two pairs of eyes of the prince and his dead father, lending the scene a sense of ambivalence and air of a pantomime. Explicitly presented as a performer in the film, the prince meets the eyes of the Other, the empty signifier that is his dead father's mask. The scene recalls Wu Hsing-kuo's dramatization of the split of the selves of Wu and King Lear in his on-stage costume change in *Lear Is Here*. The sequence of the black mask with tears streaming down its cheeks is later interpolated with the dumb-show scene. Driven by his desire for Empress Wan's hand and for revenge, the prince is implicated in the visible and invisible aspects of reality. A devoted performer of mask theater, he not only plans the dumb show dramatizing the murder of his father to catch the conscience of Emperor Li, but also appears on stage as the drummer throughout the performance. The presence of a performer behind his mask intently observing his audience turns the play-within-a-play, a theatrical device that starts its career in the Renaissance, into a bold frame for the self-reflexivity of twenty-first-century cinema. Different aesthetic and social functions of masks lead to a pointed debate between Prince Wu Luan and Empress Wan. While the former insists that a good actor performs with masks and concentrates on body language, the latter rejoins that "the most sophisticated performer uses his or her own face and turns it into a mask." One has to wonder whether she might be right, as the prince is the only principal character to be obsessed with masks throughout the film.

The long documentary-style voice-over narration at the beginning of the film establishes the historical setting of Hamlet's story in ancient China. Engineered here is a constructed sense of superiority that is articulated through the perceived historical depth of the romantic epic, a sense of seriousness that seems to override Feng's presumably less worthy comic films in contemporary settings. Feng is at pains to establish the authenticity of the Yue song and mask dance.[6] He is one of the most successful Chinese filmmakers in the comedy genre, and Ge You, the lead actor playing Emperor Li, is an acclaimed comedian. *The Banquet* was Feng's first attempt at a tragedy and period drama that was aimed at international film festivals, which may explain the need to manufacture a sense of closure, rather than an opening up of possibilities, around the cultural textures of ancient China. The film uses the idea of a lavish visual feast, as its title seems to promise, as a global vernacular.

Artists and critics of different persuasions and cultural backgrounds tend to agree on the market value of Asian visuality. Kenneth Rothwell, a scholar of Shakespeare on film, asserts that non-Anglophone filmmakers "enjoyed the luxury of reinventing the plays in purely cinematic terms, as if they were silent movies," because they did not need to "record in

English on the sound track."[7] It is useful to recall what I have termed positive stereotyping in chapter 6 (the use of masks in Huang Zuolin's *kunju*-style *Macbeth*, for example) in the tendency to see Asian theater and film as pure spectacle. The idea of a necessarily Asian visuality is implicated in a hierarchical view informed by an ideology of the print that puts spectacles to the service of textual elucidation.

Although visual beauty is commonly seen as an integral part of transnational Chinese cinema, the disparity in the film's reception raises the questions of how border-crossing works are seen and why. These debates are no less dramatic than the film itself. In fact, much more than just a metadrama of the intercultural performance, the film's reception itself is a performative act of exchanges initiated by spectacles. Heated debates about different issues ensued when this high-profile, big-budget feature film premiered at the film festivals in Venice and Cannes, and subsequently in the Sinophone world.[8] The film has been critiqued by both Chinese and Western constituencies for transgressing cultural norms. At the center of the debate is the film's dual identity. *The Banquet* was initially promoted as a Shakespearean film with martial-arts elements, but nearly all European judges found the film to be too Shakespearean in outlook to be a viable Chinese film to interest Western audiences. One critic at the Venice festival wrote, "We hope to see a Chinese movie with Chinese taste here in Italy. But we feel a bit disappointed. If the background was cut out, we could hardly tell that this was a Chinese movie."[9] Yet according to most Chinese critics, the film was a disappointing, indulgent costume epic aimed at a "completely non-Chinese audience."[10] In particular, Ge You "got laughs whenever he appeared since Chinese moviegoers are familiar with his [famous] comedy roles and found his seriousness unnatural."[11] Feng contributed to the mass culture construction of the myth about China in the same way Shakespeare's celebrity biography has been packaged in a time warp in *Shakespeare in Love*.[12] In this process, Shakespeare and spectacles of China's past have emerged repeatedly as a repository of abiding qualities of sensibility. As much as Feng's attempt to dislocate *Hamlet* via a visual method may invite skepticism, it is also part of the globalization of visual culture as a late capitalist response to the dominance of oral and print cultures. The problem goes beyond extensive knowledge or ignorance of either Shakespearean or Chinese aesthetics, and the case of *The Banquet* is not unique.[13]

Lin Zhaohua's *Richard III* (2001) was just as controversial as Feng's *The Banquet*, but for different reasons.[14] It received mixed reviews in Beijing and Berlin. Lin handled the question of visuality differently. Commissioned by the Asien-Pazifik Wochen festival of Berlin with a transnational network of funding from Japan, China, and Germany, the production starred wildly popular Chinese television stars such as Zhu Yuanyuan.[15] One of the most respected mainland Chinese avant-garde directors today, Lin refused to succumb to the logic of naturalized cultural equivalences.[16] The many political interpretations examined in preceding chapters suggest that the Cultural Revolution or Mao Zedong's rise to power as a mass murderer and dictator favored by the masses may provide powerful points of reference for directors and audiences. Instead of contemporary relevance or iconic local visual signs—a strategy commonly used by both Anglophone and Asian directors—Lin opted for formal experiments. One of the recent performances that capitalize, and indeed rely, on naturalized modern equivalences to Shakespearean setting and circumstances is Richard Loncraine and Ian McKellen's film *Richard III* (1995). In the long sequence of the climatic battle scene (Bosworth Field), set in the Battersea power station, the director is at pains to establish the credibility of the much anticipated line "A horse! A horse! My kingdom for a horse!" by trapping Richard's jeep in mud and destroying any other possible means of escape (in fact, all vehicles in sight).[17] Lin's production in Berlin was supposed to serve up a palatable portion of contemporary Chinese theater for the German and international audiences—culturally specific presentations with transferable Chinese tastes to fit on the sampling platters of international festivals. However, unlike Sulayman al-Bassam's Arab *Richard III* (RSC Complete Works festival in Stratford-upon-Avon, 2007) or Al Pacino's *Looking for Richard* (1996), which stripped or questioned English history and Shakespeare's text, Lin's production did not accommodate local cultural history or distinctively local performance styles (as in Pacino's "large incursions of urban American speech patterns").[18] Collective memory improvises and challenges history, revealing as much as it obscures. Lin's production calls to mind Leopold Lindtberg's 1962 production of *Richard III* at the Vienna Burgtheater. Forced into exile because of his Jewish origin during the Nazi period, Lindtberg not only opposed what he called "the boredom of indoctrination that is alien to art,"[19] but also refrained from any design, costume, or stylistic elements suggestive of Hitler or Nazi Germany—"too cheap an effect to mould *Richard III* into a paraphrase of recent historical events."[20]

Like his earlier production of *Hamlet,* Lin's *Richard III* thrived on the notion of theatrical doubles and extemporized games. Richard both entertained and killed. Ma Shuliang took great pride in his double role as the narrator/director and Richard of Gloucester.[21] The multimedia performance was framed by various children's games, including tag, musical chairs, hide and seek, shadow play, and other playground games. At one point, the characters turned innocent games into cruel, violent ones without Richard's guidance. With a unique take on the comedic potential of the tragedy, the production turned *Richard III* into a game space that paralleled the "kitchen table massacre" and the arcade games that Chiron and Demetrius play in Julie Taymor's film *Titus*—although in Lin's production it is the adults, not the children, who engaged in child's play.[22] Inoculated with live and prerecorded video footages, the production strategically deployed media convergence to allegorize Richard's propagandistic inclinations. The lighthearted performance became a deliberate contrast to the tragic events following the game scenes. As scenes of conspiracy and murder morphed into light-hearted exercises and games of cruelty, actors frequently appeared to be both immersed in and detached from the scenes at the same time.

Surrounded by corpses left over from an earlier game, Richard wooed Lady Anne. Close-up shots of their interaction and, alternately, their faces were projected onto the left side of the proscenium arch, separating the physical and verbal components of the seduction. The video projection simulated televised narratives that sought to replace the liveness of newsworthy events. Richard held a defenseless Lady Anne, also clad in a black suit, in his arms while giving her his full attention. While the live video footage in the wooing scene competed for the audience's divided attention, the striking prerecorded video footage at the end of the stylized murder of Clarence attempted to better the nonchalant staging of fratricide. Clarence first appeared on stage among the stagehands. He helped to erect an elegant structure that would become his own prison cell. Richard appeared briefly on stage to push Clarence into the brightly lit prison and left the stage to the two murderers. Clarence stood motionless at the center of his cell. As he described his "miserable night / . . . full of fearful dreams . . . [and] ugly sights" (1.4.2–4), the lights began to dim. The first murderer killed him with a symbolic slap on his face, with the sound effect provided by the second murderer clapping his hands: "Take that! And that! / . . . I'll drown you in the malmsey-butt within" (1.4.269–70). The death of Clarence and the reference to a keg of wine cued the stage-wide projections of gasping fish bathed in blood (shot in a fish market in Shenzhen), accompanied by light jazz music. It seemed as if the alternative aesthetics derived from the children's games came up short and had to be supplemented by a richer network of visual citations of social violence.

The same strategy of visual citation was used in the coronation scene, in which Buckingham literally orchestrated Richard's rise to power (accompanied by close-up shots of Richard's face projected at the side of the stage), with the Lord Mayor and the citizens of London singing Richard's praises—under Buckingham's direction—from within the same structure that was formerly Clarence's prison cell. After Richard exited with exaggerated bouncy, clownish movements, a prerecorded video of hundreds of ants crawling in all directions took over the stage. Similarly, in an earlier scene, after the death of Edward IV, another video appeared. A few teens were playing violent video games in an arcade. There were moments when it was no longer clear from the close-up shots whether they were just playing or engaging in an actual killing spree.

Obsessively clean in its streamlined presentation of violence, the production is far less sanguine than most twentieth-century performances. Western critics have been struck by its ongoing "cross-pollinations between different media"[23] and juxtaposition between visual pleasure and disgust, as evidenced by, among many instances, Clarence's death in a "visually pleasing prison cell" and the "unsettling stage-wide projections of gasping fish heads in pools of blood" immediately after his death.[24] Such juxtaposition between live performance on stage and video footages mediates between Shakespeare as a visual event and a textual show.

The parodic and citational impulse of Lin's *Richard III* hearkens back to Lao She's "New Hamlet" (1936) and Xiong Yuanwei's *Hamlet/Hamlet* (2000), but its significance goes beyond the dichotomized model of popularization of Shakespeare's history plays in modern times or Asian avantgarde theater in Europe. The convergence of filmic and theatrical modes of presentation might be the new "sportive tricks" Richard needs to woo the global spectator. The intercultural reading of *Richard III* shows that non-Anglophone performances of Shakespeare are not a matter of dumbing down or selling out, an enterprise at the mercy of the currency of local equivalences and the constructed quality of global vogues.[25]

The *Richard III* project has allowed Lin and his audiences in different cultural locations to see Shakespeare and their own visions of China through the eye of the Other, while *The Banquet* posed new questions about the nature of martial-arts period film and *Hamlet*, a play that has always already begun for modern English-speaking audiences. Since 1839, several generations of writers, filmmakers, and theater directors have taken imaginative approaches to engage productively with the gap of knowledge about different texts, creating various models of localization that diffuse and sustain multiple origins of plot, artistic form, and social circumstances. They did not interact with Shakespeare and China through a bilateral relationship with an original source, even though they often claim to the contrary, but instead worked in constant dialogue with a kaleidoscope of sources and modes of representation found in fictive localities. Their works bear out the troubled relationship between what is seen as the local and the global. Far from a parochial enterprise, Chinese Shakespeares have contributed to the transformation of local cultural practices and national and personal identities.

The challenge of thinking about cultural exchange at the present time is that even though the constructedness of such entities as Shakespeare and China is increasingly seen as self-evident, their encounters are often comfortably compartmentalized and typecast. The significance of the history of Chinese Shakespeares lies in its transformative power for artistic and critical endeavors, not in its evolutionary sequentiality (Did they finally get Shakespeare and Chinese opera right?) or popular use of polarity (English versus foreign Shakespeares; authentic versus inauthentic Chinas). As China occupies a transitional, multiply determined space, the differing faces of Chinese Shakespeares signal an epistemic shift, the arrival of multiple forms to engage widely circulated texts, personal history, and local consciousness. This shift is partly governed by the late capitalist market economy (as it is in the West)[26] and partly determined by the rise of the local artist's star power as a new form of cultural prestige in competition with Shakespeare's reputation.[27]

The end of almost two centuries of Chinese Shakespeares is the beginning of a fresh chapter for artists and critics, invigorated and challenged at once by the future localities yet to be created. Performing otherness is an art of re/writing as well as reading, and translation an act of obliteration as well as restoration. Historical and imagined boundaries constitute the very locality from which Shakespeare and China begin their presencing.[28] The alternating absence and presence of Shakespearean and Chinese texts throughout history suggests that new readings of intercultural signs will persist, that cultural rootedness—even if articulated differently—will continue to matter, and that visions of Shakespeare and China will remain open for future inscriptions.

Select Chronology

Year	Historical Events	Worldwide Shakespeares	Chinese Shakespeares
1596		English players tour extensively in Europe in the 1590s	Transmission of Renaissance culture begins in China
1597		"Bad" quarto of *Romeo and Juliet* published	
1598	Publication of *Peony Pavilion* by Tang Xianzu; often compared with *Romeo and Juliet*		
1602		*Hamlet* "lately acted by the Lord Chamberlain his servants" (entry in Stationers' Registrar, July 26)	
1607	John Smith founds colony of Virginia at Jamestown	*Hamlet* performed on board the *Red Dragon*, anchored near Sierra Leone	
1609	Dutch East India Company imports first shipment of tea from China	*Hamlet* performed in Socotra, Gulf of Aden (Republic of Yemen), in 1608	

Year	Historical Events	Worldwide Shakespeares	Chinese Shakespeares
1619		*Hamlet* performed by employees of the Dutch East India Company in Jayakarta, Indonesia	
1807		Charles and Mary Lamb publish *Tales from Shakespeare*, which has a great influence on the initial reception of Shakespeare in East Asia	
1839	The first Opium War (1839–1842) begins Lin Zexu publishes *Annals of the Four Continents*		First mention of Shakespeare in Chinese by Lin Zexu, who attempts to stop the opium trade
1842	China cedes Hong Kong Island to Britain for 150 years	First mention of Shakespeare in Japanese (1841 translation of a Dutch translation of an English grammar book)	
1848	Karl Marx and Friedrich Engels publish *Manifest der kommunist-ischen Partei*		
1864	China's self-strengthening movement begins	Deutsche Shakespeare-Gesellschaft founded	Rapid growth of foreign presence in such treaty ports as Shanghai and Tianjin
1867			Hong Kong Amateur Dramatic Club stages Francis Talfourd's *Shylock, or the Merchant of Venice Preserved*, revived in 1871
1877	St. John's University founded in Shanghai		Shakespeare is included in university curriculum in China
1879		Scenes from *The Taming of the Shrew* performed in English in the Gaiety Theatre in Yokohama	Guo Songtao, China's first minister to England, attends Henry Irving's *Hamlet*

Year	Historical Events	Worldwide Shakespeares	Chinese Shakespeares
1894			Yan Fu discusses Shakespeare's characters in the preface to his translation of Thomas Huxley's *Evolution and Ethics*
1895	China cedes Taiwan to Japan for fifty years		
1896	First modern Olympic Games held in Athens		The trial scene of *The Merchant of Venice* performed in English at St. Johns University, Shanghai
1898	Britain granted a ninety-nine-year lease of the New Territories (Hong Kong)		Liang Qichao's *New Rome* features Shake-speare, Voltaire, and Dante as characters
1899		Film of Herbert Beerbohn Tree's *King John*	
1904	Russo-Japanese War begins		Lin Shu and Wei Yi rewrite the Lambs' *Tales from Shakespeare*
1907	*Huaju* (spoken drama) as a new theater genre is born		
1911	Republic of China established

Colonization of Korea by Japan (1910–1945) | *Hamlet*, dir. E. G. Craig and K. S. Stanislavsky, Moscow | *The Merchant of Venice* and *Macbeth* available with Chinese annotations |
| 1913 | | *Twelfth Night*, dir. Harley Granville-Barker, London, 1912

Max Reinhardt stages ten Shakespearean plays at Deutsches Theater, Berlin

Hamlet Rajah of Denmark, The Straits Opera Company, Malaysia, 1912 | First Chinese-language performances of Shakespeare: Shanghai Eastern Girls' High School's *The Woman Lawyer* (adapted from *The Merchant of Venice* by Bao Tianxiao)

Spring Willow Society's *The Taming of the Shrew* in Changsha

Hong Kong Mummers' *Twelfth Night* |

Year	Historical Events	Worldwide Shakespeares	Chinese Shakespeares
1914	World War I begins	*Romeo and Juliet*, Geijutsu Club, trans. Tsubouchi Shōyō, Japan	First Chinese-opera Shakespeare: Ya'an Chuanju Theatre's *Hamlet* (Wang Guoren)
1915	Yuan Shikai ascends the throne as the "Emperor of the Chinese Empire," betraying the republican revolution	*The Tempest*, dir. Max Reinhardt, Berlin	Lu Jingruo's *Spring Dream*, adapted from Kawakami Otojirō's *Othello* (1903)
1919	Treaty of Versailles ends World War I May Fourth movement begins	*The Tempest* from the Lambs' *Tales from Shakespeare* translated into Korean	
1921	Irish civil war	Asta Nielsen's *Hamlet: The Drama of Vengeance* (silent film, 1920) *Hamlet*, dir. Nobuchi Akira, prod. Elan Vital, a *shingeki* theater company, Kyoto	Tian Han translates *Hamlet*, the first Shakespearean play to be translated in its entirety into Chinese
1927	Chinese civil war begins	*Macbeth*, trans. Mori Ōgai, dir. Osanai Kaoru and Aoyama Sugisaku, prod. Tsukiji Shōgekijō, Japan	First Chinese cinematic Shakespeare: *The Woman Lawyer* (*The Merchant of Venice*), dir. Qiu Yixiang (silent film)
1931	Japan takes Manchuria	*Romeo and Juliet*, dir. Arnold Szyfman, Warsaw	*A Spray of Plum Blossom*, dir. Bu Wancang (silent film inspired by *The Two Gentlemen of Verona*)
1933	Bernard Shaw visits Shanghai		
1935	Mei Lanfang and his Beijing opera troupe perform in Moscow, which inspires Bertolt Brecht to develop his Verfremdungseffekt theory	*Khoon Ka Khoon* (*Hamlet*), dir. Sohrab Modi (black-and-white film with sound, India) *Romeo and Juliet*, dir. John Gielgud, London *A Midsummer Night's Dream*, dir. Max Reinhardt (film)	A Shakespearean production becomes the degree requirements for students at the National Drama School

Year	Historical Events	Worldwide Shakespeares	Chinese Shakespeares
1936	Large number of Jews immigrate to Shanghai from Germany, Austria, and Poland in the 1930s	*Macbeth*, dir. Orson Welles, WPA Negro Theatre Project, New York	Lao She's "New Hamlet" published *The Tempest*, trans. Zhu Shenghao
1937	World War II and the second Sino-Japanese War begin The Rape of Nanjing Colonial Japanization campaign begins in Taiwan (1937–1945)	*Julius Caesar*, dir. Orson Welles, New York	*The Merchant of Venice*, dir. Yu Shangyuan, Nanjing *Romeo and Juliet*, dir. Zhang Min, Shanghai
1942	Mao Zedong, "Talk at the Yan'an Forum on Literature and Arts"		*Hamlet*, dir. Jiao Juyin, staged in a Confucian temple, Jiang'an
1944		*Henry V*, dir. Laurence Olivier (film)	Li Jianwu's *Wang Deming*, an adaptation of *Macbeth*, published
1949	People's Republic of China founded The Nationalists (KMT), led by Chiang Kai-shek, retreat to Taiwan	Sol Jun-Sik publishes first Korean translation of *Hamlet* directly from the English text	First Mandarin performance of Shakespeare in Taiwan: *Clouds of Doubt* (*Othello*), staged by the Experimental Theatre of Taipei
1954	Deng Xiaoping is appointed secretary general of the Chinese Communist Party (CCP)	*Hamlet*, dir. Nikolai Okhlopkov, Moscow *The Taming of the Shrew*, dir. Tyrone Guthrie, Stratford, Ontario	Shakespeare festival in Hong Kong, April 23
1957	European Economic Community established	*Throne of Blood* (*Macbeth*), dir. Kurosawa Akira (film) *Coriolanus*, dir. Giorgio Strehler, Milan *West Side Story* (*Romeo and Juliet*), dir. Jerome Robbins, lyrics by Stephen Sondheim, Winter Garden Theater, New York	*Much Ado About Nothing*, dir. Yevgeniya K. Lipkovskaya and Hu Dao, Shanghai *Othello*, dir. Sergei Yutkevich (Sergei Bondarchuk as Othello, 1956) screened in China

Year	Historical Events	Worldwide Shakespeares	Chinese Shakespeares
1960		Kato Taï's *Castle of Flame*, a samurai film adaptation of *Hamlet*, starring Okawa Hasizo *The Bad Sleep Well* (*Hamlet*), dir. Kurosawa Akira (film)	*Hamlet*, dir. Jiao Juyin, Beijing
1961	The CCP temporarily loosens control over art and literature	Jan Kott, *Szkice o Szekspirze* (Warsaw: Panstwowy Instytut Wydawniczy); translated as *Shakespeare Our Contemporary* (1964)	Carbon-copy revival of Lipkovskaya's *Much Ado*, dir. Hu Dao, Dalian, Shenyang, and Shangai
1966	Ten-year Cultural Revolution begins War in Vietnam	*Chimes at Midnight* (*Henry IV*), dir. Orson Welles (film, Spain/Switzerland)	All foreign writers banned in China
1967		Tom Stoppard's *Rosencrantz and Guildenstern Are Dead*, National Theatre, London	Mainland Chinese writer Liang Shiqiu moves to Taiwan and publishes the first complete Chinese translation of Shakespeare's works (forty volumes)
1979	Deng Xiaoping announces the Open Door Policy in 1978	Carmelo Bene's radical *Richard III*, championed by Gilles Deleuze in *Superpositions*	Carbon-copy revival of Lipkovskaya's *Much Ado*, dir. Hu Dao, Shanghai, and broadcast live by Shanghai Television
1981	The CCP formally condemns Mao for his role in the Cultural Revolution	*Richard II*, dir. Ariane Mnouchkine, Cartoucherie de Vincennes, France	*Measure for Measure*, dir. Tolby Robertson, Beijing People's Art Theatre
1983	Arthur Miller visits China	*Nō Hamlet*, dir. Munakata Kuniyoshi, Nō Shakespeare Kenkyūkai, Japan	First Chinese-opera Shakespeare since the Cultural Revolution: *Othello*, dir. Ma Yong'an, Beijing Experimental Jingju Theatre *A Midsummer Night's Dream*, dir. Tisa Chang, Pan Asian Repertory Theater, New York

Year	Historical Events	Worldwide Shakespeares	Chinese Shakespeares
1984	Sino-British Joint Declaration, Hong Kong	*King Lear,* dir. Ingmar Bergman, Stockholm	Shakespeare festival, Hong Kong
		1 Henry IV, dir. Ariane Mnouchkine, Paris	Shakespeare Society of China founded
			The Merchant of Venice, dir. Daniel S. P. Yang, Hong Kong Repertory Theatre
1986	Democratic Progressive Party (DPP) founded in Taiwan	*Romeo and Juliet,* dir. Michael Bogdanov, Stratford	First Shakespeare festival in mainland China (Beijing and Shanghai, April 10–23)
		Korea's Company 76 produces Tom Stoppard's *Rosencrantz and Guildenstern Are Dead*	Wu Hsing-kuo's *Kingdom of Desire* (*Macbeth*), Contemporary Legend Theater, Taiwan
1988			*One Husband Too Many,* dir. Anthony Chan (film, Hong Kong)
1989	Tiananmen Square massacre	*Kathakali King Lear,* dir. David McRuvie and Annette Leday	*Richard III,* dir. Peng Liqi, trans. Zhu Shenghao, Shanghai Theatre Academy
	Fall of the Berlin Wall	John Elsom, ed., *Is Shakespeare Still Our Contemporary?* published	
1994	China's GDP grows at an average annual rate of 10 percent	*A Midsummer Night's Dream,* dir. Ninagawa Yukio, Tokyo	Second Shakespeare festival in mainland China (Shanghai)
1997	Britain returns Hong Kong to Chinese jurisdiction	Welcome Msomi's *uMabatha* (1972) chosen as one of the six productions to open the Globe Theatre in London	*Kiss Me Nana,* dir. Liang Zhimin, Godot Theatre, Taipei; revived in 1999
	Jiang Zemin legalizes private enterprise		*LEAR,* dir. Ong Keng Sen, Singapore, Hong Kong, and Tokyo
			A Midsummer Night's Dream, dir. Daniel S. P. Yang, Hong Kong

Year	Historical Events	Worldwide Shakespeares	Chinese Shakespeares
1999	Shakespeare voted "Writer of the Millennium," BBC News	*Titus*, dir. Julie Taymor	*A Rock 'n' Roll Midsummer Night's Dream of the East*, dir. Liang Zhimin, Taipei
		King Lear, dir. Ninagawa Yukio, Tokyo, London, and Stratford	
	Chinese premier Zhu Rongji quotes *The Merchant of Venice* to endorse the legitimacy of market law	Bilingual *Othello: A Play in Black and White*, dir. Royston Abel, Edinburgh Festival	Cao Lusheng's *Who Killed the King?* (*Hamlet*), Shanghai Theatre Academy, Hong Kong
2000	Chinese-French playwright, painter, and novelist Gao Xingjian awarded the Nobel Prize for Literature	*Hamlet*, dir. Michael Almereyda	Wu Hsing-kuo's solo *Lear Is Here* premieres in the Théâtre de l'Odéon and the Théâtre du Soleil, Paris
		Hamlet, dir. Peter Brook, Paris	
	Chen Shui-bian of the Democratic Progressive Party (DPP) elected president of Taiwan	*Othello*, dir. Jonathan Bank, National Asian-American Theatre, New York	Hong Kong Experimental Shakespeare festival
			Chicken Rice War, dir. Cheah Chee Kong (film, Singapore)
			Hamlet / Hamlet, dir. Xiong Yuanwei, Hong Kong
2001	Attacks on September 11	*Scotland, PA*, dir. Billy Morrissette (film)	*Richard III*, dir. Lin Zhaohua, Berlin Asia Pacific Cultural Festival
		Takahashi Yasunari, *kyōgen* adaptation of *The Comedy of Errors*, London Globe	*Lady Macbeth*, solo *chuanju* performance by Tian Mansha, Hong Kong, Bremen (2001), Berlin (2006)
		Ang Pagpapaamo sa Maldita (*The Taming of the Shrew*), dir. Ricardo Abad, Philippines,	
		The King Is Alive, dir. Kristian Levring	

Year	Historical Events	Worldwide Shakespeares	Chinese Shakespeares
2002	Hu Jintao succeeds Jiang Zemin as president of the People's Republic of China	Sulayman Al-Bassam's *The Al-Hamlet Summit* wins the Fringe First award at the Edinburgh International Fringe Festival *A Dream in Hanoi*, dir. Tom Weidlinger (documentary film) *Maori Merchant of Venice*, dir. Don Selwyn (film, New Zealand) *The Street King*, dir. James Gavin Bedford (film)	*Search: Hamlet,* dir. Ong Keng Sen, Kronborg Castle, Denmark *Romeo and Juliet*, dir. Zhang Jian, Holo Taiwanese Opera Troupe *Crazy Scenes* (from *Macbeth, Hamlet, Lear,* and *Othello*), dir. Wei Ying-chuan, Shakespeare's Wild Sisters Company, Taiwan *Henry IV,* dir. Li Chuan-tsan and Huang Wu-shan, I Wan Jan Glove Puppet Theatre, Taipei Royal Shakespeare Company's first touring production in China: *The Merchant of Venice,* dir. Loveday Ingram "Shakespeare Is ON" organized by British Council in Hong Kong
2003	SARS outbreak	*In Search of Shakespeare,* dir. Michael Wood (BBC) *The Merchant of Venice,* dir. Michael Radford	Shakespeare in Taipei Festival
2004	Magnitude 9.3 earthquake and tsunami in Indian Ocean		Zhu Shu's five-act play *Shakespeare* (1988) adapted into a radio drama and aired during UNESCO's World Heritage Committee conference, Suzhou

Year	Historical Events	Worldwide Shakespeares	Chinese Shakespeares
2005	Beijing's National Centre for the Performing Arts opens (designed by Paul Andreu) Beijing People's Art Theatre's *Thunderstorm* (by Cao Yu) staged in Washington, D.C.	*Wheel Performance: Romeo and Juliet*, dir. Kim Jin-man, Korea, features extreme sports stunts Takahashi Yasunari's *Kyogen of Errors*, dir. Nomura Mansai, San Francisco International Arts Festival	Shanghai Jingju Company's *Hamlet* tours to Denmark's Hamlet Summer festival *A Time to Love*, dir. Huo Jianqi (film) *As You Like It*, dir. Dennis Kennedy, Central Academy of Drama, Beijing
2006	Premier Su Tseng-chang of Taiwan and other politicians quote *Julius Caesar* at length to argue for or against President Chen	*Ur-Hamlet*, dir. Eugenio Barba, Kronborg Castle, Denmark, with a cast of nō, Balinese, Indian, Afro-Brazilian, and European performers *Romeo and Juliet*, dir. Oh Tae-suk, Mokhwa Repertory Company (Korea), London	*The Banquet* (*Hamlet*), dir. Feng Xiaogang (film, Mandarin) *The Prince of the Himalayas* (*Hamlet*), dir. Sherwood Hu (film, Tibetan) "Shakespeare for Day Laborers" event: open-air *Romeo and Juliet*, dir. Jiang Zejin (Communication University of China students' *huaju* production), Beijing Mandarin–English *King Lear*, dir. David Tse, Shanghai, Chengdu, Stratford, London

Year	Historical Events	Worldwide Shakespeares	Chinese Shakespeares
2007		*As You Like It*, dir. Kenneth Branagh (HBO film) All-female *kyōgen Richard III* (*Kuni nusubito; The Country Stealer*), Setagaya Public Theater, Japan Shakespeare in Washington (January–June), "a landmark festival of theatre, music, dance, film, art, and more throughout the nation's capital"	Wu Hsing-kuo's *Lear Is Here* (2000) staged at the Lincoln Center Festival, New York, and in San Jose, California *The Witches' Sonata* (*Macbeth*), dir. Lü Boshen, Tainaner Ensemble of Taiwan, staged at the Festival d'Avignon OFF Stage production based on the 2006 film *Prince of the Himalayas*, Shanghai *Coriolanus*, dir. Lin Zhaohua, Beijing People's Art Theatre Company
2008	Magnitude 7.9 earthquake in Sichuan Province Olympic Games held in Beijing Ma Ying-Jeou of the KMT elected president of Taiwan Regular, direct flights between China and Taiwan, ending a six-decade ban	*Hamlet 2*, dir. Andrew Fleming (film)	"Eternal Shakespeare" International Festival, Beijing Lee Kuo-hsiu's *Shamlet* (1992) revived in Beijing *Romeo and Zhuyingtai*, dir. He Nian, Shanghai Dramatic Arts Center *A Midsummer Night's Dream* (in Chinese), dir. Peter Lichtenfels, Shanghai Dramatic Arts Center *Othello*, dir. Liang Zhimin, Godot Theatre, Taipei

Notes

Prologue

1. Ernest Brennecke, *Shakespeare in Germany, 1590–1700* (Chicago: University of Chicago Press, 1964), 5–6; Simon Williams, *Shakespeare on the German Stage,* vol. 1, *1586–1914* (Cambridge: Cambridge University Press, 1990), 27–45; William Shakespeare, *Hamlet,* ed. Harold Jenkins (London: Methuen, 1982), 118–22.

2. Graham Holderness, introduction to *The Al-Hamlet Summit: A Political Arabsque,* by Sulayman Al-Bassam (Hatfield: University of Hertfordshire Press, 2006), 9. The English sailors' performances of *Hamlet* on September 5 and *Richard II* on September 30, 1607, were recorded in Captain William Keeling's journals. The performance of *Hamlet* was mentioned by Frederick Boas in 1923 and Ania Loomba in 1997 but not dealt with in depth until 2001 by Gary Taylor. *The East India Company Journals of Captain William Keeling and Master Thomas Bonner, 1615–1617,* ed. M. Stachan and B. Penrose (Minneapolis: University of Minnesota Press, 1971), 24; Frederick S. Boas, *Shakespeare and the Universities and Other Studies in Elizabethan Drama* (New York: Appleton, 1923), 95; Ania Loomba, "Shakespearian Transformations," in *Shakespeare and National Culture,* ed. John J. Joughin (Manchester: Manchester University Press, 1997), 111; Gary Taylor, "*Hamlet* in Africa 1607," in *Travel Knowledge: European "Discoveries" in the Early Modern Period,* ed. Ivo Kamps and Jyotsna G. Singh (London: Palgrave, 2001), 223–48; E. K. Chambers, *William Shakespeare* (Oxford: Clarendon Press, 1930) 2:334–35; "Excerpts from the Journals of John Hearne and William Finch,

Merchants, Aboard the *Red Dragon* in 1607, en route from England to India," reprinted with annotations by Gary Taylor, in *Travel Knowledge*, ed. Kamps and Jyotsna, 211–22.

3. "Actors and directors are no longer regarded as betrayers and violators of Shakespeare's sacred texts, but are treated with respect, even deference, by academics" (Robert Shaughnessy, *The Shakespeare Effect: A History of Twentieth-Century Performance* [New York: Palgrave, 2002], 5). Stephen Greenblatt used the phrase "the dream of the master text" to critique the urge to "link certain admired scripts to a single known playwright" (general introduction to *The Norton Shakespeare*, 2nd ed., ed. Stephen Greenblatt, Walter Cohen, Jean Howard, and Katherine Maus [New York: Norton, 2008], 67–72).

4. Scholars and journalists have recently named a number of English writers as potent and palpable rivals of Shakespeare's global fame, including Charles Dickens, Jane Austen, and Samuel Beckett. Governments also compete for primacy on the global stage through cultural celebrities. Norway declared 2006 "The Year of Ibsen" and sponsored various festivals and conferences throughout the world, including a series of stage productions, radio and television shows, and a new Ibsen documentary film in Dakka, Bangladesh, in May 2006. The Bangladesh Ibsen Society was founded the next month. The year 2006, the centennial of Samuel Beckett's birth, also witnessed festivals, symposia, performances, and exhibits around the world. Dickens has a theme park dedicated to him in Chatham, England (Dickens World). Reporting on the release of British actress Emma Campbell Webster's *Lost in Austen: Create Your Own Jane Austen Adventure*, an interactive fiction game with the reader as the main character, David Gates writes, "Austen is the Virginia Woolf of 2007: a certifiably great novelist starring in books and films, yet one who might go to the same manicurist as you. Shakespeare and Dickens were pop-culture entertainers in centuries past, but as familiar as they remain, they've sunk into venerability" ("True or False: Jane Austen Outsells Alice Walker and Ann Coulter," *Newsweek*, June 23, 2007, http://www.msnbc.msn.com/id/19390924/). According to statistics, Austen, Tolkien, and Hardy ranked among the most borrowed classic authors in public libraries in Britain from 1991 to 2003, beating Shakespeare in every year. One of the possible interpretations of this data is that Shakespeare has been so fully incorporated into the British education and public life that most readers own copies of his plays and did not need to use the library. Marjorie Perloff, "Presidential Address 2006: It Must Change," *PMLA* 122, no. 3 (2007): 652–62; Chung Shin-jyh, "Cong Nanya kan Ibusen" [Ibsen Commemorated in South Asia], *Xiju xuekan* [*Taipei Theater Journal*] 4 (2006): 145–53; for the statistics, Annika Bautz, *The Reception of Jane Austen and Walter Scott: A Comparative Longitudinal Study* (London: Continuum, 2007), 131.

5. Among many popular narratives in the American media, see "China's Century," *Newsweek*, May 9, 2005.

6. In the twenty-first century, even those Shakespearean plays that express a distinctively Renaissance notion of social hierarchy continue to fascinate audiences "otherwise long ago seduced by the rival claims of middle-class social realism, of post-modern minimalism or of sheer escapism" (Michael Dobson,

introduction to *Performing Shakespeare's Tragedies Today: The Actor's Perspective*, ed. Michael Dobson [Cambridge: Cambridge University Press, 2006], 1).

7. For example, Ariane Mnouchkine (b. 1939) appropriated both Shakespeare and Asian representational practices (*jingju*, kabuki, *nō*, *kathakali*) in Théâtre du Soleil works such as *Richard II, Henry IV Part I*, and *Twelfth Night* in the 1980s. Her interculturalism in these high-profile productions has attracted both praise and criticism. Dennis Kennedy, for example, finds her "tasty oriental Shakespeare" and the "enormous cultural dislocation" problematic ("Afterword: Shakespearean Orientalism," in *Foreign Shakespeare: Contemporary Performance*, ed. Dennis Kennedy [Cambridge: Cambridge University Press, 1993], 294). Dominique Goy-Blanquet, meanwhile, justifies Mnouchkine's approach in "Shakespearean History at the Avignon Festival," in *Shakespeare's History Plays*, ed. Ton Hoenselaars (Cambridge: Cambridge University Press, 2004), 228–43.

8. Kenneth S. Rothwell, *A History of Shakespeare on Screen: A Century of Film and Television*, 2nd ed. (Cambridge: Cambridge University Press, 2004), 51; Walter Benjamin, "The Work of Art in the Age of Mechanical Reproduction," in *Illuminations*, ed. Hannah Arendt, trans. Harry Zohn (London: Pimlico, 1999), 235.

9. Victor Shklovsky, "Art as Technique," trans. Lee T. Lemon and Marion J. Reis, in *Modern Criticism and Theory: A Reader*, ed. David Lodge (London: Longman, 1988), 16–30.

10. Throughout this study, the term "globalization" refers to the global dissemination and circulation of cultural goods and what Pierre Bourdieu has termed "cultural capital" (*Distinction: A Social Critique of the Judgment of Taste*, trans. Richard Nice [Cambridge, Mass.: Harvard University Press, 1984], 2, and *The Field of Cultural Production: Essays on Art and Literature*, ed. Randal Johnson [New York: Columbia University Press, 1993]). Although those in possession of the cultural capital may not recognize its value in the same way as those who do not, it played a major role in mobilizing the asymmetrical cultural flows around the globe. See also Fredric Jameson, preface to *The Cultures of Globalization*, ed. Fredric Jameson and Masao Miyoshi (Durham, N.C.: Duke University Press, 1998), xi.

11. Ong Keng Sen, personal interview, Singapore, August 8, 2007.

12. Nicolas Standaert, "The Transmission of Renaissance Culture in Seventeenth-Century China," in *Asian Travel in the Renaissance*, ed. Daniel Carey (Oxford: Blackwell, 2004), 42–66.

13. Lord Macartney's mission has emerged as a major issue in recent studies of imperialism. James L. Hevia, *Cherishing Men from Afar: Qing Guest Ritual and the Macartney Embassy of 1793* (Durham, N.C.: Duke University Press, 1995), and *English Lessons: The Pedagogy of Imperialism in Nineteenth-Century China* (Durham, N.C.: Duke University Press, 2003), 156–92; Lydia Liu, *The Clash of Empires: The Invention of China in Modern World Making* (Cambridge, Mass.: Harvard University Press, 2004).

14. Evert Ysbrants Ides, ambassador of Russia, and his secretary, Adam Brand (d. 1713), each recorded their experiences. Their journals were translated into English in the eighteenth century and into Chinese in modern times. Evert Ysbrants Ides, *Three Years Travels from Moscow Over-land to China* (London: W. Freeman,

J. Walthoe, T. Newborough, J. Nicholson, and R. Parker, 1706); Adam Brand, *A Journal of the Embassy from Their Majesties John and Peter Alexievitz, Emperors of Muscovy over Land into China* (London: D. Brown and T. Goodwin, 1698).

15. Claudia Schnurmann, "'Wherever profit leads us, to every sea and shore . . .': The VOC, the WIC, and Dutch Methods of Globalization in the Seventeenth Century," *Renaissance Studies* 17 (2003): 474–93; Robert Markley, *The Far East and the English Imagination, 1600–1730* (Cambridge: Cambridge University Press, 2006), 64, 70–79.

16. Li Tiangang, ed., *Da Qing diguo chengshi yinxiang* [*Impressions of Nineteenth-Century Chinese Cities, Allom's Painting*] (Shanghai: Shanghai guji chubanshe, 2002), 144.

17. Theodore Huters, *Bringing the World Home: Appropriating the West in Late Qing and Early Republican China* (Honolulu: University of Hawai'i Press, 2005), 3.

18. After seeing Bottom's transformation, he says: "Bless thee, Bottom, bless thee! Thou art translated" (3.1.118–19).

19. Often lauded as a theatrical integration of multiple art forms and choreographed gesture, *xiqu* theater is commonly known as Chinese opera in the West. The word "opera" in the translation reflects a concept based on Richard Wagner's idea of *Gesamtkunstwerk*, a total artwork of music, dance, poetic, and dramatic arts. However, Chinese opera is not an accurate translation. Wang Guowei (1877–1927) defines *xiqu* as a theater in which "stories [are] imparted by singing and dancing" ("Xiqu kaoyuan" [The Origin of Traditional Theater], *Wang Guowei xiqu lunwen ji* [*Collected Essays on Drama by Wang Guowei*] [Taipei: Liren shuju, 1993], 233). As Elizabeth Wichmann-Walczak and Trevor Hay define it, "literally [meaning] theatre of sung-verse, . . . *xiqu* actually represents a complex, multifaceted conception that defies the use of a simple translation" (*Encyclopedia of Asian Theatre*, ed. Samuel L. Leiter, 2 vols. [Westport, Conn.: Greenwood Press, 2007], 2:853).

20. It further states: "[I]t is hoped [the play] may be received as the stray leaves of a Jerusalem hearty-joke. To which are added a description of the costume and the whole of the stage business" (Francis Talfourd, *Shylock; or, The Merchant of Venice Preserved* [London: Lacy, 1853]).

21. Barbara Mittler, "Defy(N)ing Modernity: Women in Shanghai's Early News-Media (1872–1915)," *Jindai Zhongguo funü shi yanjiu* [*Research on Women in Modern Chinese History*] 11 (2003): 215–60; Sun Huimin, "Minguo shiqi de nü lüshi (1927–1949)" [Women Lawyers in Shanghai in Republican China (1927–1949)] (paper presented at the XVth Biennial Conference of the European Association of Chinese Studies, Heidelberg, August 25–29, 2004).

22. Emi Suïin, "Osero," *Bungei Kurabu* 9, no. 3 (1903).

23. The Japanese play was adapted by Lu Jingruo as *Spring Dream* (*Chun meng*) and staged in Chinese by the Spring Willow Society in China, a group founded by Chinese students studying in Tokyo in 1906. Zheng Zhengqiu, ed., "Xiyang xinju" [New Western Plays], in *Xinju kaozheng baichu* [*Studies of One Hundred New Plays*] (Shanghai: Zhonghua tushu jicheng gongsi, 1919), 24; Ayako Kano, *Acting Like a Woman in Modern Japan: Theater, Gender, and Nationalism* (New York: Palgrave, 2001), 107; Siyuan Liu, "Adaptation as Appropriation: Staging Western

Drama in the First Western-Style Theatres in Japan and China," *Theatre Journal* 59, no. 3 (2007): 411–29.

24. Marshall Johnson, "Making Time: Historic Preservation and the Space of Nationality," in *New Asian Marxisms*, ed. Tani E. Barlow (Durham, N.C.: Duke University Press, 2002), 105–71; Leo T. S. Ching, *Becoming "Japanese": Colonial Taiwan and the Politics of Identity Formation* (Berkeley: University of California Press, 2001).

25. Both the Japanese colonial government and the early Chinese Nationalist regime made it a priority to assimilate Taiwanese society culturally, as evidenced by the Japanization campaign (Kominka or *huangminhua yundong*, 1937–1945) during the colonial period, the KMT-led national language (Mandarin) campaign, and the anti-Communist movement in the 1950s and 1970s.

26. Carl T. Smith, "The Hong Kong Amateur Dramatic Club and Its Predecessors," *Journal of the Hong Kong Branch of Royal Asiatic Society* 22 (1982): 218.

27. Dorothy Wong, "'Domination by Consent': A Study of Shakespeare in Hong Kong," in *Colonizer and Colonized*, ed. Theo D'haen and Patricia Krüs (Amsterdam: Rodpi, 2000), 43–56; Ng Lun Ngai-ha, *Interactions of East and West: Development of Public Education in Early Hong Kong* (Hong Kong: Chinese University Press, 1984), 74.

28. Dorothy Wong, "Shakespeare in a Hong Kong Frame," in *Shakespeare Global/Local: The Hong Kong Imaginary in Transcultural Production*, ed. Kwok-kan Tam, Andrew Parkin, and Terry Siu-han Yip (Frankfurt: Peter Lang, 2002), 63.

29. Kwok-kan Tam, Andrew Parkin, and Terry siu-han Yip, eds., preface to *Shakespeare Global/Local*, ed. Tam, Parkin, and Yip, ix.

30. Semicolonialism and semifeudalism are part of the Chinese Communist rhetoric deployed to signal the oppressive structures in China. Semicolony (*ban zhimindi*) was used by Mao Zedong and other Chinese Communists to describe late-nineteenth-century Chinese social formation in the shadow of Anglo-European imperialism. Shanghai, for example, was not under complete colonial domination or claim of sovereignty by the nations that had fractured colonial presence in the concessions. Recent scholarship has problematized such a dichotomized view of the dynamics of late Qing and early Republican Chinese society. Mao Zedong, "Zhongguo geming yu Zhongguo gongchandang" [Chinese Revolution and the Chinese Communist Party], in *Mao Zedong xuanji* [Selected Writings of Mao Zedong], ed. Central Committee of the Chinese Communist Party (Beijing: Renmin chubanshe, 1967), 589; Xia Xiaohong, *Wan Qing nüxing yü jindai Zhongguo* [Late Qing Women and Modern China] (Beijing: Beijing daxue chubanshe, 2004), 1–6; Shu-mei Shih, *The Lure of the Modern: Writing Modernism in Semicolonial China, 1917–1937* (Berkeley: University of California Press, 2001), 31, 34–36.

31. Adele Lee, "*One Husband Too Many* and the Problem of Postcolonial Hong Kong," in *Shakespeare in Hollywood, Asia, and Cyberspace*, ed. Alexander C. Y. Huang and Charles Ross (West Lafayette, Ind.: Purdue University Press, 2009); Yong Li Lan, "*Romeo and Juliets*, Local/Global," in *Shakespeare's Local Habitations*, ed. R. S. White and Krystyna Courtney (Poland: Lodz University Press, 2009).

32. *A Time to Love* (*Qingren jie*) starred Zhao Wei as Hou Jia and Lu Yi as Qu Ran; it is based on Shakespeare's *Romeo and Juliet* and An Dun's *Endless Shakespeare* (*Zhi wujin de Shashibiya*).

33. For a discussion of *The Banquet* (*Yeyan*), see the epilogue. Featuring an all-Tibetan cast, *The Prince of the Himalayas* (*Ximalaya wangzi*) was screened at the AFI Los Angeles Film Festival, Palm Spring Festival, Adelaide Festival, and elsewhere.

34. *Killing the Elder Brother and Snatching the Sister-in-Law* (*Sha xiong duo sao*) was performed in 1914 by the Ya'an Chuanju Company.

35. *A Pound of Flesh* (*Yi bang rou*) was written in 1925 by Wang Fucheng. *Qinqiang*, or Shaanxi opera, is one of the oldest forms of Chinese opera, originating in the Qin dynasty (221–207 B.C.). The Custom Renewal Society (Yisu she) was founded on August 13, 1912. Its constitution stipulated that the mission of the society was to "produce and stage both new and classical traditional Chinese theater works, to supplement social education through theater, and to [modernize and] change the local custom through dramatic works." Wang Fucheng, "*Yi bang rou*" [*A Pound of Flesh*], in *Qinqiang: Shaanxi chuantong jumu huibian* [*Qinqiang Opera: A Compendium of Shaanxi Traditional Theater Repertoire*] (Xi'an: Shaanxi Provincial Bureau of Culture, 1959), 23:9023–108.

36. Faye Chunfang Fei and William Huizhu Sun, "*Othello* and Beijing Opera: Appropriation as a Two-Way Street," *TDR: The Drama Review* 50, no. 1 (2006): 120–33.

37. For its American reception, see Lisa J. McDonnell, "Begin the Beijing: Shakespeare's *Shrew* in Jingju," in *Staging Shakespeare: Essays in Honor of Alan C. Dessen*, ed. Lena Cowen Orlin and Miranda Johnson-Haddad (Newark: University of Delaware Press, 2007), 199–226.

38. Daniel Yang and Elizabeth Wichmann-Walczak have promoted English *jingju* in university contexts in the United States.

39. *Kiss Me Nana* (*Wen wo ba Nana*), directed by Liang Zhimin (James Chi-min Liang), Godot Theatre Company, toured various cities in Taiwan from August 1 to December 19, 1997; it was revived in May 1999. The production targeted an audience under the age of thirty. Chang Yusheng, a pop star in Taiwan, composed and led the musical performance. For an in-depth review in English, see Nanette Jaynes, "Taming the Taiwanese Shrew: *Kiss Me Nana* at the Godot Theatre," in *Shakespeare Yearbook*, ed. Holger Klein and Michele Marrapodi (Lewiston, N.Y.: Edwin Mellen Press, 1999), 10:490–505.

40. The experimental production, originally designed for a small theater space (with Shakespeare's setting retained), was subsequently revised to become *Yumei and Tianlai* (*Yumei yu Tianlai*) for a major stage in Taipei in 2004.

41. Mell Gussow, "A 'Dream' Set in China," *New York Times*, April 20, 1983, and "The Many Visions of Shakespeare's 'Dream,'" *New York Times*, January 17, 1988. The Pan Asian Repertory Theatre's artistic and producing director, Tisa Chang, discusses her philosophy in "Sustaining the Project," *TDR: The Drama Review* 38, no. 2 (1994): 64–71.

42. The production starred Zhou Yemang (Lear), a Chinese movie star, and incorporated video and music. Alexander Huang, "Review of David Tse's *King Lear*,"

Shakespeare: The Journal of the British Shakespeare Association 3, no. 2 (2007): 239–42.

43. Holderness, introduction to *Al-Hamlet Summit*, by Al-Bassam, 19.

44. "Jiang Zemin guanxin Guofang Daxue peiyang gao suzhi xinxing junshi rencai" [Jiang Zemin's Addresses to National Defense University], CCTV International, December 5, 2002, http://www.cctv.com/news/china/20021205/100064 .shtml (accessed June 2008).

45. Zhu Rongji referred to the story of *A Pound of Flesh*, which he read in high school, when responding to a question about the bankruptcy of China's Guangdong International Trust and Investment Corporation (GITIC). Zhu went into such details as the three thousand ducats that Antonio borrows from Shylock. Since 1978, a line-by-line translation of the courtroom scene of *The Merchant of Venice* has been part of the standard high-school curriculum in China. Zhu warned: "Although these days if you fail to repay debts, you will not face the risk of loosing one pound of flesh, creditors will not let you go easily" ("Interview with Reporters," *China Daily*, March 16, 1999). For the play in Chinese textbooks, see Meng Xianqiang, *Zhongguo Sha xue jianshi* [*A Concise History of Shakespeare Studies in China*] (Changchun: Dongbei shifan daxue chubanshe, 1994), 48.

46. Chen's son-in-law, the first lady, and other members of his family and entourage were indicted for corruption and forgery.

47. For example, Poonam Trivedi finds Royston Abel's bilingual *Othello: A Play in Black and White* (1999) to be a powerful assertion of "postcolonial confidence to cut, critique, and rewrite the text of Shakespeare" (introduction to *India's Shakespeare: Translation, Interpretation, and Performance,* ed. Poonam Trivedi and Dennis Bartholomeusz [Newark: University of Delaware Press, 2005], 18). Abel's production won "the best entry prize at the Edinburgh festival."

48. Dennis Kennedy, "Shakespeare and the Global Spectator," *Shakespeare Jahrbuch* 131 (1995): 50–64.

49. Among the many examples is such a statement as "Lin's classical Chinese translations of Western works of fiction were a joke. Especially unforgivable is his prose translation of Shakespeare's plays" (Zhu Chuanyu, *Tan fanyi* [*On Translation*] [Taipei: Shangwu yinshuguan, 1973], 17).

50. American culture of the same period has also witnessed a tremendous anxiety over the female body in public display, as evidenced by the controversy over *Cleopatra*, directed by Cecil B. DeMille in 1934 (Claudette Colbert as Cleopatra).

51. The presentist inclination of reading the present into the past has arguably given rise to some timeless and universal classics such as Shakespeare. These canonical works are said to be ahead of their times; many premodern works are said to be postmodern in design. Hugh Grady and Terence Hawkes take one step further and argue that "we can never . . . evade the present. If it's always and only the present that makes the past speak, it speaks always and only to" ourselves and about ourselves ("Introduction: Presenting Presentism," in *Presentist Shakespeares* [London: Routledge, 2007], 5).

1. Owning Chinese Shakespeares

1. Michel Foucault uses "alterity" to refer to the concept of the Other and victimized individuals who are excluded from positions of power. Therefore, "cultural alterity" as a philosophical term can carry negative connotations, implying inferiority in a hierarchical structure. My use of cultural alterity refers to the processes by which both Chinese and Anglo-European readers define and exclude selected cultural values outside of a given group's normative expectations.

2. Terence Hawkes, *Meaning by Shakespeare* (London: Routledge, 1992), 3.

3. Arthur F. Kinney, *Shakespeare by Stages: An Historical Introduction* (Oxford: Blackwell, 2003).

4. Inga-Stina Ewbank's observation of the lack of reciprocity between Shakespeareans in the United States and Great Britain and in non-Anglophone countries (including Europe) a decade ago still applies: "[S]eminars on translation are now an inalienable part of Shakespeare Conferences and World congresses," but very few native English speakers attend them, which suggests that the field is "an interesting and harmless occupation for researchers abroad" ("Shakespeare Translation as Cultural Exchange," *Shakespeare Survey* 48 [1995]: 1).

5. Patrice Pavis, "Wilson, Brook, Zadek: An Intercultural Encounter?" in *Foreign Shakespeare: Contemporary Performance*, ed. Dennis Kennedy (Cambridge: Cambridge University Press, 1993), 270.

6. Sonia Moore, *The Stanislavski System* (New York: Penguin, 1984), 28.

7. Artists and critics work through localities that may manifest themselves as James Joyce's Dublin, Jean Baudrillard's Los Angeles, Walter Benjamin's Paris, and others. See also Michael Neill, "Post-Colonial Shakespeare? Writing Away from the Centre," in *Post-Colonial Shakespeares*, ed. Ania Loomba and Martin Orkin (London: Routledge, 1998), 168.

8. Fredric Jameson has argued that individual texts or works are always part of a larger social formation: texts are "reconstituted in the form of the great collective . . . discourse of which a text is little more than an individual *parole* or utterance" (*The Political Unconscious: Narrative as a Socially Symbolic Art* [Ithaca, N.Y.: Cornell University Press, 1981], 18, 76). Kate McLuskie has suggested that the packaging of Shakespearean productions seems as interesting as the product "in the endless game of pass the parcel" ("*Macbeth/Umabatha*: Global Shakespeare in a Post-colonial Market," *Shakespeare Survey* 58 [1999]: 155).

9. Recent revisionary efforts have recast the received postcolonial wisdom from such figures as Homi Bhabha and Arjun Appadurai in productive frameworks. Xiaomei Chen argues against the assumption that "indigenous cultural appropriation of the Other" has necessarily negative effects (imperialistic colonization or self-colonization), while Claire Conceison takes issue with the conventional "binaristic hierarchy of hegemony" in postcolonialism and Occidentalism. Xiaomei Chen, *Occidentalism: A Theory of Counter-Discourse in Post-Mao China*, 2nd ed. (Lanham, Md.: Rowman & Littlefield, 2002), 7; Claire Conceison, *Significant Other: Staging the American in China* (Honolulu: University of Hawai'i Press, 2004), 52. See also Leo Ou-fan Lee, *Shanghai Modern: The Flowering of a New*

Urban Culture in China, 1930–1945 (Cambridge, Mass.: Harvard University Press, 1999), 308–9; and Andrew F. Jones, *Yellow Music: Media Culture and Colonial Modernity in the Chinese Jazz Age* (Durham, N.C.: Duke University Press, 2001), 57.

10. Neill, "Postcolonial Shakespeare?" 168.

11. Xudong Zhang, "On Some Motifs in the Chinese 'Cultural Fever' of the Late 1980s," *Social Text* 39 (1994): 145.

12. Gayatri Chakravorty Spivak, *Other Asias* (Oxford: Blackwell, 2003); Prasenjit Duara, *Sovereignty and Authenticity: Manchukuo and the East Asian Modern* (New York: Rowman & Littlefield, 2004); Liao Ping-hui, "Taiwan Under Japanese Colonial Rule, 1895–1945: History, Culture, Memory," in *Taiwan Under Japanese Colonial Rule, 1895–1945: History, Culture, Memory*, ed. Liao Ping-hui and David Der-wei Wang (New York: Columbia University Press, 2006), 1–15.

13. A recent example from the field of performance studies is Leslie Hill and Helen Paris, eds., *Performance and Place* (New York: Palgrave, 2006), especially part 3, "On Location," 101–47. Two recent works in Shakespeare studies attempt to refocus the field on local interpretations of Shakespeare: Martin Orkin, *Local Shakespeares: Proximations and Power* (London: Routledge, 2005); and Sonia Massai, ed., *World-wide Shakespeares: Local Appropriations in Film and Performance* (London: Routledge, 2006).

14. Homi K. Bhabha, *The Location of Culture* (London: Routledge, 1994), 162.

15. Arjun Appadurai, "Globalization and the Research Imagination," *International Social Science Journal* 51 (1999): 231.

16. Rather than to ridicule the "follies" of criticism in William Hazlitt's style. He famously derided the futility of literary criticism by announcing that if one wishes to appreciate the glory of human achievement, he should read Shakespeare, but if one wishes to view the follies of human ingenuity, he can simply read Shakespeare's commentators.

17. Dennis Kennedy wrote over a decade ago: "We have not even begun to develop a theory of cultural exchange that might help us understand what happens when Shakespeare travels abroad. . . . It is much more important than linguistic analysis, textual examination, psychological assessments, historical research, or any of the Anglo-centered occupations scholars have traditionally valued and perpetuated" (afterword to *Foreign Shakespeare*, ed. Kennedy, 301). Ten years on, there have been no dramatic improvements. John Russell Brown lamented the lack of interest among Shakespeareans in non-Western theatrical adaptations: "[T]oday most theatres in Europe and North America occupy only a part of the spectrum of what theatre can be and we have become so used to accepting this that . . . we view Shakespeare's plays through this distorting filter" (*New Sites for Shakespeare: Theatre, the Audience and Asia* [London: Routledge, 1999], 3).

18. Patrice Pavis, "Introduction: Towards a Theory of Interculturalism in Theatre?" in *The Intercultural Performance Reader*, ed. Patrice Pavis (London: Routledge, 1996), 1. Antony Tatlow, meanwhile, insists that we think globally "to make sense of these practices [of intercultural reading], even if not everything can be encompassed" (*Shakespeare, Brecht, and the Intercultural Sign* [Durham, N.C.: Duke University Press, 2001], 31).

1. OWNING CHINESE SHAKESPEARES

19. The same is true for exchanges between other European thinkers and China. Franklin Perkins bemoans the lack of interest among scholars in the relationships between Leibniz and China: "[E]even when people know that Leibniz had a life-long interest in China and directed his considerable energy and political skills to encouraging cultural exchange—the topic remains strange and peripheral to the concerns of a philosopher engaged with philosophy's history" (*Leibniz and China: A Commerce of Light* [Cambridge: Cambridge University Press, 2004], ix).

20. Françoise Lionnett and Shu-mei Shih, "Introduction: Thinking Through the Minor, Transnationally," in *Minor Transnationalism*, ed. Françoise Lionnett and Shu-mei Shih (Durham, N.C.: Duke University Press, 2005), 7; Charles Taylor and Amy Gutman, *Multilingualism and the "Politics of Recognition": An Essay* (Princeton, N.J.: Princeton University Press, 1992).

21. Jonathan Bate, "How Shakespeare Conquered the World," *Harper's Magazine*, April 2007, 40, 41.

22. Dennis Kennedy, introduction to *Foreign Shakespeare*, ed. Kennedy, 16.

23. James J. Y. Liu writes, "I shall not deal with twentieth-century Chinese theories, except those held by purely traditionalist critics, since these have been dominated by one sort of Western influence or another, be it Romanticist, Symbolist, or Marxist, and do not possess the same kind of value and interest as do traditional Chinese theories, which constitute a largely independent source of critical ideas" (*Chinese Theories of Literature* [Chicago: University of Chicago Press, 1975], 5). See also Rey Chow, *Woman and Chinese Modernity: The Politics of Reading between West and East* (Minnesota: University of Minnesota Press, 1991), 33.

24. "How far one can go before Shakespeare is no longer really Shakespeare?" (Murray Levith, *Shakespeare in China* [London: Continuum, 2004], 83).

25. Kathleen McLuskie, "Unending Revels: Visual Pleasure and Compulsory Shakespeare," in *A Concise Companion to Shakespeare on Screen*, ed. Diana E. Henderson (Oxford: Blackwell, 2006), 238–49; Thomas Cartelli and Katherine Rowe, *New Wave Shakespeare on Screen* (Cambridge: Polity, 2007), 97–98.

26. In his commentary to the French version of Carmelo Bene's Italian adaptation of *Richard III*, Gilles Deleuze applauds Bene's avant-garde adaptation and argues that "adaptation" (as a literary genre and political tool) can open up new space for arts by pursuing different aesthetics trajectories. Deleuze views the author and the idea of the original as tyrannical and feudalistic, representing a despotic order. Yet his notion of adaptation is idealistic. Gilles Deleuze, "Un manifeste de moins," in *Superpositions*, ed. Carmelo Bene and Gilles Deleuze (Paris: Éditions de Minuit, 1979), 85–131.

27. Linda Hutcheon, *A Theory of Adaptation* (New York: Routledge, 2006), 6; Roland Barthes, *Image—Music—Text*, trans. Stephen Heath (New York: Hill and Wang, 1977), 160.

28. Or what Alan C. Dessen calls "the Blame Game, the academic process of fault finding wherein the director becomes a vandal sacking the sacred text" ("Teaching What's Not There," in *Shakespeare in Performance: A Collection of Essays*, ed. Frank Occhiogrosso [Newark: University of Delaware Press, 2003], 112).

29. A *New Yorker* cartoon usefully summarizes the common attitude toward film adaptations of literary works and in general adapted works: two goats are eating a pile of film cans when one goat remarks: "Personally, I liked the book better." Fidelity still figures in several areas. Operating on the assumption that we are now in a posttheoretical moment, David Kastan proposes to "*restore* Shakespeare's artistry to the earliest conditions of its realization and intelligibility" (my italics) (*Shakespeare After Theory* [New York: Routledge, 1999], 16, 31). See also James Naremore, introduction to *Film Adaptation,* ed. James Naremore (New Brunswick, N.J.: Rutgers University Press, 2000), 2.

30. "Shakespeare's plays rarely allow Chinese stylization. If you add these flavours, you are murdering Shakespeare" (Daniel Yang, in Fong Chee Fun [Gilbert], *Xianggang huaju fangtan lu* [*Interviews of Hong Kong Spoken Drama Personalities*] [Hong Kong: Xianggang xiju gongcheng, 2000], 67). Behind this attitude is a powerful but unexamined assumption: that an unadulterated text is even possible in the sense of authenticity that is here implied. Yang is the former producing director of the Colorado Shakespeare Festival (1977–1981, 1985–1990) and artistic director of the Hong Kong Repertory Theatre (1990–2001).

31. Feng claimed that his film was an adaptation of *Hamlet* with "authentic" Chinese flavors set in ancient China in a period known as the Five Dynasties and Ten Kingdoms. Changes have been made to the world of *Hamlet* along the lines of the Oedipal subtext of Laurence Olivier's film. For example, Empress Wan, the close parallel to Gertrude in this film, harbors illicit desires for her stepson, Prince Wu Luan, the equivalent to Hamlet.

32. See the epilogue.

33. Stanley Fish, "Interpreting the *Variorum,*" in *Reader-Response Criticism: From Formalism to Post-Structuralism,* ed. Jane Tompkins (Baltimore: Johns Hopkins University Press, 1980), 164–84.

34. I have taken this notion from Jacques Derrida: "Mimesis . . . is not the representation of one thing by another, the relation of resemblance or identification between two beings, the reproduction of a product of nature by a product of art. It is not the relation of two products but of two productions. And of two freedoms" ("Economimesis," *Diacritics* 11, no. 3 [1981]: 9).

35. One popular argument for Shakespeare's universality evokes the notion of timelessness that remains fixated on particular imaginations of Shakespearean characters, language, and meaning, failing to recognize that what has been perceived as timeless actually reveals shifting constructions of the works' timeliness. If the plays were "timeless," the ways they were performed would have remained unchanged. The vitality and viability of Shakespeare as a cultural institution is deeply rooted in each generation's complicit desire to see the plays in its mind's eye. The plays' elasticity further aided the illusion of a Shakespearean essence— something naturalized, not natural.

36. Diana E. Henderson opens her new book by tackling the question: Given the "remarkable range and freedom of Shakespeare in performance during [the past] decades, which have brought the plays to larger audiences and new cultural

locations . . . . Can there still be an alternative Shakespeare?" (*Alternative Shakespeares 3* [London: Routledge, 2008], 1–2). Similarly, in his critique of the notion of authenticity as "a licensed regime of faithful performance," W. B. Worthen argues that "the rhetoric of authenticity or fidelity, whatever its particular signs, is realized within our contemporary system of theatrical performance . . . that includes a wide range of non-Shakespearean alternatives [and] a wide range of performance technologies" (*Shakespeare and the Force of Modern Performance* [Cambridge: Cambridge University Press, 2003], 215).

37. After having argued for "alternative" Shakespeares for the past decade, Hugh Grady and Terence Hawkes still feel the pressure of theorizing from the margins. They open their latest book by stating: "What is 'presentism'? It's easier to begin with what it's not" (*Presentist Shakespeares* [London: Routledge, 2007], 1).

38. Kenneth S. Rothwell, *A History of Shakespeare on Screen: A Century of Film and Television*, 2nd ed. (Cambridge: Cambridge University Press, 2004), 183.

39. Sarah Bernhadt was the first female Hamlet on film (1900), as has recently been fully documented in Tony Howard, *Woman as Hamlet: Performance and Interpretation in Theatre, Film and Fiction* (Cambridge: Cambridge University Press, 2007).

40. E. H. Carr critiques the problematic model of historiography as "scissors-and-paste history without meaning or significance" (*What Is History?* [Harmondsworth: Penguin, 1964], 29).

41. Take Orson Welles's *Touch of Evil* (1958), for example. When bringing it into the purview of Shakespeare scholarship for the first time, Scott L. Newstok had to go to great lengths to prove the "subterranean" relationship between the film and *Othello* with two lists of similarities between the film and the play in terms of the frame of the time "that passes on stage and on screen," interracial relationships, and other areas (*"Touch* of Shakespeare: Welles Unmoors *Othello,"* *Shakespeare Bulletin* 23, no. 1 [2005]: 33–35, 47–48).

42. Compare G. W. F. Hegel's conception of knowledge: "Das Bekannte überhaupt ist darum, weil es bekannt ist, nicht erkannt" ("Vorrede," in *Phänomenologie des Geistes,* Werke in zwanzig Bänden [Frankfurt: Suhrkamp, 1980], 3:35).

43. Ayanna Thompson, "Practicing a Theory/Theorizing a Practice: An Introduction to Shakespearean Colorblind Casting," in *Colorblind Shakespeare: New Perspectives on Race and Performance,* ed. Ayanna Thompson (New York: Routledge, 2006), 22.

44. Sonia Massai, "Defining Local Shakespeares," in *World-wide Shakespeares,* ed. Massai, 9.

45. Ramona Wray, "Shakespeare on Film in the New Millennium," *Shakespeare* 3, no. 2 (2007): 277.

46. For reasons of economy, it suffices to say that by now there is a unanimous consensus that there is no longer a single "origin" of Shakespearean texts, nor are there only a limited number of imperfect versions of a play like *Hamlet* (Q1, Q2, and so on). The logic of print and performance has generated an indefinite number of textual origins: Alexander Pope's, Edmond Malone's, and Gary Taylor's *Hamlets,* among others.

47. Eric Hayot, Haun Saussy, and Steven G. Yao, eds., *Sinographies: Writing China* (Minneapolis: University of Minnesota Press, 2008); Lisa Lowe, *Critical Terrains: French and British Orientalisms* (Ithaca, N.Y.: Cornell University Press, 1991); Gayatri Chakravorty Spivak, *A Critique of Postcolonial Reason: Toward a History of the Vanishing Present* (Cambridge, Mass.: Harvard University Press, 1999).

48. Among the numerous instances, it suffices to cite one recent example. In a feature article on Hangzhou, the upscale travel magazine *Condé Nast Traveler* indulges in cultural essentialism. China seems to be conveniently antithetical to the West: "Travel within China is famously infamous, a rapidly improving brew of timeless antiquities and turbid masses, sublime insights and ruinous encounters. Privacy and individual space hardly exist, apologizing may be rude and staring polite, and laughter can indicate discomfort, not happiness. Nodding, like pushing and shoving, means nothing at all" (Patrick Symmes, "China Lost and Found," *Condé Nast Traveler*, October 2007, 226). Mainland Chinese pianist Lang Lang's interview in the same magazine is no less binaristic: "Americans understand [only] part of China. But every country has its own way of thinking, and Americans should learn more about Chinese traditions, such as Confucius and legendary stories—which are as important to knowing China as Shakespeare is to understanding the West" (Dorinda Elliott, "A Conversation with Lang Lang," *Condé Nast Traveler*, July 2008, 28). With over 830,000 copies sold per issue in 2007 on average, the magazine is a useful measure of popular discourses about China.

49. François Jullien, *La Valeur allusive des catégories originales de l'interprétation poétique dans la tradition chinoise: contribution à une réflexion sur l'altérité interculturelle* (Paris: École française d'Extrême-Orient, 1985); François Jullien and Thierry Merchaisse, *Penser d'un Dehors (la Chine): Entretiens d'Extrême-Occident* (Paris: Seuil, 2000).

50. Rey Chow reasons that this tendency on the part of the Chinese intellectuals is a "historically conditioned paranoid reaction to the West, [which] easily flips over and turns into narcissistic, megalomaniac affirmation of China." She attributes the "compulsion to emphasize the Chinese dimension to all universal questions" to recent world history and the "preemptive Western hegemony, which expressed itself militarily and territorially in the past, and expresses itself discursively in the present" (introduction to *Modern Chinese Literary and Cultural Studies in an Age of Theory: Reimagining a Field*, ed. Rey Chow [Durham, N.C.: Duke University Press, 2000], 2–3).

51. Carol Fisher Sorgenfrei, "The State of Asian Theatre Studies in the American Academy," *Theatre Survey* 47, no. 2 (2006): 220.

52. Patricia Sieber, *Theaters of Desire: Authors, Readers, and the Reproduction of Early Chinese Song-Drama, 1300–2000* (New York: Palgrave, 2003), 4. See also Prasenjit Duara, *Rescuing History from the Nation: Questioning Narratives of Modern China* (Chicago: University of Chicago Press, 1995), 33–50; and Craig Clunas, *Fruitful Sites: Garden Culture in Ming Dynasty China* (Durham, N.C.: Duke University Press, 1995), 9–15.

53. Xudong Zhang, "The Making of the Post-Tiananmen Intellectual Field: A Critical Overview," in *Whither China? Intellectual Politics in Contemporary China*, ed. Xudong Zhang (Durham, N.C.: Duke University Press, 2001), 1 (my italics).

54. Michel Foucault, *The Order of Things: An Archaeology of the Human Sciences* (New York: Vintage Books, 1994), xix.

55. C.T. Hsia, "Obsession with China," in *A History of Modern Chinese Fiction* (New Haven, Conn.: Yale University Press, 1961), 533–54.

56. David Der-wei Wang, "Afterword: Chinese Fiction for the Nineties," in *Running Wild: New Chinese Writers*, ed. David Der-wei Wang and Jeanne Tai (New York: Columbia University Press, 2004), 252–53.

57. Gloria Davies notes that "Chinese critical inquiry is predominantly undertaken in the general interest of advancing the national culture, it tends characteristically to include a moral evaluation as well as an inspection of utility . . . with a view to determining whether an idea . . . will benefit China." The result is a form of "transcendent unity conceived of as the telos of a perfected China enlightened by Reason, Democracy, Science, Chineseness, etc." (*Worrying About China: The Language of Chinese Critical Inquiry* [Cambridge, Mass.: Harvard University Press, 2007], 11, 241). Although Davies rightly locates the source of Chinese patriotic anxiety, her study employs the same vague terms used by those Chinese intellectuals being critiqued.

58. Xiao Yang Zhang proposes to "summarize the essential characteristics of Western and Chinese cultures through the symbolism of the sun and the moon" (*Shakespeare in China: A Comparative Study of Two Traditions and Cultures* [Newark: University of Delaware Press, 1996], 90).

59. See, for example, Patrice Pavis's hourglass model of filtering of the "source" culture into "target" culture, and studies claiming influence of this model in *Theatre at the Crossroads of Culture*, trans. Loren Kruger (London: Routledge, 1992), 4; Li Ruru, *Shashibiya: Staging Shakespeare in China* (Hong Kong: Hong Kong University Press, 2003), 195–96, 116 (diagram); and Jacqueline Lo and Helen Gilbert, "Towards a Topography of Cross-Cultural Theatre Praxis," *Drama Review* 46, no. 3 (2002): 31–53. Some scholars avoid the term "adaptation" or "appropriation" and resort to neologism such as "Shake-shifting" or "Shakesploitation," but this does not solve the problem entirely. Richard Burt, "Afterword: T(e)en Things I Hate About Girlene Shakesploitation Flicks in the Late 1990s, or, Not-So-Fast Times at Shakespeare High," in *Spectacular Shakespeare: Critical Theory and Popular Cinema*, ed. Courtney Lehmann and Lisa S. Starks (Madison, N.J.: Fairleigh Dickinson University Press, 2002), 205–32; Diana E. Henderson, *Collaborations with the Past: Reshaping Shakespeare Across Time and Media* (Ithaca, N.Y.: Cornell University Press, 2006).

60. Peter Holland, "Touring Shakespeare," in *The Cambridge Companion to Shakespeare on Stage*, ed. Stanley Wells and Sarah Stanton (Cambridge: Cambridge University Press, 2002), 194–211.

61. In *Shakespeare in China*, Zhang treats the Chinese reading positions as necessarily Confucian (pre-1949) or Marxist (post-1949), ignoring the nuances of

the space within and between Shakespearean texts and Chinese cultural practices (artistic movements, genres, or claims made in the name of collective history). While Zhang's book and Tetsuo Anzai, Soji Iwasaki, Holger Klein, and Peter Milward S. J., eds., *Shakespeare in Japan* (Lewiston, N.Y.: Edwin Mellen Press, 1999), are flawed by an oversimplification and generalization of self-reflexive antitheses between the two "great" traditions, certainly not all the works that fall into this category are problematic. Some of them have specific missions, such as chronicling the reception of an author in a specific culture for the first time; others concentrate on personal accounts of select aspects of cross-cultural influence. Monica Matei-Chesnoiu, *Shakespeare in the Romanian Cultural Memory* (Madison, N.J.: Fairleigh Dickinson University Press, 2006); Robert Wardy, *Aristotle in China: Language, Categories, and Translation* (Cambridge: Cambridge University Press, 2000); Andrew F. Jones, "Gramophone in China," in *Yellow Music: Media Culture and Colonial Modernity in the Chinese Jazz Age* (Durham, N.C.: Duke University Press, 2001), 53–72.

62. Shu-mei Shih uses the notion of Sinophone communities in her study of the flows of images across geopolitical borders, although she focuses on the contemporary period when "it is possible to live virtually in multiple social contexts at the same time" (*Visuality and Identity: Sinophone Articulations Across the Pacific* [Berkeley: University of California Press, 2007], 12–13).

63. When a Taiwanese parody of *Hamlet* titled *Shamlet* (dir. Lee Kuo-hsiu, Pingfeng Performance Workshop, 1992) was staged in Shanghai by mainland Chinese director Liu Yun and the Shanghai Modern People's Theatre in 1994, the jokes and topical allusions lost their currency. Alexander C. Y. Huang, "*Shamlet:* Shakespeare as a Palimpsest," in *Shakespeare Without English: The Reception of Shakespeare in Non-Anglophone Countries,* ed. Sukanta Chaudhuri and Chee Seng Lim (New Delhi: Pearson Longman, 2006), 21–45.

64. Compare Pierre Bourdieu, "The Field of Cultural Production, or: The Economic World Reversed," in *The Field of Cultural Production: Essays on Art and Literature,* ed. Randal Johnson (New York: Columbia University Press, 1993), 29–73.

65. Anthony Dawson rightly observes that the "recent celebrations of the 'global' might seem a bit straitened, overly eager to find in the local the possibility of escape from an oppressiveness which is too easily identified as 'Western' or 'European,' as if those terms were themselves single and uncomplicated. The local can be as much of a straitjacket as the universal" ("Reading Kurosawa Reading Shakespeare," in *Concise Companion to Shakespeare on Screen,* ed. Henderson, 158).

66. For example, Levith's *Shakespeare in China* has been compared with Zhang's *Shakespeare in China:* "Although the books overlap somewhat," a book review tells us, Levith deals with Shakespeare in Hong Kong and Taiwan, which is not treated at all by Zhang (Edward Berry, "Review of Murray Levith's *Shakespeare in China,*" *Modern Philology* 105, no. 2 [2007]: 409–10). How many "new" adaptations a study covers is often used as the sole yardstick to measure contributions.

67. Mark Thornton Burnett, "The Local and the Global," in *Filming Shakespeare in the Global Marketplace* (New York: Palgrave Macmillan, 2007), 63.

68. Hugh Grady freely admits: "Shakespearian criticism has long been in search of the authentic Shakespearian meaning, and almost every critic, including this one, writes as if s/he had come to be in possession of it" (*The Modernist Shakespeare: Critical Texts in a Material World* [Oxford: Clarendon Press, 1991], 1).

69. Rustom Bharucha, *Theatre and the World: Performance and the Politics of Culture* (London: Routledge, 1993), 1–2.; J. R. Mulryne, "The Perils and Profits of Interculturalism and the Theatre Art of Tadashi Suzuki," in *Shakespeare and the Japanese Stage*, ed. Takashi Sasayama, J. R. Mulryne, and Margaret Shewring (Cambridge: Cambridge University Press, 1998), 71–93; Tatlow, *Shakespeare, Brecht*, 6, 189–218.

70. Ania Loomba, "Shakespeare and the Possibilities of Postcolonial Performance," in *A Companion to Shakespeare and Performance*, ed. Barbara Hodgdon and W. B. Worthen (London: Blackwell, 2005), 136.

71. Robert Shaughnessy, *The Shakespeare Effect: A History of Twentieth-Century Performance* (New York: Palgrave, 2002), 7.

72. An example is the earliest book-length study of Shakespeare on silent film: Robert Hamilton Ball, *Shakespeare on Silent Film: Strange Eventful History* (New York: Theatre Arts Books, 1968). The situation may be changed by Judith Buchanan, *Shakespeare on Silent Film: An Excellent Dumb Discourse* (Cambridge: Cambridge University Press, 2009). As for films after the silent period, Kurosawa remains the sole token East Asian filmmaker to be analyzed (or mentioned) in many studies, including Roger Manvell, *Shakespeare and the Film* (London: Dent, 1971), xv; Rothwell, *History of Shakespeare on Screen;* Judith Buchanan, *Shakespeare on Film* (New York: Pearson Longman, 2005); Stephen M. Buhler, *Shakespeare in the Cinema: Ocular Proof* (Albany: State University of New York Press, 2002); and Dawson, "Reading Kurosawa Reading Shakespeare," 155–75.

73. Zhen Zhang, "Cosmopolitan Projections: World Literature on Chinese Screens," in *A Companion to Literature and Film*, ed. Robert Stam and Alessandra Raengo (Oxford: Blackwell, 2004), 145.

74. If one wishes to grasp the shape of the entire theatrical experience, he or she would do well to attend the live performance or utilize performance archives. The task of performance criticism does not lie in merely describing the events. More and more critics have found narrowly defined "firsthand" studies inadequate. Timothy Billings writes in a book review: "Li . . . mentions a personal acquaintance or offers a personal observation every few pages . . . . Others will undoubtedly . . . rewrite . . . this stage history . . . more analytically, theoretically, and methodically" ("Review of *Shashibiya* by Li Ruru," *Shakespeare Quarterly* 57, no. 4 [2006]: 495).

75. Bhabha, *Location of Culture*, 193, 207–9. See also Arjun Appardurai, *Modernity at Large: Cultural Dimensions of Globalization* (Minneapolis: University of Minnesota Press, 1996), 4.

76. Duara, *Rescuing History from the Nation*, 17, 19–20.

77. Theodore Huters notes that "both Chinese scholarship and Western sinol-ogy, whether working from the paradigm of 'modernization,' 'enlightenment,' or even 'socialist revolution,' have over the years tended to take for granted the inevi-tability of the transformation of modern China into something that resembles the modern West more than it resembles China before . . . 1850" (*Bringing the World Home: Appropriating the West in Late Qing and Early Republican China* [Honolulu: University of Hawai'i Press, 2005], 6).

78. "History seeks to convince by truth, and succumbs to falsehood. Heritage exaggerates and omits, candidly invents and frankly forgets, and thrives on ig-norance or error. . . . Heritage uses historical traces and tells historical tales. But these tales and traces are stitched into fables closed to critical scrutiny. . . . Heri-tage is not a testable or even plausible version of our past; it is a declaration of faith in that past" (David Lowenthal, "Fabricating Heritage," *History and Memory* 10 [1998]: 7–8).

79. Richard Eyre claims that "you go into a theatre an individual and you emerge an audience" (Richard Eyre and Nicholas Wright, *Changing Stages: A View of British Theatre in the Twentieth Century* [London: Bloomsbury Press, 2000]). See also Herbert Blau, *The Audience* (Baltimore: Johns Hopkins University Press, 1990), 9–11; and Barbara Hodgdon, "Introduction: Viewing Acts," *Shakespeare Bulletin* 25, no. 3 (2007): 1–10.

2. Shakespeare in Absentia

1. Jacques Derrida, *Of Grammatology*, trans. Gayatri Spivak (Baltimore: Johns Hopkins University Press, 1997), 8, 49.

2. Theodore Huters, *Bringing the World Home: Appropriating the West in Late Qing and Early Republican China* (Honolulu: University of Hawai'i Press, 2005), 19.

3. *Yangwu* was an umbrella term for both diplomatic maneuvers and the at-tempt to institutionalize translation and adoption of Western knowledge, espe-cially technological and scientific knowledge, between the 1860s and 1890s.

4. Liang Qichao, "Xin min shuo" [On the New Citizens], in *Yinbing shi quanji* [*Collected Essays from the Ice-drinking Studio*] (Taipei: Wenhua tushu, 1973), 67.

5. Joseph Goodrich, an American scholar living in China at this time, noted in 1911 that "the desire to secure [the] 'new learning' [from the West]" even spread into rural districts in "the coming China" (*The Coming China* [Chicago: McClurg, 1911], 202–3).

6. Heinrich Fruehauf, "Urban Exoticism in Modern and Contemporary Chi-nese Literature," in *From May Fourth to June Fourth: Fiction and Film in Twentieth-Century China*, ed. Ellen Widmer and David Der-wei Wang (Cambridge, Mass.: Harvard University Press, 1993), 133; Craig Clunas, *Pictures and Visuality in Early Modern China* (Princeton, N.J.: Princeton University Press, 1997), 173.

7. Frank Dikötter, *Exotic Commodities: Modern Objects and Everyday Life in China* (New York: Columbia University Press, 2007), 2–3.

8. Yu Guifen, *Xifeng dongjian: Zhong Ri shequ xifang wenhua de bijiao yanjiu* [*The Spread of Western Wind to the East: A Comparative Study of the Ways in Which China and Japan Appropriated Western Cultures*] (Taipei: Taiwan shangwu yin-shuguan, 2003), 126.

9. A dozen Japanese books were also translated. A Ying [Qian Xingcun], ed., *Wan Qing wenxue congchao: Xiaoshuo xiqu yanjiu juan* [*A Compendium of Late Qing Literature: Research on Fiction and Drama*] (Beijing: Xinhua shudian, 1960), 1. See also Zou Zhenhuan, *Ershi shiji Shanghai fanyi chuban yu wenhua bianqian* [*Twentieth-Century Shanghai's Translation Industry and Cultural Change*] (Nanning: Guangxi jiaoyu chubanshe, 2000), and *Yingxiang Zhongguo jindai shehui de yibai zhong yizuo* [*One Hundred Most Influential Translated Works in Modern Chinese Society*] (Beijing: Zhongguo duiwai fanyi chuban gongsi, 1996). Zou's compilation indicates that most of the Chinese translations of German and Russian texts—often incomplete—were based on English or Japanese versions.

10. It was reprinted as a monograph in 1922 by Zhonghua shuju in Shanghai. By March 1936, it had gone through the eighth printing.

11. J. C. Trewin, *The Night Has Been Unruly* (London: Hale, 1957), 19–20. For evaluative comments on Garrick's project, see Christian Deelman, *The Great Shakespeare Jubilee* (New York: Viking Press, 1964).

12. Lin Zexu, trans. and ed., *Sizhou zhi* [*Annals of Four Continents*] (Shanghai: Zhuyitang, 1891), reprinted in Lin Zexu, *Sizhou zhi*, annotated by Zhang Man (Beijing: Huaxia chubanshe, 2002), 117.

13. Hsin-pao Chang, *Commissioner Lin and the Opium War* (Cambridge, Mass.: Harvard University Press, 1964), 134–45.

14. Lin, *Sizhou zhi*, 117.

15. Emanuel van Meteren (1558–1612), an Antwerp merchant and Dutch consul for England from 1583 to 1612, wrote that "the English are a clever, handsome, and well-made people, but, like all islanders, of a weak and tender nature. . . . The people are bold, courageous, ardent, and cruel in war, fiery in attack [*vyerich int aengrijpen*], and having little fear of death" (translated in *England as Seen by Foreigners in the Days of Elizabeth and James the First*, ed. William Brenchley Rye [1865; reprint, New York: Bloom, 1967], 69–70).

16. England in 1764 accounted for 63 percent of China's imports from Western Europe, and it took "47 percent of China's exports to Western Europe" (Hu Sheng, *From the Opium War to the May Fourth Movement*, 2 vols., trans. Dun J. Li [Beijing: Foreign Language Press, 1991], 1:29).

17. Gary Taylor, "The Incredible Shrinking Bard," in *Shakespeare and Appropriation*, ed. Christy Desmet and Robert Sawyer (London: Routledge, 1999), 197.

18. Thomas Milner, *An Account of the Great British Empire* [*Daying guo zhi*], trans. Mu Weilian (Shanghai: Mohai shuyuan, 1856).

19. Guo Songtao, *Guo Songtao riji* [*The Diary of Guo Songtao*], 4 vols. (Changsha: Hunan renmin chubanshe, 1982), 3:267–68.

20. Develto Zelotos Sheffield [Xie Weilou], *The History of the World* [*Wanguo tongjian*] (Shanghai: American Presbyterian Press, 1882), quoted in Zhang Siyang,

Xu Bin, and Zhang Xiaoyang, *Shashibiya yinlun* [*Preface to Shakespeare*] (Beijing: Zhongguo xiju chubanshe, 1989), 516.

21. Preface to *Haiwai qitan* [*Strange Tales from Overseas*] (Shanghai: Dawen she, 1903) (my translation). The passage in Chinese is quoted in Zhou Zhaoxiang, *Hanyi "Hamuleite" yanjiu* [*A Study of Chinese Translations of "Hamlet"*] (Hong Kong: Chinese University of Hong Kong Press, 1981), 10.

22. Sun Yuxiu used the phrases "of all ages" and "of all nations" in English, in "Ou Mei xiaoshuo congtan" [Collected Discussions of European and American Fiction], *Xiaoshuo yuebao* [*Short Story Magazine*], May 1913, 13.

23. Dorinda Elliott, "A Conversation with Lang Lang," *Condé Nast Traveler*, July 2008, 28. See also chapter 1, note 48.

24. Ric Charlesworth, *Shakespeare, the Coach* (Sydney: Pan Macmillan, 2004); John O. Whitney and Tina Packer, *Power Plays: Shakespeare's Lessons in Leadership and Management* (New York: Simon and Schuster, 2000), translated into Chinese as *Quanli juchang: Shashibiya lingdao ke* (Beijing: Zhongxin chubanshe, 2005) and into German as *Powerplays: Was Chefs von Shakespeare lernen können* (Munich: Deutsches Verlags-Anstalt, 2001); Rolf Breitenstein, *Shakespeare para managers* (Barcelona: Plaza and Janes, 2000); George Weinberg and Dianne Rowe, *Will Power! Using Shakespeare's Insights to Transform Your Life* (New York: St. Martin's Press, 1996); Jess Winfield, *What Would Shakespeare Do? Personal Advice from the Bard* (Berkeley, Calif.: Seastone, 2000); Kenneth Adelman and Normand Augustine, *Shakespeare in Charge: The Bard's Guide to Leading and Succeeding on the Business Stage* (New York: Hyperion-Talk-Miramax, 1999), translated into Chinese by Liang Xiaoying as *Shaweng shangxueyuan: Shashibiya chuanshou ni Hafo shangxueyuan mei jiao de gongke* [*Shakespeare Business School: Shakespeare Teaches Lessons Not Offered at Harvard Business School*] (Beijing: Jixie gongye chubanshe, 2002; Taipei: Jingdian chuanxun, 2001), and many others.

25. Tian Min, *Shashibiya yu xiandai xiju* [*Shakespeare and Modern Drama*] (Beijing: Zhongguo shehui kexue chubanshe, 2006), 1; Cao Shujun, *Shashibiya de chuntian zai Zhongguo* [*It Is Springtime for Shakespeare in China*] (Hong Kong: Tianma tushu, 2002), 1; Perng Ching-hsi, introduction to *Faxian Shashibiya: Taiwan Sha xue lunshu xuanji* [*Discovering Shakespeare: Shakespeare Studies in Taiwan*], ed. Perng Ching-hsi (Taipei: Maotouying, 2000), 9; Cao Shujun and Sun Fuliang, *Shashibiya zai Zhongguo wutai shang* [*Shakespeare on the Chinese Stage*] (Shenyang: Harbin chubanshe, 1989), 42; Zhang Chong, ed., *Tong shidai de Shashibiya: Yujing, huwen, duozhong shiyu* [*Shakespeare Our Contemporary: Contexts, Intertexts, and Multiple Perspectives*] (Shanghai: Fudan daxue chubanshe, 2005), 1; Zhang Chong, introduction to *Chung-wai wenxue* [*Chung-wai Literary Monthly*] 33, no. 11 (2005): 11 (special issue on Shakespeare); Lu Gusun quotes Goethe for the same effect, in *Shashibiya shi jiang* [*Ten Lectures of Shakespeare*] (Shanghai: Fudan daxue chubanshe, 2005), 1–2.

26. Such as "Shakespeare frequently displays a romantic tendency and . . . traditional Chinese drama manifests a classical style" (Xiao Yang Zhang, *Shakespeare in China: A Comparative Study of Two Traditions and Cultures* [Newark: University

of Delaware Press, 1996], 23, 93) or Shakespeare's "beautiful writing" and "deep understanding of the human condition" (Li Ruru, *Shashibiya: Staging Shakespeare in China* [Hong Kong: Hong Kong University Press, 2003], 227).

27. Sun Fuliang wrote, "There is a shining star in the galaxy of world cultural history emitting rays of glorious light. That is William Shakespeare" (Sun Fuliang, Cao Shujun, and Liu Minghou, eds., *Shanghai guoji Shashibiya xijujie lunwen ji* [*A Collection of Essays from the Shanghai International Shakespeare Festival*] [Shanghai: Shanghai wenyi chubanshe, 1996], 1).

28. Yu Kwang-chung, "Xiu suo nankai de jin yaoshi" [The Golden Key that Cannot Open a Rotten Lock], in *Shashibiya de shisihangshi* [*Shakespeare's Sonnets*], trans. Liang Zongdai (Taipei: Chunwenxue, 1992), reprinted in *Faxian Shashibiya*, ed. Perng, 19.

29. Matthew Arnold, *Culture and Anarchy: An Essay in Political and Social Criticism* (London: Smith, Elder, 1869), viii.

30. Douglas M. Lanier, "Shakespeare *Noir*," *Shakespeare Quarterly* 53, no. 2 (2002): 161.

31. Yan Fu, "Daoyan 16: Jinwei pian" [Section 16 of the General Introduction: On Microevolution], in *Tianyan lun* [*Evolution and Ethics*] (1894; reprint, Taipei: Shangwu yinshu guan, 1987), 1:40n.

32. Yan Fu, "*Tianyan lun* yili yan" [Notes on Translating *Evolution and Ethics*, 1894], in *Yan Fu yanjiu ziliao* [*Research Materials on the Study of Yan Fu*], ed. Niu Yangshan and Sun Hongni (Fuzhou: Haixia wenyi chubanshe, 1990), 117–19.

33. Yan is commonly recognized as a major translator and commentator of his time. James Reeve Pusey, *China and Charles Darwin* (Cambridge, Mass.: Council on East Asian Studies, Harvard University, 1983), 5; Benjamin Schwartz, *In Search of Wealth and Power: Yen Fu and the West* (Cambridge, Mass.: Belknap Press of Harvard University Press, 1964), 91.

34. *Xixue qimeng shiliu zhong* [*Introduction to Sixteen Western Works*] (Shanghai: Zhu yi tang, 1896).

35. Meng Xianqiang also erroneously claimed that "the first introduction of Shakespeare [into China by Lin Zexu] was so silent that almost nobody noticed it" ("The Reception of Shakespeare in China: A Historical Overview," in *Shakespeare Global/Local: The Hong Kong Imaginary in Transcultural Production*, ed. Kwok-kan Tam, Andrew Parkin, and Terry Siu-han Yip [Frankfurt: Peter Lang, 2002], 116).

36. Kim C. Sturgess, *Shakespeare and the American Nation* (Cambridge: Cambridge University Press, 2004), 9.

37. For a critical evaluation of Henry Irving's *Hamlet* in the Lyceum Theatre, see Alan Hughes, "*Hamlet*: 31 October 1874, 30 December 1878," in *Henry Irving, Shakespearean* (Cambridge: Cambridge University Press, 1981), 27–87; and Richard Foulkes, *Performing Shakespeare in the Age of Empire* (Cambridge: Cambridge University Press, 2002), 106–7.

38. *Guo Songtao riji* [*The Diary of Guo Songtao*] (Changsha: Hunan renmin chubanshe, 1981–1983), 3:743. See also *Guo Songtao: Lundun yu Bali riji* [*Guo Songtao:*

The London and Paris Diary], comp. Zhong Shuhe and Yang Jian (Changsha: Yuelu shushe, 1984), 873.

39. Foulkes, *Performing Shakespeare*, 105.

40. Ibid., 106.

41. *Era*, November 1, 1874, quoted in ibid.

42. Henry Irving. "An Actor's Notes on Shakespeare No. 2, Hamlet and Ophelia Act III Scene I," *Nineteenth Century*, May 1877.

43. Bram Stoker, *Personal Reminiscences of Henry Irving* (London: Macmillan, 1906), 2:78.

44. Zeng Jize, *Shixi riji* [*Diary of a Diplomatic Mission in the West*], ed. Zhang Xuanhao (Changsha: Hunan renmin chubanshe, 1981), 66.

45. Zeng Jize, *Chushi Ying Fa Eguo riji* [*Diaries Kept on Diplomatic Missions to England, France, and Russia*], ed. Zhong Shuhe (Changsha: Yuelu shushe, 1985), 184.

46. "Wednesday, September 18. We went this morning to Court, in consequence of an invitation from the [Qianlong] Emperor, to see the Chinese comedy and other diversions given on the occasion of his birthday. . . . Last of all was the grand pantomime, which, from the approbation it met with, is, I presume, considered as a first rate effort of invention and ingenuity. It seemed to me, as far as I could comprehend it, to represent the marriage of the Ocean and the Earth" (*An Embassy to China: Lord Macartney's Journal, 1793–1794*, ed. J. L. Cranmer-Byng [London: Longman, 1962], 136–38, quoted in Wilt Idema, "Performances on a Three-tiered Stage: Court Theatre During the Qianlong Era," in *Ad Seres et Tungusos Festschrift für Martin Gimm zu seinem 65. Geburtstag am 25. Mai 1995*, ed. Lutz Bieg, Erling von Mende, and Martina Siebert [Wiesbaden: Harrassowitz Verlag, 2000], 212–13).

47. Laura Bohannan, "Shakespeare in the Bush," *Natural History*, August–September 1966, 28–33.

48. The reactions of Guo, Zeng, and the Tivs to *Hamlet* remind us that cultures do not clash with one another; epistemologies and localities do, to adapt Lydia Liu's concept, in *The Clash of Empires: The Invention of China in Modern World Making* (Cambridge, Mass.: Harvard University Press, 2006), 1–4.

49. Zeng Jize wrote in a letter to Chen Junchen from Paris that "when I first left China, I wrote diaries and sent them to the translation bureau [*yishu*]. I do not know how the Shanghai publisher got the manuscript and published it. I am enclosing one copy for your perusal." The letter was dated September 21, "the eighth year of the Guangxu reign [1882]" (quoted in Zhong Shuhe, "Zeng Jize zai waijiao shang de gongxian" [Zeng Jize's Contribution to Chinese Foreign Relations], in *Zeng Jize: Chushi Ying Fa Eguo riji* [*Zeng Jize: Diaries on Diplomatic Missions to England, France, and Russia*], ed. Zhong Shuhe [Changsha: Yuelu shushe, 1985], 39).

50. Amy Freed, *The Beard of Avon* (New York: Samuel French, 2004). The play premiered on June 1, 2001 (South Coast Repertory Theater, Costa Mesa, California), under the direction of David Emmes, starring Douglas Weston (William Shakespeare), Richard Doyle (Richard Burbage, Sir Francis Walsingham, and Old Colin), Nike Doukas (Queen Elizabeth), and others. Zhu Shu's *Shashibiya*

(*Shakespeare*) is a five-act *huaju* play. Although it has never been staged, it was adapted as a radio drama and aired during UNESCO's Twenty-Eighth World Heritage Committee conference in Suzhou in 2004. The play was first published in *Jiangsu xiju congkan* [*Jiangsu Journal of Drama*] 3 (1988) and reprinted, with revisions, in *Shashibiya gushi ji* [*The Complete Stories from Shakespeare*], ed. Tu Sheng, Xi Ning, and Zhao Xing (Beijing: Zhongguo xiju chubanshe, 2002), 2:775–853.

51. Joseph R. Levenson, *Liang Ch'i-ch'ao and the Mind of Modern China* (Berkeley: University of California Press, 1970), 199–202; Xiaobing Tang, *Global Space and the Nationalist Discourse of Modernity: The Historical Thinking of Liang Qichao* (Stanford, Calif.: Stanford University Press, 1996), 7.

52. Liang Qichao, *New Rome* (*Xin Luoma*), in Giuliano Bertuccioli, *La letteratura cinese* (Milan: Sansoni, 1968), 319–25, and William Dolby, *A History of Chinese Drama* (London: Elek, 1976), 198–201. All the Chinese- and English-language studies overlooked *New Rome*, including Murray J. Levith, *Shakespeare in China* (London: Continuum, 2004); Zhang, *Shakespeare in China*; Li, *Shashibiya*; and Cao and Sun, *Shashibiya zai Zhongguo*. Some studies of *chuanqi* mention *New Rome* in passing as an example of "antifeudalist" propaganda, such as Zuo Pengjun, *Jindai chuanqi zaju yanjiu* [*A Study of Modern Chuanqi and Zaju*] (Guangdong: Guangdong gaodeng jiaoyu cubanshe, 2001), 122.

53. *Chuanqi* referred to short fiction in the Tang dynasty (618–907), drama in the late Yuan (1280–1368), and southern drama (in contrast to northern *zaju*) from the early Qing (1644–1911) on. Catherine Swatek, "*Chuanqi*," in *Encyclopedia of Asian Theatre*, ed. Samuel L. Leiter, 2 vols. (Westport, Conn.: Greenwood Press, 2007), 1:122. However, it should be noted that the relationship between southern drama (*nanxi*) and *chuanqi* is a topic of debate.

54. Liang, *New Rome*, in Dolby, *History of Chinese Drama*, 201.

55. Ibid., 199.

56. Liang, *Xin Luoma* [*New Rome*], in *Wan Qing wenxue*, ed. A Ying, 519 (my translation).

57. Recent works on the rise of English literature as a discipline and institution include Terry Eagleton, "The Rise of English Studies," in *Literary Theory: An Introduction* (Minneapolis: University of Minnesota Press, 1996), 15–46; Gerald Graff, *Professing Literature* (Chicago: University of Chicago Press, 1989); and Franklin Court, *Institutionalizing English Literature: The Culture and Politics of Literary Study, 1750–1900* (Stanford, Calif.: Stanford University Press, 1992).

58. Rebecca E. Karl, "Creating Asia: China in the World at the Beginning of the Twentieth Century," *American Historical Review* 103, no. 4 (1998): 1096–118.

59. Compare Mei Lanfang's theater-going account in his memoir, *Wutai shenghuo sishi nian: Mei Lanfang huiyilu* [*Forty Years on Stage: Mei Lanfang's Memoir*] (Beijing: Tuanjie chubanshe, 2005), 1:177.

60. For a study of Wang's play, see Rebecca E. Karl, *Staging the World: Chinese Nationalism at the Turn of the Twentieth Century* (Durham, N.C.: Duke University Press, 2002), 27–52.

61. Rebecca E. Karl, "Staging the World in Late-Qing China: Globe, Nation, and Race in a 1904 Beijing Opera," *Identities* 6, no. 4 (2000): 551.

62. Liu Yazi, in *Ershi shiji da wutai* [*Great Twentieth-Century Stage*], in *Wan Qing wenxue*, ed. A Ying, 176–77, translation adapted from Dolby, *History of Chinese Drama*, 278n.6.

63. Jing Tsu, *Failure, Nationalism, and Literature: The Making of Modern Chinese Identity, 1895–1937* (Stanford, Calif.: Stanford University Press, 2005), 222.

64. David V. Mason, "Who Is the Indian Shakespeare? Appropriation of Authority in a Sanskrit *A Midsummer Night's Dream*," *New Literary History* 34, no. 4 (2003): 639.

65. Harold Bloom argues that in our day "there are many signs that global self-consciousness increasingly identifies with Hamlet, Asia, and Africa included" (*Shakespeare: The Invention of the Human* [New York: Riverhead Books, 1998], 430). However, the formation of a "global" or transnational "self-consciousness" is an exceedingly complex phenomenon, as the introduction of Western ideas and literature into China in the late nineteenth century testifies. The Chinese "self-consciousness" does not identify itself with Shakespearean characters. Rather, it transforms the characters to support its reformation.

66. Biographical details of Shakespeare are found in "Shï'aikupï'a zhuan" [A Biography of Shakespeare], *Dalu bao* [*Continental Magazine*, 1904]; "Yesibi zhuan" [Biography of Shakespeare], in *Jin shijie liushi mingren hua zhuan* [*Pictorial Biography of Sixty Renowned Figures in the Modern World*, 1907]; and "Shakepiya zhuan" [Biography of Shakespeare], in *Shijie mingren zhuanlüe* [*Short Biography of Famous Figures of the World*, 1908]. See also Ge Baoquan, "Shashibiya zuopin zai Zhongguo" [Shakespeare's Works in China], *Shashibiya yanjiu* [*Shakespeare Studies*] 1 (1983): 332.

67. Zhang, Xu, and Zhang, *Shashibiya yinlun*, 516–17.

68. "China Ten Years Hence," *Northern China Herald*, January 4, 1907, 20–21.

69. Su Manshu's autobiographical novel, published in March 1912, is titled *Duanhong ling yan ji* [*Lost and Alienated Wild Swans and Geese*]. Liu Wuji, *Manshu dashi jinian ji* [*A Collection of Essays in Honor of Master Manshu*] (Taipei: Taiwan shidai shuju, 1975), 172.

70. Lin Shu and Wei Yi, "Yin bian yan yu xu" [Preface to *An English Poet Reciting from Afar*], in *Wan Qing wenxue congchao: Xiaoshuo xiqu yanjiu juan* [*A Compendium of Late Qing Literature: Materials on Fiction and Drama*], ed. A Ying (Taipei: Xin wenfeng chuban gongsi, 1989), 2:208.

71. Stephen Owen, "Du Fu," in *An Anthology of Chinese Literature: Beginnings to 1911*, ed. Stephen Owen (New York: Norton, 1996), 413.

72. Zheng Peikai, *Tang Xianzu yu wan Ming wenhua* [*Tang Xianzu and Late Ming Culture*] (Taipei: Yunchen wenhua, 1995), 3; Cyril Birch, introduction to *The Peony Pavilion: Mudan Ting*, by Tang Xianzu (Boston: Cheng and Tsui, 1980), ix; Aoki Masaru, *Zhongguo jinshi xiqu shi* [*A History of Chinese Theater in the Ming and Qing Dynasties*], trans. Wang Jilu (Taipei: Shangwu, 1988), 230.

73. Zhao Jingshen, "Tang Xianzu yu Shashibiya" [Tang Xianzu and Shakespeare], *Wenyi chunqiu* [*Annals of Literature and Art*] 1 (1946), quoted in Mao Xiaotong, *Tang Xianzu yanjiu ziliao huibian* [*Collected Reprints of Articles on Tang Xianzu Studies*] (Shanghai: Shanghai guji, 1986), 727–33. See also Xu Shuofang, "Tang

Xianzu yu Shashibiya" [Tang Xianzu and Shakespeare], in *Lun Tang Xianzu yu qita* [*On Tang Xianzu and Other Issues*] (Shanghai: Shanghai guji, 1983), 73–90.

74. Aoki, *Zhongguo jinshi*, 230. For further details on the analogy of Tang Xianzu and Shakespeare in Chinese academe, see Chen Kaixin, "Kunju *Mudan ting* wutai yishu yanjin zhi tantao" [A Performance History of *Peony Pavilion*] (M.A. thesis, National Taiwan University, 1999), 1–2.

75. Quoted in Zheng Peikai, "Yumingtang qian zhao fu mu: Tang Xianzu yu *Mudan ting*" [Dawns Warmed and Twilights Shadowed by My White Camellia Hall: Tang Xianzu and *The Peony Pavilion*], in *Cha zi yan hong Mudan ting: Sibainian qingchun zhi meng* [*Deepest Purple, Brightest Scarlet: Four Hundred Years of Youthful Dreams*], ed. Lin Jiaohong (Taipei: Yuanliu, 2004), 19.

76. Catherine C. Swatek, *"Peony Pavilion" Onstage: Four Centuries in the Career of a Chinese Drama* (Ann Arbor: Center for Chinese Studies, University of Michigan, 2002), 193–96; Lawrence W. Levine, *Highbrow/Lowbrow: The Emergence of Cultural Hierarchy in America* (Cambridge, Mass.: Harvard University Press, 1994) 21–24, 31, 36.

77. Ian Bartholomew, "Breathing New Life into a Classic," *Taipei Times*, April 24, 2004, 16.

78. Ibid.

79. Zheng, "Yumingtang qian zhao fu mu," 18–21.

80. Liang Qichao, "Yinbing shi shihua" [Notes on Poetry from the Ice-drinking Studio], *Xinmin yuekan* [*New People's Monthly*] 5 (1902): 8, reprinted in *Yinbingshi shihua* [*Notes on Poetry from the Ice-drinking Studio*] (Beijing: Renmin wenxue, 1959), 4. See also Liang Qichao, in *Yinbing shi wenji* [*Collected Essays from the Ice-drinking Studio*] (Taipei: Xinxing, 1967), 4:76.

81. Tsemou Hsu (Xu Zhimo), "Art and Life" [in English], *Chuangzao jikan* [*Creation Quarterly*] 2, no. 1 (1992), reprinted in *Modern Chinese Literary Thought: Writings on Literature, 1893–1945*, ed. Kirk A. Denton (Stanford, Calif.: Stanford University Press, 1996), 175.

82. Hsu, "Art and Life," 175

83. Lu Xun, "Moluo shi li shuo" [On the Power of Mara Poetry, 1908], in *Lu Xun quanji* [*The Complete Works of Lu Xun*] (Beijing: Renmin yishu chubanshe, 1980), 1:64.

84. Thomas Carlyle, *On Heroes, Hero-worship and the Heroic in History* (London: Oxford University Press, 1946), 148.

85. Lu Xun, "Moluo shi li shuo," 64.

86. Lu Xun, "On the Power of Mara Poetry," in *Modern Chinese Literary Thought*, ed. Denton, 108.

87. Sun Yuxiu, "Ou Mei xiaoshuo congtan," in *Xiaoshuo yuebao*, November 1913, translated in Denise Gimpel, *Lost Voices of Modernity: A Chinese Popular Fiction Magazine in Context* (Honolulu: University of Hawai'i Press, 2001), 161.

88. Frances Teague, *Shakespeare and the American Popular Stage* (Cambridge: Cambridge University Press, 2006), 3.

89. The tagline of the festival connected Shakespeare to "great culture": "'To be or not to be' may be the world's most famous question—but for six months, the

only place to be is D.C. for this spectacular celebration of William Shakespeare's influence on great culture and entertainment" (http://www.kennedy-center.org/programs/festivals/06–07/shakespeare/home.html [accessed June 2008]). Over one hundred events by more than sixty arts organizations were presented in the John F. Kennedy Center for the Performing Arts and elsewhere. In April 2007, Public Radio International (PRI) aired a radio documentary, "Shakespeare in American Life" (produced by Richard Paul and narrated by Sam Waterston), presented by the Folger Library to celebrate its seventy-fifth anniversary (http://www.shakespeareinamericanlife.org/).

90. The initiative aimed to support a nationwide, hundred-community tour of Shakespeare. See http://www.nea.gov/news/news03/ShakespeareAnnounce.html (accessed June 2008).

91. Student demonstration against the Treaty of Versailles settlement on May 4, 1919, in Tiananmen Square in Beijing marked the beginning of decades of contradictory nationalist and cultural projects to reform China. The May Fourth era saw radical iconoclasm and attempts to transplant Western cultural and political models.

92. Although Ibsen and his contemporaries often argue for the value of theater as social criticism, recent scholarship has questioned this tendency to take their claims at face value. Toril Moi challenges traditional theories of the opposition between realism and modernism by resituating Ibsen in European visual culture, asserting Ibsen's position as a major writer of modernity on par with Baudelaire and Flaubert, in Henrik Ibsen and the Birth of Modernism: Art, Theater, Philosophy (Oxford: Oxford University Press, 2006).

93. Benedict Anderson theorizes the nation as an "imagined political community," one that is imagined as both "inherently limited and sovereign," a fraternity based on a "deep, horizontal comradeship" (Imagined Communities: Reflections on the Origin and Spread of Nationalism [London: Verso, 1991], 6–7).

94. Antony Tatlow uses the term "intercultural sign" to refer to meanings and values produced by the act of performing and reading between cultures, in Shakespeare, Brecht, and the Intercultural Sign (Durham, N.C.: Duke University Press, 2001), 30–31.

3. Rescripting Moral Criticism

1. Compare Julie Sanders, Adaptation and Appropriation (London: Routledge, 2006), 46.

2. Wen-hsin Yeh, The Alienated Academy: Culture and Politics in Republican China, 1919–1937 (Cambridge, Mass.: Harvard University Press, 1990), 75.

3. St. John's University, ed., St. John's University, 1879–1929 (Shanghai, 1929), 15.

4. Zhang Siyang, ed., Shashibiya da cidian [Encyclopedic Dictionary of Shakespeare] (Beijing: Shangwu yinshuguan, 2001), 1369–71.

5. Yeh, Alienated Academy, 73.

6. "With the backing of an increasingly wealthy and influential body of alumni, this event received extensive coverage in the social pages of the Shanghai papers

as well. Friends and families of students and alumni eagerly attended the performances, arriving in private chauffeured vehicles and dressed in fashionable clothing, each paying several *yuan* for admission and donation" (ibid.).

7. *The New Shakespeare Society's Transactions* (London: Trübner, 1874–1904); Frederick James Furnivall, "The New Shakespeare Society: The Founder's Prospectus Revised," supplement to *Transactions of the New Shakespeare Society*, 1st ser., vol. 1 (1874); Hugh Grady, *The Modernist Shakespeare: Critical Texts in a Material World* (Oxford: Clarendon Press, 1991), 41–44.

8. Improvisation played a major role in early *huaju* and *shinpa* theaters in China and Japan, as the leader of Japan's *shingeki* (new theater) Shimamura Hōgetsu (1871–1918) reminds us: "An actor may memorize only the main points [like a *kabuki* performer]; as for details of the exact words, an actor might just freely make them up on the spot" (quoted in Ayako Kano, *Acting Like a Woman in Modern Japan: Theater, Gender, and Nationalism* [New York: Palgrave, 2001], 175–76). The advocates of new theater argued for the importance of memorizing the lines and against the improvisational mode.

9. Yeh, *Alienated Academy*, 62.

10. Griffith John, "The Holy Spirit in Connection with Our Works," in *Records of the General Conference of the Protestant Missionaries of China Held at Shanghai, May 10–24, 1977*, ed. American Presbyterian Mission (Shanghai: American Presbyterian Mission Press, 1877), 32, quoted in Loren William Crabtree, "Christian Colleges and the Chinese Revolution, 1840–1940: A Case Study in the Impact of the West" (Ph.D. diss., University of Minnesota, 1969), 70.

11. Francis Lister Hawks Pott, in *St. John's University*, ed. St. John's University, 7–8.

12. David Der-wei Wang, *Fin-de-siècle Splendor: Repressed Modernities of Late Qing Fiction, 1849–1911* (Stanford, Calif.: Stanford University Press, 1997), 3.

13. Guy S. Alitto, *The Last Confucian: Liang Shuming and the Chinese Dilemma of Modernity* (Berkeley: University of California Press, 1979).

14. Compare André Lefevere, "Chinese and Western Thinking on Translation," in *Constructing Cultures: Essays on Literary Translation*, ed. Susan Bassnett and André Lefevere (Clevedon, Eng.: Multilingual Matters, 1998), 14–15.

15. Meng Xianqiang, *Zhongguo Shaxue jianshi* [*A Brief History of Shakespeare in China*] (Changchun: Dongbei shifan daxue chubanshe, 1994), 4.

16. One of the earliest performances in Japanese was titled *The Strange Affair of the Flesh of the Bosom* (*The Merchant of Venice*). Toyoda Minoru, *Shakespeare in Japan: An Historical Survey* (Tokyo: Iwanami shoten, 1940), 61.

17. His mother died in 1895. Lin Shu, author's footnote to "Poem Composed on My Seventieth Birthday," manuscript, Fujian Provincial Library; Zhang Juncai, *Lin Shu pingzhuan* [*A Critical Biography of Lin Shu*] (Beijing: Zhonghua shuju, 2007), 61.

18. Charles Lamb and Mary Lamb, *Plot Outlines of Shakespeare's Dramatic Works* [*Sha shi yuefu benshi*], annotated by Kan Tsao-ling (Shanghai: Shangwu yinshuguan, 1922). Although the only extant edition is from 1922, according to Com-

mercial Press's advertisements in *Xiaoshuo yuebao* [*Short Story Magazine*], November 1910 and January 1911, the book was already available before October 1910.

19. *Xiaoshuo yuebao* 1, no. 5 (1910).

20. Mission statement, in *Xiaoshuo yuebao* 1, no. 1 (1910). The periodical's focus shifted in different phases. Wang Yunzhang was the editor in chief from August 1910 to October 1919, after which Shen Yanbing (Mao Dun) took over.

21. *Xiaoshuo yuebao* 7, no. 3 (1916) and 8, no. 2 (1917). The submission guidelines varied in different phases of the magazine. For details about Lin's payment, see Michael Hill, "Lin Shu, Inc.: Translation, Print Culture, and the Making of an Icon in Modern China" (Ph.D. diss., Columbia University, 2008), 188.

22. *Short Story Magazine* was closely connected to the "mandarin duck and butterfly literature" (*yuanyang hudie pai*) of the time. Denise Gimpel has outlined the controversy over the magazine's place in modern Chinese literary history in *Lost Voices of Modernity: A Chinese Popular Fiction Magazine in Context* (Honolulu: University of Hawai'i Press, 2001), 3–4.

23. Compare Jing M. Wang, *When "I" Was Born: Women's Autobiography in Modern China* (Madison: University of Wisconsin Press, 2008), 45.

24. Zheng Zhengqiu, *Xinju kaozheng bai chu* [*Textual Criticism on a Hundred Spoken-Drama Plays*] (Shanghai: Shangwu yinshuguan, 1919), 1–29.

25. *Xiaoshuo yuebao* 7, no. 5 (1916).

26. Walter Benjamin, "The Task of the Translator," in *Illuminations*, ed. Hannah Arendt, trans. Harry Zohn (London: Fontana, 1992), 70–82.

27. Jacques Derrida, "Des tours de babel," trans. Joseph F. Graham, in *Difference in Translation*, ed. Joseph F. Graham (Ithaca, N.Y.: Cornell University Press, 1985), 165–238, and "Roundtable on Translation," trans. Peggy Kamuf, in *The Ear of the Other: Otobiography, Transference, Translation*, ed. Christie V. McDonald (New York: Schocken Books, 1985), 91–161.

28. Zhang, *Lin Shu pingzhuan*, 40–42.

29. A degree granted in the nationwide civil-service exam in China. The system was adopted in A.D. 606 and abandoned in 1905.

30. As defined in chapter 2.

31. Lin Shu and Wei Yi, "*Yin bian yan yu xu*" [Preface to *An English Poet Reciting from Afar*], in *Wan Qing wenxue congchao: Xiaoshuo xiqu yanjiu juan* [*A Compendium of Late Qing Literature: Materials on Fiction and Drama*], ed. A Ying (Taipei: Xin wenfeng chuban gongsi, 1989), 2:208.

32. Lin and Wei, "*Yin bian yan yu xu*," 208.

33. Quoted in Joan Coldwell, ed., *Charles Lamb on Shakespeare* (Gerrards Cross, Eng.: Smythe, 1978), 11.

34. Some recent editions were published by Puffin (1994), Wordsworth Editions (1999), Echo Library (2006), and Penguin (2007).

35. Charles Marowitz, "Shakespeare Recycled," *Shakespeare Quarterly* 38, no. 4 (1987): 467–78, 475.

36. Charles Lamb and Mary Lamb, *Tales from Shakespeare* (London: Dent, 1963), vi.

37. Lamb, "On the Tragedies of Shakespeare" (1811), in *Charles Lamb on Shakespeare*, ed. Coldwell, 29.

38. Calvin S. Brown, "Requirements for Admission in English," *Modern Language Notes* 12, no. 1 (1897): 32. Brown was a faculty member at Vanderbilt University.

39. Lamb and Lamb, *Tales from Shakespeare*, v.

40. Ibid., 290.

41. Sun Chongtao, *Nanxi luncong* [*On Southern Drama*] (Beijing: Zhonghua shuju, 2001), 127.

42. Chen Duo and Ye Changhai, eds., *Zhongguo lidai julun xuanzhu* [*Selected Chinese Dramatic Criticism*] (Changsha: Hunan wenyi chubanshe, 1987), 457–58; Lin Shu, "Tales from Shakespeare," in *Chinese Theories of Theater and Performance from Confucius to the Present*, trans. and ed. Faye Chunfang Fei (Ann Arbor: University of Michigan Press, 1999), 116.

43. Samuel Smiles presents Shakespeare as a commendable self-made man who rose from "a very humble rank" to become a success in the world of theater (*Self-Help; with Illustrations of Character and Conduct* [London: John Murray, 1859], 8). The Japanese translation of the prosaic homilies in Smiles's book was taken as a sourcebook of Western morality: Samuel Smiles, *Saikoku risshihen* [*Stories of Successful Lives in the West*], trans. Nakamura Masanao (Tokyo, 1871). See also Yasunari Takahashi, "*Hamlet* and the Anxiety of Modern Japan," *Shakespeare Survey* 48 (1995): 99.

44. Zheng Shifeng, *Xieshou ji* [*The Story of Bloody Hands*], in *Lanyuan jicui: Wushi nian Zhongguo kunju yanchu juben xuan* [*Collection of the Best Plays from the Orchid Garden: The Performance Texts of Kunju in China from the Past Fifty Years*], ed. Wang Wenzhang (Beijing: Wenhua yishu chubanshe, 2000), 2:227–58.

45. Lin Shu and Wei Yi, *Yingguo shiren yinbian yanyu* [*An English Poet Reciting from Afar*] (Shanghai: Shangwu yinshuguan, 1904), 1.

46. Lamb and Lamb, *Tales from Shakespeare*, 72.

47. James Andreas, "Canning the Classic: Race and Ethnicity in the Lambs' *Tales from Shakespeare*," in *Reimagining Shakespeare for Children and Young Adults*, ed. Naomi J. Miller (New York: Routledge, 2003), 98–106.

48. Lin and Wei, *Yingguo shiren yinbian yanyu*, 63–64.

49. Ibid., 63.

50. Lamb and Lamb, *Tales from Shakespeare*, 256.

51. Lin and Wei, *Yingguo shiren yinbian yanyu*, 64.

52. Ibid., 67.

53. Lin Shu and Wei Yi, *Gui zhao* [*A Ghost's Summons*], in *Qing wenxue congchao*, ed. A Ying, 2:77.

54. Lin and Wei, *Yingguo shiren yinbian yanyu*, 67.

55. Lin and Wei, *Gui zhao*, 77.

56. Lamb and Lamb, *Tales from Shakespeare*, 268–69.

57. I thank Haiyan Lee for sharing her insights with me.

58. Lin and Wei, "*Yin bian yan yu xu*," 1–2.

59. Wang Xiaonong, "Ti *Yingguo shiren yin bian yan yu* ershi shou [Twenty Poems Dedicated to *An English Poet Reciting from Afar*]," in *Wan Qing wenxue congchao*, ed. A Ying, 2:588–90.

60. His comment testified to the appeal of Lin's rendition: "One of my favorite . . . playwright[s] is Shakespeare, and my fondness for Shakespeare's plays started from reading Lin Shu's *Tales* when I was a little boy. As soon as I was able to read the original English, I was eager to get hold of a Shakespeare play, because Lin's translation of Shakespeare's fantasy world was so fresh in my young mind" (quoted in Li, *Shashibiya*, 16).

61. "[Those] novels translated by Lin Shu were very popular. I was unconsciously influenced by and attracted to *Yinbian yanyu* [Lin's translation of the Lambs' *Tales from Shakespeare*]. I've read *The Tempest*, *Hamlet*, *Romeo and Juliet*, and other plays in the original, but they were not as appealing as Lin's fairytale narratives" (Guo Moruo, "Wo de tongnian" [My Childhood], in *Moruo wenji* [*Collected Writings of Moruo*] [Beijing: Renmin wenxue chubanshe, 1958], 6:114).

62. Tu Sheng, Xi Ning, Zhao Xing, and Wu Zhuan, *Shashibiya xiju gushi quanji* [*The Complete Stories from Shakespeare*] (Beijing: Zhongguo xiju chubanshe, 2001), 1:22.

63. Fu Sinian, *Fu Mengzhen xiansheng ji* [*Collected Writings by Mr. Fu Mengzhen*] (Taipei: Fu Mengzhen xiansheng yizhu bianji weiyuanhui, 1952), 6:30. To Salarino's rhetorical question: "Why, I am sure, if [Antonio] forfeit, thou wilt not take his flesh: what's that good for?" Shylock responds: "To bait fish withal . . . Hath not a Jew eyes? Hath not a Jew hands, organs, dimensions, senses, affections, passions? If you prick us, do we not bleed? . . . And if you wrong us, shall we not revenge?" (3.1.51–67)

64. "*Tales from Shakespeare*, Charles Lamb and Mary Lamb" is printed on the spine and front cover of Xiao Qian, *Yuedu Shashibiya: Yong bu xiemu de bei xi ju* [*Reading Shakespeare: Eternal Tragedies and Comedies*] (Tianjin: Baihua wenyi chubanshe, 2004).

65. Liu Hongyan, trans., *Shashibiya gushi ji* [*Tales from Shakespeare*] (Taichung: Haodu, 2005), 5. I have quoted from the Lambs' text that corresponds to the Chinese passages in Liu's translation: *Tales from Shakespeare*, vii. See also Chen Jingmin and Shen Mo, trans., *Shashibiya gushi ji* [*Tales from Shakespeare*] (Taipei: Yuyan gongchang, 2004).

66. André Lefevere, "Prewrite," in *Translation, Rewriting, and the Manipulation of Literary Fame* (London: Routledge, 1992), 1.

67. Hamlet's image is so widely appropriated (on stage, on screen, and in literary works) that Douglas Bruster conjectures that if there were a Shakespeare Museum, it would "definitely have some kind of *Hamlet* wing" with many Hamlets on exhibit (*To Be or Not to Be* [London: Continuum, 2007], 7).

68. Jane Smiley, *A Thousand Acres* (New York: Knopf, 1991); Johann Wolfgang von Goethe, *Wilhelm Meisters Lehrjahre* (1796); A. S. Byatt, *The Virgin in the Garden* (New York: Knopf, 1978), for example.

69. Christopher Reed, *Gutenberg in Shanghai: Chinese Print Capitalism, 1876–1937* (Vancouver: University of British Columbia Press, 2004), 207.

70. Margreta de Grazia, *"Hamlet" Without Hamlet* (Cambridge: Cambridge University Press, 2007), 7–22.

71. Theodore Huters, *Bringing the World Home: Appropriating the West in Late Qing and Early Republican China* (Honolulu: University of Hawai'i Press, 2005), 2.

72. W. A. P. Martin, *The Awakening of China* (New York: Doubleday, Page, 1907).

73. Heiner O. Zimmermann, "Is Hamlet Germany? On the Political Reception of *Hamlet*," in *New Essays on Hamlet*, ed. Mark Thornton Burnett and John Manning (New York: AMS Press, 1994), 299; Ludwig Börne, "*Hamlet* von Shakespeare," in *Gesammelte Schriften* (Leipzig: Hesse, 1908), 2:436.

74. David Der-wei Wang, "Melancholy Laughter: Farce and Melodrama in Lao She's Fiction," in *Fictional Realism in Twentieth-Century China: Mao Dun, Lao She, Shen Congwen* (New York: Columbia University Press, 1992), 111–56.

75. Frederic Jameson, "Third World Literature in the Era of Multinational Capitalism," *Social Text: Theory/Culture Ideology* 15 (1986): 65–88.

76. *The Golden Lotus: A Translation from the Chinese Original of the Novel, Chin P'ing Mei*, trans. Clement Egerton (London: Routledge, 1939).

77. Wang, "Melancholy Laughter," 126.

78. Hu Feng, "Realism: A Correction" [Xianshizhuyi de xiuzheng, 1936], in *Modern Chinese Literary Thought: Writings on Literature, 1893–1945*, ed. Kirk Denton (Stanford, Calif.: Stanford University Press, 1996), 355.

79. Wang, "Melancholy Laughter," 126.

80. Lao She, *Er Ma* [*The Two Mas*] (Shanghai: Shangwu yinshuguan, 1931), 1–2; Wang, "Melancholy Laughter," 126–27.

81. "So memorierte ich, und so übte ich mich, und glaubte nach und nach mit meinem Helden zu einer Person zu warden" (Johann Wolfgang von Goethe, *Weilhelm Meisters Lehrjahre: Ein Roman*, ed. Hans-Jürgen Schings [Munich: Carl Hanser Verlag, 1988], 215).

82. Wang, "Melancholy Laughter," 126.

83. Lao She, "Xin Hanmuliede" [New Hamlet], in *Lao She xiaoshuo quanji* [*Complete Collection of Lao She's Novels*] (Wuhan: Changjiang wenyi chubanshe, 2004), 10:443, translation adapted from Wang, "Melancholy Laughter," 126.

84. Lao She, "Xin Hanmuliede," 443–44.

85. Ibid., 444.

86. Translation revised from Lao She, "Dr. Mao," in *Chinese Wit and Humor*, ed. George Kao (New York: Coward-McCann, 1946), 310–11.

87. *Lu Xun quanji* [*Complete Works of Lu Xun*] (Beijing: Renmin wenxue chubanshe, 1981), 5:57.

88. G. Lowes Dickinson, "An Essay on the Civilizations of India, China, and Japan," in *Letters from John Chinaman and Other Essays* (London: George Allen and Unwin, 1946), 71–72.

89. Lao She, "Xin Hanmuliede," 448–49 (my translation).

90. Ibid., 458.

91. Ibid., 458–59. "Painting feet on a snake (*hua she tian zu*)" is a Chinese proverb describing an unnecessary action—the opposite of bringing coal to Newcastle.

92. For a study of the achievement of the Pre-Raphaelites and the Victorian tradition of illustrating Shakespeare's plays, especially individual characters displaying emotional intensity, see John Christian, "Shakespeare in Victorian Art," in *Shakespeare in Art*, ed. Jane Martineau and Desmond Shawe-Taylor (London: Merrell, 2003), 217–21. See also Stuart Sillars, *Painting Shakespeare: The Artist as Critic, 1720–1820* (Cambridge: Cambridge University Press, 2006), 306.

93. Lao She, "Xin Hanmuliede," 459.

94. *Mr. Hamlet of Broadway* was staged by Ned Wayburn in the Casino Theater, December 23, 1908. Frances Teague, *Shakespeare and the American Popular Stage* (Cambridge: Cambridge University Press, 2006), 102.

4. Silent Film and Early Theater

1. For studies that explore the significance of Chen's groundbreaking essay, see Zhang Xiangbing, "Lun Chen Duxiu zai woguo xiqu gaige shi shang de diwei" [Chen Duxiu's Place in the History of Drama Reform in China], *Ji'nan xuebao* [*Ji'nan Journal*] 3 (1986): 54–64; and Fu Xiaohang, "Chen Duxiu de xiqu lunwen" [Chen Duxiu's Essay on Drama], *Xiqu yanjiu* [*Drama Research*] 8 (1983): 220–26.

2. San Ai (Chen Duxiu), "Lun xiqu" [On Chinese Music Drama], *Anhui suhua bao* [*Anhui Vernacular News*], September 10, 1904, reprinted in *Xin xiaoshuo* 2, no. 2 (1905), and *Zhongguo lidai julun xuanzhu* [*Selected Chinese Dramatic Criticism*], ed. Chen Duo and Ye Changhai (Changsha: Hunan wenyi chubanshe, 1987), 460–62, translation revised from Chen Duxiu, "On Chinese Music Drama," in *Chinese Theories of Theatre and Performance from Confucius to the Present*, ed. and trans. Faye Chunfang Fei (Ann Arbor: University of Michigan Press, 1999), 117–18.

3. Translation revised from Chen, "On Chinese Music Drama," 120.

4. Yao Yiwei, "Yuan zaju zhong de beiju guan chutan" [A Preliminary Attempt at the Tragic Consciousness in the *Zaju* of the Yuan Dynasty], in *Xiju yu wenxue* [*Drama and Literature*] Lianjing pinglun series 8 (Taipei: Lianjing chubanshe, 1989), 13.

5. Jiang Guanyun, in *Wan Qing wenxue congchao: Xiaoshuo xiqu yanjiu juan* [*A Compendium of Late Qing Literature: Research on Fiction and Drama*], ed. A Ying (Beijing: Zhonghua shuju, 1960), 50–52.

6. *Wang Guowei xiqu lunwen ji* [*Wang Guowei's Works on Traditional Chinese Drama*] (Taipei: Liren, 1992); Patricia Sieber, *Theaters of Desire: Authors, Readers, and the Reproduction of Early Chinese Song-Drama, 1300–2000* (New York: Palgrave, 2003), 22.

7. Fu Sinian, "Xiju gailiang gemianguan" [Aspects of Theater Reform], *Xin qingnian* [*New Youth*], October 15, 1918, 5. For a discussion of Fu Sinian, Qian Xuantong, and other critics' conception of mimesis in Chinese theater, see Jingsong Chen, "To Make People Happy, Drama Imitates Joy: The Chinese Theatrical Concept of *Mo*," *Asian Theatre Journal* 14, no. 1 (1997): 38–55.

8. Xu Huaizhong, *Zhongguo xiandai xiaoshuo lilun piping de bianqian* [The Vicissitudes of Modern Chinese Fiction Theory and Criticism] (Shanghai: Shanghai wenyi chubanshe, 1990), 38.

9. Xu Banmei, *Huaju chuangshiqi huiyilu* [Memoir of the Founding Era of Spoken Drama] (Beijing: Zhongguo xiju chubanshe, 1957), 24; Siyuan Liu, "The Impact of *Shinpa* on Early Chinese *Huaju*," *Asian Theatre Journal* 23, no. 2 (2006): 345.

10. Compare Walter Benjamin, "The Task of the Translator," in *Illuminations*, ed. Hannah Arendt, trans. Harry Zohn (New York: Harcourt, Brace, 1968), 69–82.

11. Wang Yiqun, "Shaju yanchu zai wuoguo wutai shang de bianqian" [The Development of Shakespearean Performances on the Chinese Stage], in *Shashibiya zai Zhonguo* [Shakespeare in China] (Shanghai: Wenyi chubanshe, 1987), 94.

12. Li Ming, "*Luomi'ou yu Zhuliye*—gongyan hou de pingjia" [A Review of the Production of *Romeo and Juliet*], *Da gong bao zengkan* [Dagong Daily Supplement], June 8, 1937.

13. Tang Wen, "*Luomi'ou yu Zhuliye*—canguan caipai" [My Impression of the Dress Rehearsal of *Romeo and Juliet*], *Da gong bao zengkan*, June 8, 1937.

14. Wang, "Shaju yanchu," 94.

15. *Shanghai Post*, June 3, 1937, 5.

16. Tang, "*Luomi'ou yu Zhuliye*," 14.

17. Xiong Foxi, "Danchun zhuyi" [Econimism], in *Foxi lunju* [Foxi on Drama] (Beijing: Pushe, 1928), 17.

18. Li, "*Luomi'ou yu Zhuliye*," 14. See also Ma Ling, "*Luomi'ou yu Zhuliye* zhi wo jian" [Review of *Romeo and Juliet*], *Da gong bao zhengkan*, June 17, 1937, 14.

19. The Japanese surrendered on August 15, 1945.

20. Si Ming, review of *The Hero of a Tumultuous Time*, *Zhongguo zhoubao* [China Weekly], May 13, 1945.

21. Li Quan, "*Luanshi Yingxiong* guan hou de pingjia" [An Evaluation of *The Hero of a Tumultuous Time*], *Haibao* [Shanghai News], May 2, 1945.

22. Poshek Fu, *Passivity, Resistance, and Collaboration: Intellectual Choices in Occupied Shanghai, 1937–1945* (Stanford, Calif.: Stanford University Press, 1993), 96–109.

23. Li Jianwu, "Yu youren shu" [A Letter to My Friend], *Shanghai wenhua* [Shanghai Culture], July 1946, 28–29.

24. Li Jianwu, *Wang Deming*, in *Li Jianwu juzuo xuan* [Selected Plays by Li Jianwu], ed. Zhang Jie (Beijing: Zhongguo xiju chubanshe, 1982), 440.

25. Ibid.

26. *Wenzhang* 1–4 (January–July 1946).

27. Ke Ling, preface to *Li Jianwu juzuo xuan*, ed. Zhang, 11.

28. Zhang Siyang, ed., *Shashibiya da cidian* [Encyclopedic Dictionary of Shakespeare] (Beijing: Shangwu, 2001), 1437.

29. Li Jianwu, "Preface [to *Ah shi na*]," *Wenxue zazhi* [Literature Magazine], July 1947, 10.

30. Meng Xianqiang, *Zhongguo Shaxue jianshi* [A Concise History of Shakespeare Studies in China] (Changchun: Dongbei shifan daxue chubanshe, 1994), 148.

31. Maurice Hindle, *Studying Shakespeare on Film* (New York: Palgrave Macmillan, 2007), 19–20.

32. Luke McKernan and Olwen Terris, eds., *Walking Shadows: Shakespeare in the National Film and Television Archive* (London: British Film Institute, 1994), 81–82.

33. Robert Hamilton Ball, *Shakespeare on Silent Film* (New York: Theatre Arts, 1968), 76.

34. Jack J. Jorgens, *Shakespeare on Film* (Bloomington: Indiana University Press, 1977), 1.

35. Zhen Zhang has identified some twenty silent films that are "apparent" adaptations. As she recognizes, adaptation can take many forms "with some having more visible umbilical cords linked to original sources and others outlandishly incarnating into something nebulous or different" ("Cosmopolitan Projections: World Literature on Chinese Screens," in *A Companion to Literature and Film*, ed. Robert Stam and Alessandra Raengo [Oxford: Blackwell, 2004], 151).

36. A "comprehensive coverage of Chinese film in its historical, cultural, geopolitical, generic, thematic, and textual aspects," Yingjin Zhang and Zhiwei Xiao, eds., *The Encyclopaedia of Chinese Film* (London: Routledge, 1998), does not include these films, nor does Chou Hui-ling's more up-to-date *Biaoyan Zhongguo: Nü mingxing, biaoyan wenhua, shijue zhengzhi 1910–1945* [*Performing China: Actresses, Performance Culture, Visual Politics, 1910–1945*] (Taipei: Rye Field Publications, 2004). Scholarly works in Chinese also overlook them. Huang Zhiwei, ed., *Lao Shanghai dianying* [*Old Shanghai Films*] (Shanghai: Wenhui chubanshe, 1998); *Zhongguo dianying dacidian* [*Dictionary of Chinese Films*] (Shanghai: Shanghai cishu chubanshe, 1995).

37. Tan Chunfa, *Kai yidai xianhe: Zhongguo dianying zhi fu Zheng Zhengqiu* [*The Pathbreaker: Zheng Zhengqiu, the Father of Chinese Cinema*] (Beijing: Guoji wenhua chuban gongsi, 1992).

38. Sarah E. Stevens, "Figuring Modernity: The New Woman and the Modern Girl in Republican China," *NWSA Journal* 15, no. 3 (2003): 82–103.

39. Rey Chow, *Woman and Chinese Modernity: The Politics of Reading Between West and East* (Minnesota: University of Minnesota Press, 1991), 86.

40. Zheng Zhengqiu, "Zhongguo yingxi de qucai wenti" [On the Question of Chinese Film's Subject], *Mingxing tekan—xiao pengyou hao* [*Bright Stars Magazine*], June 1925, 5.

41. Yang Jingyuan, "Yuan Changying he Shashibiya" [Yuan Changying and Shakespeare], *Waiguo wenxue yanjiu* [*Foreign Literature Studies*], April 1994, 1–3.

42. Yu Zhiping, "Shanghai Zhongxi nüshu zayi" [Remembering the Shanghai McTyeire School], *Minguo chunqiu* [*Republican History*], January 1997, 61–62.

43. Chen Danyan, *Shanghai de jinzhi yuye* [*Shanghai Princess*] (Beijing: Zuojia chubanshe, 1999), 20.

44. "Meanings . . . are not so much 'transformed' when concepts pass from the guest language to the host language as invented within the local environment of the latter" (Lydia H. Liu, *Translingual Practice: Literature, National Culture, and Translated Modernity in China, 1900–1937* [Stanford, Calif.: Stanford University Press, 1995], 26).

45. Hu Ying, *Tales of Translation: Composing the New Woman in China, 1898–1918* (Stanford, Calif.: Stanford University Press, 2000), 5.

46. Zhang, "Cosmopolitan Projections," 148–49.

47. *Nü lüshi* (*The Woman Lawyer*, also known as *Rouquan*) premiered in Shanghai's Grand Central Theatre (Zhongyang daxiyuan). *Shen bao* [*Shanghai News*], March 20, 1927, 4; Huang, ed., *Lao Shanghai dianying*, 31. I thank Don Marion of the University of Minnesota Library and Huei-min Sun of the Academia Sinica, Taiwan, for helping me locate a number of references.

48. Zhongguo dianying yishu yanjiu zhongxin [China Film Art Research Center] and Zhongguo dianying ziliao guan [China Film Archive], eds., *Zhongguo yingpian dadian—gushi pian, xiqu pian, 1905–1930* [*Encyclopedia of Chinese Films: 1905–1930*] (Beijing: Zhongguo dianying chubanshe, 1996), 130; *Zhongguo dianying dacidian*, 720.

49. William Shakespeare, *The Merchant of Venice*, trans. Perng Ching-hsi (Taipei: Lianjing, 2006), 1–43.

50. Janet Adelman, *Blood Relations: Christian and Jew in "The Merchant of Venice"* (Chicago: University of Chicago Press, 2008).

51. Quoted in Alfred Hickling, "Sit Down and Shut Up," *Observer*, June 12, 2002, 16.

52. *The Merchant of Venice*, directed by Loveday Ingram, toured Malaysia, Japan, China, and elsewhere.

53. Ian Bartholomew, in *China Daily*, May 21, 2002.

54. Li Ruru quoted Tian's response nonchalantly as a "bright spot" to demonstrate "Shakespeare . . . is not dead" in what seems to be a pessimistic future for staging Shakespeare in China, in *Shashibiya: Staging Shakespeare in China* (Hong Kong: Hong Kong University Press, 2003), 230. Li and other Chinese scholars did not address the epistemological gap between modern Chinese and Western criticism of the play, taking for granted the Chinese negligence of racial and religious issues in nearly all of Shakespeare's plays. Fan Shen, "Shakespeare in China: *The Merchant of Venice*," *Asian Theatre Journal* 5, no. 1 (1988): 23–37.

55. There was a vibrant Jewish community in Shanghai in the 1940s. Jonathan Goldstein, ed., *The Jews of China*, 2 vols. (Armonk, N.Y.: Sharpe, 1999); Lois Ruby, *Shanghai Shadows* (New York: Holiday House, 2006); *Forever Nostalgia: The Jews in Shanghai* (Shanghai: Shanghai Municipal Tourism Administrative Commission, 1998); Berl Falbaum, ed., *Shanghai Remembered: Stories of Jews Who Escaped to Shanghai from Nazi Europe* (Royal Oak, Mich.: Momentum Books, 2005).

56. "Gongxie nü lüshi chuting zhi diyi ren" [The First Woman Lawyer to Appear in the Court], *Shen bao*, March 3, 1921, 10; "First Woman Lawyer in Shanghai," *North-China Herald*, March 5, 1921, 2; Sun Huimin, "Women Lawyers in Shanghai, 1927–1949" [Minguo shiqi Shanghai de nü lüshi, 1927–1949] (paper presented at the XVth Biennial Conference of the European Association of Chinese Studies, University of Heidelberg, August 25–29, 2004).

57. Dan Weng, "Wei nüjie huanying nü lüshi" [Let Us Welcome Women Lawyers], *Jing bao* [*Crystal*], January 27, 1921, 2.

58. Madame Wei Tao-ming, *My Revolutionary Years* (New York: Scribner, 1943), 145–46. The number is very small when compared with the 1,263 male members. "Lüshi gonghui huiyuan renshu ji chengjie nianbiao, 25 niandu" [Member Directory and Annual Reviews, 1936], Shanghai Bar Association Files (Shanghai lüshi gonghui dang'an), Shanghai Archives (Shanghai dang'an guan), Q190-1-13739, 190.

59. Liao Weng, "Zhifen bu rang xumei" [Women Are as Capable as Men], *Jingang zuan* [*Diamond*], September 5, 1932, 1.

60. Compare Chou's account of the media attention given to actresses in Shanghai in the 1930s, in *Biaoyan Zhongguo*, chap. 2.

61. Xiao Zhen, "Haosheng nü lüshi" [An Impassioned Woman Lawyer], *Jing bao*, July 28, 1933, 3.

62. Lin Shu and Wei Yi, *Yingguo shiren yinbian yanyu* [*An English Poet Reciting from Afar*] (Shanghai: Shangwu yinshuguan, 1904), 31, 32, 36.

63. Ibid., 33.

64. *Yingxi zazhi* [*Film Magazine*], April 1931, 11–12; Zhang, "Cosmopolitan Projections," 158.

65. Zhang, "Cosmopolitan Projections," 158.

66. *Yingxi zazhi*, April 1931, 11–12.

67. *As You Like It* (2.7.139–40). The passage reads "All the world's a stage" in *The Riverside Shakespeare*, 2nd ed., ed. G. Blakemore Evans (Boston: Houghton Mifflin, 1997).

68. The Chinese intertitle reads, "zhifen jiangjun de bense."

69. *Yingxi zazhi*, October 1, 1931, 42; Zhang, "Cosmopolitan Projections," 158, 163.

70. The Chinese transliteration of Thurio bears negative connotations.

71. Zhen Zhang, "Bodies in the Air: The Magic of Science and the Fate of the Martial Arts Film in China," *Post Script* 20, nos. 2–3 (2001): 43–60, and "Cosmopolitan Projections," 155.

72. Anne Barton, "Introduction to *The Two Gentlemen of Verona*," in *Riverside Shakespeare*, ed. Evans, 179.

73. Mary Beth Rose, "Introduction to *The Two Gentlemen of Verona*," in *William Shakespeare: The Complete Works*, ed. Stephen Orgel and A. R. Braunmuller (New York: Penguin Books, 2002), 113.

74. The ending reminds us of Valentine's comment at the end of the play, "one feast, one house, one happiness" (5.4.173), although the film literally ends with "one house" in that all four characters are now related through not only marriage but familial relations.

5. Site-Specific Readings

1. "As imagination bodies forth / The forms of things unknown, the poet's pen / Turns them to shapes, and gives to airy nothing / A local habitation" (*A Midsummer Night's Dream*, 5.1.14–17).

2. Compare Irena R. Makaryk and Joseph G. Price, "Introduction: When Worlds Collide: Shakespeare and Communisms," in *Shakespeare in the Worlds of Communism and Socialism*, ed. Irena R. Makaryk and Joseph G. Price (Toronto: University of Toronto Press, 2006), 5–6.

3. John Russell Brown, "Theatrical Pillage in Asia: Redirecting the Intercultural Traffic," *New Theatre Quarterly* 14, no. 1 (1998): 12.

4. Dennis Kennedy, "Shakespeare and the Global Spectator," *Shakespeare Jahrbuch* 131 (1995): 50.

5. Compare Philip Auslander, *Liveness: Performance in a Mediatized Culture*, 2nd ed. (London: Routledge 2008).

6. Infuriated, Queen Elizabeth intimated: "I am Richard II, know ye not that?" E. K. Chambers, *William Shakespeare: A Study of Facts and Problems* (Oxford: Clarendon Press, 1930), 2:327. See also Stephen Greenblatt, Walter Cohen, Jean E. Howard, and Katharine Eisaman Maus, eds., *The Norton Shakespeare* (New York: Norton, 1997), 943–44, 2555.

7. *The Merchant of Venice* has frequently been used as a parable for the Holocaust. Hanan Snir's 1995 production was a unique site-specific performance. To celebrate the fiftieth anniversary of the liberation of the largest concentration camp on German soil, the Deutsches Nationaltheater staged the play in the notorious Buchenwald concentration camp, located outside Weimar. Former Jewish prisoners of the camp were both in the audience and on stage. Three of them played the Jewish roles. At center stage hung the cynical slogan that was once on display at the entrance to the concentration camp, "Jedem das Seine," which means "To each his own," but could also be taken to mean "Everyone gets what he deserves." Snir brought the localities of the play and its performance (as well as his own historicity) to bear on the fictional and historical events. He argues that "today, after the Holocaust and pogroms in other countries," *The Merchant of Venice* is racist and anti-Semitic "even if Shakespeare had not intended it to be so" (quoted in Rüdiger Schaper, "Der Kaufmann von Buchenwald: Ein Shakespeare zum Gedenktag am Deutschen Nationaltheater Weimar," *Süddeutsche Zeitung*, April 11, 1995). I thank Christa Jansohn for her help in collecting German texts relevant to this production. Directed by Hanan Snir (with text adapted from A. W. von Schlegel's German translation), the production was staged by the Deutsches Nationaltheater Weimar on April 8, 1995. Representative reviews include Frank Quilitzsch, "Spiel, Jude, spiel! Ein Israeli inszenierte den *Kaufmann von Venedig*," *Berliner Zeitung*, April 11, 1995; Thomas Bickelhaupt, "Der Shakespeare der SS: Ums Leben spielen: *Kaufmann von Venedig* in Weimar," *Frankfurter Allgemeine*, April 11, 1995; and Werner Schulze-Reimpell, "Shylock in Buchenwald," *Stuttgarter Zeitung*, April 20, 1995.

8. Edward Said, *Orientalism* (New York: Pantheon, 1978), 9.

9. Karl Marx often quotes from Aeschylus, Sophocles, Shakespeare, and Goethe. For example, Marx quotes the Schlegel-Tieck German translation of *Timon of Athens* (4.3) to support his argument about the power of money in bourgeois society. Karl Marx, in *The Marx-Engels Reader*, ed. Robert C. Tucker (New York: Norton, 1972), 80–81; Karl Marx, *Economic and Philosophic Manuscripts of*

1844, trans. Martin Milligan (Buffalo: Prometheus Books, 1988). Marx's daughter Eleanor recalled in 1895 that "Shakespeare was the Bible of [their] house, seldom out of our hands or mouths." By the time she was six, she "knew scene upon scene of Shakespeare by heart" ("Recollections of Mohr," in *Marx and Engels on Literature and Art: A Selection of Writings,* ed. Lee Baxandall and Stefan Morawski [St. Louis: Telos Press, 1973], 147).

10. *Yu Shangyuan xiju lunwen ji* [*Collective Essays on Drama by Yu Shangyuan*] (Wuhan: Changjiang wenyi chubanshe, 1986), 28.

11. Quoted in Drama Review Section, *Zhongyang ribao* [*Central Daily News*], 1937.

12. Cao Shujun and Sun Fuliang, *Shashibiya zai Zhongguo wutai shang* [*Shakespeare on the Chinese Stage*] (Harbin: Ha'erbin chubanshe, 1989), 99.

13. In the 1920s, Sun Yat-sen (1866–1925), the Nationalist leader, sought assistance for China's national unification from the Soviet Union after his plea for aid to the Western democratic nations was ignored. The Soviet Union worked with both the KMT and the CCP for political expediency.

14. Boris Andreevich Lavrenyov (1891–1959) wrote *Razlom* in 1927 in honor of the tenth anniversary of the Great October Socialist Revolution. The heroic-revolutionary play remained in continuous production in Moscow for some fifty years. Boris Lavrenev, *Razlom* (Leningrad: GIKhl, 1932).

15. Constantine Tung, introduction to *Drama in the People's Republic of China,* ed. Constantine Tung and Colin Mackerras (Albany: State University of New York Press, 1987), 12.

16. Brooks Atkinson concluded that "sincere and painstaking though this *Hamlet* may be, it is not yet ready for Broadway" ("The Play," *New York Times,* December 18, 1942, 38).

17. Fu Xiangmo, "Guan Sha weng de shijie da beiju" [Attending a Performance of a World-Class Tragedy by Shakespeare], *Guoli xiju zhuanke xuexiao xiaoyou tongxun yuekan* [*Alumni Monthly Newsletter of the National Drama School*], June 18, 1942, reprinted in *Zhongguo zaoqi xiqu huakan* [*Early Chinese Drama Gazettes*] (Beijing: Quanguo tushuguan wenxian suowei fuzhi zhongxin, 2006), 37:115.

18. Cao and Sun, *Shashibiya zai Zhongguo,* 105.

19. Zhang Qihong, "Rang shangdi jianglin renjian: Zai Zhongguo Shashibiya Yanjiuhui chengli dahui shang de fayan" [Let God Descend to the Human World: A Speech to the First Convention of the Shakespeare Society of China], *Qingnian yishu* [*Youth Art*] 1 (1985): 7, translated in Fan Shen, "Shakespeare in China: The Merchant of Venice," *Asian Theatre Journal* 5, no. 1 (1988): 29–30.

20. Lao She, "Xin Hanmuliede" [New Hamlet], in *Lao She xiaoshuo quanji* [*The Complete Collection of Lao She's Fiction*], ed. Shu Ji and Shu Yi (Wuhan: Changjiang wenyi chubanshe, 2004), 10:443–59; David Der-wei Wang, *Fictional Realism in Twentieth-Century China: Mao Dun, Lao She, Shen Congwen* (New York: Columbia University Press, 1996), 126.

21. Lu Gu-sun, "Hamlet Across Space and Time," *Shakespeare Survey* 36 (1988): 56.

22. Cao and Sun, *Shashibiya zai Zhongguo,* 49.

23. Alexander C. Y. Huang, "*Shamlet*: Shakespeare as a Palimpsest," in *Shakespeare Without English: The Reception of Shakespeare in Non-Anglophone Countries*, ed. Sukanta Chaudhuri and Chee Seng Lim (Delhi: Pearson Longman, 2006), 211–21.

24. Ludwig Tieck, "Bemerkungen über einige Charaktere im 'Hamlet', und über die Art, wie diese auf der Bühne dargestellt werden könnten," in *Kritische Schriften* (Leipzig: Brockhaus, 1848–52), 3:243–98.

25. Ferdinand Freiligrath, "Deutschland ist Hamlet," in *Werke*, ed. Julius Schwering (Berlin: Bong, 1909) 2:71–73, translated in *Hamlet: A New Variorum Edition of Shakespeare*, ed. Horace Howard Furness (London: Lippincott, 1877), 376–78. See also *Poems from the German of Ferdinand Freiligrath* (Leipzig: Bernhard Tauchnitz, 1871), 201–4.

26. For a study of *Hamlet* as political allegory in Germany, see Heiner O. Zimmermann, "Is Hamlet Germany? On the Political Reception of *Hamlet*," in *New Essays on Hamlet*, ed. Mark Thornton Burnett and John Manning (New York: AMS Press, 1994), 293–318.

27. Jiang Tao, "Lun Zhongguo Shaju wutai shang de daoyan yishu" [Directing Shakespeare on the Chinese stage], *Xiju* [*Drama*] 3 (1996): 107.

28. Quoted in Tian Benxiang, *Zhongguo xiandai bijiao xiju shi* [*A Comparative History of Modern Chinese Drama*] (Beijing: Wenhua yishu chubanshe, 1993), 453.

29. Atkinson, "The Play," 38.

30. The script was translated by Liang Shiqiu.

31. The revival of the production was given a slightly different title, *Danmai wangzi Hamuleite* (*Danish Prince Hamlet*). It was staged at the Huangjiayakou Experimental Theater in Chongqing on November 17, 1942, and in the Guotai Theater (Guotai Da Xiyuan) in the same city from December 9 to 19, 1942.

32. Cao and Sun, *Shashibiya zai Zhongguo*, 104.

33. Jiang, "Lun Zhongguo Shaju," 106.

34. Jiao Juyin, "Guanyu *Hamuleite*" [About *Hamlet*], in *Jiao Juyin wenji* [*Collected Works of Jiao Juyin*] (Beijing: Wenhua yishu chubanshe, 1988), 2:167–68.

35. Boyd M. Johnson, "Executive Order 12333: The Permissibility of an American Assassination of a Foreign Leader," *Cornell International Law Journal* 25 (1992): 421n.129.

36. Fu, "Guan Sha weng," 118.

37. Jiang, "Lun Zhongguo Shaju," 107.

38. Xiao Yang Zhang, *Shakespeare in China: A Comparative Study of Two Traditions and Cultures* (Newark: University of Delaware Press, 1996), 216.

39. It is of interest to note that a few months before *Hamlet* was staged in the Guotai Theater in Chongqing, a Chinese play bearing strong resemblance to *Hamlet* was also performed there. The five-act Chinese historical play *Qu Yuan* by Guo Moruo (1892–1978), one of the most widely recognized modern Chinese historians and writers, was staged by the Chinese Dramatic Art Society (Zhonghua Juyi She) and directed by Chen Liting in April 1942. The titular character Qu Yuan is a historical figure who has become an icon of the melancholic Confucian politician wronged by his emperor. Many of Guo's contemporaries pointed out the

similarities—in terms of characterizations of Hamlet and Qu Yuan and dramatic techniques—between Guo and Shakespeare.

40. Wu Ningkun and Li Yikai, *A Single Tear: A Family's Persecution, Love, and Endurance in Communist China* (New York: Atlantic Monthly Press, 1993), 34.

41. Ibid., 100.

42. Ibid., 35.

43. Pierre Ryckmans, "Are Books Useless? An Extract from the 1996 Boyer Lecture," *Australian Humanities Review: An Electronic Journal* (December 1996–February 1997), http://www.lib.latrobe.edu.au/AHR/ (accessed June 2007).

44. Wu and Li, *Single Tear*, 100–101.

45. Ibid., 101.

46. Wu was interviewed by CNN on February 1997, for *Cold War* (episode 15); his book and experience were also covered in Judith Shapiro, "22 Years as Class Enemy," *New York Times*, February 28, 1993.

47. Primo Levi, *Se questo è un uomo* (Turin: De Silva, 1947), and *Survival in Auschwitz: The Nazi Assault on Humanity*, trans. Stuart Woolf (New York: Simon and Schuster, 1996).

48. Ernie O'Malley to Molly Childers, November 26–December 1, 1923, quoted in *Prisoners: The Civil War Letters of Ernie O'Malley*, ed. Richard English and Cormac O'Malley (Dublin: Poolbeg, 1991), 89; Peadar O'Donnell, *The Gates Flew Open* (London: Jonathan Cape, 1932), 150. See also Richard English, "Shakespeare and the Definition of the Irish Nation," in *Shakespeare and Ireland: History, Politics, Culture,* ed. Mark Thornton and Ramona Wray (London: Macmillan, 1997), 136–51.

49. Mao Zedong's "Talks at the Yan'an Forum on Literature and Art" was delivered at a congregation of CCP cadres in May 1942. Mao spoke twice at the historic meeting in the CCP's revolutionary headquarters in Yan'an. His lectures were published in the *Jiefang ribao [Liberation Daily]* on October 19, 1943. Mao Zedong "Zai Yan'an wenyi zuotan hui shang de jianghua," in *Mao Zedong xuanji [Selected Works of Mao Zedong]* (Beijing: Renmin chubanshe, 1990), 804.

50. Stephen Orgel, afterword to *Shakespeare, Memory and Performance,* ed. Peter Holland (Cambridge: Cambridge University Press, 2006), 349.

51. *Much Ado About Nothing,* directed by Yevgeniya K. Lipkovskaya, translated by Zhu Shenghao, staged by the Shanghai Theatre Academy (1957); revived by the Shanghai Theatre Academy's Experimental Huaju Theatre Company, directed by Hu Dao and Wu Li (1961); revived by the Shanghai Youth Huaju Theatre Company (Shanghai qingnian huaju tuan), directed by Hu Dao (1979). The production was staged by graduates of the Program for Acting Teachers (*biaoyan shizi jinxiu ban*) of the Shanghai Theatre Academy. The 1957 production was very popular and was performed from June 19 to July 1, and again from September 1 to 10, in the Experimental Theatre of the Shanghai Theatre Academy. The performances were attended by over sixteen thousand people, a very large audience considering that the small theater seated only some five hundred people. The same year, the production was staged for thirteen nights in the Youth Art Theater (Qingnian yishu

juchang) and People's Theater (Renmin juchang) in Beijing between September 25 and October 27. It was staged for an additional eleven nights in the People's Grand Theater (Renmin da wutai) in Shanghai between November 23 and December 1, 1957. Zhang Siyang et al., eds., *Shashibiya da cidian* [*Encyclopedic Dictionary of Shakespeare*] (Beijing: Shangwu yinshu guan, 2001), 1377. The 1961 production was staged in the Shanghai Art Theater (Shanghai yishu juchang) from May 16 to June 12 and from July 1 to 9, 1961. The revived production toured Dalian and Shenyang in northeastern China in July and August 1961. It was staged in Shanghai again from November 11 to 16, 1961. The 1979 production was performed on April 21 and broadcast live by Shanghai Television.

52. Haiyan Lee, "Love and Loathing in Socialist China," in *Revolutionary Discourse in China: Words and Their Stories*, ed. Ban Wang (Leiden: Brill, forthcoming). I thank Haiyan Lee for sharing her unpublished manuscript.

53. Walter Benjamin, "The Work of Art in the Age of Mechanical Reproduction," in *Illuminations*, ed. Hannah Arendt, trans. Harry Zohn (London: Pimlico, 1999), 214.

54. Terence Hawkes, *Shakespeare in the Present* (London: Routledge, 2002), 3.

55. Ros King, "Dramaturgy: Beyond the Presentism/Historicism Dichotomy," *Shakespearean International Yearbook* 7 (2007): 6–21; David Scott Kastan, *Shakespeare After Theory* (London: Routledge, 1999); Lisa Jardine, *Reading Shakespeare Historically* (London: Routledge, 1996).

56. Sun Yu, "Zanmei zhengzhi, caizhi, han youyi de shipian: Shashibiya de xiju *Wushi shengfei* guanhou" [Poetry in Praise of Righteousness, Wisdom, and Friendship: My Impression of the Production of the Shakespearean Comedy, *Much Ado About Nothing*], *Liaoning ribao* [*Liaoning Daily*], September 2, 1961.

57. Li Ruru, interview with Hu Dao, September 1998 and January 2001 (*Shashibiya: Staging Shakespeare in China* [Hong Kong: Hong Kong University Press, 2003], 60).

58. The scene corresponded to act 5, scene 4, of the original play. Beilitesi (Beatrice) was played by Zhu Xijun, and Baidini (Benedick) was played by Jiao Huang. *Wushi shengfei* [*Much Ado About Nothing*], stage bill, Shanghai Youth Huaju Theater Company, 1979.

59. Liu Fan, "Xiang nimen xuexi, xiang nimen kanqi: Xie gei Shanghai xiju xueyuan shiyan huaju tuan" [Learning from You, Looking onto You: A Letter to the Shanghai Theatre Academy's Experimental Huaju Company], *Liaoning ribao*, September 2, 1961.

60. Cao and Sun, *Shashibiya zai Zhongguo*, 116–17.

61. Lu Hai, "Kan *Wushi shengfei*" [Watching *Much Ado About Nothing*], *Qingdao ribao* [*Qingdao Daily*], August 1, 1962.

62. Sun, "Zanmei zhengzhi."

63. Dong Youdao, "*Wushi shengfei* de wutai diaodu: Liepukefusikaya de daoyan shoufa" [The Mise-en-scène of *Much Ado About Nothing*: Lipkovskaya's Directing Method], *Xinmin wanbao* [*New Citizen Evening News*], November 30, 1957.

64. "New China" was a term deployed by the CCP to describe the socialist state founded in 1949.

65. *Twelfth Night*, translated by Zhu Shenghao, directed by Gennadi Kazansky, Beijing Polytechnic School of Film Art (Beijing dianying zhuanke xuexiao), graduating class, 1957; *Twelfth Night*, translated by Cao Weifeng, directed by Ling Zhihao, Shanghai Film Actors' Theater Company (Shanghai dianying yanyuan jutuan), 1958; revived in 1959 and 1962 with the same translation and director.

66. In the earlier phase of Chinese Shakespeare (in the Republican China period [1911–1949]), *Macbeth* was staged as a political allegory against Yuan Shikai, who restored the imperial government and crowned himself as emperor.

67. Hu Dao, "*Wushi shengfei* shi ge zenyang de xiju?" [What Kind of Comedy Is *Much Ado About Nothing?*], *Xinmin wanbao*, May 22, 1961.

68. Yevgeniya Konstantinovna Lipkovskaya, "Xiju yishu de jiben tedian" [The Basic Features of Dramatic Art], trans. Sha Jin, in *Yuan bao* [*Newsletter of Shanghai Theatre Academy*] 8 (Shanghai: Shanghai Theatre Academy, 1956), 13.

69. Yevgeniya Konstantinovna Lipkovskaya, "Sulian zhuanjia Ye Kang Liepukefusikaya zai biaoyan shizi jinxiuban di yi tang biaoyanke shang de jianghua" [The Soviet Expert Yevgeniya Konstantinovna Lipkovskaya's Talk at the First Acting Class for the Acting Teachers' Program], trans. Sha Jin, in *Yuan bao* 7 (Shanghai: Shanghai Theatre Academy, 1956), 8.

70. Constantin Stanislavski, *An Actor Prepares*, trans. Elizabeth Reynolds Hapgood (New York: Theatre Arts Books, 1972), 51.

71. Lipkovskaya, "Sulian zhuanjia," 8.

72. Mao Zedong, "Baihua qifang, baijia zhengming fangzhen de guanche" [How to Enforce the Policy of "Letting A Hundred Flowers Bloom and A Hundred Schools Contend"], in *Zhongguo xiandai wenxue shi cankao ziliao: Zhongguo geming wenxue de xin jieduan* [*Reference Materials of Modern Chinese Literary History: The New Epoch of Chinese Revolutionary Literature, 1949–1958*], ed. Beijing shifan daxue zhongwenxi xiandai wenxue jiaoxue gaige xiaozu (Beijing: Gaodeng jiaoyu chubanshe, 1959), 3:475.

73. Li, *Shashibiya*, 56.

74. Friedrich Engels, introduction to *Dialectics of Nature*, ed. and trans. Clemens Dutt (New York: International Publishers, 1960), 2–3.

75. Friedrich Engels, "Letter to Ferdinand Lassalle, May 18, 1859," in *Marx and Engels on Literature and Art*, ed. Baxandall and Morawski, 109.

76. The phrase Marx and Engels used in their letters on this subject was "Shakespeare's vivacity and wealth of action" (Karl Marx, "Letter to Ferdinand Lassalle, April 19, 1859," in *Marx and Engels on Literature and Art*, ed. Baxandall and Morawski, 145).

77. Alexander Anikst, "Shakespeare—A Writer of the People" (1959), in *Shakespeare in the Soviet Union: A Collection of Articles*, trans. Avril Pyman, comp. Roman Samarin and Alexander Nikolyukin (Moscow: Progress Publishers, 1966), 113.

78. Ibid., 138.

79. Meng Xianqiang, *Zhongguo Shaxue jianshi* [*A Concise History of Shakespeare Studies in China*] (Changchun: Dongbei shifan daxue chubanshe, 1994), 35.

80. Mikhail M. Morozov, *Shakespeare on the Soviet Stage*, trans. David Magarshack (London: Soviet News, 1947).

81. Mikhail M. Morozov, *Shashibiya zhuan* [*Shakespeare's Life*], trans. Xu Haiyan and Wu Junzhong (Changsha: Hunan renmin chubanshe, 1984).

82. A. A. Anikst, "Byt' ili ne byt' u nas Gamletu?" *Teatr* 3 (1955): 62, translated in David Gillespie, "Adapting Foreign Classics: Kozintsev's Shakespeare," in *Russian and Soviet Film Adaptations of Literature, 1900–2001: Screening the Word*, ed. Stephen Hutchings and Anat Vernitski (London: Routledge, 2005), 87.

83. Mao, "Zai Yan'an wenyi zuotan hui shang de jianghua," 828.

84. Ibid., 827.

85. Chen Shouzhu, "Guanyu xiju wenti" [On the Question of Comedy], *Wenhui bao* [*Wenhui Daily*], March 2, 1961, 3.

86. Editorial Committee, ed., *Shashibiya quanji* [*Complete Works of Shakespeare*] (Beijing: Renmin wenxue chubanshe, 1978), 1:9.

87. Friedrich Engels, "Landscape," *Telegraph für Deutschland* 123, August 1840, in *Karl Marx and Frederick Engels: Collected Works*, vol. 2, *Frederick Engels, 1838–42*, trans. Richard Dixon et al. (London: Lawrence & Wishart, 1975), 95–101, and *The Condition of the Working Class in England*, ed. and trans. W. O. Henderson and W. H. Chaloner (New York: Macmillan, 1958).

88. Engels, "Landscape," 100.

89. In 1398: "[Armenia] is most merye londe, with herbes, corne, wodes and fruyte" (J. Trevisa, trans., Bartholomaeus Anglicus's *De Proprietatibus Rerum* f. 172); in 1596: "To mery London, my most kindly Nurse" (Edmund Spenser, *Prothalamion* 128); in 1816: "Their moonlight walks and merry evening games" (Jane Austen, *Emma* 1. iv.52, cited in *Oxford English Dictionary*, 2nd ed. [Oxford: Oxford University Press, 1989]).

90. A recent example is Julian Barnes, *England, England* (London: Jonathan Cape, 1998). In the novel, a series of circumstances returned modern England to a pastoral, preindustrialized state.

91. Karl Marx, "Critique of the Gotha Program," in *Karl Marx and Friedrich Engels, Selected Works* (Moscow: Foreign Languages Publishing House, 1949), 2:23; Karl Marx and Friedrich Engels, *The German Ideology* (New York: International Publishers, 1960), 22.

92. Maurice Meisner, *Marxism, Maoism, and Utopianism: Eight Essays* (Madison: University of Wisconsin Press, 1982), 26, 29. Meisner notes that Marx's "idyllic and almost pastoral vision of communism was entirely in harmony with the Maoist expectation of the time" (192). Frederic Wakeman Jr. traces Mao's utopian vision to Kang Youwei's syncratic utopianism, in *History and Will: Philosophical Perspectives of Mao Tse-tung's Thought* (Berkeley: University of California Press, 1973), 115–36.

93. "*Wushi shengfei*: Si mu xiju" [*Much Ado About Nothing*: A Comedy in Four Acts], play script, March 1961, manuscript in the Archive of Shanghai Youth Huaju Theater (Shanghai qingnian huaju tuan dang'an).

94. Anne Barton, "Introduction to *Much Ado About Nothing*," in *The Riverside Shakespeare*, ed. G. Blakemore Evans (Boston: Houghton Mifflin, 1997), 366–98, 361.

95. Hu, "*Wushi shengfei* shi ge zenyang de xiju?"

96. Wang Qibang, "Tantan huaju *Wushi shengfei* he ta de yanchu" [A Few Words on the *Huaju* Performance of *Much Ado About Nothing*], *Shenyang wanbao* [*Shenyang Evening Post*], August 29, 1961.

97. Hu, "*Wushi shengfei* shi ge zenyang de xiju?"

98. Konstantin Stanislavsky, *Stanislavski Produces Othello*, trans. Helen Nowak (New York: Theatre Arts Books, 1963), 6.

99. Anne Bogart, *A Director Prepares* (London: Routledge, 2001), 22.

100. Jonathan Spence, *The Search for Modern China* (New York: Norton, 1990), 589.

101. Geoffrey Francis Hudson, Richard Lowenthal, and Roderick MacFarquhar, *The Sino-Soviet Dispute* (New York: Praeger, 1961), 42–45.

102. John King Fairbank and Merle Goldman, *China: A New History* (Cambridge, Mass.: Belknap Press of Harvard University Press, 1998), 368.

103. Hu, "*Wushi shengfei* shi ge zenyang de xiju?"; Liu, "Xiang nimen xuexi"; Sun, "Zanmei zhengzhi."

104. Li, *Shashibiya*, 59.

105. Zhu Xijuan, "Wo yan Beitelisi" [Me Playing Beatrice], *Shanghai xiju* [*Shanghai Theater*] 2 (1980): 29.

106. Perry Link, *The Uses of Literature: Life in the Socialist Chinese Literary System* (Princeton, N.J.: Princeton University Press, 2000), 10. For a study of Stalin and Gorky's socialist realism, see Harold Swayze, *Political Control of Literature in the USSR, 1946–1959* (Cambridge: Cambridge University Press, 1962).

107. Stanley Wells, foreword to *Shakespeare, Memory and Performance*, ed. Peter Holland (Cambridge: Cambridge University Press, 2006), xx.

108. I thank Djelal Kadir for bringing to my attention the parallel between Borges's story and the paradoxical reproducibility of Shakespeare's plays as texts and as performances. Jorge Luis Borges, "Pierre Menard, Author of the *Quixote*," in *Everything and Nothing*, trans. Donald A. Yates, James E. Irby, John M. Fein, and Eliot Weinberger (New York: New Directions, 1999), 5.

109. The production had a cast of over sixty, including dancers from the Shanghai Dancers' Association and the Yindu Art School (Yindu yiyuan jinxiu xuexiao), and realistic set and props including fountains, horses, motorcycles, and a convertible.

110. Cao Shujun, "*Wushi shengfei* guangchang ju" [The "Plaza Open-Air Theater" of *Much Ado About Nothing*], *Xin wutai* [*New Stage*], December 9, 1995, 5.

111. Chang Chuangze, "Changmian da, huanjing chao, yanyuan lei: Shouci guangchang huaju liangxiang muji" [Grand Setting, Noisy Environment, Exhausted Actors: Witness of the First Open-Air *Huaju*], *Qingnian bao* [*Youth News*], November 20, 1995.

112. Rehearsal script, "*Wushi shengfei*" *yanchu ben* [*Prompt Book of "Looking for Trouble"*], trans. Zhu Shenghao (Shanghai: Shanghai huaju yishu zhongxin, 1995), 38. The scene (act 4) corresponds to 5.4.117–19 of the original.

113. Cao, "*Wushi shengfei* guangchang ju," 5.

114. Yu Luosheng's rehearsal notes on October 10, 1995, transcribed and edited by Liao Jingfeng, manuscript in the Archive of the Shanghai Center for the Huaju Art (Shanghai huaju yishu zhongxin).

115. Clifford Geertz, *Negara: The Theatre State in Nineteenth Century Bali* (Princeton, N.J.: Princeton University Press, 1988), 136. Contrary to the case of Chinese Shakespeare in this period, the elaborate performances examined by Geertz were "not means to political ends, " but "the ends themselves" because "power served pomp, not pomp power" (13).

6. Why Does Everyone Need Chinese Opera?

1. Gore Vidal, *Screening History* (London: Abacus, 1992), 2; Wendy Everett, "Introduction: From Frame to Frame: Images in Transition," in *The Seeing Century: Film, Vision, and Identity*, ed. Wendy Everett (Amsterdam: Rodopi, 2000), 6.

2. For more information on *xiqu*, see the prologue.

3. Frederic Jameson argues that multinational capitalism is defined by two features, "the transformation of reality into images" and the "fragmentation of time into a series of perpetual presents." As image becomes a transferable commodity, it dominates the social space by purging previously privileged forms of expression. Stuart Hall connects the rise of global mass culture to the availability of "the image which crosses and re-crosses linguistic frontiers much more rapidly and more easily" (*Cultural Turns: Selected Writings on the Postmodern, 1983–1998* [London: Verso, 1998], 20, and *Postmodernism, or, the Cultural Logic of Late Capitalism* [Durham, N.C.: Duke University Press, 1991], 68). See also Stuart Hall, "The Local and the Global: Globalization and Ethnicity," in *Culture, Globalization, and the World-System*, ed. Anthony King (Minneapolis: University of Minnesota Press, 1997), 27.

4. Dennis Kennedy, "Introduction: Shakespeare Without His Language," in *Foreign Shakespeare: Contemporary Performance*, ed. Dennis Kennedy (Cambridge: Cambridge University Press, 1993) 1, 5, reprinted, with revisions, as "Shakespeare Without His Language," in *Shakespeare, Theory, and Performance*, ed. James C. Bulman (London: Routledge, 1996), 133–48, 6.

5. This is a familiar scenario with many traditional Asian performances of Shakespeare. A case in point is Kurosawa Akira's internationally acclaimed film *Throne of Blood* (based on *Macbeth*). Kurosawa was regarded by his Japanese peers as so Westernized that his name was often printed in *katakana*, used to write transliterations of non–East Asian names or foreign-derived loan words in Japanese.

6. Dennis Kennedy, *Looking at Shakespeare: A Visual History of Twentieth-Century Performance*, 2nd ed. (Cambridge: Cambridge University Press, 2001), 288, 293.

7. Dennis Kennedy, "Shakespeare and the Global Spectator," *Shakespeare Jahrbuch* 131 (1995): 50–64.

8. John Gillies, "Shakespeare Localized: An Australian Looks at Asian Practice," in *Shakespeare Global/Local: The Hong Kong Imaginary in Transcultural Production*, ed. Kwok-kan Tam, Andrew Parkin, and Terry Siu-han Yip (Frankfurt: Peter Lang, 2002), 101.

9. John Russell Brown, "Foreign Shakespeare and English-speaking Audiences," in *Foreign Shakespeare*, ed. Kennedy, 32; John Russell Brown, *New Sites for Shakespeare: Theatre, the Audience and Asia* (London: Routledge, 1999), 130.

10. Daphne Pi-Wei Lei, *Operatic China: Staging Chinese Identity Across the Pacific* (New York: Palgrave Macmillan, 2006), 255.

11. Brown, *New Sites for Shakespeare*.

12. Antony Tatlow, *Shakespeare, Brecht, and the Intercultural Sign* (Durham, N.C.: Duke University Press, 2001), 198.

13. J. Philip Brockbank, "Shakespeare Renaissance in China," *Shakespeare Quarterly* 39, no. 2 (1988): 195–204.

14. Dennis Bartholomeusz, "Shakespeare Imagines the Orient: The Orient Imagines Shakespeare," in *Shakespeare and Cultural Traditions: The Selected Proceedings of the International Shakespeare Association World Congress, Tokyo, 1991*, ed. Roger Pringle, Tetsuo Kishi, and Stanley Wells (Newark: University of Delaware Press, 1994), 201.

15. Ibid., 199.

16. Quoted in Brockbank, "Shakespeare Renaissance," 195.

17. Cao Shujun, *Shashibiya de chuntian zai Zhongguo* [*It Is the Spring Time for Shakespeare in China*] (Hong Kong: Tianma tushu, 2002), 2.

18. Matthew Gurewitsch, "A Cast of One for 'King Lear,'" *Wall Street Journal*, July 10, 2007, eastern edition, D5.

19. Faye Chunfang Fei and William Huizhu Sun, "*Othello* and Beijing Opera: Appropriation as a Two-Way Street," *TDR: The Drama Review* 50, no. 1 (2006): 122.

20. Xiao Yang Zhang argued from the premise that adaptation is possible because Shakespearean and traditional Chinese theaters share a great deal of similarities, in *Shakespeare in China: A Comparative Study of Two Traditions and Cultures* (Newark: University of Delaware Press, 1996), 62–172. Li Ruru wrote that "the Chinese character with which *xi* [theater] is written conveys the idea of what *xi* is. This character is made up of two components: one of which is *xu* (false), and the other is *ge* (dagger . . .). So in Chinese mentality, theatre is always the 'false . . . fight,'" and it stands to reason that "Shakespeare and Chinese indigenous theatre [Beijing opera] agree entirely" (*Shashibiya: Staging Shakespeare in China* [Hong Kong: Hong Kong University Press, 2003], 192).

21. Tatlow, *Shakespeare, Brecht*, 198.

22. Qi Rushan, *Qi Rushan huiyilu* [*Qi Rushan's Memoir*] (Beijing: Zhongguo xiju chubanshe, 1998), 126–85; Joshua Goldstein, *Drama Kings: Players and Publics in the Re-creation of Peking Opera, 1870–1937* (Berkeley: University of California Press, 2007), 134–71, 264–89.

23. Kwai-Cheung Lo, *Chinese Face/Off: The Transnational Popular Culture of Hong Kong* (Urbana: University of Illinois Press, 2005), 180.

24. *Think Korea 2006: Korea-UK Mutual Visit Year*, program booklet (London: Korean Cultural Centre and the Embassy of the Republic of Korea, 2006), 21. The same passage can also be found in the production description: Barbican Centre, http://www.barbican.org.uk/theatre/event-detail.asp?id=4276 (accessed July 2007). The Mokhwa Repertory Company's *Romeo and Juliet* was staged from November 23 to December 9, 2006, at the Pit, as part of the bite 2006 (July–December); tickets were £15 apiece, and all performances were sold out.

25. Charles Spencer, "A *Macbeth* Made in Taiwan," *Daily Telegraph*, November 16, 1990.

26. Tatlow, *Shakespeare, Brecht*, 200.

27. Ibid., 201.

28. Lois Potter, "The Spectacle of *Macbeth*," *Times Literary Supplement*, November 13, 1987, 1253.

29. "Art thou not, fatal vision, sensible / To feeling as to sight? or art thou but / A dagger of the mind, a false creation / Proceeding from the heat-oppressed brain? / I see thee yet, in form as palpable / As this which now I draw" (*Macbeth* 2.1.35–41).

30. Cao Shujun and Sun Fuliang, *Shashibiya zai Zhongguo wutai shang* [*Shakespeare on the Chinese Stage*] (Shenyang: Harbin chubanshe, 1989) 195.

31. Harold Bloom, *Shakespeare: The Invention of the Human* (New York: Riverhead Books, 1998), 430; G. Wilson Knight, *The Shakespearean Tempest* (London: Milford, 1932), 3–4.

32. Brown believes that Shakespeare's plays in foreign languages often seem more "political and polemical" than in English. He attributed this phenomenon to the fact that "a director will underline his chosen political interpretation in many ways that are non verbal," and the alien signifying practice prompts the audience to pay more attention to these nonverbal signs. A contemporary translation is "more attuned to contemporary parlance" and moves the play "closer to our own political consciousness" ("Foreign Shakespeare," 26). Along the same line, Kennedy argues that "foreign performances may have a more direct access to the power of [Shakespeare's] plays," because they "contemporize the meanings of the plays" ("Introduction," 5–6).

33. Walter Ong, *Orality and Literacy: The Technologizing of the Word* (London: Routledge, 1982), 132.

34. The play was written by Shao Hongchao and his associates, including Weng Ouhong. This production was staged again at the first Chinese Shakespeare Festival in Beijing in 1986.

35. A typical *jingju* painted-face character would be a supernatural being or a man of great physical strength or mental power. The role type is often used to present vigorous, violent, or crafty characters. Elizabeth Wichmann, *Listening to Theatre: The Aural Dimension of Beijing Opera* (Honolulu: University of Hawai'i Press, 1991), 10.

36. One of the most important features of painted-face roles is the brightly colored patterns of the makeup that covers the entire face from the forehead to

the jawline. Thus it was considered revolutionary for a *hualian* to perform without makeup.

37. During the 1950s and the early 1960s, only a limited number of foreign films were approved by the state and imported. Four films of Shakespeare were screened in public: the Soviet *Twelfth Night* and *Othello* (with Chinese subtitles), Laurence Olivier's *Hamlet* (dubbed in Chinese), and *Richard III* (with Chinese subtitles). These films had an enormous influence on Chinese performances of Shakespeare. Ma Yong'an was not the only Chinese actor inspired by them. Xiong Yuanwei incorporated Olivier's *Hamlet* into his multimedia Cantonese *huaju* adaptation called *Hamlet, Hamlet* (Hong Kong, 2001) with video clips projected onto screens on the stage. In 1958, Sun Daolin dubbed Olivier's film version of *Hamlet* in Chinese (Shanghai Film Studio), using Bian Zhilin's translation. His recitation of the "To be, or not to be" soliloquy (3.1.55–87) remained in the Chinese collective cultural memory. Sun's reading was subsequently made into a radio play that had a wide audience. His dubbing in "Stanislavsky's method, complemented by internal monologue and psychological depth," according to Sun in an interview, has achieved a new height in its presentation of compounding values of life and death that Olivier "fail[ed] to address." Zhu Haining, "Zuo daxie de ren: Sun Daolin maodie zhi nian de rensheng ganwu [A Name to Be Capitalized: Interview of Sun Daolin]," *Dazhong dianying* [*Popular Cinema*], March 2002. Sun also records in detail the process of dubbing the Olivier film in his autobiography, which has become a hit among mainland Chinese readers who retain a collective memory of Sun's voice, especially during the turbulent years of the Cultural Revolution when radio was the only form of entertainment imaginable. Sun Daolin, *Zoujin yangguang* [*Walking into the Sun*] (Shanghai: Shanghai renmin chubanshe, 1997).

38. *Othello* (1956), directed by Sergei Yutkevitch, starred Sergei Bondarchuk (Othello), Irina Skobesteva (Desdemona), and Andrei Popov (Iago). The 108-minute black-and-white film adaptation won "Best Director" at Cannes.

39. Ma Yong'an, interview with Alexander Huang, Beijing, September 4, 2002.

40. Ibid.

41. Frank Dikötter, *The Discourse of Race in Modern China* (London: Hurst, 1992), 15, 38–39, 89, 149. See also Frank Dikötter, ed., *The Construction of Racial Identities in China and Japan: Historical and Contemporary Perspectives* (London: Hurst, 1997).

42. The production was staged in Tokyo's Hongo-za on June 1 and 2, 1907, and in Shanghai's Lyceum Theatre (Lanxin juchang) by Wang Zhongsheng in October of the same year, in *jingju* style.

43. Ayanna Thompson, "Practicing a Theory/Theorizing a Practice: An Introduction to Shakespearean Colorblind Casting," in *Colorblind Shakespeare: New Perspectives on Race and Performance*, ed. Ayanna Thompson (New York: Routledge, 2006), 1.

44. August Wilson, *The Ground on Which I Stand* (New York: Theatre Communication Group, 1996) (speech presented at the eleventh Biennial Theatre Communication Group National Conference, Princeton University, June 26, 1996), quoted in Thompson, "Practicing a Theory," 1.

45. Fei and Sun, "*Othello* and Beijing Opera," 125.

46. *Student Wife* is a *huaju* play by Yu Luosheng, adapted from Wang Zhousheng's eponymous novel. It was staged by the Shanghai Dramatic Arts Center in 1995, with a record box-office success. According to Claire Conceison, it sold out "its two-month run at the highest ticket prices ever charged by a Shanghai professional theatre company up until that time" (*Significant Other: Staging the American in China* [Honolulu: University of Hawai'i Press, 2004], 137, 139, 264–65). A former United States Information Service diplomat fluent in Mandarin, Richard Daly costarred in the popular television series *A Beijinger in New York* (*Beijingren zai Niuyue*, 1993).

47. Ania Loomba, foreword to *Colorblind Shakespeare*, ed. Thompson, xiv.

48. Ibid., xv.

49. Li believes that the play "is organized in eight acts" (*Shashibiya*, 181). This discrepancy probably arose out of the translation of the Chinese concept of "act," (*chang*), which is based on changes of aria suits and melodies. The concepts of "act" and "scene" divisions based on scene changes are alien to *jingju*. In my interview with Ma Yong'an, he referred to the first "scene" as merely a prologue.

50. My translation, based on Li, *Shashibiya*, 180–81.

51. Brockbank, "Shakespeare Renaissance," 201.

52. On the role of director in Chinese opera, see Megan Evans, "The Emerging Role of the Director in Chinese Xiqu," *Asian Theatre Journal* 24, no. 2 (2007): 470–504.

53. Elizabeth Wichmann-Wlaczak and Catherine Swatek, "*Jingju* Role Types," in *Encyclopedia of Asian Theatre*, ed. Samuel L. Leiter (Westport, Conn.: Greenwood Press, 2007), 2:626. Definitions of the *laosheng* role type vary in different genres of Chinese opera. For example, in *kunqu* (*kunju*), it refers to a "bearded, high-status older [male character]" (625).

54. Ma Yong'an performed this last scene for me without music accompaniment during the interview. The lines transcribed are from his performance.

55. Ma interview.

56. Ibid.

57. Deng Xiaoping, "Zai Zhongguo wenxue yishu gongzuo zhe di si ci daibiao dahui shang de zhuci" [Congratulatory Remark at the Fourth Chinese Literary and Artistic Workers' Congress], in *Deng Xiaoping wenxuan* [*Selected Writings of Deng Xiaoping*] (Beijing: Renmin chubanshe, 1983) 182.

58. The revolutionary model theater did not use traditional Chinese-opera costumes and introduced the trend of seeking contemporized meanings in a stylized theater employing partly traditional forms. For a detailed account of Western influences on the performing style and dramatic structure of the model revolutionary theater, see Chen Xiaomei, "The Making of a Revolutionary Stage: Chinese Model Theatre and Its Western Influences," in *East of West: Cross-Cultural Performance and the Staging of Difference*, ed. Claire Sponsler and Xiaomei Chen (New York: Palgrave, 2000), 125–40.

59. Daniel S. P. Yang, interviews with theater practitioners, in "Theatre Activities in Post-Cultural Revolution China," in *Drama in the People's Republic of China*,

ed. Constantine Tung and Colin Mackerras (Albany: State University of New York, 1987), 176.

60. There are eighteen ranks, with the eighteenth rank being the lowest. A *jingju* actor who had just finished his or her training was not ranked. In the first year, an actor received a wage for "practical training," which was approximately US$20 a month. After being promoted to the eighteenth rank, the actor was paid approximately US$25 a month. Salary for the actors of the highest rank, *wenyi yiji* (first rank in literature and art) or *guojia yiji yanyuan* (the first-rate actor of the nation), was approximately US$192 a month (RMB 336). Yang collected this data in the 1980s in multiple field research trips ("Theatre Activities," 177).

61. In fact, of the 2,524 plays produced in mainland China in 1980, only 176 were *huaju* productions. Chinese-opera productions made up more than 87 percent (2,209) of the total number of plays produced. *Zhongguo xiju nianjian [Chinese Theatre Annual]* (Beijing, 1981), 296–303. Statistics also indicate that theaters were thriving. According to the statistics of the *Zhongguo xiju nianjian,* of the 275 new plays published in mainland Chinese journals, 139 were Chinese-opera dramas and 114 were *huaju* plays in the Western tradition (289–95). In 1981, there was a 45 percent increase in the number of new plays published. In 1981, 389 new plays were published. *Zhongguo xiju nianjian [Chinese Theatre Annual]* (Beijing: Zhongguo xiju chubanshe, 1982), 555.

62. *Zhongguo xiju nianjian* (1982), 173. Theater tickets remained affordable for the general public, according to Yang's field research in 1981, 1983, and 1985. Ticket prices range from around US$1.50 (1980s currency exchange rate) for an "all-star Beijing opera performance" to US$0.30 for an "average show in a medium-sized city." The factory wages were between US$30 and $40 a month. Monthly rent was under $4. The audience at these performances represented a cross section of society. However, it was difficult to tell a person's occupation, because most people wore gray or blue clothing, a legacy of the Cultural Revolution. High-ranking government officials, such as the mayor or party leaders, were usually invited to attend the performance for reasons ranging from promoting to sanctioning the performance. While the audience at *huaju* productions was more "civilized" and quieter during the performances, the audience at the traditional theaters still retained the practice of cracking melon seeds and shouting during the performance (as a way of applauding their favorite actors). Yang, "Theatre Activities," 171–72.

63. Perry Link did not specify which edition it was, but it is likely that the statistics refer to Zhu Shenghao's complete translation. Link suspects that the purchase was made as "a bow to a 'standard' great Western writer" (*The Uses of Literature* [Princeton, N.J.: Princeton University Press, 2000], 170). However, the number of copies of Shakespeare circulated is greater than many Chinese novels, which is significant in a period when most reprinted and published literature was fiction, not drama.

64. *Romeo and Juliet,* directed by Huang Zuolin, Zhuang Zejing, and Ji Qiming, translated by Cao Yu, Shanghai People's Art Theater (Shanghai renmin yishu juyuan), 1980.

65. Cao and Sun, *Shashibiya zai Zhongguo,* 127.

66. I have adopted Adrian Hsia's translation of Huang Zuolin's term *xieyi* (literally, "painting the intentions"), in "Huang Zuolin's Ideal of Drama and Bertolt Brecht," in *Drama in the People's Republic of China*, ed. Tung and Mackerras, 160. Huang did not settle on any translation, although he has attempted to translate it as "intrinsicalistic theatre" and essentialism. Sun Huizhu and Gong Bo'an, "Huang Zuolin de xiju xieyi shuo" [Huang Zuolin's *Xieyi* Theater], *Xiju yishu* [*Theatre Art*], no. 4 (1983): 7–8.

67. Graduation production of the Actor Training Program for Tibetan Students [Zangzu biaoyan ban], Shanghai Theatre Academy, Tibetan translation by Mengnan Jiangcun, based on Cao Yu's Chinese translation, directed by Xu Qiping. The production was staged in Shanghai in April 1981, and in Beijing on May 22, 1981, by invitation of the State Department of Culture (Wenhua bu). The cast, acting teachers, and director were honored with the title "Advanced Unit of Education" (*xianjin jiaoxue jiti*) by the State Department of Culture on June 17, 1981. The production was staged in Lhasa in early 1982. Juliet was played by De Yang, and Romeo was played by Duobu Ji. Li Xiao, ed., *Shanghai huaju zhi* [*Annals of Huaju in Shanghai*] (Shanghai: Baijia chubanshe, 2002), 182–83.

68. Cao and Sun, *Shashibiya zai Zhongguo*, 129.

69. The play was adapted by Xu Fen and codirected by Cao Ping and Tian Mansha. It was produced by the Youth Chuanju Company of the Sichuan Province Sichuan Opera Conservatory (Sichuan sheng chuanju xuexiao qingnian chuanju tuan), with lighting design by Xing Xin and music by Lan Tian. The play was staged in Chengdu, Sichuan, and then at the Twelfth Macau Art Festival in March 2001, as well as the Bremen Shakespeare aus Asien (Shakespeare from Asia) Festival, March 14, 16, and 17, 2001.

70. Tian Mansha, interview with Alexander Huang, March 15, 2004.

71. The play was adapted by Wang Anqi and directed by the Hong Kong film director Xu Ke (Tsui Hark). Shi Rufang, "*Baofeng yu* shouci deng 'Tai': Mofashi da chang pihuang" [*The Tempest* to Appear on the Taiwanese Stage for the First Time: The Magician Sings Beijing Opera Tunes], *Biaoyan yishu* [*Performing Arts Review*] 135 (2004): 72.

72. Lai Tingheng, "Wu Hsing-kuo jiang yanchu Shaju *Baofeng yu*" [Wu Hsing-kuo to Perform Shakespeare's *The Tempest*], *Zhongshi wanglu yiwen cun* [Art Village section of *China Times*], May 24, 2004, http://news.chinatimes.com/Chinatimes/newscontent/newscontent-artnews/0,3457,112004052400176+110513+20040524+C9352430,00.html.

73. Fei and Sun, "*Othello* and Beijing Opera," 127.

74. Yi Kai, "Zhanxin de tiandi, juda de biange: Shoujie Shashibiya xijujie wutai yanchu guangan" [Brave New World and Great Changes: Reflections on the Five Chinese Opera Productions at the First Chinese Shakespeare Festival], *Xiqu yishu* [*Chinese Opera Arts*] 4 (1986): 6, translated in Fei and Sun, "*Othello* and Beijing Opera," 126.

75. Shu-mei Shih, *Visuality and Identity: Sinophone Articulations Across the Pacific* (Berkeley: University of California Press, 2007), 8.

76. "The fantasy of a pictorial turn, of a culture totally dominated by images, has now become a real technical possibility on a global scale" (W. J. T. Mitchell, *Picture Theory: Essays on Verbal and Visual Representation* [Chicago: University of Chicago Press, 1994], 16). See also Guy Debord, *The Society of the Spectacle*, trans. Donald Nicholson-Smith (New York: Zone Books, 1995), 26–27.

77. "Global mass culture . . . remains centered in the West. That is to say, Western technology, the concentration of capital, the concentration of techniques, the concentration of advanced labor in the Western societies, and the stories and imagery of Western societies: these remain the driving powerhouse of this global mass culture. In that sense, it is centered in the West and it always speaks English" (Hall, "Local and the Global," 28).

7. Disowning Shakespeare and China

1. Wu Hsing-kuo's metatheatrical comments on his eyes and Lear's eyes—and the blind spots in their visions—coincide with Jacques Lacan's concept of the gaze, in *Quatre concepts fondamentaux de la psychanalyse*, vol. 11, *Le Séminaire de Jacques Lacan* (Paris: Seuil, 1973). Lacan uses the floating skull in Holbein's painting *The Ambassadors* (1533) as an example of the object-gaze. Driven by his desire, the spectator is implicated in the perceived invisibility and visibility of different aspects of reality. The subject is unable to fully perceive the objects within his field of vision.

2. Wearing a *jingju* martial-role undercoat as an actor would be backstage.

3. Wu's virtuosity in the innovative solo performance is discussed in Matthew Gurewitsch, "A Cast of One for 'King Lear,'" *Wall Street Journal*, July 10, 2007, eastern edition, D5

4. I will cite the Lincoln Center Festival version and then fill in additional details from earlier versions performed in Paris (2000) and Taipei (2004). Conceived, directed, and performed by Wu Hsing-kuo, *Lear Is Here* (*Li'er zaici*) has toured the United States, Asia, and Europe. The Lincoln Center performance was supported by the Alice Tully Foundation, Asian Cultural Council, Josie Robertson Fund for Lincoln Center, the National Endowment for the Arts, public funds from the city and state of New York, and Taiwan's Council for Cultural Affairs.

5. See the prologue and chapter 6.

6. Barbara Hodgdon, "Stratford's Empire of Shakespeare; or, Fantasies of Origin, Authorship, and Authenticity: The Museum and the Souvenir," in *The Shakespeare Trade: Performances and Appropriations* (Philadelphia: University of Pennsylvania Press, 1998), 191–240.

7. Several critics have noted the dimension of the personal in contemporary Shakespearean performance, including Robert Lepage's one-man performance *Elsinore* (based on *Hamlet*) and Michael Almereyda's film *Hamlet*. Margaret Jane Kidnie calls Lepage's production "one performer's experiential encounter with 'Hamlet'" ("Dancing with Art: Robert Lepage's *Elsinore*," in *World-wide*

Shakespeares: Local Appropriations in Film and Performance, ed. Sonia Massai [London: Routledge, 2005], 140). Similarly, Mark Burnett writes that "the idea that filmmaking/video-making provides a means of writing a personal script is most fully encoded in Almereyda's *Hamlet*. His camera dwells repeatedly on Hamlet's auteurial eyes, as if alerting us to the ways in which he visualizes a history that is otherwise absent" (*Filming Shakespeare in the Global Marketplace* [New York: Palgrave Macmillan, 2007], 52).

8. *King Lear,* directed by Jean-Luc Godard (Cannon Films, 1988). Screenplay by Jean-Luc Godard, with Peter Sellars as William Shakespeare Jr., the Fifth. Peter Donaldson regards Godard's film as a "modernized, fragmented, constantly self-interrupting work, only part of which derives from Shakespeare's text." He believes Godard uses the film to "address the limits of his control over his work" ("Disseminating Shakespeare: Paternity and Text in Jean-Luc Godard's *King Lear,*" in *Shakespearean Films/Shakespearean Directors* [Boston: Unwin Hyman, 1990], 189–90). See also Anthony R. Guneratne, *Shakespeare, Film Studies, and the Visual Cultures of Modernity* (New York: Palgrave Macmillan, 2008), chap. 5; and Alan Walworth, "Cinema *Hysterica Passio:* Voice and Gaze in Jean-Luc Godard's *King Lear,*" in *The Reel Shakespeare: Alternative Cinema and Theory,* ed. Lisa S. Starks and Courtney Lehmann (Madison, N.J.: Fairleigh Dickinson University Press, 2002), 59–94.

9. This thirty-minute performance premiered in Kwai Tsing Theatre as part of the Hong Kong Experimental Shakespeare Festival, March 16 to 19, 2000. The play was revived in Taipei (May 25–27, 2001) for four performances by the Off-PW (Wai biaofang shiyan tuan), a subsidiary of the Performance Workshop that was inaugurated on October 6, 2000, in Taipei.

10. I use the term "cultural prestige" to highlight the tension between the artist's claim of personal difference (for example, in an autobiographical play such as Wu's *Lear Is Here*) and Shakespeare's universal currency. Pascale Casanova argues that the world of letters—with Paris as its symbolic center of gravity—is governed by the economy of cultural prestige, in *The World Republic of Letters,* trans. M. B. DeBevoise (Cambridge, Mass.: Harvard University Press, 2004), 9. James English theorizes a different aspect of this cultural value in his study of literary prizes, *The Economy of Prestige: Prizes, Awards, and the Circulation of Cultural Value* (Cambridge, Mass.: Harvard University Press, 2005), 264.

11. *The Daily Telegraph's* summer 2006 advertisement of its sports section in London's Underground stations (Paddington and elsewhere) prominently featured a digitally re-created portrait of Shakespeare and the line: "SPORT. We've got the greatest writers."

12. The ad appeared in newspapers and online media in Taiwan, including *China Times* (*Zhongshi dianzi bao,* http://news.chinatimes.com [accessed November 2003]) and *United Daily News* (*Lianhe xinwen wang,* http://udn.com [accessed April 2003]) between April and November 2003. In the advertisement, "Shakespeare" was used as an icon of Englishness and the global stature of the English language. The line from *Hamlet* was supposed to communicate a sense of cultural sophistication through English language education. However, it ironically connected the English classes to things irrelevant to that purpose, things evoked

by the line "To be, or not to be," such as the image of Hamlet or Renaissance skepticism.

13. Two more recent examples of big-time Shakespeare in China are the government-subsidized Chinese Shakespeare festivals of 1986 and 1994.

14. Quoted in Michael D. Bristol, *Big-time Shakespeare* (London: Routledge, 1996), 3.

15. Shen Lin, "Shakespeare, 'Theirs' and 'Ours'" (International Conference on Shakespeare Performance in the New Asias, National University of Singapore, June 27–30, 2002).

16. Albert Hunt and Geoffrey Reeves, *Peter Brook* (Cambridge: Cambridge University Press, 1995), 44.

17. Alexander C. Y. Huang, "Impersonation, Autobiography, and Cross-Cultural Adaptation: Lee Kuo-Hsiu's *Shamlet*," *Asian Theatre Journal* 22, no. 1 (2005): 122–37.

18. The Golden Bough Theatre's performance style fuses Jerzy Grotowski–inspired body language and Taiwanese opera (*gezai xi*).

19. *Hamlet / Hamlet* was directed by Xiong Yuanwei and produced in Cantonese by three Hong Kong theater companies: Amity Drama Club (Zhichun jushe), Shatian Spoken Drama Theatre (Shatian huaju tuan), and the Fourth Line Theatre (Di si xian jushe) in January 2000.

20. Xiong Yuanwei, "From Classics to Modernity: Director's Notes on *Hamlet / Hamlet*," *Hong Kong Drama Review* [*Xianggang xiju xuekan*] 2 (2000): 93.

21. "Contact zone" is a phrase used by Mary Louise Pratt to theorize the geographical and cultural space where colonial conflicts occur and hybrid identities are formed or resisted, in *Imperial Eyes: Studies in Travel Writing and Transculturation* (London: Routledge, 1992).

22. Tu Wei-ming is one of the scholars who have promoted the idea that "authentic" Confucian culture is located outside mainland China, where Marxist-Maoism dominated the cultural landscape up until the early 1990s. Tu coined the term "cultural China" to refer to global sites where Chinese identity is formulated, in "Cultural China: The Periphery as the Center," *Daedalus* 120, no. 2 (1991): 1–32, reprinted in *The Living Tree: The Changing Meaning of Being Chinese Today*, ed. Tu Wei-ming (Stanford, Calif.: Stanford University Press, 1994), 1–34.

23. Colonized by the Dutch (1624–1662) and ruled by the Chinese Ming loyalist Zheng Chenggong from 1662 to 1683, Taiwan was subsequently governed by the Chinese Qing imperial court (1683–1895). After China's defeat in the first Sino-Japanese War in 1895, Taiwan was ceded to Japan for fifty years. China's Nationalist Party took over Taiwan at the end of Japanese colonial period in 1945 after Mao Zedong's army defeated them and drove them out of mainland China (the PRC was founded in 1949). The KMT moved the central government of the Republic of China (ROC) to Taiwan, and claimed sovereignty over mainland China until the late 1980s.

24. Michelle Yeh, "Frontier Taiwan: An Introduction," in *Frontier Taiwan: An Anthology of Modern Chinese Poetry*, ed. Michelle Yeh and N. G. D. Malmqvist (New York: Columbia University Press, 2001), 50–51.

25. Jon von Kowallis considers Stan Lai an American Asian rather than an Asian American, in "The Diaspora in Postmodern Taiwan and Hong Kong Film: Framing Stan Lai's *The Peach Blossom Land* with Allen Fong's *Ah Ying*," in *Transnational Chinese Cinemas: Identity, Nationhood, Gender*, ed. Sheldon Hsiao-peng Lu (Honolulu: University of Hawai'i Press, 1997), 169.

26. Stan Lai, "Specifying the Universal," *TDR: The Drama Review* 38, no. 2 (1994): 33.

27. *Xiangsheng* (crosstalk) is a form of traditional Chinese standup comedy generally featuring either a monologue or two people engaged in rapid, bantering dialogue.

28. Lai, "Specifying the Universal," 33, 37.

29. Quoted in Tao Qingmei and Hou Shuyi, *Chana zhong: Lai Shengchuan de juchang yishu [Flash of a Moment: Stan Lai's Theater Art]* (Taipei: Shibao wenhua, 2003), 97.

30. Ma Sen, *Zhongguo xiandai xiju de liangdu xi chao [The Two Western Tides of Modern Chinese Drama]* (Tainan: Wenhua shenghuo xinzhi chubanshe, 1991), revised as *Xi chao xia de Zhongguo xiandai xiju [Modern Chinese Drama Under the Western Tides]* (Taipei: Shulin, 1994).

31. Another example is the protagonist's decision in *A Man from Wuling (Wuling ren*, 1972) to stay in the mundane world to defend humanity rather than escape to a readily accessible utopia.

32. *Snow in August*, a musical theater piece, was commissioned by the National Guoguang Jingju Company in Taiwan in 1997. Its hybridity both in form and in content posed an enormous difficulty for stage representation. Therefore, the play was not staged until December 19, 2002. Its world premiere in Taipei was directed by Gao himself, with a cast of *jingju* performers and acrobats who employed movements and singing methods that combined *jingju*, modern dance, and other performing idioms, featuring the ninety-musician National Symphony Orchestra (NSO) of Taiwan, four percussionists, a fifty-member chorus, and an all-star cast including Wu Hsing-kuo (Huineng), Ye Furun (Hongren), Tsao Fu-yung (Shenxiu), Huang Fa-kuo (Huiming), and Tang Wen-hua (Yinzong). The music was composed by Xu Shuya, a Chinese composer based in France, and directed by Marc Trautmann. The piece was choreographed by Lin Hsiu-wei, with stage design by Nie Guangyan, costume design by Yip Kam Tim, and lighting design by Philippe Grosperrin. The production, with the same cast and stage design but French musicians (L'Opéra de Marseille, Orchestre et Chœurs de l'Opéra de Marseille), was staged in France in January 2005. The title was *La Neige en août*, and the program note indicated that it was an *épopée*, which is an epic poem or cycle.

33. Lai also completed the Chinese translation and voice-over for a video based on Matthieu Ricard's memoirs.

34. Stan Lai, "Statement About *The Thirty-seven-fold Practice of a Bodhisattva*," stage bill, Hong Kong Experimental Shakespeare Festival, March 9, 2000, 3–4.

35. Ibid., 4.

36. Lai writes, "Political events always affect the way we work as well as with what we work" ("Specifying the Universal," 37).

37. Ibid.

38. Prior to its performance during the annual Globe to Globe Festival at the reconstructed Shakespeare's Globe in London (July 6–17, 1999), the production was staged in Italy, the Netherlands, France, and Spain in 1989; in Singapore and Edinburgh in 1990; in Portugal in 1993 and 1994; and in Germany in 1994 and 1996.

39. Susan Bennett's comments in a different context are in *Performing Nostalgia: Shifting Shakespeare and the Contemporary Past* (London: Routledge, 1996), 51.

40. A cross-check with major Chinese editions demonstrates that Lai did not use Liang Shiqiu's, Fang Ping's, Zhu Shenghao's, Bian Zhilin's, or Yang Shipeng's (Daniel Yang) translations of *King Lear.*

41. Jan Kott, *Shakespeare Our Contemporary*, trans. Boleslaw Taborski (London: Routledge, 1967).

42. James Howe, *A Buddhist's Shakespeare: Affirming Self-Deconstructions* (Rutherford, N.J.: Fairleigh Dickinson University Press, 1994), 182–85.

43. Lai, "Statement," 4–5.

44. Peggy Phelan, "Reconstructing Love: *King Lear* and Theatre Architecture," in *A Companion to Shakespeare and Performance*, ed. Barbara Hodgdon and W. B. Worthen (Oxford: Blackwell, 2005), 22; Lyell Asher, "Lateness in *King Lear*," *Yale Journal of Criticism* 13, no. 2 (2000): 209–28.

45. Stan Lai, *Lear and the Thirty-seven-fold Practice of a Bodhisattva* [*Pusa zhi sanshiqi zhong xiuxing zhi Li'er wang*], play script. I thank Stan Lai for making the script available to me.

46. Stanley Cavell, "The Avoidance of Love: A Reading of *King Lear*," in *Must We Mean What We Say: A Book of Essays* (New York: Scribner, 1969), 290.

47. Lai, *Lear and the Thirty-seven-fold Practice*, 17.

48. Ibid., 17–18.

49. Lai, "Statement," 5.

50. Ibid., 4.

51. Richard Halpern, *The Poetics of Primitive Accumulation: English Renaissance Culture and the Genealogy of Capital* (Ithaca, N.Y.: Cornell University Press, 1991), 215; Kaara L. Peterson, "*Historica Passio*: Early Modern Medicine, *King Lear*, and Editorial Practice," *Shakespeare Quarterly* 57, no. 1 (2006): 1–22; Richard Flatter, "Sigmund Freud on Shakespeare," *Shakespeare Quarterly* 2 no. 4 (1951): 368–69; Coppélia Kahn, "The Absent Mother in *King Lear*," in *Rewriting the Renaissance: The Discourse of Sexual Difference in Early Modern Europe*, ed. Margaret W. Ferguson, Maureen Quilligan, and Nancy J. Vickers (Chicago: University of Chicago Press, 1985), 35; Jane Adelman, *Suffocating Mothers: Fantasies of Maternal Origin in Shakespeare's Plays, "Hamlet" to "The Tempest"* (New York: Routledge, 1992), 128. See also Sholom J. Kahn, "Enter Lear Mad," *Shakespeare Quarterly* 8, no. 3 (1957): 311–29.

52. Lai, "Statement," 3.

53. Arthur Holmberg, "The Liberation of Lear," *American Theatre*, July–August, 1988), 12, quoted in Bennett, *Performing Nostalgia*, 39.

54. W. E. B. Du Bois, *The Souls of Black Folk*, ed. David W. Blight and Robert Gooding-Williams (Boston: Bodford Books, 1997), 12.

55. Nancy Guy, *Peking Opera and Politics in Taiwan* (Urbana: University of Illinois Press, 2005), 2–4.

56. Wu Hsing-kuo, "Director's Note," in *Lincoln Center Festival, July 10–July 29, 2007* (New York: Playbill, 2007), 19.

57. In terms of actor training in the United States, solo performance is used as one of the pedagogical tools to help actors understand the relationship between the performing self and the characters. The National Theatre Conservatory of the Denver Center for the Performing Arts, for example, requires second-year students to complete a solo Shakespeare project that involves the intensive study of a character.

58. *King Lear*, stage bill, the Contemporary Legend Theatre, July 2007.

59. The role types in *Lear Is Here* include a wide sampling of the traditional character types found in *jingju*: *laosheng* (middle-aged male character), *wusheng* (combatant male role), *huadan* (vivacious and animated female role), *qingyi* (singing female role), *chousheng* (male clown), *guimendan* (noble or aristocratic young female role), *xiaosheng* (young male), *jing* (vigorous male role), and *mo* (supporting male role). Wu performs Lear in the *laosheng* role type in act 1. The performing style of act 3 aligns itself with postmodern speech drama; the only character is Wu himself (the performer as a character), who circles the stage without any Beijing-opera facial pattern or movement.

60. Wu, "Director's Note," 19.

61. Wu Hsing-kuo, "Wo yan beiju renwu" [I Perform Tragic Characters], *Shijie ribao* [*World Journal*], November 1, 2006, J8.

62. Wu, *Li'er zai ci* [*Lear Is Here*], program notes (Taipei version), unpaged (my translation).

63. Wu, "Director's Note," 19.

64. Yong Li Lan, "Shakespeare and the Fiction of the Intercultural," in *Companion to Shakespeare and Performance*, ed. Hodgdon and Worthen, 547.

65. Bristol, *Big-time Shakespeare*, 36.

66. Wu, *Lear Is Here*, act 1.

67. Chen Shih-Shih, "Wu Hsing-kuo Brings *King Lear* to Chinese Opera in One-man Show," *Taiwan News*, July 6, 2001; Chou Mei-hui, "Faguo Yangguang jutuan chuangban ren fang Tai" [Ariane Mnouchkine, Founder of Le Théâtre du Soleil, Visits Taiwan to Attend Wu Hsing-kuo's *Lear Is Here*], *Lianhe bao* [*United Daily News*], August 31, 2001, 14. In addition to her positive responses to the Paris and Taipei productions (covered by local media), Ariane Mnouchkine has been quoted praising *Lear Is Here*, emphasizing the actor's search for the character King Lear: "What a great performer seeking King Lear on the stage!" (Contemporary Theatre Archive, http://www.cl-theatre.com.tw/main.htm [accessed in May 2006]). Her theater philosophy, which fuses styles and contents from disparate cultures, led her to endorse the Contemporary Legend Theatre's intercultural politics in their engagements with Shakespeare, Greek tragedy, and other Western dramas.

68. Eugenio Barba wrote, "[Wu] shook the tradition of *jingju*; he also shook the understanding of Shakespeare" (quoted in *King Lear*, stage bill, 3–4); Mo Yan considered Wu's *Lear* to be "a profound work" that "leaves the audience immense

space of meditation" (13–14). For excerpts of other reviews, including one by Louis Helmer (director of the World Music Theatre Festival, Amsterdam), see *King Lear,* stage bill.

69. Donaldson, "Disseminating Shakespeare," 219.

70. Bennett sees the film as an instance of "avant-garde filmmaking conducted in the face (and against the grain) of commercial profit-drive" (*Performing Nostalgia*, 39). See also Susan Bennett, "Godard and Lear: Trashing the Can(n)on," *Theatre Survey* 39, no. 1 (1998): 11.

Epilogue

1. Compare William Childers, *Transnational Cervantes* (Toronto: University of Toronto Press, 2006), 242. He suggests that an intercultural reading of canonical literature (such as an Americanized reading of *Los trabajos de Persiles y Sigismunda*) can serve readers in both the culture that is closer to and the culture that is further from the contexts of such literature.

2. Ian Bartholomew was commenting on the disparity between the English and Chinese receptions of the production. The production in London was ill received, but the performances in China (with Chinese supertitles) attracted rave reviews. During a Shanghai television interview, the director and actors emphasized the new meanings generated by the new cultural location of the production. Bartholomew stated: "In England, the audience tends to laugh at Shylock's humiliation. Here [in China] they seem stunned into silence" (quoted in Alfred Hickling, "Sit Down and Shut Up," *Guardian,* June 12, 2002, quoted in Maria Jones, *Shakespeare's Culture in Modern Performance* [New York: Palgrave, 2003], 100).

3. The spectator, as Ella Shohat writes of the visual pleasure of the Other in cinema, "is subliminally invited on an ethnographic tour of a celluloid preserved culture" ("Gender and Culture of Empire: Toward a Feminist Ethnography of the Cineam," in *Visions of the East: Orientalism in Film,* ed. Matthew Bernstein and Gaylyn Studlar [New Brusnwick, N.J.: Rutgers University Press, 1997], 32).

4. Rey Chow, "Digging an Old Well: The Labor of Social Fantasy in a Contemporary Chinese Film," in *Reinventing Film Studies,* ed. Christine Gledhill and Linda Williams (London: Arnold, 2000), 403; Meaghan Morris, "Introduction: Hong Kong Connections," in *Hong Kong Connections: Transnational Imagination in Action Cinema,* ed. Meaghan Morris, Siu Leung Li, and Stephen Chan Ching-kiu (Durham, N.C.: Duke University Press, 2005), 1–3.

5. In general, there are two categories of martial-arts films: the sword-fighting knight-errant (*wuxia*) genre, informed by dynastic fantasy literature, and the kungfu genre in contemporary settings, which was shaped by Bruce Lee and Jackie Chan.

6. The music was composed by Tan Dun, who is known for his Grammy- and Oscar-winning scores for *Crouching Tiger, Hidden Dragon* and *Hero*.

7. Kenneth S. Rothwell, *A History of Shakespeare on Screen: A Century of Film and Television,* 2nd ed. (Cambridge: Cambridge University Press, 2004), 160.

8. With a US$20 million budget, *The Banquet* (*Yeyan*) is, in the standard of Chinese cinema, a big-budget film by a director who was not widely known internationally.

9. Mo Hong'e, "Venice Critics Want a More Chinese 'Banquet,'" *Xinhua News* September 5, 2006, http://news.xinhuanet.com/english/2006–09/05/content _5050440.htm (accessed June 10, 2007).

10. Kozo writes, "*The Banquet* is a member of that suddenly popular Asian Cinema genre: the indulgent, overproduced costume epic aimed at a completely non-Chinese audience many thousands of miles away" (http://www.lovehkfilm .com/panasia/banquet.htm [accessed June 10, 2007]).

11. Mo, "Venice Critics."

12. Richard Burt, "*Shakespeare in Love* and the End of the Shakespearean: Academic and Mass Culture Constructions of Literary Authorship," in *Shakespeare, Film, Fin de Siècle*, ed. Mark Thornton Burnet and Ramona Wray (London: Macmillan, 2000), 203–31.

13. Widely regarded in Japan as a director with too much Western influence, Kurosawa Akira is known outside Japan as an iconic Japanese filmmaker. But Asian artists are not the only ones to champion the aesthetic possibilities of intercultural visuality. Ariane Mnouchkine's *Richard II* (Paris, 1981), Trevor Nunn's *Henry IV* (London, 1982), and Adrian Noble's *Henry V* (Stratford, 1984) are prime examples of productions that thrive on a visual feast. While, as Jan Kott observes, a distrust of politics in the theater has driven directors to search for "new visual expression[s]," the market law has played a larger role in the pursuit of visualization as a global vernacular in *The Banquet* (quoted in Charles Marowitz, "Kott, Our Contemporary," *American Theatre*, October 1988, 100).

14. Man Yanwen, "Huaju *Licha sanshi* shouyan yinxiang" [Impressions of (Lin Zhaohua's) *Huaju Richard III*], *Beijing wanbao* [*Beijing Evening News*], February 17, 2001; Yan Huandong, "Qing bie zeguai guanzhong" [Do Not Blame the Audience], *Zhongguo wenhua bao* [*China Culture Daily*], March 26, 2001.

15. Based on the Chinese translation of *Richard III* by Liang Shiqiu; major funding secured by Ueda Misako in Japan.

16. Lin Zhaohua is best known as the director who discovered Gao Xingjian, the French-Chinese Nobel literature laureate (2000), in the 1980s. Together with Gao, Lin emerged as a key figure in avant-garde theater. He began his career in 1951 with the preeminent, state-funded, Beijing People's Arts Theatre (BPAT) as a follower of Stanislavsky's psychological realism, as dictated by the Soviet–Chinese Communist ideology, but became increasingly rebellious against orthodoxy after he formed his own company, the Lin Zhaohua Workshop, in 1989, when the Chinese economic reform released theater artists from the confining infrastructure endorsed and sponsored by the state. He has moved from the BPAT's homogenizing routine of mimetic realism to interpolations that call for superimposed styles and rewritings of seminal texts at the heart of Chinese and Western cultures, including Lu Xun and Shakespeare.

17. Other examples abound: Billy Morrissette's *Scotland PA* (2001) lucidly translates Macbeth's Scotland to a fast-food joint in mid-twentieth-century

Pennsylvania by lowering the register of Shakespeare's tragedy; Baz Luhrmann's *William Shakespeare's Romeo + Juliet* (1996) relies on the lyrical transformation of the inexplicable feud in Verona to perfectly explicable twentieth-century gang culture and corporate war in Verona Beach; and Simon McBurney's *Measure for Measure* (Complicite, National Theatre, London, May 2004; revived in 2006) featured prisoners in orange jumpsuits reminiscent of the U.S. military detention camp in Guantánamo Bay, unabashedly presentist in the blunt commentary on the Iraq War. Taking a step beyond "Shakespeare in modern dress," the production made extensive use of surveillance devices to signal the contemporary connections to the world of *Measure for Measure*. In dim light, the face of Angelo (Paul Rhys) could well be mistaken for that of Peter Mandelson, a trusted adviser to Tony Blair. The word "war" in Angelo's press conferences ushered in images of George W. Bush on screen. For an in-depth analysis of the production, see P. A. Skantze, "Uneasy Coalitions: Culpability, Orange Jumpsuits and *Measure for Measure*," *Shakespeare* 3, no. 1 (2007): 63–71.

18. Al Pacino focused on the tension between the American actor and the British tradition (and between the acting profession and academia) and experimentation with media and facetiousness (farcical visits to Shakespeare's birthplace). Contemporary China, a country in the midst of rapid transformation, shares a similarly uneasy relationship with the British tradition represented by *Richard III*. Critics have observed the ways in which *Looking for Richard* plays off the tensions between British and American performance traditions by "compress[ing] long speeches into shorter ensembles of speech-actions, and unmoors entire passages in order to restructure our experience of the play" (Thomas Cartelli and Katherine Rowe, *New Wave Shakespeare on Screen* [Cambridge: Polity, 2007], 98).

19. Erwin Leiser, *Leopold Lindtberg: Schriften—Bilder—Dokumente* (Zurich: Musik and Theater, 1985), 14, translated in Manfred Draudt, "Shakespeare's English Histories at the Vienna Burgtheater," in *Shakespeare's History Plays: Performance, Translation and Adaptation in Britain and Abroad*, ed. Ton Hoenselaars (Cambridge: Cambridge University Press, 2004), 198.

20. Draudt, "Shakespeare's English Histories," 198.

21. Ma Shuliang, "Wo wei Licha kuang" [Gone Crazy for Richard], *Beijing qingnian bao* [*Beijing Youth Daily*], June 20, 2001.

22. Peter Donaldson, "Game Space/Tragic Space: Julie Taymor's *Titus*," in *A Companion to Shakespeare and Performance*, ed. Barbara Hodgdon and W. B. Worthen (Oxford: Blackwell, 2005), 457–77; Carol Chillington Rutter, *Shakespeare and Child's Play: Performing Lost Boys on Stage and Screen* (London: Routledge, 2007), 34–95.

23. Cartelli and Rowe, *New Wave Shakespeare*, 42.

24. Paul Prescott, *Richard III: A Guide to the Text and Its Theatrical Life* (New York: Palgrave Macmillan, 2006), 101–2.

25. In film studies, as well as in performance studies, the notion of cultural discount has been proposed to account for the dominance of particular performance idioms. It has been argued that a work with "degree zero" cultural specificity will travel better than one that requires extensive decoding. Colin Hoskins

and Rolf Mirus, "Reasons for the U.S. Domination of the International Trade in Television Programmes," *Media, Culture, and Society* 10, no. 4 (1988): 499–516. Scott Robert Olson has further connected the global circulation of specific performances to transparency, a textual apparatus that "allows audiences to project indigenous values, beliefs, rites, and rituals into imported media or the use of those devices." Transparency also refers to narrative structures that "easily blend into other cultures" (*Hollywood Planet: Global Media and the Competitive Advantage of Narrative Transparency* [Mahwah, N.J.: Erlbaum, 1999], 5). The assumption behind the cultural logic of nil particularity is clearly problematic. Charles R. Acland has observed that "signs of cultural specificity may be precisely the qualities prized by international audiences" (*Screen Traffic: Movies, Multiplexes, and Global Culture* [Durham, N.C.: Duke University Press, 2003], 34).

26. Susan Bennett, "Shakespeare on Vacation," in *Companion to Shakespeare and Performance,* ed. Hodgdon and Worthen, 507.

27. The cases of Shakespeare in Japan and Korea in the 1990s share some of the same anxieties. Commenting on the modernist localized Shakespeare in Japan, John Gillies observes that a Japanese Shakespeare emerged as a sign of "the endurance and reassertiveness of the local in the face of global value," contrary to the common expectation that the local will be "erased or compromised" when Shakespeare's plays are performed "beyond the Western pale" ("Afterword: Shakespeare Removed: Some Reflections on the Localization of Shakespeare in Japan," in *Performing Shakespeare in Japan,* ed. Minami Ryuta, Ian Carruthers, and John Gillies [Cambridge: Cambridge University Press, 2001], 236–37). In a study of Lee Yountaek's production of Hamlet that premiered in Seoul in 1996, Yeeyon Im is more pessimistic, writing that Korean performances of Shakespeare reflect "the impasse of contemporary Korean society, whose postcolonial reality is obscured by an optimistic idea of interculturalism" ("The Location of Shakespeare in Korea: Lee Yountaek's *Hamlet* and the Mirage of Interculturality," *Theatre Journal* 60, no. 2 [2008]: 257–76).

28. As Martin Heidegger posits, "a boundary is not that at which something stops but . . . that from which something begins its presencing" (quoted in Homi Bhabha, *The Location of Culture* [London: Routledge, 1994], 1).

Select Bibliography

Novels, Films, Stage Productions, Television Documentaries

Bank, Jonathan, dir. *Othello*. National Asian-American Theatre Company. Connelly Theatre, New York, February 10–March 4, 2000. Joshua Spafford (Othello), Joel de la Fuente (Iago), Andy Pang (Cassio), Tina Horii (Desdemona), Jennifer Kato (Bianca).

Bu Wancang 卜萬蒼, dir. *Yi jian mei* 一剪梅 [*A Spray of Plum Blossom*]. Black-and-white silent film. Lianhua Studio, 1931. Ruan Lingyu 阮玲玉 (Hu Zhuli), Lin Chuchu (Shi Luohua).

Cao Ping 曹平, dir. *Makebai furen* 馬克白夫人 [*Lady Macbeth*]. Perf. Tian Mansha 田蔓莎. Sichuan sheng chuanju xuexiao 四川省川劇學校 [Sichuan Provincial Chuanju Conservatory]. Bremen, 2001.

Chan, Anthony Yau 陳友, dir. *Yiqi liangfu* 一妻兩夫 [*One Husband Too Many*]. Cantonese. Golden Harvest Entertainment, Hong Kong, 1988.

Chang, Tisa, dir. *A Midsummer Night's Dream*. Mandarin–English production. Pan Asian Repertory Theatre. New York, April 1983. Lu Yu (Theseus and Oberon), Jodi Long (Hippolyta and Titania), Elizabeth Sung (Hermia), Koji Okamura (Lysander).

Chung Hsing-lin (Chuan-hsing) 鍾幸玲 / 鍾傳幸, dir. *The Taming of the Shrew: Adapted from Shakespeare's Play for Jingju Performance*. Denison University, Granville, Ohio, April 11–12, 15–19, 2003.

Feng Xiaogang 馮小剛, dir. *Yeyan* 夜宴 [*The Banquet*; released in North America as *The Legend of Black Scorpion*]. Mandarin. Huayi Brothers and Media Asia, China and Hong Kong, 2006. Zhang Ziyi (Empress Wan; Gertrude), Ge You (Emperor Li; Claudius), Daniel Wu (Prince Wu Luan; Hamlet), Zhou Xun (Qing Nü; Ophelia), Ma Jingwu (General Yin; Polonius), Huang Xiaoming (Yin Zhun; Laertes).

He Nian 何念, dir. *Luo Mi'ou yu Zhu Yingtai* 羅密歐與祝英台 [*Romeo and Zhu Yingtai*]. Shanghai huaju yishu zhongxin 上海話劇藝術中心 [Shanghai Dramatic Arts Center]. Shanghai, May 8–25, 2008. Qian Fang (Zhu Wanying; Juliet), Guo Jingfei (Luo Guo; Romeo).

Hu, Sherwood 胡雪華, dir. *Ximalaya wangzi* 喜馬拉雅王子 [*The Prince of the Himalayas*]. Tibetan. Hus Entertainment and Shanghai Film Studios, China, 2006. Purba Rgyal (Prince Lhamoklodan; Hamlet). Stage version premiered at the Shanghai Grand Theatre in May 2007 and the Poly Theatre in Beijing in June 2007.

Huang Zuolin 黃佐臨, dir. *Luanshi yingxiong* 亂世英雄 [*The Hero of a Tumultuous Time*]. Kugan xiju xiuyang xueguan 苦幹戲劇修養學館 [Bitter Toilers Drama School]. Shanghai, April 1945. Shi Hui (Wang Deming), Dan Ni (Dugu Xiu).

Huang Zuolin, and Li Jiayao 李家耀, dir. *Xieshou ji* 血手記 [*The Story of Bloody Hands*]. Shanghai kunju yuan 上海崑劇院 [Shanghai Kunju Theatre]. Edinburgh and London, 1986.

Huo Jianqi 霍建起, dir. *Qingren jie* 情人結 [*A Time to Love*]. Cantonese. Beijing Starlight International Media, 2005.

Ingram, Loveday, dir. *The Merchant of Venice*. Royal Shakespeare Company. The Pit, London, 2001; Poly Plaza Theatre, Beijing, May 23–26, 2002; Shanghai Dramatic Arts Centre, May 30–June 2, 2002. Ian Bartholomew (Shylock), Hermione Gulliford (Portia), Ian Gelder (Antonio), Chris Jarman (Prince of Morocco), Darren Tunstall (Launcelot).

Jiao Juyin 焦菊隱, dir. *Hamuleite* 哈姆雷特 [*Hamlet*]. Mandarin. Guoli xiju zhuanke xuexiao 國立戲劇專科學校 [National Drama School]. Jiang'an, June 2–7, 1942. Wen Xiying (Hamlet), Chen Jingxian (Claudius), Peng Houjun (Gertrude), Luo Shui (Ophelia).

Lai, Stan 賴聲川, dir. *Pusa zhi sanshiqi zhong xiuxing zhi Li'er wang* 菩薩之三十七種修行之李爾王 [*Lear and the Thirty-seven-fold Practice of a Bodhisattva*]. Biaoyan gongzuo fang 表演工作坊 [Performance Workshop]. Hong Kong, March, 2000. Li Jianchang, Liu Liangzuo, Na Weixun, Jigme Khyentse Rinpoche (voice-over).

Lao She 老舍. "Xin Hanmuliede" 新韓穆烈德 [New Hamlet]. *Hazao ji* 蛤藻集 [*Clams and Seaweed*]. Shanghai: Kaiming shudian, 1936.

Liang Qichao 梁啓超. *Xin Luoma* 新羅馬 [*New Rome*]. In *Wan Qing wenxue congchao: Xiaoshuo xiqu yanjiu juan* 晚清文學叢鈔小說戲曲研究卷 [*A Compendium of Late Qing Literature: Research on Fiction and Drama*], edited by A Ying, 518–48. Beijing: Zhonghua shuju, 1960.

Lin Shu 林紓. *Hengli diwu ji* 亨利第五紀 [*Henry V*]. *Xiaoshuo shijie* 小說世界 [*Story World*] 12, nos. 9–10 (November 26–December 4, 1925).

Lin Shu 林紓 and Chen Jialin 陳家麟. *Hengli diliu yishi* 亨利第六遺事 [*Henry VI*]. Shanghai: Shangwu yinshuguan, 1916.

——. *Hengli disi ji* 亨利第四紀 [*Henry IV*]. *Xiaoshuo yuebao* 小說月報 [*Short Story Magazine*] 7, nos. 2–4 (February–April 1916).

——. *Kaiche yishi* 凱徹遺事 [*Julius Caesar*]. *Xiaoshuo yuebao* 小說月報 [*Short Story Magazine*] 7, nos. 5–7 (May–July 1916).

——. *Leichade ji* 雷差得紀 [*Richard II*]. *Xiaoshuo yuebao* 小說月報 [*Short Story Magazine*] 7, no. 1 (January 1916).

Lin Shu 林紓 and Wei Yi 魏易. *Yingguo shiren yinbian yanyu* 英國詩人吟邊燕語 [*An English Poet Reciting from Afar*]. Shanghai: Shangwu yinshuguan, 1904.

Lin Zhaohua 林兆華, dir. *Licha sanshi* 里查三世 [*Richard III*]. Produced by Ueda Misako. Zhongyang shiyan huaju tuan 中央實驗話劇團 [Central Experimental Huaju Theater] and Sunwen daxue Lin Zhaohua gongzuo shi 孫文大學林兆華工作室 [Lin Zhaohua Workshop of the Sun Wen University]. Beijing, February 16–March 2, 2001; Berlin, September 22–24, 2001.

Lipkovskaya, Yevgeniya K., dir. *Wushi shengfei* 無事生非 [*Looking for Trouble (Much Ado About Nothing)*]. Shanghai xiju xueyuan 上海戲劇學院 [Shanghai Theatre Academy]. Shanghai and Beijing, 1957. Dir. Hu Dao and Wu Li, Shanghai Theatre Academy's Experimental Huaju Theatre Company. Shanghai, Dalian, and Shenyang, 1961. Dir. Hu Dao, Shanghai Youth Huaju Theatre Company. Shanghai, 1979.

Ong, Keng Sen 王景生, dir. *LEAR*. Script by Rio Kishida. TheatreWorks, Singapore, and Japan Foundation Asia Center. Tokyo, Osaka, and Fukuoka, 1997. Naohiko Umewaka (Old Man and Mother), Jiang Qihu (Older Daughter), Peeramon Chomdhavat (Younger Daughter).

Qiu Qixiang 裘芭香 and Li Songfu 李松父, dir. *Nü lüshi (Rouquan)* 女律師, 肉券 [*The Woman Lawyer*]. Screenplay by Shao Cunren 邵邨人. Black-and-white silent film. Tianyi Film, 1927. Hu Die (Bao Qixia; Portia), Jin Yuru (Bai Shanyi; Bassanio), Xiao Tiandai (Xue Luke; Shylock).

Tian Han 田漢. "Hamengleite" 哈孟雷特 [*Hamlet*]. *Shaonian Zhongguo* 少年中國 [*Youth China*] 2, no. 12 (1921). In *Tian Han quanji* 田漢全集 [*The Complete Works of Tian Han*]. Vol. 19. Shijiazhuang: Huashan wenyi chubanshe, 2000.

Tse, David Ka-shing 謝家聲, dir. *King Lear*. Mandarin–English production. Yellow Earth Theatre, London, and Shanghai Dramatic Arts Center. The Cube at the Royal Shakespeare Theatre, Stratford-upon-Avon, October–November 2006; London, Nottingham, Guildford, Wolverhampton, Liverpool, Shanghai, and Chengdu.

Tong Sanqiang 童三強 and Lu Jing 魯婧, dir. *Ling juli jiechu Weinisi shangren* 零距離接觸威尼斯商人 [*RSC Visits China*]. Shanghai Oriental Television, 2002.

Wang Fucheng 王輔成. *Yibang rou* 一磅肉 [*A Pound of Flesh*]. In *Qinqiang: Shaanxi chuantong jumu huibian* 秦腔—陝西傳統劇目匯編 [*Qinqiang Opera: A Compendium of Traditional Repertoire in Shaanxi*], 23:9023–108. Xi'an: Shaanxi Provincial Bureau of Culture, 1959.

Wang Rongyu 王榮裕, dir. *Luo Mi'ou yu Zhu Liye* 羅密歐與朱麗葉 [*Romeo and Juliet*]. Taiwanese–Mandarin production. Jinzhi yanshe 金枝演社 [Golden Bough Theatre]. Taipei, May 2003.

Wu Hsing-kuo 吳興國, dir. and perf. *Li'er zaici* 李爾在此 [*Lear Is Here*]. Dangdai chuanqi juchang 當代傳奇劇場 [The Contemporary Legend Theatre]. Paris and New York, 2000; Taipei, 2001; Tokyo, Macao, and Seoul, 2002–2003; London, Singapore, and Hong Kong, 2003; Taipei, Prague, London, and Holstebro (Denmark), 2004; Berlin, March 24–25, 2006; Shanghai, May 2006; San Jose, California, May 26–27, 2007; New York, July 12, 2007; Tainan, Taiwan, July 2008.

Yu Luosheng 俞洛生, dir. *Wushi shengfei* 無事生非 [*Looking for Trouble* (*Much Ado About Nothing*)]. Shanghai renmin yishu juyuan 上海人民藝術劇院 [Shanghai People's Art Theater]. Shanghai, November 16–19, 1995. Wang Guojing (Don Pedro), Li Guoliang (Don John), Yu Butao (Claudio), An Hanjin (Benedick), Geng Ge (Hero), Liu Wanling (Beatrice).

Zhang Min 章泯, dir. *Luo Mi'ou yu Zhu Liye* 羅密歐與朱麗葉 [*Romeo and Juliet*]. Shanghai yeyu shiyan jutuan 上海業餘實驗劇團 [Shanghai Amateur Experimental Theatre Company]. Carlton Theatre, Shanghai, 1937.

Zheng Bixian 鄭碧賢, dir. *Aosailuo* 奧賽羅 [*Othello*]. Experimental Jingju Company of Beijing (renamed Beijing Jingju Company). Beijing, May 1983; Shanghai and Tianjin, 1987. Ma Yong'an 馬永安 (Othello), Li Yalang (Desdemona).

Sources in European Languages

Acland, Charles R. *Screen Traffic: Movies, Multiplexes, and Global Culture*. Durham, N.C.: Duke University Press, 2003.

Adelman, Jane. *Suffocating Mothers: Fantasies of Maternal Origin in Shakespeare's Plays, "Hamlet" to" The Tempest."* New York: Routledge, 1992.

Adelman, Kenneth, and Normand Augustine. *Shakespeare in Charge: The Bard's Guide to Leading and Succeeding on the Business Stage*. New York: Hyperion-Talk-Miramax, 1999.

Adorno, Theodore W., and Max Horkheimer. "The Culture Industry: Enlightenment as Mass Deception." In *Dialectics of Enlightenment: Philosophical Fragments*, 94–136. Edited by Gunzelin Schmid Noerr. Translated by Edmund Jephcott. Stanford, Calif.: Stanford University Press, 2002.

Aebischer, Pascale, Edward J. Esche, and Nigel Wheale, eds. *Remaking Shakespeare: Performance Across Media, Genres, and Cultures*. New York: Palgrave Macmillan, 2003.

Al-Bassam, Sulayman. *The Al-Hamlet Summit: A Political Arabsque*. Hatfield: University of Hertfordshire Press, 2006.

Alcoff, Linda Martín, and Eduardo Mendieta, eds. *Identities: Race, Class, Gender, and Nationality*. Oxford: Blackwell, 2003.

Alitto, Guy S. *The Last Confucian: Liang Shuming and the Chinese Dilemma of Modernity*. Berkeley: University of California Press, 1979.

Anderegg, Michael. *Cinematic Shakespeare*. Lanham: Rowman & Littlefield, 2004.

Anderson, Benedict. *Imagined Communities: Reflections on the Origin and Spread of Nationalism*. Rev. ed. London: Verso, 1991.

Anderson, Marston. *The Limits of Realism: Chinese Fiction in the Revolutionary Period*. Berkeley: University of California Press, 1990.

Ang, Ien. *On Not Speaking Chinese: Living Between Asia and the West*. London: Routledge, 2001.

Anikst, Alexander. "Shakespeare: A Writer of the People." In *Shakespeare in the Soviet Union: A Collection of Articles*, translated by Avril Pyman, compiled by Roman Samarin and Alexander Nikolyukin, 113–39. Moscow: Progress Publishers, 1966.

Appadurai, Arjun. *Modernity at Large: Cultural Dimensions of Globalization*. New Delhi: Oxford University Press, 1997.

Arnold, Matthew. *Culture and Anarchy: An Essay in Political and Social Criticism*. London: Smith, Elder, 1869.

Ball, Robert Hamilton. *Shakespeare on Silent Film: Strange Eventful History*. New York: Theatre Arts Books, 1968.

Barker, Harley Granville. *Prefaces to Shakespeare*. 5 vols. London: Sidgwick and Jackson, 1927–1947.

Barthes, Roland. *Image—Music—Text*. Translated by Stephen Heath. New York: Hill and Wang, 1977.

Bassnett, Susan, and André Lefevere. *Constructing Cultures: Essays on Literary Translation*. Clevedon, Eng.: Multilingual Matters, 1998.

Baudrillard, Jean. *Le Système des objets*. Paris: Gallimard, 1968.

Benjamin, Walter. "The Task of the Translator." In *Illuminations*, 70–82. Edited by Hannah Arendt. Translated by Harry Zohn. London: Fontana, 1992.

——. "The Work of Art in the Age of Mechanical Reproduction." In *Illuminations*, 211–44. Edited by Hannah Arendt. Translated by Harry Zohn. London: Pimlico, 1999.

Bennett, Susan. "Shakespeare on Vacation." In *A Companion to Shakespeare and Performance*, edited by Barbara Hodgdon and W. B. Worthen, 494–508. Oxford: Blackwell, 2005.

Berry, Edward. "Review of *Shakespeare in China*, by Murray Levith." *Modern Philology* 105, no. 2 (2007): 409–10.

Betruccioli, Giuliano. *La letteratura cinese*. Milan: Sansoni, 1968.

Bhabha, Homi K. *The Location of Culture*. London: Routledge, 1994.

Bharucha, Rustom. *The Politics of Cultural Practice: Thinking Through Theatre in an Age of Globalization*. New Delhi: Oxford University Press, 2001.

Bickelhaupt, Thomas. "Der Shakespeare der SS: Ums Leben spielen: *Kaufmann von Venedig* in Weimar." *Frankfurter Allgemeine*, April 11, 1995.

Billings, Timothy. "Review of *Shashibiya*, by Li Ruru." *Shakespeare Quarterly* 57, no. 4 (2006): 494–96.

Blau, Herbert. *The Audience*. Baltimore: Johns Hopkins University Press, 1990.

Bloom, Harold. *Shakespeare: The Invention of the Human*. New York: Riverhead Books, 1998.

Bogart, Anne. *A Director Prepares*. London: Routledge, 2001.

Bohannan, Laura. "Shakespeare in the Bush." In *Conformity and Conflict*, edited by James P. Spradley and David W. McCurdy, 35–44. Boston: Allyn and Bacon, 1999.

Borges, Jorge Luis. *Everything and Nothing*. Translated by Donald A. Yates, James E. Irby, John M. Fein, and Eliot Weinberger. New York: New Directions, 1999.

Börne, Ludwig. *Gesammelte Schriften*. Leipzig: Hesse, 1908.

Bourdieu, Pierre. *Distinction: A Social Critique of the Judgment of Taste*. Translated by Richard Nice. Cambridge, Mass.: Harvard University Press, 1984.

——. *The Field of Cultural Production: Essays on Art and Literature*. Edited by Randal Johnson. New York: Columbia University Press, 1993.

Brand, Adam. *A Journal of the Embassy from Their Majesties John and Peter Alexievitz, Emperors of Muscovy over Land into China*. London: D. Brown and T. Goodwin, 1698 [Bodleian Library].

Brandon, James R. "Some Shakespeare(s) in Some Asia(s)." *Asian Studies Review* 20, no. 3 (1997): 1–26.

Breitenstein, Rolf. *Shakespeare para managers*. Barcelona: Plaza and Janes, 2000.

Brennecke, Ernest. *Shakespeare in Germany, 1590–1700*. Chicago: University of Chicago Press, 1964.

Bristol, Michael D. *Big-time Shakespeare*. London: Routledge, 1996.

Brockbank, J. Philip. "Shakespeare Renaissance in China." *Shakespeare Quarterly* 39, no. 2 (1988): 195–204.

Brown, Calvin S. "Requirements for Admission in English." *Modern Language Notes* 12, no. 1 (1897): 32.

Brown, John Russell. *New Sites for Shakespeare: Theatre, the Audience and Asia*. London: Routledge, 1999.

Bruckner, D. J. R. "New Clarity from a Colorblind *Othello*." *New York Times*, February 7, 2000.

Bruster, Douglas. *To Be or Not to Be*. London: Continuum, 2007.

Buchanan, Judith. *Shakespeare on Film*. New York: Pearson Longman, 2005.

——. *Shakespeare on Silent Film: An Excellent Dumb Discourse*. Cambridge: Cambridge University Press, 2009.

Buhler, Stephen M. *Shakespeare in the Cinema: Ocular Proof*. Albany: State University of New York Press, 2002.

Bühnenspiegel im fernen Osten. Shanghai: Deutschen Theater-Verein, 1926–1943.

Bulman, James C., ed. *Shakespeare, Theory, and Performance*. London: Routledge, 1996.

Burnett, Mark Thornton. "The Local and the Global." In *Filming Shakespeare in the Global Marketplace*, 47–65. New York: Palgrave Macmillan, 2007.

Burt, Richard. "Shakespeare and Asia in Postdiasporic Cinemas: Spin-offs and Citations of the Plays from Bollywood to Hollywood." In *Shakespeare, the Movie, II: Popularizing the Plays on Film, TV, Video, and DVD*, edited by Richard Burt and Lynda E. Boose, 265–303. London: Routledge, 2003.

Carlson, Marvin. *The Haunted Stage: The Theatre as Memory Machine*. Ann Arbor: University of Michigan Press, 2001.

Carlyle, Thomas. *On Heroes, Hero-Worship, and the Heroic in History*. Berkeley: University of California Press, 1993.

Cartelli, Thomas, and Katherine Rowe. *New Wave Shakespeare on Screen*. Cambridge: Polity, 2007.

Cartmell, Deborah, and Michael Scott, eds. *Talking Shakespeare: Shakespeare into the Millennium.* New York: Palgrave, 2001.

Casanova, Pascale. *The World Republic of Letters.* Translated by M. B. DeBevoise. Cambridge, Mass.: Harvard University Press, 2004.

Cavell, Stanley. *Must We Mean What We Say: A Book of Essays.* New York: Scribner, 1969.

Chang, Tisa. "Sustaining the Project." *TDR: The Drama Review* 38, no. 2 (1994): 64–71.

Charlesworth, Ric. *Shakespeare, the Coach.* Sydney: Pan Macmillan, 2004.

Chatenet, Jean. *Shakespeare sur la scène française depuis 1940.* Paris: Minard, 1962.

Chaudhuri, Sukanta, and Chee Seng Lim, eds. *Shakespeare Without English: The Reception of Shakespeare in Non-Anglophone Countries.* Delhi: Pearson Longman, 2006.

Chen, Xiaomei. *Acting the Right Part: Political Theater and Popular Drama in Contemporary China.* Honolulu: University of Hawai'i Press, 2002.

——. *Occidentalism: A Theory of Counter-Discourse in Post-Mao China.* 2nd ed. Lanham, Md.: Rowman & Littlefield, 2002.

——. "Performing the Nation: Chinese Drama and Theater." In *The Columbia Companion to Modern East Asian Literature,* edited by Joshua S. Mostow, Kirk A. Denton, Bruce Fulton, and Sharalyn Orbaugh, 437–45. New York: Columbia University Press, 2003.

Childers, William. *Transnational Cervantes.* Toronto: University of Toronto Press, 2006.

Ching, Leo T. S. *Becoming "Japanese": Colonial Taiwan and the Politics of Identity Formation.* Berkeley: University of California Press, 2001.

Chow, Rey. *The Age of the World Target: Self-Referentiality in War, Theory, and Comparative Work.* Durham, N.C.: Duke University Press, 2006.

——, ed. *Modern Chinese Literary and Cultural Studies in an Age of Theory: Reimagining a Field.* Durham, N.C.: Duke University Press, 2000.

——. *Woman and Chinese Modernity: The Politics of Reading Between West and East.* Minnesota: University of Minnesota Press, 1991.

Chow, Tse-tsung. *The May Fourth Movement.* Cambridge, Mass.: Harvard University Press, 1960.

Cohn, Ruby. *Modern Shakespeare Offshoots.* Princeton, N.J.: Princeton University Press, 1976.

Coldwell, Joan, ed. *Charles Lamb on Shakespeare.* Gerrards Cross, Eng.: Smythe, 1978.

Conceison, Claire. *Significant Other: Staging the American in China.* Honolulu: University of Hawai'i Press, 2004.

Court, Franklin. *Institutionalizing English Literature: The Culture and Politics of Literary Study, 1750–1900.* Stanford, Calif.: Stanford University Press, 1992.

Crabtree, Loren William. "Christian Colleges and the Chinese Revolution, 1840–1940: A Case Study in the Impact of the West." Ph.D. diss., University of Minnesota, 1969.

Culler, Jonathan. *The Literary in Theory*. Stanford, Calif.: Stanford University Press, 2007.

Davenant, William. "*Macbeth (1674)*." In *Five Restoration Adaptations of Shakespeare*, edited by Christopher Spencer, 33–108. Urbana: University of Illinois Press, 1965.

Davies, Gloria. *Worrying About China: The Language of Chinese Critical Inquiry*. Cambridge, Mass.: Harvard University Press, 2007.

Davis, A. R. "Out of 'Uncle Tom's Cabin,' Tokyo 1907: A Preliminary Look at the Beginnings of the Spoken Drama in China." *Journal of the Oriental Society of Australia* 4, nos. 1–2 (1968–1969): 33–49.

Dawson, Anthony B. "International Shakespeare." In *The Cambridge Companion to Shakespeare on Stage*, edited by Stanley Wells and Sarah Stanton, 174–93. Cambridge: Cambridge University Press, 2002.

De Grazia, Margreta. *"Hamlet" Without Hamlet*. Cambridge: Cambridge University Press, 2007.

Debord, Guy. *The Society of the Spectacle*. Translated by Donald Nicholson-Smith. New York: Zone Books, 1995.

Deelman, Christian. *The Great Shakespeare Jubilee*. New York: Viking Press, 1964.

Deleuze, Gilles. "Un manifeste de moins." In *Superpositions*, 85–131. Edited by Carmelo Bene and Gilles Deleuze. Paris: Éditions de Minuit, 1979.

Denton, Kirk A., ed. *Modern Chinese Literary Thought: Writings on Literature, 1893–1945*. Stanford, Calif.: Stanford University Press, 1996.

Derrida, Jacques. "Différance." In *Margins of Philosophy*, 1–27. Translated by Alan Bass. Chicago: University of Chicago Press, 1982.

——. "Economimesis." *Diacritics* 11, no. 3 (1981): 3–25.

——. *Of Grammatology*. Translated by Gayatri Spivak. Baltimore: Johns Hopkins University Press, 1997.

——. "Roundtable on Translation." In *The Ear of the Other: Otobiography, Transference, Translation*, 91–161. Edited by Christie V. McDonald. Translated by Peggy Kamuf. New York: Schocken Books, 1985.

——. "Des Tours de Babel." In *Difference in Translation*, edited by Joseph F. Graham, 209–48. Ithaca, N.Y.: Cornell University Press, 1985.

Desmet, Christy, and Robert Sawyer, eds. *Shakespeare and Appropriation*. London: Routledge, 1999.

Dessen, Alan C. *Rescripting Shakespeare: The Text, the Director, and Modern Productions*. Cambridge: Cambridge University Press, 2002.

Dickinson, G. Lowes. *Letters from John Chinaman and Other Essays*. London: George Allen and Unwin, 1946.

Dikötter, Frank, ed. *The Construction of Racial Identities in China and Japan: Historical and Contemporary Perspectives*. London: Hurst, 1997.

——. *Exotic Commodities: Modern Objects and Everyday Life in China*. New York: Columbia University Press, 2007.

Dobson, Michael, ed. *Performing Shakespeare's Tragedies Today: The Actor's Perspective*. Cambridge: Cambridge University Press, 2006.

Dolby, William. *A History of Chinese Drama*. London: Elek, 1976.

Dollimore, Jonathan, and Alan Sinfield, eds. *Political Shakespeare: Essays in Cultural Materialism.* Manchester: Manchester University Press, 1985.

Donaldson, Peter. "Disseminating Shakespeare: Paternity and Text in Jean-Luc Godard's *King Lear.*" In *Shakespearean Films / Shakespearean Directors,* 189–90. Boston: Unwin Hyman, 1990.

——. "Game Space/Tragic Space: Julie Taymor's *Titus.*" In *A Companion to Shakespeare and Performance,* edited by Barbara Hodgdon and W. B. Worthen, 457–77. Oxford: Blackwell, 2005.

Draudt, Manfred. "Shakespeare's English Histories at the Vienna Burgtheater." In *Shakespeare's History Plays: Performance, Translation and Adaptation in Britain and Abroad,* edited by Ton Hoenselaars, 196–212. Cambridge: Cambridge University Press, 2004.

Du Bois, W. E. B. *The Souls of Black Folk.* Edited by David W. Blight and Robert Gooding-Williams. Boston: Bodford Books, 1997.

Duara, Prasenjit. *Rescuing History from the Nation: Questioning Narratives of Modern China.* Chicago: University of Chicago Press, 1995.

Eagleton, Terry. "The Rise of English Studies." In *Literary Theory: An Introduction,* 15–46. Minneapolis: University of Minnesota Press, 1996.

Egan, Gabriel. *Shakespeare and Marx.* Oxford: Oxford University Press, 2004.

Elsom, John. *Is Shakespeare Still Our Contemporary?* London: Routledge, 1989.

Engels, Friedrich. *The Condition of the Working Class in England.* Edited and translated by W. O. Henderson and W. H. Chaloner. New York: Macmillan, 1958.

——. *Dialectics of Nature.* Edited and translated by Clemens Dutt. New York: International Publishers, 1960.

——. "Landscape." In *Karl Marx and Frederick Engels: Collected Works.* Vol. 2, *Frederick Engels, 1838–42,* 95–101. Translated by Richard Dixon et al. London: Lawrence & Wishart, 1975.

English, James F. *The Economy of Prestige: Prizes, Awards, and the Circulation of Cultural Value.* Cambridge, Mass.: Harvard University Press, 2005.

English, Richard, and Cormac O'Malley, eds. *Prisoners: The Civil War Letters of Ernie O'Malley.* Dublin: Poolbeg, 1991.

Erne, Lucas, and Margaret Jane Kidnie, eds. *Textual Performances: The Modern Reproduction of Shakespeare's Drama.* Cambridge: Cambridge University Press, 2004.

Erven, Eugène van. *The Playful Revolution: Theatre and Liberation in Asia.* Bloomington: Indiana University Press, 1992.

Esche, Edward J., ed. *Shakespeare and His Contemporaries in Performance.* Aldershot: Ashgate, 2000.

Everett, Wendy, ed. *The Seeing Century: Film, Vision, and Identity.* Amsterdam: Rodopi, 2000.

Ewbank, Inga-Stina. "Shakespeare Translation as Cultural Exchange." *Shakespeare Survey* 48 (1995): 1–12.

Eyre, Richard, and Nicholas Wright. *Changing Stages: A View of British Theatre in the Twentieth Century.* London: Bloomsbury Press, 2000.

Falbaum, Berl, ed. *Shanghai Remembered: Stories of Jews Who Escaped to Shanghai from Nazi Europe.* Royal Oak, Mich.: Momentum Books, 2005.

Fei, Faye Chunfang, ed. and trans. *Chinese Theories of Theater and Performance from Confucius to the Present.* Ann Arbor: University of Michigan Press, 1999.

Fei, Faye Chunfang, and William Huizhu Sun. "*Othello* and Beijing Opera: Appropriation as a Two-Way Street." *TDR: The Drama Review* 50, no. 1 (2006): 120–33.

Fischlin, Daniel and Mark Fortier, eds. *Adaptations of Shakespeare: A Critical Anthology of Plays from the Seventeenth Century to the Present.* London: Routledge, 2000.

Fish, Stanley "Interpreting the *Variorum.*" In *Reader-Response Criticism: From Formalism to Post-Structuralism,* edited by Jane Tompkins, 164–84. Baltimore: Johns Hopkins University Press, 1980.

Fotheringham, Richard, Christa Jansohn, and R. S. White, eds. *Shakespeare's World / World Shakespeares: The Selected Proceedings of the International Shakespeare Association World Congress, Brisbane, 2006.* Newark: University of Delaware Press, 2008.

Foucault, Michel. *The Order of Things: An Archaeology of the Human Sciences.* New York: Vintage Books, 1994.

Foulkes, Richard, ed. *Shakespeare and the Victorian Stage.* Cambridge: Cambridge University Press, 1986.

Freiligrath, Ferdinand. "Deutschland ist Hamlet." In *Werke,* 2:71–73. Edited by Julius Schwering. Berlin: Bong, 1909.

Freud, Sigmund. "The Theme of the Three Caskets." In *The Standard Edition of the Complete Psychological Works of Sigmund Freud.* Vol. 12, *Case History of Schreber, Papers on Technique, and Other Works (1911–1913).* Translated by James Strachey, in collaboration with Anna Freud, Alix Strachey, and Alan Tyson. London: Hogarth Press, 1958.

Fu, Poshek. "Mapping Shanghai Cinema Under Semi-Occupation." In *Between Shanghai and Hong Kong: The Politics of Chinese Cinemas,* 1–50. Stanford, Calif.: Stanford University Press, 2003.

Gates, Henry Louis, Jr. "'Authenticity,' or the Lesson of Little Tree." *New York Times Book Review,* November 24, 1991, 1.

Geertz, Clifford. *The Interpretation of Cultures.* New York: Basic Books, 1973.

Gillies, John. "Shakespeare Localized: An Australian Looks at Asian Practice." In *Shakespeare Global/Local: The Hong Kong Imaginary in Transcultural Production,* edited by Kwok-kan Tam, Andrew Parkin, and Terry Siu-han Yip, 101–13. Frankfurt: Peter Lang, 2002.

Gimpel, Denise. *Lost Voices of Modernity: A Chinese Popular Fiction Magazine in Context.* Honolulu: University of Hawai'i Press, 2001.

Goethe, Johann Wolfgang von. *Wilhelm Meisters Lehrjahre: Ein Roman.* Edited by Hans-Jürgen Schings. Munich: Carl Hanser Verlag, 1988.

——. "Zum Shakespeares Tag." In *Shakespeare-Rezeption: Die Diskussion um Shakespeare in Deutschland.* Vol. 1, *Ausgewählte Texte von 1741 bis 1788,* 98–101. Introduction, notes, and bibliography by Hansjürgen Blinn. Berlin: Schmidt, 1982.

Goldman, Merle. *Literary Dissent in Communist China.* Cambridge, Mass.: Harvard University Press, 1981.

Goldstein, Jonathan. *The Jews of China.* 2 vols. Armonk, N.Y.: Sharpe, 1999.

Goldstein, Joshua. *Drama Kings: Players and Publics in the Re-creation of Peking Opera, 1870–1937.* Berkeley: University of California Press, 2007.

Goodrich, Joseph King. *The Coming China.* Chicago: McClurg, 1911.

Grady, Hugh, and Terence Hawkes. "Introduction: Presenting Presentism." In *Presentist Shakespeares,* 1–5. London: Routledge, 2007.

Greenblatt, Stephen. *Marvelous Possessions: The Wonder of the New World.* Chicago: University of Chicago Press, 1991.

Guo Songtao. *The First Chinese Embassy to the West, Translated from the Journals of Kuo Sung-t'ao, Liu His-hung and Chang Te-yi.* Translated by J. D. Frodsham. Oxford: Oxford University Press, 1974.

Gurewitsch, Matthew. "A Cast of One for 'King Lear.'" *Wall Street Journal,* July 10, 2007, eastern edition, D5.

Gussow, Mel. "A 'Dream' Set in China." *New York Times,* April 20, 1983, 26.

——. "The Many Visions of Shakespeare's 'Dream.'" *New York Times,* January 17, 1988.

Guy, Nancy. *Peking Opera and Politics in Taiwan.* Urbana: University of Illinois Press, 2005.

Hall, Stuart, and Paul du Gay, eds. *Questions of Cultural Identity.* London: Sage, 1996.

Hawkes, Terence. *Shakespeare in the Present.* London: Routledge, 2002.

Hayot, Eric, Haun Saussy, and Steven G. Yao, eds. *Sinographies: Writing China.* Minneapolis: University of Minnesota Press, 2008.

Hegel, G. W. F. *Phänomenologie des Geistes.* Werke in zwanzig Bänden, vol. 3. Frankfurt: Suhrkamp, 1980.

Henderson, Diana E. *Collaborations with the Past: Reshaping Shakespeare Across Time and Media.* Ithaca, N.Y.: Cornell University Press, 2006.

——, ed. *A Concise Companion to Shakespeare on Screen.* London: Blackwell, 2006.

Hill, Leslie, and Helen Paris, eds. *Performance and Place.* New York: Palgrave, 2006.

Hill, Michael. "Lin Shu, Inc.: Translation, Print Culture, and the Making of an Icon in Modern China." Ph.D. diss., Columbia University, 2008.

Hockx, Michel, ed. *The Literary Field of Twentieth-Century China.* Richmond, Eng.: Curzon Press, 1999.

Hodgdon, Barbara. *The Shakespeare Trade: Performance and Appropriations.* Philadelphia: University of Pennsylvania Press, 1998.

Hoenselaars, Ton, ed. *Shakespeare and the Language of Translation.* London: Arden Shakespeare, 2004.

Holland, Peter. "Touring Shakespeare." In *The Cambridge Companion to Shakespeare on Stage,* edited by Stanley Wells and Sarah Stanton, 194–211. Cambridge: Cambridge University Press, 2002.

Howard, Jean E., and Scott Cutler Shershow, eds. *Marxist Shakespeare*. London: Routledge, 2001.

Howard, Roger. *Le Théâtre chinois contemporain*. Brussels: La Renaissance du livre, 1978.

Howe, James. *A Buddhist's Shakespeare: Affirming Self-Deconstructions*. Rutherford, N.J.: Fairleigh Dickinson University Press, 1994.

Hsia, C. T. *A History of Modern Chinese Fiction*. New Haven, Conn.: Yale University Press, 1961.

Hu, Shi. *The Chinese Renaissance*. Chicago: University of Chicago Press, 1934.

Huang, Alexander C. Y. "Asian Shakespeares in Europe: From the Unfamiliar to the Defamiliarized." *Shakespearean International Yearbook* 8 (2008): 51–70.

——. "Cosmopolitanism and Its Discontents: The Dialectics between the Global and the Local in Lao She's Fiction." *MLQ: Modern Language Quarterly* 69, no. 1 (2008): 97–118.

——. "Impersonation, Autobiography, and Cross-Cultural Adaptation." *Asian Theatre Journal* 22, no. 1 (2005): 122–37.

Hughes, Alan. *Henry Irving, Shakespearean*. Cambridge: Cambridge University Press, 1981.

Hutcheon, Linda. *A Theory of Adaptation*. New York: Routledge, 2006.

Hutchings, Stephen, and Anat Vernitski, eds. *Russian and Soviet Film Adaptations of Literature, 1900–2001: Screening the Word*. London: Routledge, 2005.

Huters, Theodore. *Bringing the World Home: Appropriating the West in Late Qing and Early Republican China*. Honolulu: University of Hawai'i Press, 2005.

——. "Ideologies of Realism in Modern China: The Hard Imperatives of Imported Theory." In *Politics, Ideology, and Literary Discourse in Modern China: Theoretical Interventions and Cultural Critique*, edited by Liu Kang and Xiaobing Tang, 147–73. Durham, N.C.: Duke University Press, 1993.

Idema, Wilt L. "Performances on a Three-tiered Stage: Court Theatre During the Qianlong Era." In *Ad Seres et Tungusos Festschrift für Martin Gimm zu seinem 65. Geburtstag am 25. Mai 1995*, edited by Lutz Bieg, Erling von Mende, and Martina Siebert, 201–19. Wiesbaden: Harrassowitz Verlag, 2000.

Ides, Evert Ysbrants. *Three Years Travels from Moscow Over-land to China*. London: W. Freeman, J. Walthoe, T. Newborough, J. Nicholson, and R. Parker, 1706.

Im, Yeeyon. "The Location of Shakespeare in Korea: Lee Yountaek's *Hamlet* and the Mirage of Interculturality." *Theatre Journal* 60, no. 2 (2008): 257–76.

Irving, Henry. "An Actor's Notes on Shakespeare No. 2, Hamlet and Ophelia Act III Scene I." *Nineteenth Century*, May 1877.

Jameson, Fredric. *The Political Unconscious: Narrative as a Socially Symbolic Art*. Ithaca, N.Y.: Cornell University Press, 1981.

——. "Third World Literature in the Era of Multinational Capitalism." *Social Text: Theory/Culture Ideology* 15 (1986): 65–88.

Jameson, Fredric, and Masao Miyoshi, eds. *The Cultures of Globalization*. Durham, N.C.: Duke University Press, 1998.

Jardine, Lisa. *Reading Shakespeare Historically*. London: Routledge, 1996.

Jauss, Hans Robert. *Toward an Aesthetic of Reception*. Translated by Timothy Bahti. Brighton: Harvester Press, 1982.

Jaynes, Nanette. "Taming the Taiwanese Shrew: *Kiss Me Nana* at the Godot Theatre." In *Shakespeare Yearbook*, edited by Holger Klein and Michele Marrapodi, 10:490–505. Lewiston, N.Y.: Edwin Mellen Press, 1999.

Johnson, Linda Cooke. *Shanghai: From Market Town to Treaty Port, 1074–1858*. Stanford, Calif.: Stanford University Press, 1995.

Johnson, Marshall. "Making Time: Historic Preservation and the Space of Nationality." In *New Asian Marxisms*, edited by Tani E. Barlow, 105–71. Durham, N.C.: Duke University Press, 2002.

Jorgens, Jack J. *Shakespeare on Film*. Bloomington: Indiana University Press, 1977.

Joughin, John J., ed. *Shakespeare and National Culture*. Manchester: Manchester University Press, 1997.

Jullien, François. *La Valeur allusive des catégories originales de l'interprétation poétique dans la tradition chinoise: Contribution à une réflexion sur l'altérité interculturelle*. Paris: École française d'Extrême-Orient, 1985.

Kahn, Coppélia. "The Absent Mother in *King Lear*." In *Rewriting the Renaissance: The Discourse of Sexual Difference in Early Modern Europe*, edited by Margaret W. Ferguson, Maureen Quilligan, Nancy J. Vickers, and Catherine R. Stimpson, 33–49. Chicago: University of Chicago Press, 1985.

Kahn, Sholom J. "Enter Lear Mad." *Shakespeare Quarterly* 8, no. 3 (1957): 311–29.

Kamps, Ivo, and Jyotsna G. Singh, eds. *Travel Knowledge: European "Discoveries" in the Early Modern Period*. New York: Palgrave, 2001.

Kano, Ayako. *Acting Like a Woman in Modern Japan: Theater, Gender, and Nationalism*. New York: Palgrave, 2001.

Kantorowicz, Ernst H. *The King's Two Bodies: A Study in Medieval Political Theology*. Princeton, N.J.: Princeton University Press, 1997.

Karl, Rebecca E. *Staging the World: Chinese Nationalism at the Turn of the Twentieth Century*. Durham, N.C.: Duke University Press, 2002.

Kastan, David Scott. *Shakespeare After Theory*. London: Routledge, 1999.

Kennedy, Dennis. "Afterword: Shakespearean Orientalism." In *Foreign Shakespeare: Contemporary Performance*, edited by Dennis Kennedy, 290–303. Cambridge: Cambridge University Press, 1993.

——. *Looking at Shakespeare: A Visual History of Twentieth-Century Performance*. 2nd ed. Cambridge: Cambridge University Press, 2001.

——. "Shakespeare and the Global Spectator." *Shakespeare Jahrbuch* 131 (1995): 50–64.

Knoppers, Laura Lunger, and Gregory M. Colon Semenza, eds. *Milton in Popular Culture*. New York: Palgrave, 2006.

Kott, Jan. *Shakespeare Our Contemporary*. Translated by Boleslaw Taborski. London: Routledge, 1967.

Kowallis, Jon Eugene von. "The Diaspora in Postmodern Taiwan and Hong Kong Film: Framing Stan Lai's *The Peach Blossom Land* with Allen Fong's *Ah Ying*."

In *Transnational Chinese Cinemas: Identity, Nationhood, Gender*, edited by Sheldon Hsiao-peng Lu, 169–86. Honolulu: University of Hawai'i Press, 1997.

Lacan, Jacques. *Quatre concepts fondamentaux de la psychanalyse*. Vol. 11, *Le Séminaire de Jacques Lacan*. Edited by Jacques-Alain Miller. Paris: Seuil, 1973.

Lai, Stan. "Specifying the Universal." *TDR: The Drama Review* 38, no. 2 (1994): 33–37.

——. "Statement About the *Thirty-seven-fold Practice of a Bodhisattva*." Stage bill. Hong Kong Experimental Shakespeare Festival, March 9, 2000.

Lamb, Charles, and Mary Lamb. *Tales from Shakespeare*. Edited by Julia Briggs. London: Guernsey Press, 1993.

——. *Tales from Shakespeare*. Puffin Classics. London: Puffin Books, 1994.

——. *Tales from Shakespeare*. Wordsworth Children's Classics. Ware: Wordsworth Editions, 1999.

——. *Tales from Shakespeare*. Teddington: Echo Library, 2006.

——. *Tales from Shakespeare*. Penguin Classics. London: Penguin, 2007.

Lanier, Douglas. *Shakespeare and Modern Popular Culture*. Oxford: Oxford University Press, 2002.

Lee, Leo Ou-fan. *Shanghai Modern: The Flowering of a New Urban Culture in China, 1930–1945*. Cambridge, Mass.: Harvard University Press, 1999.

Lefevere, André. *Translation, Rewriting, and the Manipulation of Literary Fame*. London: Routledge, 1992.

Lehmann, Courtney. *Shakespeare Remains: Theatre to Film, Early Modern to Postmodern*. Ithaca, N.Y.: Cornell University Press, 2002.

Lei, Daphne Pi-Wei. *Operatic China: Staging Chinese Identity Across the Pacific*. New York: Palgrave Macmillan, 2006.

Leiser, Erwin. *Leopold Lindtberg: Schriften—Bilder—Dokumente*. Zurich: Musik and Theater, 1985.

Leiter, Samuel L., ed. *Shakespeare Around the Globe: A Guide to Notable Postwar Revivals*. New York: Greenwood Press, 1986.

Levenson, Joseph. *Liang Ch'i-ch'ao and the Mind of Modern China*. Berkeley: University of California Press, 1970.

Levi, Primo. *Se questo è un uomo*. Turin: De Silva, 1947.

——. *Survival in Auschwitz: The Nazi Assault on Humanity*. Translated by Stuart Woolf. New York: Simon and Schuster, 1996.

Levith, Murray J. *Shakespeare in China*. London: Continuum, 2004.

Li, Ruru. *Shashibiya: Staging Shakespeare in China*. Hong Kong: Hong Kong University Press, 2003.

Liao, Ping-hui. "Taiwan Under Japanese Colonial Rule, 1895–1945: History, Culture, Memory." In *Taiwan Under Japanese Colonial Rule, 1895–1945: History, Culture, Memory*, edited by Liao Ping-hui and David Der-wei Wang, 1–15. New York: Columbia University Press, 2006.

Lilley, Rozanna. "The Romance of the Marginal: Zuni Icosahedron." In *Staging Hong Kong: Gender and Performance in Transition*, edited by Rozanna Lilley, 89–147. Richmond: Curzon Press, 1998.

Link, Perry. *The Uses of Literature*. Princeton, N.J.: Princeton University Press, 2000.

Lionnett, Françoise, and Shu-mei Shih, eds. *Minor Transnationalism*. Durham, N.C.: Duke University Press, 2005.

Liu, Haiping, and Lowell Swortzell, eds. *Eugene O'Neill in China: An International Centenary Celebration*. New York: Greenwood Press, 1992.

Liu, James J. Y. *Chinese Theories of Literature*. Chicago: University of Chicago Press, 1975.

Liu, Lydia H. *The Clash of Empires: The Invention of China in Modern World Making*. Cambridge, Mass.: Harvard University Press, 2006.

——. *Translingual Practice: Literature, National Culture, and Translated Modernity: China, 1900–1927*. Stanford: Stanford University Press, 1995.

Liu, Siyuan. "Adaptation as Appropriation: Staging Western Drama in the First Western-Style Theatres in Japan and China." *Theatre Journal* 59, no. 3 (2007): 411–29.

Lowenthal, David. "Fabricating Heritage." *History and Memory* 10 (1998): 5–24.

Mackerras, Colin. *The Chinese Theatre in Modern Times: From 1840 to the Present Day*. Amherst: University of Massachusetts Press, 1975.

Makaryk, Irena R., and Joseph Price, eds. *Shakespeare in the Worlds of Communism and Socialism*. Toronto: University of Toronto Press, 2006.

Marcus, Leah. *Puzzling Shakespeare: Local Reading and Its Discontents*. Berkeley: University of California Press, 1988.

Martin, W. A. P. *The Awakening of China*. New York: Doubleday, Page, 1907.

Marx, Eleanor. "Recollections of Mohr." In Karl Marx and Friedrich Engels, *Marx and Engels on Literature and Art: A Selection of Writings*, 147–48. Edited by Lee Baxandall and Stefan Morawski. St. Louis: Telos Press, 1973.

Marx, Karl. *Economic and Philosophic Manuscripts of 1844*. Translated by Martin Milligan. Buffalo, N.Y.: Prometheus Books, 1988.

Marx, Karl, and Friedrich Engels. *Marx and Engels on Literature and Art: A Selection of Writings*. Edited by Lee Baxandall and Stefan Morawski. St. Louis: Telos Press, 1973.

Massai, Sonia, ed. *World-wide Shakespeares: Local Appropriations in Film and Performance*. London: Routledge, 2005.

McLuskie, Kathleen. "Unending Revels: Visual Pleasure and Compulsory Shakespeare." In *A Concise Companion to Shakespeare on Screen*, edited by Diana E. Henderson, 238–49. Oxford: Blackwell, 2006.

Meisner, Maurice. *Marxism, Maoism, and Utopianism: Eight Essays*. Madison: University of Wisconsin Press, 1982.

Merlin, Bella. *Beyond Stanislavsky: The Psycho-Physical Approach to Actor Training*. New York: Routledge, 2001.

Mignolo, Walter D. *Local Histories / Global Designs: Coloniality, Subaltern Knowledges, and Border Thinking*. Princeton, N.J.: Princeton University Press, 2000.

Mittler, Barbara. "Defy(N)ing Modernity: Women in Shanghai's Early News-Media (1872–1915)." *Jindai Zhongguo funü shi yanjiu* [*Research on Women in Modern Chinese History*] 11 (2003): 215–60.

Morozov, Mikhail M. *Shakespeare on the Soviet Stage*. Translated by David Magarshack. London: Soviet News, 1947.

Neill, Michael. "Post-Colonial Shakespeare? Writing Away from the Centre." In *Post-Colonial Shakespeares*, edited by Ania Loomba and Martin Orkin, 164–85. London: Routledge, 1998.

Newstok, Scott L. "*Touch* of Shakespeare: Welles Unmoors *Othello.*" *Shakespeare Bulletin* 23, no. 1 (2005): 29–86.

Ng, Lun Ngai-ha. *Interactions of East and West: Development of Public Education in Early Hong Kong*. Hong Kong: Chinese University Press, 1984.

O'Neil, Catherine. *With Shakespeare's Eyes: Pushkin's Creative Appropriation of Shakespeare*. Newark: University of Delaware Press, 2003.

Orkin, Martin. *Local Shakespeares*. London: Routledge, 2005.

Owen, Stephen, ed. *An Anthology of Chinese Literature: Beginnings to 1911*. New York: Norton, 1996.

Pavis, Patrice. *Theatre at the Crossroads of Culture*. Translated by Loren Kruger. London: Routledge, 1992.

Perkins, Franklin. *Leibniz and China: A Commerce of Light*. Cambridge: Cambridge University Press, 2004.

Perloff, Marjorie. "Presidential Address 2006: It Must Change." *PMLA* 122, no. 3 (2007): 652–62.

Phelan, Peggy. "Reconstructing Love: *King Lear* and Theatre Architecture." In *A Companion to Shakespeare and Performance*, edited by Barbara Hodgdon and W. B. Worthen, 13–35. Oxford: Blackwell, 2005.

Pronko, Leonard Cabell. *Theater East and West: Perspectives Toward a Total Theater*. Berkeley: University of California Press, 1967.

Pusey, James Reeve. *China and Charles Darwin*. Cambridge, Mass.: Council on East Asian Studies, Harvard University, 1983.

Reed, Christopher. *Gutenberg in Shanghai: Chinese Print Capitalism, 1876–1937*. Vancouver: University of British Columbia Press, 2004.

Rothwell, Kenneth S. *A History of Shakespeare on Screen: A Century of Film and Television*. 2nd ed. Cambridge: Cambridge University Press, 2004.

Russell, Bertrand. *The Problem of China*. New York: Century, 1922.

Rye, William Brenchley, ed. *England as Seen by Foreigners in the Days of Elizabeth and James the First*. New York: Benjamin Bloom, 1967.

Ryuta, Minami, Ian Carruthers, and John Gillies, eds. *Performing Shakespeare in Japan*. Cambridge: Cambridge University Press, 2001.

Said, Edward W. *Orientalism*. New York: Pantheon, 1978.

Sanders, Julie. *Adaptation and Appropriation*. London: Routledge, 2006.

Saussy, Haun. "Là, tout n'est qu'ordre et beauté: The Surprises of Applied Structuralism." In *Reading East Asian Writing: The Limits of Literary Theory*, edited by Michel Hockx and Ivo Smits, 39–71. London: RoutledgeCurzon, 2003.

Schaper, Rüdiger. "Der Kaufmann von Buchenwald: Ein Shakespeare zum Gedenktag am Deutschen Nationaltheater Weimar." *Süddeutsche Zeitung*, April 11, 1995.

Schwartz, Benjamin. *In Search of Wealth and Power: Yen Fu and the West*. Cambridge, Mass.: Belknap Press of Harvard University Press, 1964.

Shanghai Kunju Theatre: Macbeth, the Peony Pavilion, the Woman Warrior—The First Ever European Tour of the Most Exciting Company in China. Souvenir Program. Shanghai Kunju Theatre, Autumn 1987.

Shaughnessy, Robert. *The Shakespeare Effect: A History of Twentieth-Century Performance.* New York: Palgrave, 2002.

Shih, Shu-mei. *Visuality and Identity: Sinophone Articulations Across the Pacific.* Berkeley: University of California Press, 2007.

Shohat, Ella. "Gender and Culture of Empire: Toward a Feminist Ethnography of the Cinema." In *Visions of the East: Orientalism in Film,* edited by Matthew Bernstein and Gaylyn Studlar, 19–68. New Brunswick, N.J.: Rutgers University Press, 1997.

Sieber, Patricia. *Theaters of Desire: Authors, Readers, and the Reproduction of Early Chinese Song-Drama, 1300–2000.* New York: Palgrave, 2003.

Sillars, Stuart. *Painting Shakespeare: The Artist as Critic, 1720–1820.* Cambridge: Cambridge University Press, 2006.

Sinfield, Alan. "Give an account of Shakespeare and Education, showing why you think they are effective and what you have appreciated about them. Support your comments with precise references." In *Political Shakespeare: Essays in Cultural Materialism,* edited by Jonathan Dollimore and Alan Sinfield, 134–57. Manchester: Manchester University Press, 1985.

Singh, Jyotsna. "The Postcolonial/Postmodern Shakespeare." In *Shakespeare: World Views,* edited by Heather Kerr, Robin Eaden, and Madge Mitton, 29–43. Newark: University of Delaware Press, 1996.

Smiles, Samuel. *Self-Help; with Illustrations of Character and Conduct.* London: John Murray, 1859.

Snow, Lois Wheeler. *China on Stage: An American Actress in the People's Republic.* New York: Random House, 1972.

Sorgenfrei, Carol Fisher. "The State of Asian Theatre Studies in the American Academy." *Theatre Survey* 47, no. 2 (2006): 217–23.

Spence, Jonathan. *The Search for Modern China.* New York: Norton, 1990.

Spivak, Gayatri Chakravorty. *Other Asias.* Oxford: Blackwell, 2003.

Sponsler, Claire, and Chen Xiaomei. *East of West: Cross-Cultural Performance and the Staging of Difference.* New York: Palgrave, 2000.

St. John's University, ed. *St. John's University, 1879–1929.* Shanghai, 1929.

Stanislavski, Constantin. *An Actor Prepares.* Translated by Elizabeth Reynolds Hapgood. New York: Theatre Arts Books, 1972.

——. *My Life in Art.* Translated by J. J. Robins. Boston: Little, Brown, 1937.

Stevens, Sarah E. "Figuring Modernity: The New Woman and the Modern Girl in Republican China." *NWSA Journal* 15, no. 3 (2003): 82–103.

Stoker, Bram. *Personal Reminiscences of Henry Irving.* 2 vols. London: Macmillan, 1906.

Sturgess, Kim C. *Shakespeare and the American Nation.* Cambridge: Cambridge University Press, 2004.

Talfourd, Francis. *Shylock; or, The Merchant of Venice Preserved.* London: Lacy, 1853.

Tam, Kwok-kan. *Ibsen in China, 1908–1997: A Critical-Annotated Bibliography of Criticism, Translation and Performance*. Hong Kong: Chinese University Press, 2001.

Tam, Kwok-kan, Andrew Parkin, and Terry Siu-han Yip, eds. *Shakesperae Global/ Local: The Hong Kong Imaginary in Transcultural Production*. Frankfurt: Peter Lang, 2002.

Tang, Xiaobing. *Global Space and the Nationalist Discourse of Modernity: The Historical Thinking of Liang Qichao*. Stanford, Calif.: Stanford University Press, 1996.

Tatlow, Antony. *Shakespeare, Brecht, and the Intercultural Sign*. Durham, N.C.: Duke University Press, 2001.

Taylor, Charles, and Amy Gutman. *Multilingualism and the "Politics of Recognition": An Essay*. Princeton, N.J.: Princeton University Press, 1992.

Taylor, Gary. "The Incredible Shrinking Bard." In *Shakespeare and Appropriation*, edited by Christy Desmet and Robert Sawyer, 197–205. London: Routledge, 1999.

Thompson, Ayanna, ed. *Colorblind Shakespeare: New Perspectives on Race and Performance*. New York: Routledge, 2006.

Trivedi, Poonam. "Reading 'Other Shakespeares.'" In *Remaking Shakespeare: Performance Across Media, Genres, and Cultures*, edited by Pascale Aebischer, Edward J. Esche, and Nigel Wheale, 56–73. New York: Palgrave, 2003.

Tsu, Jing. *Failure, Nationalism, and Literature: The Making of Modern Chinese Identity, 1895–1937*. Stanford, Calif.: Stanford University Press, 2005.

Tu, Wei-ming, ed. *The Living Tree: The Changing Meaning of Being Chinese Today*. Stanford, Calif.: Stanford University Press, 1994.

Wakeman, Frederic, Jr. *History and Will: Philosophical Perspectives of Mao Tse-tung's Thought*. Berkeley: University of California Press, 1973.

Waley, Arthur. *The Opium War Through Chinese Eyes*. London: Allen and Unwin, 1958.

Wang, David Der-wei. *Fictional Realism in Twentieth-Century China: Mao Dun, Lao She, Shen Congwen*. New York: Columbia University Press, 1992.

Wardy, Robert. *Aristotle in China: Language, Categories, and Translation*. Cambridge: Cambridge University Press, 2000.

Whitney, John O., and Tina Packer. *Power Plays: Shakespeare's Lessons in Leadership and Management*. New York: Simon and Schuster, 2000.

Wichmann, Elizabeth. *Listening to Theatre: The Aural Dimension of Beijing Opera*. Honolulu: University of Hawai'i Press, 1991.

Widmer, Ellen, and David Der-wei Wang, eds. *From May Fourth to June Fourth: Fiction and Film in Twentieth-Century China*. Cambridge, Mass.: Harvard University Press, 1993.

Williams, Raymond. *Marxism and Literature*. Oxford: Oxford University Press, 1977.

Winfield, Jess. *What Would Shakespeare Do? Personal Advice from the Bard*. Berkeley: Seastone, 2000.

Wong, Dorothy. "'Domination by Consent': A Study of Shakespeare in Hong Kong." In *Colonizer and Colonized*, edited by Theo D'haen and Patricia Krüs, 43–56. Amsterdam: Rodpi, 2000.

Worthen, W. B. *Shakespeare and the Force of Modern Performance.* Cambridge: Cambridge University Press, 2003.

Wu, Hsing-kuo. "Director's Note." In *Lincoln Center Festival, July 10–July 29, 2007.* Stage bill. New York: Playbill, 2007.

Wu, Ningkun, and Li Yikai. *A Single Tear: A Family's Persecution, Love, and Endurance in Communist China.* New York: Atlantic Monthly Press, 1993.

Yeh, Michelle, and N. G. D. Malmqvist, eds. *Frontier Taiwan: An Anthology of Modern Chinese Poetry.* New York: Columbia University Press, 2001.

Yeh, Wen-hsin. *The Alienated Academy: Culture and Politics in Republican China, 1919–1937.* Cambridge, Mass.: Harvard University Press, 1990.

Yong, Li Lan. "Shakespeare and the Fiction of the Intercultural." In *A Companion to Shakespeare and Performance,* edited by Barbara Hodgdon and W. B. Worthen. Oxford: Blackwell, 2005.

Zhang, Ning. *L'Appropriation par la Chine du théâtre occidental: Un autre sens de l'Occident (1978–1989).* Paris: L'Harmattan, 1998.

Zhang, Xiao Yang. *Shakespeare in China: A Comparative Study of Two Traditions and Cultures.* Newark: University of Delaware Press, 1996.

Zhang, Xudong. "On Some Motifs in the Chinese 'Cultural Fever' of the Late 1980's." *Social Text* 39 (1994): 129–56.

Zhang, Yingjin, and Zhiwei Xiao. *The Encyclopedia of Chinese Film.* London: Routledge, 1998.

Zhang, Zhen. "Bodies in the Air: The Magic of Science and the Fate of the Martial Arts Film in China." *Post Script* 20, nos. 2–3 (2001): 43–60.

——. "Cosmopolitan Projections: World Literature on Chinese Screens." In *A Companion to Literature and Film,* edited by Robert Stam and Alesandra Raengo, 144–63. Oxford: Blackwell, 2004.

Zimmermann, Heiner O. "Is Hamlet Germany? On the Political Reception of *Hamlet.*" In *New Essays on Hamlet,* edited by Mark Thornton Burnett and John Manning, 293–318. New York: AMS Press, 1994.

Sources in Chinese and Japanese

A Ying 阿英 [Qian Xingcun], ed. *Wan Qing wenxue congchao: Xiaoshuo xiqu yanjiu juan* 晚清文學叢鈔小說戲曲研究卷 [*A Compendium of Late Qing Literature: Research on Fiction and Drama*]. Beijing: Zhonghua shuju, 1960.

Ai Yuese 艾約瑟 [A. Joseph], ed. and trans. *Xixue qimeng shiliu zhong* 西學啟蒙十六種 [*Introduction (for Beginners) to Sixteen Western Works*]. Shanghai: Zhuyi tang, 1896.

Anikst, Alexander. *Shashibiya zhuan* 莎士比亞傳 [*Biography of Shakespeare*]. Translated by An Guoliang. Beijing: Zhongguo xiju chubanshe, 1984.

Aoki Masaru 青木正兒. *Shina kinsei gikyoku shi* (Japanese, 1930). *Zhongguo jinshi xiqu shi* 中國近世戲曲史 [*A History of Chinese Theater in the Ming and Qing Dynasties*]. Translated by Wang Jilu 王吉廬. Taipei: Shangwu yinshuguan, 1988.

Beijing daxue 北京大學, 北京師範大學, 北京師範學院中文系中國現代文學教研室, eds. *Wenxue yundong shiliao xuan* 文學運動史料選 [*Selected Historical Materials of Literary Movements*]. Vol. 1. Shanghai: Shanghai jiaoyu chubanshe, 1979.

Cai Yuanpei 蔡元培. *Zhongguo xin wenxue daxi daolun ji* 中國新文學大系導論集 [*Collected Introductions to "Compendium of Modern Chinese Literature"*]. Shanghai: Liangyou fuxing tushu, 1940.

Cao Shujun 曹樹鈞. *Shashibiya de chuntian zai Zhongguo* 莎士比亞的春天在中國 [*It Is Springtime for Shakespeare in China*]. Hong Kong: Tianma tushu youxian gongsi, 2002.

——. "*Wushi shengfei* guangchang ju"《無事生非》廣場劇 [The "Plaza Open-Air Theater" of *Much Ado About Nothing*]. *Xin wutai* 新舞台 [*New Stage*] 9 (1995): 5.

Cao Shujun and Sun Fuliang 孫福良. *Shashibiya zai Zhongguo wutai shang* 莎士比亞在中國舞台上 [*Shakespeare on the Chinese Stage*]. Shenyang: Harbin chubanshe, 1989.

Chen Danyan 陳丹燕. *Shanghai de jinzhi yuye* 上海的金枝玉葉 [*Shanghai Princess*]. Beijing: Zuojia chubanshe, 1999.

Chen Duxiu 陳獨秀. "Dong xi minzu genben sixiang zhi chayi" 東西民族根本思想之差異 [Fundamental Differences Between Eastern and Western Peoples' Modes of Thinking]. *Qingnian zazhi* 青年雜誌 [*Youth Magazine*] 1, no. 4 (1915). In *Wusi qianhou dongxi wenhua lunzhan wenxuan* 五四前後東西文化論戰文選 [*Debates About East–West Cultural Issues Around the May Fourth Period*], edited by Chen Song, 12–15. Beijing: Zhongguo shehui kexue yuan, 1985.

——. "Lun Xiqu" 論戲曲 [On Chinese Music Drama]. *Anhui suhua bao* 安徽俗話報 [*Anhui Vernacular News*], September 10, 1904.

Chen Jia 陳嘉. "Cong *Hamuleite* he *Aosailuo* de fenxi laikan Shashibiya de pingjia wenti" 從《哈姆雷特》和《奧賽羅》的分析來看莎士比亞的評價問題 [Toward an Evaluation of Shakespeare: Analyses of *Hamlet* and *Othello*]. *Nanjing daxue xuebao: Wenke* 南京大學學報:文科 [*Nanjing University Journal: Humanities Section*] 8, no. 2 (1964): 34–59.

Chen Jingzhi 陳敬之. *Wenxue yanjiu hui yu Chuangzao she* 文學研究會與創造社 [*The Literary Research Association and the Creation Society*]. Taipei: Chengwen chubanshe, 1986.

Chen Kaixin 陳凱莘. "Kunju *Mudan ting* wutai yishu yanjin zhi tantao" 崑劇《牡丹亭》舞台藝術演進之探討 [A Performance History of *Peony Pavilion*]. M.A. thesis, Graduate Institute of Drama and Theater, National Taiwan University, 1999.

Chen Shouzhu 陳瘦竹. "Guanyu xiju wenti" 關於喜劇問題 [On the Question of Comedy]. *Wenhui bao* 文匯報 [*Wenhui Daily*], March 2, 1961, 3.

Cheng Fangwu 成仿吾. "Chuangzao she yu Wenxue yanjiu hui" 創造社與文學研究會 [The Creation Society and the Literary Research Association]. *Chuangzao jikan* 創造季刊 [*Creation Quarterly*] 1, no. 4 (1923).

Chou Hui-ling 周慧玲. *Biaoyan Zhongguo: Nü mingxing, biaoyan wenhua, shijue zhengzhi, 1910–1945* 表演中國:女明星, 表演文化, 視覺政治 1910–1945 [*Perform-*

ing China: Actresses, Performance Culture, Visual Politics, 1910–1945]. Taipei: Rye Field Publications, 2004.

Deng Xiaoping 鄧小平. "Zai Zhongguo wenxue yishu gongzuo zhe di si ci daibiao dahui shang de zhuci" 在中國文學藝術工作者第四次代表大會上的祝詞 [Congratulatory Remark at the Fourth Chinese Literary and Artistic Workers' Congress]. In *Deng Xiaoping wenxuan* 鄧小平文選 [*Selected Writings of Deng Xiaoping*]. Beijing: Renmin chuban she, 1983.

Dianying cidian bianwei hui 電影辭典編委會, eds. *Zhongguo dianying dacidian* 中國電影大辭典 [*Dictionary of Chinese Films*]. Shanghai: Shanghai cishu chubanshe, 1995.

Dong Youdao 董友道. "Wushi shengfei de wutai diaodu: Liepukefusikaya de daoyan shoufa" 《無事生非》的舞台調度—列普柯夫斯卡雅的導演手法 [The Mise-en-scène of *Much Ado About Nothing*: Lipkovskaya's Directing Method]. *Xinmin wanbao* 新民晚報 [*New Citizen Evening News*], November 30, 1957.

Fang Jiaji 方家驥 and Zhu Jianming 朱建明, eds. *Shanghai kunju zhi* 上海崑劇誌 [*Annals of Shanghai Kun Opera*]. Shanghai: Shanghai wenhua chubanshe, 1998.

Fang Ping 方平. "Cao Xueqin yu Shashibiya" 曹雪芹與莎士比亞 [Cao Xueqin and Shakespeare]. *Wenyi lilun yanjiu* 文藝理論研究 [*Theoretical Studies of Literature and Art Quarterly*] 3 (1981): 132–36.

Fong Chee Fun (Gilbert). *Xianggang huaju fangtan lu* 香港話劇訪談錄 [*Interviews of Hong Kong Spoken Drama Personalities*]. Hong Kong: Xianggang xiju gongcheng, 2000.

Fu Sinian 傅斯年. *Fu Mengzhen xiansheng ji* 傅孟真先生集 [*Collected Writings by Mr. Fu Mengzhen*]. Vol. 6. Edited by Fu Mengzhen xiansheng yizhu bianju weiyuanhui. Taipei: Taiwan University, 1952.

Fu Xiangmo. "Guan Shaweng de shijie da beiju" 觀莎翁的世界大悲劇 [Attending a Performance of a World-Class Tragedy by Shakespeare]. *Guoli xiju zhuanke xuexiao xiaoyou tongxun yuekan* 國立戲劇專科學校校友通訊月刊 [*Alumni Monthly Newsletter of the National Drama School*], June 18, 1942, 1–5.

Ge Baoquan 戈寶全. "Shashibiya zuopin zai Zhongguo" 莎士比亞作品在中國 [Shakespeare's Works in China]. *Shijie wenxue* 世界文學 [*World Literature*], May 1964. *Shashibiya yanjiu* 莎士比亞研究 [*Shakespeare Studies*] 1 (1983): 332–42.

Guo Songtao 郭松燾. *Guo Songtao: Lundun yu Bali riji* 郭松燾: 倫敦與巴黎日記 [*Guo Songtao: London and Paris Diary*]. Compiled by Zhong Shuhe and Yang Jian. Changsha: Yuelu shushe, 1984.

——. *Guo Songtao riji* 郭松燾日記 [*The Diary of Guo Songtao*]. Edited by Hunan People's Press. 4 vols. Changsha: Hunan Renmin chubanshe, 1981–1983.

Hong Shen 洪深. "Xiandai xiju daolun" 現代戲劇導論 [General Introduction to Modern Drama]. In *Zhongguo xinwenxue daxi daolun xuanji* 中國新文學大系導論選集 [*An Anthology of Selected Introductions to "Compendium of Modern Chinese Literature"*], edited by Zheng Zhenduo et al. Hong Kong: Yiqun chubanshe, 1961.

Hu Dao 胡導. "*Wushi shengfei* shi ge zenyang de xiju" 《無事生非》是個怎樣的喜劇 [What Kind of Comedy is *Much Ado About Nothing*?]. *Xinmin wanbao* 新民晚報 [*New Citizen Evening News*], May 22, 1961.

Hu Feng 胡風. "Xianshi zhuyi de xiuzheng" 現實主義的修正 [Realism: A Correction, 1936]. In *Modern Chinese Literary Thought: Writings on Literature, 1893–1945*, edited by Kirk Denton, 345–55. Stanford, Calif.: Stanford University Press, 1996.

———. "Xianshi zhuyi zai jintian" 現實主義在今天 [Realism Today]. *Shishi xinbao* 時事新報 [*Current Affairs*], January 1, 1944. In *Hu Feng pinglun ji* 胡風評論集 [*Collection of Hu Feng's Literary Criticism*], 2:319–23. Beijing: Renmin wenxue, 1984.

Hu Shi 胡適. "Chongfen shijiehua yu quanpan xihua" 充分世界化與全盤西化 [Total Globalization and Wholesale Westernization]. In *Hu Shi wencun* 胡適文存 [*Collected Works of Hu Shi*], 4:541–44. Taipei: Yuandong tushu, 1971.

———. "Wenxue jinhua guannian yu xiju gailiang" 文學進化觀念與戲劇改良 [Drama Reform and the Concept of Literary Evolution]. *Xin qingnian* 新青年 [*New Youth*] 5, no. 4 (1918). In *Zhongguo xin wenxue daxi* 中國新文學大系 [*Compendium of Modern Chinese Literature*], edited by Zhao Jiabi, 1:376–86. Shanghai: Liangyou tushu gongsi, 1935.

Hu Weimin 胡偉民. "Guoqu de zuji" 過去的足跡 [Footsteps in the Past]. In *Hu Weimin yanjiu* 胡偉民研究 [*Study of Hu Weimin*], edited by Zhang Yu, 144–58. Beijing: Zhongguo xiju yishu chubanshe, 1999.

Huang Long 黃龍. "Cao Xueqin yu Shashibiya" 曹雪芹與莎士比亞 [Cao Xueqin and Shakespeare]. *Wenjiao ziliao jianbao* 文教資料簡報 [*Brief Reports on Recent Studies of Culture and Education*] 6 (1982): 93–98.

Huang Zhiwei, ed. *Lao Shanghai dianying* 老上海電影 [*Old Shanghai Films*]. Shanghai: Wenhui chubanshe, 1998.

Huang Zuolin 黃佐臨. *Wo yu xieyi xiju guan* 我與寫意戲劇觀 [*My Conception of Theater as Impressionism and Stylization*]. Edited by Jiang Liu. Beijing: Zhongguo xiju chubanshe, 1990.

Jiang Qing 江青. "Tan jingju geming" 談京劇革命 [On Revolutionalizing Beijing Opera]. In *Mao zhuxi de geming wenyi luxian shengli wansui* 毛主席的革命文藝路線勝利萬歲 [*Long Live the Victory of Chairman Mao's Revolutionary Literary Axiom*]. Xi'an: Shaanxi renmin chubanshe, 1972.

Jiang Tao 江濤. "Lun Zhongguo Shaju wutai shang de daoyan yishu" 論中國莎劇舞台上的導演藝術 [Directing Arts of Shakespearean Performance on the Chinese Stage]. *Xiju* 戲劇 [*Drama*] 3 (1996): 105–26.

Jiao Juyin 焦菊隱. "Guanyu *Hamuleite*" 關於哈姆雷特 [About *Hamlet*]. In *Jiao Juyin wenji* 焦菊隱文集 [*Collected Writings by Jiao Juyin*], 167–68. Beijing: Zhongguo xiju chubanshe, 1988.

Kang Youwei 康有為. "Guanxi ji" 觀戲記 [Reflections on Theatrical Performances (I) Saw]. In *Qingyi bao quanbian* 清議報全編 [*Complete Collection of Qingyi Newspaper*]. Vol. 25. 1899. In *Jindai Zhongguo shiliao congkan sanbian* 近代中國史料叢刊三編 [*Collectanea of Source Material on the History of Modern China*], edited by Shen Yunlong 沈雲龍, 15:161–68. Taipei: Wenhai chubanshe, 1986.

Ke Ling 柯靈. "Xuyan" 序言 [Preface]. In *Li Jianwu juzuo xuan* 李健吾劇作選 [*Selected Plays by Li Jianwu*], 1–16. Edited by Zhang Jie. Beijing: Zhongguo xiju chubanshe, 1982.

Kuang Yinghui 匡映輝, ed. *Shashibiya Zhongwen ziliao suoyin, 1902–1984* 莎士比亞中文資料索引 [*Chinese Bibliography on Shakespeare, 1902–1984*]. Beijing: Zhongyang xiju xueyuan xiju zazhishe, 1984.

Lamb, Charles, and Mary Lamb. *Shashi yuefu benshi* 莎氏樂府本事 [*Plot Outlines of Shakespeare's Dramatic Works*]. Annotated by Kan Tsao-ling. Shanghai: Shangwu yinshuguan, 1922.

——. *Shashibiya gushi ji* 莎士比亞故事集 [*Tales from Shakespeare*]. Translated by Chen Jingmin and Shen Mo. Taipei: Yuyan gongchang, 2004.

——. *Shashibiya gushi ji* 莎士比亞故事集 [*Tales from Shakespeare*]. Translated by Liu Hongyan. Taichung: Haodu, 2005.

——. *Yuedu Shashibiya: Yong bu xiemu de bei xi ju* 閱讀莎士比亞: 永不謝幕的悲喜劇 [*Reading Shakespeare: Tragedies and Comedies that Never End*]. Translated by Xiao Qian. Tianjin: Baihua wenyi chubanshe, 2004.

Li Jianwu 李健吾. *Wang Deming* 王德明. In *Li Jianwu juzuo xuan* 李健吾劇作選 [*Selected Plays by Li Jianwu*], 417–88. Edited by Zhang Jie. Beijing: Zhongguo xiju chubanshe, 1982.

——. "Xu" 序 [Preface to *Ah shi na*]. *Wenxue zazhi* 文學雜誌 [*Literature Magazine*] 2, no. 10 (1947).

——. "Yu youren shu" 與友人書 [A Letter to My Friend]. *Shanghai wenhua* 上海文化 [*Shanghai Culture*] 6 (1946): 28–29.

Li Ming 黎明. "*Luomi'ou yu Zhuliye*: Gongyan hou de pingjia" 羅密歐與朱麗葉——公演後的評價 [A Review of the Production of *Romeo and Juliet*]. *Da gong bao zengkan* 大公報贈刊 [*Dagong Daily Supplement*], June 8, 1937.

Li Quan 李荃. "*Luanshi Yingxiong* guanhou de pingjia" 亂世英雄觀後的評價 [An Evaluation of *The Hero of a Tumultuous Time*]. *Haibao* 海報 [*Shanghai News*], May 2, 1945.

Li Suyuan 酈蘇元 and Hu Jubin 胡菊彬. *Zhongguo wusheng dianying shi* 中國無聲電影史 [*A History of Chinese Silent Film*]. Beijing: Zhongguo dianying chubanshe, 1996.

Li Xiao 李曉, ed. *Shanghai huaju zhi* 上海話劇志 [*Annals of Huaju in Shanghai*]. Shanghai: Baijia chubanshe, 2002.

Liang Qichao 梁啟超. *Yinbingshi shihua* 飲冰室詩話 [*Notes on Poetry from the Ice-drinking Studio*]. Beijing: Renmin wenxue chubanshe, 1959.

Lin Zexu 林則徐, trans. and ed. *Sizhou zhi* 四洲志 [*Annals of Four Continents*]. Edited and annotated by Zhang Man. Beijing: Huaxia chubanshe, 2002.

Lipkovskaya, Yevgeniya K. "Sulian zhuanjia Ye Kang Liepukefusikaya zai biaoyan shizi jinxiuban di yi tang biaoyanke shang de jianghua" 蘇聯專家葉康列普科夫斯卡雅在表演師資進修班第一堂表演課上的講話 [The Soviet Expert Yevgeniya Konstantinovna Lipkovskaya's Talk at the First Acting Class for the Acting Teachers' Program]. Translated by Sha Jin. In *Yuan bao* 院報 [*Newsletter of the Shanghai Theater Academy*] 7, 7–14. Shanghai: Shanghai Theater Academy, 1956.

Liu Fan 劉凡. "Xiang nimen xuexi, xiang nimen kanqi: Xie gei Shanghai xiju xueyuan shiyan huaju tuan" 向你們學習 向你們看齊——寫給上海戲劇學院實驗話劇團 [Learning from You, Looking onto You: A Letter to the Shanghai

Theatre Academy's Experimental Huaju Company]." *Liaoning ribao* 遼寧日報 [*Liaoning Daily*], September 2, 1961.

Liu Yonglai. "Xinxian, youqu, qipuo: Shanghai yanchu guangchang Shaju *Wushi shengfei*" 新鮮、有趣、氣魄—上海演出廣場莎劇《無事生非》[Fresh, Fascinating, Magnificent: The Open-air Shakespeare, *Much Ado About Nothing*, in Shanghai]. *Xiju dianying bao* 戲劇電影報 [*Drama and Film*], December 1995, 9.

Lu Hai 魯海. "Kan *Wushi shengfei*" 看《無事生非》[Watching *Much Ado About Nothing*]. *Qingdao ribao* 青島日報 [*Qingdao Daily*], August 1, 1962.

Lu Qian 盧前. *Zhongguo xiju gailun* 中國戲劇概論 [*A General Introduction to Chinese Drama*]. Zhongguo wenxue balun 中國文學八論 , no. 6. Hong Kong: Nanguo, 1961.

Lu Xun 魯迅. *Lu Xun quanji* 魯迅全集 [*The Complete Works of Lu Xun*]. Beijing: Renmin yishu chubanshe, 1981.

Ma Sen 馬森. *Zhongguo xiandai xiju de liangdu xi chao* 中國現代戲劇的兩度西潮 [*The Two Western Tides of Modern Chinese Drama*]. Tainan: Wenhua shenghuo xinzhi chubanshe, 1991.

Ma Shuliang 馬畫良. "Wo wei Licha kuang" 我為理查狂 [Gone Crazy for Richard]. *Beijing qingnian bao* 北京青年報 [*Beijing Youth Daily*], June 20, 2001.

Man Yanwen. "Huaju *Licha sanshi* shouyan yinxiang" 話劇理查三世首演印象 [Impressions of (Lin Zhaohua's) *Huaju Richard III*]. *Beijing wanbao* 北京晚報 [*Beijing Evening News*], February 17, 2001.

Mao Dun 茅盾. "Wenxue yu rensheng" 文學與人生 [Literature and Life]. In *Mao Dun zhuanji* 茅盾專集 [*Collection of Writings by and About Mao Dun*], 1:2:1052–56. Fuzhou: Fujian renmin chubanshe, 1982.

Mao Zedong 毛澤東. "Baihua qifang, baijia zhengming fangzhen de guanche" 百花齊放, 百家爭鳴方針的貫徹 [How to Enforce the Policy of "Letting a Hundred Flowers Bloom and a Hundred Schools Contend"]. In *Zhongguo xiandai wenxue shi cankao ziliao: Zhongguo geming wenxue de xin jieduan* 中國現代文學史參考資料: 中國革命文學的新階段 [*Reference Materials of Modern Chinese Literary History: The New Epoch of Chinese Revolutionary Literature, 1949–1958*], edited by Beijing shifan daxue zhongwenxi xiandai wenxue jiaoxue gaige xiaozu, 3:474–79. Beijing: Gaodeng jiaoyu chubanshe, 1959.

——. "Zai Yan'an wenyi zuotan hui shang de jianghua" 在延安文藝座談會上的講話 [Talks at the Yan'an Forum on Literature and Art]. In *Mao Zedong xuanji* 毛澤東選集 [*Selected Works of Mao Zedong*], 804–35. Beijing: Renmin chubanshe, 1990.

Mei Lanfang 梅蘭芳. *Wutai shenghuo sishi nian* 舞台生活四十年 [*Forty Years on Stage: Mei Lanfang's Memoir*]. 2 vols. Edited by Xu Jichuan. Beijing: Tuanjie chubanshe, 2005.

Meng Xianqiang 孟憲強. *Zhongguo shaxue jianshi* 中國莎學簡史 [*A Concise History of Shakespeare Studies in China*]. Changchun: Dongbei shifan daxue chubanshe, 1994.

Milner, Thomas. *Daying guo zhi* 大英國誌 [*An Account of the Great British Empire*]. Translated and compiled by Mu Weilian 慕維廉. Shanghai: Mohai shuyuan, 1856.

Morozov, Mikhail M. *Shashibiya zai Sulian* 莎士比亞在蘇聯 [*Shakespeare in the Soviet Union*]. Translated by Wu Ningkun 巫寧坤. Shanghai: Pingming chubanshe, 1953.

——. *Shashibiya zhuan* 莎士比亞傳 [*Shakespeare's Life*]. Translated by Xu Haiyan and Wu Junzhong. Changsha: Hunan renmin chubanshe, 1984.

Niu Yangshan 牛仰山 and Sun Hongni 孫鴻霓, eds. *Yan Fu yanjiu ziliao* 嚴復研究資料 [*Research Materials on the Study of Yan Fu*]. Fuzhou: Haixia wenyi chubanshe, 1990.

Ouyang Yuqian 歐陽予倩. "Huiyi Chunliu" 回憶春柳 [Reminiscence of the Spring Willow Society]. In *Zhongguo huaju yundong wushi nian shiliao ji, 1907–1957* 中國話劇運動五十年史料集 1907–1957 [*An Anthology of Historical Documents Related to the First Five Decades of the Chinese Spoken Drama Movement, 1907–1957*], edited by Tian Han et al., 13–47. Hong Kong: Wenhua ziliao gongyingshe, 1978.

——. "Tan wenming xi" 談文明戲 [On Civilized Drama]. In *Zhongguo huaju yundong wushi nian shiliao ji, 1907–1957* 中國話劇運動五十年史料集 1907–1957 [*An Anthology of Historical Documents Related to the First Five Decades of the Chinese Spoken Drama Movement, 1907–1957*], edited by Tian Han et al., 48–108. Hong Kong: Wenhua ziliao gongyingshe, 1978.

Qi Rushan 齊如山. *Qi Rushan huiyilu* 齊如山回憶錄 [*Qi Rushan's Memoir*]. Beijing: Zhongguo xiju chubanshe, 1998.

Shanghai qingnian huaju tuan 上海青年話劇團. "*Wushi shengfei*: Si mu xiju" 《無事生非》: 四幕喜劇. [*Much Ado About Nothing*: A Four-Act Comedy]. Play script, March 1961. Shanghai qingnian huaju tuan dang'an 上海青年話劇團檔案 [Archive of Shanghai Youth Huaju Theater].

Shanghai yishu yanjiu suo 上海藝術研究所 [Shanghai Arts Institute], ed. *Zhongguo xiqu quyi cidian* 中國戲曲曲藝辭典 [*Dictionary of Chinese Xiqu Art*]. Shanghai: Shanghai cishu chubanshe, 1981.

Shanxisheng xiju yanjiu suo 山西省戲劇研究所 [The Shanxi Province Drama Institute], ed. *Zhongguo bangzi xi jumu da cidian* 中國梆子戲劇目大辭典 [*Dictionary of Chinese Bangzi Opera Repertoire*]. Taiyuan: Shanxi renmin chubanshe, 1991.

Sheffield, Devello Zelotos [Xie Weilou 謝衛樓]. *Wanguo tongjian* 萬國通鑑 [*The History of the World*]. Shanghai: American Presbyterian Press, 1882.

Shen Congwen 沈從文. "Yiban huo teshu" 一般或特殊 [Universal or Restricted]. *Jinri pinglun* 今日評論 [*Criticism Today*] 1, no. 4 (1939). In *Wenxue yundong shiliao xuan* 文學運動史料選 [*Selections of Historical Materials of Literary Movements*], 4:253–57. Shanghai: Shanghai jiaoyu chubanshe, 1979.

Shi Rufang 施如芳, "*Baofeng yu shouci deng 'Tai'*: Mofashi da chang pihuang" 《暴風雨》首次登「台」: 魔法師大唱皮黃 [*The Tempest* to Appear on the Taiwanese Stage for the First Time: The Magician Sings Beijing Opera Tunes], *Biaoyan yishu* 表演藝術 [*Performing Arts Review*] 135 (2004): 72.

Smiles, Samuel. *Saikoku risshihen* 西国立志編 [*Stories of Successful Lives in the West*]. Translated by Nakamura Masanao 中村正直. Tokyo, 1871.

Song Baozhen 宋寶珍 and Wang Weiguo 王衛國. *Zhongguo huaju* 中國話劇 [*Chinese Spoken Drama*]. Beijing: Wenhua yishu chubanshe, 1999.

Suïin Emi. "Osero." In *Bungei kurabu* 文芸倶楽部, 9:no. 3. Tokyo: Hakubunsha
博文館, 1903.

Sun Chongtao 孫崇濤. *Nanxi luncong* 南戲論叢 [*On Southern Drama*]. Beijing:
Zhonghua shuju, 2001.

Sun Daolin 孫道臨. *Zoujin yangguang* 走進陽光 [*Walking into the Sun*]. Shanghai:
Shanghai renmin chubanshe, 1997.

Sun Fuliang孫福良, Cao Shujin曹樹鈞, and Liu Minghou 劉明厚, eds. *Shanghai
guoji Shashibiya xijujie lunwen ji* 上海國際莎士比亞戲劇節論文集 [*A Collection of Essays from the Shanghai International Shakespeare Festival*]. Shanghai:
Shanghai wenyi chubanshe, 1996.

Sun Huizhu 孫惠柱 and Gong Bo'an. "Huang Zuolin de xiju xieyi shuo" 黃佐臨
的戲劇寫意說 [Huang Zuolin's Xieyi Theater]. *Xiju yishu* 戲劇藝術 [*Theatrical
Art*] 4 (1983): 7–8.

Sun Yu 孫芋. "Zanmei zhengzhi, caizhi, he youyi de shipian: Shashibiya de xiju
Wushi shengfei guanhou" 讚美正直、才智、和友誼的詩篇—莎士比亞的戲劇
「無事生非」觀後 [A Poetry in Praise of Righteousness, Wisdom, and Friendship: My Impression of the Production of the Shakespearean Comedy, *Much
Ado About Nothing*]. *Liaoning ribao* 遼寧日報 [*Liaoning Daily*], September 2,
1961.

Tan Chunfa 譚春發. *Kai yidai xianhe: Zhongguo dianying zhifu Zheng Zhengqiu* 開
一代先河: 中國電影之父鄭正秋 [*The Pathbreaker: Zheng Zhengqiu, the Father of
Chinese Cinema*]. Beijing: Guoji wenhua chuban gongsi, 1992.

Tang Wen 唐汶. "*Luomi'ou yu Zhuliye*: Canguan caipai" 羅密歐與朱麗葉—參觀
彩排 [My Impression of the Dress Rehearsal of *Romeo and Juliet*]." *Dagong bao
zengkan* 大公報贈刊 [*Dagong Daily Supplement*], June 8, 1937.

Tao Qingmei 陶慶梅 and Hou Shuyi 侯淑儀, eds. *Chana zhong: Lai Shengchuan
de juchang yishu* 刹那中—賴聲川的劇場藝術 [*Flash of a Moment: Stan Lai's
Theater Art*]. Taipei: Shibao wenhua, 2003.

Tian Benxiang 田本相, ed. *Zhongguo xiandai bijiao xiju shi, 1907–1957* 中國現
代比較戲劇史 1907–1957 [*A Comparative History of Modern Chinese Drama,
1907–1957*]. Beijing: Wenhua yishu chubanshe, 1993.

Tu Sheng 土生, Xian Ning 洗寧, Zhao Xing 肇星, and Wu Zhuan 武專, eds.
Shashibiya xiju gushi quanji 莎士比亞戲劇故事全集 [*The Complete Stories from
Shakespeare*]. 2 vols. Beijing: Zhongguo xiju chubanshe, 2001.

Wang Guowei 王國維. "Xiqu kaoyuan" 戲曲考原 [The Origin of Traditional The-
ater]. In *Wang Guowei xiqu lunwen ji* 王國維戲曲論文集 [*Collected Essays on
Drama by Wang Guowei*], 231–60. Taipei: Liren shuju, 1993.

Wang Qibang 汪齊邦. "Tantan huaju *Wushi shengfei* he ta de yanchu" 談談話劇
《無事生非》和它的演出 [A Few Words on the *Huaju* Performance of *Much
Ado About Nothing*]. *Shenyang wanbao* 瀋陽晚報 [*Shenyang Evening Post*], August 29, 1961.

Wang Shiwei 王實味. "Ye baihe hua" 野百合花 [Wild Lily]. *Jiefang ribao* 解放日
報 [*Liberation Daily*], March 17 and 23, 1942. In *Zhongguo xiandai wenxue shi
cankao ziliao: Zhongguo geming wenxue de xin jieduan, 1942–1949* 中國現代文

學史參考資料: 中國革命文學的新階段 1942–1949 [*Reference Materials of Modern Chinese Literary History: The New Epoch of Chinese Revolutionary Literature, 1942–1949*], edited by Beijing shifan daxue zhongwenxi xiandai wenxue jiaoxue gaige xiaozu, 2:235–40. Beijing: Gaodeng jiaoyu chubanshe, 1959.

Wang Shouyue 王瘦月. "*Xinju shi xu*" 新劇史序 [Introduction to *The History of New Drama*]. In *Xinju shi* 新劇史 [*The History of New Drama*], edited by Zhu Shuangyun 朱雙雲, 1–2. Shanghai: Xinju xiaoshuo she, 1914.

Wang Xiaonong 汪笑儂. "Ti *Yingguo shiren yin bian yan yu* ershi shou" 題英國詩人吟邊燕語二十首 [Twenty Poems Dedicated to *An English Poet Reciting from Afar*]. In *Wan Qing wenxue congchao: Xiaoshuo xiqu yanjiu juan* 晚清文學叢鈔: 小說戲曲研究卷 [*A Compendium of Late Qing Literature: Materials on Fiction and Drama*], edited by A Ying, 2:588–90. Taipei: Xin wenfeng chuban gongsi, 1989.

Wu Hsing-kuo 吳興國. "Wo yan beiju renwu" 我演悲劇人物 [I Perform Tragic Characters]. *Shijie ribao* 世界日報 [*World Journal*], November 1, 2006, J8.

Wu Xinlei 吳新雷. "Cao Fu xin shiliao chutan" 曹頫新史料初探 [A Preliminary Study of New Historical Materials on Cao Fu]. *Jianghai xuekan* 江海學刊 [*Jianghai Journal*] 1 (1983): 71–74.

Wushi shengfei 無事生非 [*Much Ado About Nothing*]. Stage bill. Shanghai qingnian huaju tuan 上海青年話劇團 [Shanghai Youth Huaju Company], 1979.

Xiong Yuanwei 熊源偉. "Cong jingdian zouxiang xiandai: *Hamuleite/Hamuleite* daoyan gousi" 從經典走向現代:《哈姆雷特／哈姆雷特》導演構思 [From Classics to Modernity: Director's Notes on *Hamlet/Hamlet*]. *Xianggang xiju xuekan* 香港戲劇學刊 [*Hong Kong Drama Review*] 2 (2000): 91–100.

Xiong Yuezhi 熊月之 and Ma Xueqiang, eds. *Shanghai de waiguo ren, 1842–1949* 上海的外國人 1842–1949 [*Foreigners in Shanghai, 1842–1949*]. Shanghai: Shanghai guji chubanshe, 2003.

Xu Banmei 徐半梅. *Huaju chuangshi qi huiyilu* 話劇創始期回憶錄 [*Reminiscences of the Beginning of Spoken Drama*]. Beijing: Zhongguo xiju chubanshe, 1957.

Xu Zhimo 徐志摩 [Hsu Tsemou]. "Art and Life." *Chuangzao jikan* 創造季刊 [*Creation Quarterly*] 2, no. 1 (1992).

Yan Fu 嚴復. *Tianyan lun* 天演論 [*Evolution and Ethics*]. Taipei: Shangwu yinshuguan, 1987.

Yan Huandong 閻煥東. "Qing bie zeguai guanzhong" 請別責怪觀眾 [Do Not Blame the Audience]. *Zhongguo wenhua bao* 中國文化報 [*China Culture Daily*], March 26, 2001.

Yang Jingyuan 楊靜遠. "Yuan Changying he Shashibiya" 袁昌英和莎士比亞 [Yuan Changying and Shakespeare]. *Waiguo wenxue yanjiu* 外國文學研究 [*Foreign Literature Studies*], April 1994, 1–3.

Yao Yiwei 姚一葦. *Xiju yu wenxue* 戲劇與文學 [*Drama and Literature*]. Taipei: Lianjing chubenshe, 1989.

Yu Kwang-chung 余光中. "Xiu suo nankai de jin yaoshi" 鏽鎖難開的金鑰匙 [The Golden Key that Cannot Open a Rotten Lock]. In *Faxian Shashibiya: Taiwan Sha xue lunshu xuanji* 發現莎士比亞:台灣莎學論述選集 [*Discovering Shakespeare:*

Shakespeare Studies in Taiwan], edited by Perng Ching-hsi 彭鏡禧, 17–29. Taipei: Maotouying, 2000.

Yu Shangyuan 余上沅. "Women weisheme gongyan shaju" 我們為什麼公演莎劇 [Why We Perform Shakespeare (The Merchant of Venice)]. In Jieshao Shashibiya tekan 介紹莎士比亞特刊 [Introducing Shakespeare: A Pamphlet], 61–66. Nanjing: National Drama School, 1937.

Yu Zhiping 于芷萃. "Shanghai Zhongxi nüshu zayi" 上海中西女塾雜憶 [Remembering Shanghai McTyeire School]." Minguo chunqiu 民國春秋 [Republican History], January 1997, 61–62.

Zeng Jize 曾紀澤. Chushi Ying Fa Eguo riji 出使英法俄國日記 [Diaries Kept on Diplomatic Missions to England, France, and Russia]. Edited by Zhong Shuhe. Changsha: Yuelu shushe, 1985.

——. Shixi riji 使西日記 [Diary of a Diplomatic Mission in the West]. Edited by Zhang Xuanhao. Changsha: Hunan Renmin Chubanshe, 1981.

Zhang Chong 張沖, ed. Tong shidai de Shashibiya: Yujing, huwen, duozhong shiyu 同時代的莎士比亞：語境、互文、多種視域 [Shakespeare Our Contemporary: Contexts, Intertexts, and Multiple Perspectives]. Shanghai: Fudan daxue chubanshe, 2005.

Zhang Daofan 張道藩. "Women suo xuyao de wenyi zhengce" 我們所需要的文藝政策 [The Cultural and Literary Policy We Need]. Wenyi xianfeng 文藝先鋒 [Pioneer of Literature and Art] 1, no. 6 (1942).

Zhang Juncai 張俊才. Lin Shu pingzhuan 林紓評傳 [A Critical Biography of Lin Shu]. Beijing: Zhonghua shuju, 2007.

Zhang Junxiang 張駿祥 and Cheng Jihua 程季華, eds. Zhongguo dianying da cidian 中國電影大辭典 [Encyclopedia of Chinese Cinema]. Shanghai: Shanghai cishu chubanshe, 1995.

Zhao Pinsan 趙品三. "Guanyu zhongyang geming genjudi huaju gongzuo de huiyi" 關於中央革命根據地話劇工作的回憶 [My Recollection of My Work in the Huaju Theater in the Central Base of Revolution: Yan'an]. In Zhongguo huaju yundong wushi nian shiliao ji, 1907–1957 中國話劇運動五十年史料集 1907–1957 [An Anthology of Historical Documents Related to the First Five Decades of the Chinese Spoken Drama Movement, 1907–1957], edited by Tian Han et al., 183–97. Hong Kong: Wenhua ziliao gongyingshe, 1978.

Zheng Shifeng 鄭拾風. Xieshou ji 血手記 [The Story of Bloody Hands]. In Lanyuan jicui: Wushi nian Zhongguo kunju yanchu juben xuan 蘭苑集萃：五十年中國崑劇演出劇本選 [Collection of the Best Plays from the Orchid Garden: The Performance Texts of Kunju in China from the Past Fifty Years], edited by Wang Wenzhang, 2:227–58. Beijing: Wenhua yishu chubanshe, 2000.

Zheng Zhenduo 鄭振鐸. "Guangming yundong de kaishi" 光明運動的開始 [The Beginning of the Movement of Enlightenment]. Xiju 戲劇 [Drama] 1, no. 3 (1921).

Zheng Zhengqiu 鄭正秋. "Zhongguo yingxi de qucai wenti" 中國影戲的取材問題 [On the Question of Chinese Film's Subject]. Mingxing tekan: Xiao pengyou hao 明星特刊 [Bright Stars Magazine] 2 (1925).

Zhongguo dianying yishu yanjiu zhongxin 中國電影藝術研究中心 [China Film Art Research Center] and Zhongguo dianying ziliao guan 中國電影資料館 [China Film Archive], eds. *Zhongguo yingpian dadia: Gushi pian, xiqu pian, 1905–1930* 中國影片大典—故事片戲曲片, 1905–1930 [*Encyclopedia of Chinese Films, 1905–1930*]. Beijing: Zhongguo dianying chubanshe, 1996.

Zhongguo xiju nianjian bianji bu 《中國戲劇年鑑》編輯部, eds. *Zhongguo xiju nianjian* 中國戲劇年鑑 [*Chinese Theater Annual*]. Beijing: Zhongguo xiju chubanshe, 1983.

Zhou Zhaoxiang 周兆祥. *Hanyi Hamuleite yanjiu* 漢譯《哈姆雷特》研究 [*A Study of "Hamlet" in Chinese Translation*]. Hong Kong: Chinese University Press, 1981.

Zhu Xijuan 祝希娟. "Wo yan Beitelisi" 我演貝特麗絲 [Me Playing Beatrice]. *Shanghai xiju* 上海戲劇 [*Shanghai Theater*] 2 (1980): 27–29.

Zou Zhenhuan 鄒振環. *Yingxiang Zhongguo jindai shehui de yibaizhong yizuo* 影響中國近代社會的一百種譯作 [*Hundred Most Influential Translated Works in Modern Chinese Society*]. Beijing: Zhongguo duiwai fanyi chuban gongsi, 1996.

Index

Conquering Jun Mountain (*Ding Junshan*), 112. *See also* Cultural Revolution.
Contemporary Legend Theatre (Dangdai chuanqi), 13, 169, 191–92, 196–97, 202–3, 217–18, 223–24, 230. *See also* Lin Hsiu-wei; Wu Hsing-kuo
cosmopolitanism, 90, 96, 101–2, 112–14, 118–19
cultural alterity, 23, 54, 258n.1
cultural ownership, 18, 31, 197
cultural prestige, perceived, 131–35, 197–98; theory of, 302n.10
Cultural Revolution, 9, 28, 39, 130, 141, 145–46, 159–60, 172, 177, 180, 188, 235; and *Hamlet*, 19, 126, 139–40; and *Much Ado About Nothing* (1957), 126, 129, 144–48, 150–51, 154–58, 289n.51; and *Much Ado About Nothing* (1961 and 1979), 144, 146–61, 289n.51. *See also* censorship; Mao Zedong; Marx, Karl; patronage
Cymbeline, and *Ring Evidence* (*Huan zheng*; Lin Shu), 80

Dazai Osamu, 87
Deng Xiaoping, 13, 17, 168, 188–89
Derrida, Jacques, 47, 76, 261n.34
Dickens, Charles, 252n.4
Ding Ling, 113

Eliot, T. S., 87, 140
Engels, Friedrich, 151–52, 154–55, 291n.76
English Poet Reciting from Afar, An (*Yingguo shiren yinbian yanyu*; Lin Shu), 7, 71–87, 96

Feng Xiaogang, 20, 33, 230–34, 261n.31
festivals, 10, 33, 230; *The Banquet* at, 33, 233–34; Berlin Asia Pacific Cultural Festival, 228; in China, 168–69, 171, 176, 181, 187, 220;

Colorado Shakespeare Festival, 200; Edinburgh Festival, 218; Globe to Globe Festival, 305n.38; in Hong Kong, 11, 13, 218; Hong Kong Experimental Shakespeare Festival, 208–9; and international audiences, 68; Lin Zhaohua's *Richard III* at, 235–36; Lincoln Center Festival, 196–97, 301n.4; New York Shakespeare Festival, 179; Royal Shakespeare Company Complete Works Festival, 14–16, 230, 235; Shakespeare in Taipei Festival, 10, 14; Shakespeare in Washington, 65, 274n.89; in Taipei, 13, 218; Wu Hsing-kuo's *The Kingdom of Desire* at, 169
fidelity, discourse of, 18, 31–34, 120, 145, 261n.29
Foucault, Michel, 37, 258n.1
Freed, Amy, 57, 271n.50
Fu Sinian, 86, 104

Gao Xingjian, 206, 304n.32, 308n.16
gezaixi. *See* Taiwanese opera
global cultural marketplace, 23, 30, 191, 194
global spectator, 169–70, 192–93, 237–38
global vernacular. *See* vernacular
globalization: definition and theorization of, 29–31, 253n.10; and locality, 26–28; as performance, 3–4, 14–15, 201–2, 234–37; rhetoric of, 42–43
Godard, Jean-Luc, 196, 201, 228, 302n.8
Goethe, Johann Wolfgang von, 49, 64, 91, 218
Golden Bough Theatre (Jinzhi yanshe), 200. See also *Romeo and Juliet*; Wang Rongyu
Grady, Hugh, 266n.68
Guan Hanqing, 65
Guo Songtao, 55–57, 61

Sun and Fan Yisong, 14; film of, by Sergei Yutkevich, 177, 297n.38; production of, by Kawakami Otojirō, 9–10, 103; and *Touch of Evil*, 262n.41. *See also* racial otherness

CHINESE VERSIONS OF: *Aosailuo*, 176–87, 296n.34; *Ashina*, 108, 111; *The Black General* (*Hei du*; Lin Shu), 80; *Clouds of Doubt*, 10; *Spring Dream*, 103, 254n.23

Otojirō Kawakami, 9–10, 103

Pacino, Al, 309n.18
Pai, Hsien-yung (Kenneth), 63
parody, 33, 87–88, 91, 94, 96–97, 200, 219
patronage, 10–11, 13, 171, 217, 252n.4. *See also* censorship
Peking opera. *See* Beijing opera
Peony Pavilion, The (*Mudan ting*; Tang Xianzu), 62–63
Performance Workshop (Biaoyan gongzuo fang), 202–9
Pericles, and *Providential Reunion* (*Shen he*; Lin Shu), 80
postcolonial studies, 11, 258n.9; and colorblind casting, 178–80; and locality criticism, 25–27. *See also* colonialism; racial otherness; semicolonialism
Pound, Erza, 76, 96
Pound of Flesh, A (*Yi bang rou* [*The Merchant of Venice*]; Wang Fucheng), 13, 70, 115, 256n.35, 257n.45
presentism, 19, 33, 66, 142–45, 153, 160
Prince of the Himalayas, The (*Ximalaya wangzi* [*Hamlet*]; Sherwood Hu), 12, 35
pseudo-translation, 84. *See also* Lin Shu

qinqiang. *See* Shaanxi opera
Qiu Yixiang, 115–18, 123
Qu Yuan, 52, 132, 288n.39

racial otherness, 4, 8, 17, 19, 36, 115–16, 177–82; in *The Black Slave's Cry to Heaven*, 179; and colorblind casting, 179–81; lack of, 178–80; and Ma Yong'an, 177–87, 192–93; in *The Woman Lawyer*, 8, 115–18, 120
Ran (*King Lear*; Kurosawa), 12, 208
realism, 9, 102–6, 132–33, 144–52, 205; and Chinese opera and spoken drama, 173–74, 190; socialist, 159–60. *See also* Huang Zuolin; Mao Zedong; May Fourth movement; Stanislavsky, Konstantin
religious rhetoric, 6–8, 17, 115–16; and autobiographical performance, 20, 197–99, 205–16, 227; and translation, 74. *See also* Buddhism; Christianity
Richard II, 14, 57, 127; and *Leichade ji* (Lin Shu), 73; performance of, on *Red Dragon*, 1, 251n.2; production of, by Ariane Mnouchkine, 14, 308n.13
Richard III, 6, 20, 228, 230, 234–37, 253n.7, 260n.26, 297n.37; 309n.18; film of, by Ian McKellen, 235; and *Looking for Richard*, 309n.18; production of, by Lin Zhaohua, 20, 228, 234–38; production of, by Sulayman al-Bassam, 235
Rinpoche, Jigme Khyentse, 196–97, 207–10, 213–14
Romeo and Juliet, 12; and *The Peony Pavilion*, 62–63; production of, by Nancy Meckler, 15; production of, by Oh Tae-suk, 174–75; *William Shakespeare's Romeo + Juliet*, as adaptation of, 12, 63, 308n.17
CHINESE VERSIONS OF: *Chicken Rice War*, 12; *Committing the Crime of Passion* (*Zhu qing*; Lin Shu), 80; *One Husband Too Many*, 12; performance of, by Huang Hsiang-lian, 218; production of, by Huang Zuolin, 189–90; production of, by